European Industrial Relations

European Industrial Relations

The Challenge of Flexibility

edited by
Guido Baglioni and Colin Crouch

 SAGE Publications

London ● Newbury Park ● New Delhi

Chapter 1 © Guido Baglioni 1990
Chapter 2 © Armand Spineux 1990
Chapter 3 © Bruno Amoroso 1990
Chapter 4 © Denis Segrestin 1990
Chapter 5 © Otto Jacobi and Walther Müller-Jentsch 1990
Chapter 6 © Serafino Negrelli and Ettore Santi 1990
Chapter 7 © Jelle Visser 1990
Chapter 8 © Mario Pinto 1990
Chapter 9 © Jordi Estivill and Josep M. de la Hoz 1990
Chapter 10 © Gösta Rehn and Birger Viklund 1990
Chapter 11 and Afterword © Colin Crouch 1990

First published 1990, first paperback edition 1991 Reprinted 1992

 SAGE Publications Ltd
28 Banner Street
London EC1Y 8QE

SAGE Publications Inc
2111 West Hillcrest Drive
Newbury Park, California 91320

SAGE Publications India Pvt Ltd
32, M-Block Market
Greater Kailash – I
New Delhi 110 048

British Library Cataloguing in Publication data

European industrial relations: the challenge of flexibility.
1. Europe. Industrial relations
I. Baglioni, Guido II. Crouch, Colin, 1944–
331'.094

ISBN 0-8039-8242-9
ISBN 0-8039-8544-4 pbk

Library of Congress catalog card number 89-063772

Typeset by Mayhew Typesetting, Bristol, England
Printed in Great Britain by Billing and Sons Ltd, Worcester

Contents

Preface

This study was sponsored by the Commission of the European Communities, funded by the Commission and by the National Research Council of Italy, and conducted by the Centro di Studi e Sindacali (CESOS) of Rome.

The authors of the national reports are: Otto Jacobi and Walther Müller-Jentsch for Germany, Colin Crouch for Britain, Denis Segrestin for France, Serafino Negrelli and Ettore Santi for Italy, Jordi Estivill and Josep M. de la Hoz for Spain, Gösta Rehn and Birger Viklund for Sweden, Armand Spineux for Belgium, Jelle Visser for the Netherlands, Bruno Amoroso for Denmark, and Mario Pinto for Portugal.

The study was directed and co-ordinated by Guido Baglioni, with the advice and collaboration of Colin Crouch. Corrado Squarzon handled the organization of the study through its various stages. The co-ordinator would like to acknowledge the valuable assistance of Colin Crouch and Corrado Squarzon, as well as of Carlo Savoini and Gaetano Zingone of the EC.

Shortly after the study was completed, on 1 April 1988, we were profoundly saddened by the premature death of Ettore Santi, the co-author of the Italian report, of a sudden heart attack. We mourn Ettore's loss and remember him with admiration and affection.

List of Contributors

Bruno Amoroso, Institut for Samfundsokonomi og planlægning, Roskilde Universitetscenter

Guido Baglioni, Dipartimento di Economia, Università degli Studi di Milano; president, Centro di Studi Sociali e Sindacali (CESOS), Rome

Colin Crouch, Fellow of Trinity College, Oxford

Jordi Estivill, Gabinete d'Estudios Sociales, Universidad de Barcelona

Josep M. de la Hoz, Gabinete d'Estudios Sociales, Universidad de Barcelona

Otto Jacobi, Institut für Sozialforschung, Johann-Wolfgang-Goethe Universität, Frankfurt am Main

Walther Müller-Jentsch, Fachbereich Soziologie, Universität–GHS, Paderborn

Serafino Negrelli, CESOS, Rome

Mario Pinto, Universita Cattolica, Lisbon

Gösta Rehn, Social Research Institute, Stockholm University

Ettore Santi, deceased; formerly secretary general of CESOS, Rome

Denis Segrestin, Laboratoire de Sociologie du Travail et des Relations Professionnelles, Conservatoire National des Arts et Métiers, Paris

Armand Spineux, Faculté des Sciences Economiques, Sociales et Politiques, Université Catholique de Louvain

Birger Viklund, Arbetslivscentrum, Stockholm

Jelle Visser, Sociologisch Instituut, Universiteit van Amsterdam

Abbreviations

General

EC	European Community
ETUC	European Trades Union Council
ICFTU	International Congress of Free Trade Unions
ILO	International Labour Office
NATO	North Atlantic Treaty Organization
OECD	Organization for Economic Co-Operation and Development
VAT	Value-Added Tax

Belgium

AR	Arrêté Royal (Royal Decree)
ASBL	association sans but lucratif (non-profit-making association)
CE	conseil d'entreprise (works council)
CGSLB	Confédération Générale des Syndicats Libéraux de Belgique (General Confederation of Liberal Trade Unions in Belgium)
CNT	Conseil National du Travail (National Council of Labour)
CP	commission paritaire (joint commission)
CSC	Confédération des Syndicats Chrétiens (Confederation of Christian Trade Unions)
CSHE	comité de sécurité, d'hygiène et d'embellissement des locaux de travail (committee for safety, health and workplace environmental improvement)
CVP	Catholiek Vlaamse Partij (Catholic Flemish Party)
FEB	Fédération des Entreprises de Belgique (Federation of Belgian Companies)
FGTB	Fédération Générale des Travailleurs de Belgique (General Federation of Belgian Workers)
INAMI	Institut National d'Assurance contre la Maladie et

l'Invalidité (National Institute for Sickness and
Disability Insurance)
PME   petites et moyennes entreprises (small and medium-
sized firms)
PRL   Parti Réformateur Libéral (Liberal Reform Party)
PS   Parti Socialiste (Socialist Party)
PSC   Parti Social Chrétien (Christian Social Party)
PVV   Partij voor Vrijheid en Veruitgang (Party for
Freedom and Progress)
SETCA   Syndicat des Employés Techniciens et Cadres (Union
of Technical and Managerial Staffs)
SP   Socialistich Partij (Socialist Party)

Denmark

AC   Akademikernes Centralorganisation (Central
Organization of Professions)
BST–Centre (Safety Committees and Service Centre)
DA   Dansk Arbejdsgiverforening (Confederation of
Danish Employers)
FTF   Fællesråd for Tjenestemænd og Funktionærer
(Federation of Civil Servants and Salaried
Employees)
HK   Handels- og Kontorfunktionærernes Forbund i
Danmark (Commercial and Clerical Employees'
Union of Denmark)
HR   Håndværksråd (Council of Smaller Firms)
IR   Industriråd (Council of Industry)
LO   Landsorganisation i Danmark (Danish Federation of
Trade Unions)
LR   Landbrugsråd (Agricultural Council)
Metal   Centralorganisation af Metalarbejdere (Central
Organization of Metalworkers)
SID   Specialarbejderforbund i Danmark (General Workers'
Union of Denmark)

France

CFDT   Confédération française démocratique du travail
(French Democratic Confederation of Labour)
CFTC   Confédération française des travailleurs chrétiens
(French Confederation of Christian Workers)
CGC (or CGC–CFE) Confédération générale des cadres –
Confédération française de l'encadrement (General

	Confederation of Mangerial Staffs – French Confederation of Managerial Staffs)
CGPME	Confédération générale des petites et moyennes entreprises (General Confederation of Small and Medium-sized Enterprises)
CGT	Confédération générale du travail (General Confederation of Labour)
CHS–CT	Comité d'hygiène, de sécurité et des conditions de travail (Committee for health, safety and working conditions)
CNPF	Conseil national du patronat français (National Council of French Employers)
FO (or CGT–FO)	Force ouvrière (Workers' Strength)
INSEE	Institut national de la statistique et des études économiques (National Institute for Statistics and Economic Studies)
SNPMI	Syndicat national des petites et moyennes industries (National Union of Small and Medium-sized Industries)
TUC	Travaux d'utilité collective (Works of Public Use; temporary employment offered to young unemployed people, with public subsidy)

Germany (West)

AFG	Arbeitsförderungsgesetz (Labour Promotion Act)
CDU	Christlich-Demokratische Union (Christian Democratic Union)
CSU	Christlich-Soziale Union (Christian Social Union)
DGB	Deutscher Gewerkschaftsbund (German Trade Union Federation)
FDP	Freie Demokratische Partei (Free Democratic (Liberal) Party)
IG Metall, IGM	Industriegewerkschaft Metall (Metalworkers' Union)
SPD	Sozialdemokratische Partei Deutschlands (German Social Democratic Party)
SVR	Sachverständigenrat zur Begutachtung der gesamtwirtschaftlichen Entwicklung (Council of Economic Experts)

Italy

ASAP   Associazione Sindacale delle Aziende Petrolchimiche (Employers' Association for the Petrochemical Industry)

Assolombarda   (Lombardy Employers' Association)

CGIL   Confederazione Generale Italiana del Lavoro (General Italian Confederation of Labour)

CIG   Cassa Integrazione Guadagni (Short-term Earnings Compensation Fund)

CISL   Confederazione Italiana Sindacati Lavoratori (Italian Confederation of Workers' Unions)

Cobas   comitati di base (rank-and-file committees)

Confindustria   (Confederation of Italian Industrialists)

ENI   Ente Nazionale Idrocarburi (National Hydrocarbons Agency)

Federmeccanica   (Engineering Industry Employers' Association)

FISAFS   Federazione Italiana Sindacati Autonomi delle Ferrovia dello Stato (Italian Federation of Independent Unions in State Railways)

GEPI   gestioni a partecipazioni industriali (state industrial management and holding company)

INPS   Istituto Nazionale della Previdenza Sociale (National Institute for Social Security)

Intersind   (Public Sector Industrial Employers' Association)

IRI   Istituto per la Ricostruzione Industriale (Institute for Industrial Reconstruction)

Istat   Istituto Centrale di Statistica (Central Statistical Institute)

PCI   Partito Comunista Italiano (Italian Communist Party)

SIP   Società per l'Esercizio Telefonico (National Telephone Corporation)

UIL   Unione Italiana dei Lavoratori (Italian Union of Workers)

Netherlands

AWV   Algemene Werkgevers-Vereniging (General Association of Employers)

CBS   Centraal Bureau van de Statistiek (Central Statistical Office)

CNV   Christelijk Nationaal Vakverbond (Christian National Trade Union Federation)

CPB	Centraal Plan Bureau (Central Planning Office)
FME	Federatie Metaal- en Electrotechnische Industrie (Federation of Employers in the Metal and Electrotechnical Industry)
FNV	Federatie Nederlandse Vakbeweging (Federation of Dutch Trade Unions)
MHP	Federatie van Middelbaar en Hoger Personeel (Federation of White-collar Employees)
NCW	Nederlands Christelijk Werkgeversverbond (Dutch Christian Employers' Association)
NKV	Nederlands Katholiek Vakverbond (Dutch Catholic Union Federation)
NVV	Nederlands Verbond van Vakverenigingen (Dutch Federation of Trade Unions)
RCO	Raad van Centrale Ondernemersorganisaties (Council of Central Employers' Associations)
SAE	Ministerie van Socialie Zaken en Werkgelegenheid, until 1981 Ministerie van Sociale Zaken (Ministry of Social Affairs and Employment, until 1981 Ministry of Social Affairs)
SER	Sociaal-Economische Raad (Social-Economic Council)
SvA	Stichting van de Arbeid (Foundation of Labour)
VNO	Verbond van Nederlandse Ondernemingen (Confederation of Dutch Enterprises)
WRR	Wetenschappelijke Raad voor het Regeringsbeleid (Scientific Council of Government Policy)

Portugal

CAP	Confederação da Agricultura Portuguesa (Confederation of Portuguese Agriculture)
CCP	Confederação do Comércio Português (Confederation of Portuguese Commerce)
CDS	Centro Democrático Social (Social Democratic Centre)
CGTP–IN	Confederação Geral dos Trabalhadores Portugueses – Intersindical Nacional (General Confederation of Portuguese Workers – National Trade Union Confederation)
CIP	Confederação da Indústria Portuguesa (Confederation of Portuguese Industry)
CNEP	Consilio Nacional da Economia Portuguesa (National Council for the Portuguese Economy)

CPCS	Consilio Permanente por Concertação Sociala (Permanent Council for Social Concertation)
IN	Intersindical Nacional (later CGTP–IN, q.v.) (National Trade Union Confederation)
PCP	Partido Comunista Português (Portuguese Communist Party)
PPM	Partido Popular Monárquico (Popular Monarchist Party)
PRD	Partido Renovador Democrático (Party for Democratic Renewal)
PS	Partido Socialista (Socialist Party)
PSD	Partido Social Democrata (Social Democratic Party)
UGT	União Geral de Trabalhadores (General Workers' Union)

Spain

ABI	Acuerdo Bàsico Interconfederal (Basic Interconfederal Agreement)
AES	Acuerdo Económico y Social (Economic and Social Agreement)
AI	Acuerdo Interconfederal (Interconfederal Agreement)
AMI	Acuerdo Marco Interconfederal (Interconfederal Mark Agreement)
ANE	Acuerdo Nacional sobre el Empleo (National Agreement on Employment)
AP	Alianza Popular (Popular Alliance)
CCOO	Comisiones Obreras (Workers' Commissions)
CDS	Centro Democràtico Social (Social Democratic Centre)
CEOE	Confederación Española de Organizaciones Empresariales (Spanish Confederation of Employers Organizations)
CNT	Confederación Nacional de Trabajadores (National Confederation of Workers)
COS	Coordinadora Organizaciones Sindicales (Co-ordination of Trade Union Organizations)
ELA/STV	Solidaridad de Trabajadores Vascos (Basque Workers' Solidarity)
INE	Instituto Nacional de Estadistica
INTG	Intersindical Nacional de Trabajadores Gallega (National Federation of Galician Workers)
IVA	Impuesto sobre el Valor Anadido (Value-Added Tax)
LOLS	Ley Organica de Libertad Sindical (Organic Law on Union Freedom)

PDP	Partido Democràtico Popular (Democratic People's Party)
PSOE	Partido Socialista Obrero Español (Socialist Workers' Party of Spain)
UCD	Unión de Centro Democràtico (Democratic Centre Union)
UGT	Unión General de Trabajadores (General Union of Workers)
USO	Unión Sindical Obrera (Workers' Union)

Sweden

KFO	Kooperationens Förhandlingsorganisation (Employer Organization for Co-operative Sector)
KTK	Kommunaltjänstemannakartell (Cartel of Salaried Local Government Employees' Union)
LO	Landsorganisation (Trade Union Confederation)
PKF	Privattjänstemannakartell (Cartel of Salaried Employees' Unions in Industry and Services)
PTK	Privattjänstemannakartell (Cartel of Salaried Employees' Unions in the Private Sector)
SACO–SR	Centralorganisation SACO–SR (Central Organization of Unions of the Professions)
SAF	Svenska Arbetsgivarförening (Swedish Employers' Federation)
SALF	Svenska Arbetsledareförbund (Swedish Union of Supervisors and Foremen)
SAV	Statens Avtalverk (State Bargaining Agency)
SFO	Statens Förhandlingsorganisation (Employer Organizations for State-owned Industries)
SIF	Svenska Industritjänstemannaförbund (Swedish Union of Clerical and Technical Employees in Industry)
SKAF	Svenska Kommunalarbetareförbund (Swedish Local Government Employees' Union)
TCO	Tjänstemännens Centralorganisation (Central Organization of Salaried Employees' Unions)
TCO–S	(TCO section for state employees)

United Kingdom

| AEU | Amalgamated Engineering Union (formerly AUEW) |
| AUEW | Amalgamated Union of Engineering Workers (now known as AEU, q.v.) |

BL   British Leyland (motor-manufacturing company)
CBI   Confederation of British Industry
EETPU   Electrical, Electronic and Plumbing Trades Union
GCHQ   Government Communications Headquarters
            (intelligence-gathering headquarters)
GMBATU or GMB   General, Municipal, Boilermaking and
            Allied Trades Union
LEA   local education authority
MSC   Manpower Services Commission
NCB   National Coal Board
NUM   National Union of Mineworkers
TASS   Technical, Administrative and Scientific Staffs Union
TGWU   Transport and General Workers' Union
TUC   Trades Union Congress

1

Industrial Relations in Europe in the 1980s

Guido Baglioni

This study has employed the method of comparative analysis. In the summary and analysis I have sought to apply criteria that are generally accepted or that I felt were appropriate to the material (Baglioni, 1988). If the objects of a comparison have been properly defined, the analysis should identify the similarities and differences between the nations considered. The identification of the factors underlying the conditions and changes, whether common or specific to a particular country, moreover, may bring to light elements or explanation of how industrial relations systems work. Finally, through a typology of industrial relations, we have sought to ascertain in each country the presence or absence of a series of specified, important features, in order both to assess the extent of the changes that have taken place in industrial relations during these years and to check whether these changes have accentuated or diminished the elements of transnational convergence.

The study, and particularly the analytical synthesis, is not designed to furnish information or statistical updates on the economy or the labour market. A vast specialized literature is available on these topics. Rather, our purpose is to distil the principal elements in the evolution of the direction of change in industrial relations. Our attention has consequently focussed on qualitative rather than quantitative aspects (Blanpain, 1982; Schregle, 1981).

The study was conducted on the basis of a detailed programme of observation, and it deals with virtually all the principal aspects and dimensions of industrial relations. The decision to take this approach reflects the need for an overall framework covering a large number of countries and based on careful use of empirical data. This need arises from the fact that the literature and the discussion of industrial relations have frequently offered excessive generalizations, insufficiently well grounded, lacking in careful and accurate use of empirical documentation, and with an exaggerated penchant for brilliant theorization.

This analytical synthesis first gives a brief description of the state of industrial relations in Europe before the turn of the decade, followed by an account of the conditions, processes, decisions and interaction in the course of the 1980s. It then compares the present state of affairs with that prevailing previously. Finally, it notes the essential points on questions concerning the present and future of industrial relations.

1   Industrial relations before the turn of the decade

During the 1970s the trend in income distribution and in industrial relations was favourable to labour and its representatives. In other words, unions continued to make new gains, in Europe and even in the United States. Specifically, there was progress in regulations governing employment contracts, an extension of the scope of collective bargaining, and advances in union rights and, in some countries, in industrial democracy.

A significant feature, in many ways unprecedented in the history of industrial relations, was that these gains were made at a time when the long post-war expansion had finally come to an end, a time of oil shock, crisis and recession. These events, together with others no less important, such as the massive resurgence of unemployment, did not appear to give rise to any substantial constraints on industrial relations or to diminish either the political or the bargaining power or the recognition of the unions.

The incongruity between the poor performance of the economy and the progressive advance in the objectives and accomplishments of trade union action was the focus of debate during the 1970s, but all in all the potential incompatibility between this action and the structural conditions did not give rise to notable changes in industrial relations either by government decision or through private employer initiative. Regulatory actions in the decade concentrated almost exclusively, as we know, on guidelines for wage increases and the cost of labour. The instrument chosen was usually some form of incomes policy (almost never compulsory, in reality), which diminished the independence of the industrial relations system and spread more or less institutionalized relations between the state and the union and employer organizations.[1]

Objectively, the most profound challenge to the workings and the arrangement of industrial relations was already present in the later 1970s – but, with a few harbingers and exceptions, it was not manifest until after the turn of the decade.

In the 1970s, the panorama of industrial relations is here summarized by a typology based on the standard elements, such as levels of bargaining; but it also takes explicit account of the situation in the 1980s, mentioning such elements as employers' strategies of worker involvement. It should therefore facilitate a comparison between the previous and the present decade. The typology[2] has been used in each of the national reports included in this volume.

In the late 1970s there was still a high degree of recognition of the legitimacy and the positive role of the trade unions. This satisfactory position reflected traditional status in some countries, the support of political equilibria, or the strength acquired by the unions in industrial action and bargaining; often enough, all three.

At the same time, there was widespread use of the institutions and practices of concertation,[3] except in Portugal, where this would only begin in the 1980s. The logic of concertation continued in countries where it was well established (Sweden, Belgium, Denmark), albeit with perceptible strains and signs of wear and tear in some countries (Germany, Belgium, Netherlands). Elsewhere (France and Spain) it was significantly institutional in nature, undertaken markedly at government initiative. In the United Kingdom, finally, concertation yielded few results, even under the requisite conditions (a pro-labour government), while in Italy, in less propitious circumstances, there was experimentation with concertation, albeit more in practice than in proclamation.

Collective bargaining at the national level between unions and employer associations – mainly, though not exclusively, via industry-wide agreements – was very common and at times decisive. It was found in all countries, though less broadly in Spain and Portugal. National collective bargaining sometimes took place under the control and guidance of the national union confederations or legislation (Sweden, Denmark, the Netherlands). Elsewhere, it was conducted more autonomously and in conjunction with bargaining at less extensive levels (regional in Germany, company-level in Italy and especially in Britain). Collective bargaining was supplemented and interwoven with experiments in industrial democracy[4] in only a few northern countries, most notably Germany, Sweden and Denmark.

Collective bargaining based fundamentally on decentralized negotiation, particularly company-level contracts – characteristic of typically 'pluralist' models of industrial relations[5] – were also quite common. However, there were exceptions, the most significant being Germany (with a centralized contract structure) as well as the Netherlands (where unions have traditionally had little strength at the company level) and Portugal. In some cases, such as Britain and Italy, decentralized bargaining was largely independent of the higher levels. Elsewhere (Sweden, Belgium, Denmark, Spain), decentralized bargaining was essentially supplementary to the regulations laid down by centralized pacts. As a rule, the vigorous extension of bargaining decentralization does not correspond to situations of union weakness either at the company level or outside.

Management strategies of worker participation, that is involvement of workers in the problems of the firm, using company-level union representation, were of scant significance. In some countries, such experiences are virtually non-existent. In others, such as France and Spain, they were of only small importance and in any case were not widespread. Obviously, this description does not apply to experiments in participation against a background of industrial democracy.

Management strategies, aiming at worker participation via direct relations with the workers, that is, without or in opposition to union structures, were simply absent in some countries, such as Sweden, where union representatives are in full control and furnish complete protection. In other countries where worker protection was quite comprehensive, such efforts have been exceptional and of little importance. This applies, for instance, to Britain and Belgium, where participatory schemes are offered mainly to white-collar workers. Somewhat more experience in this line is found in France, where schemes concern working conditions, hours and technical change.

The situation differed notably with respect to management strategies to establish industrial relations with diminished regulation and narrowed scope for bargaining, but without proposals or experiments in participation. Such strategies have been aimed at traditional employment contracts (full-time, permanent) in more than one country (France, Spain, Portugal, and also the UK and Belgium). They were even more commonly adopted with respect to atypical employment (part-time, temporary jobs, secondary labour). The range of situations is wide, from countries in which such action is exceptional (Sweden, Belgium) to intermediate circumstances (Britain, especially for women), to the typical informal economy (France, Spain, Portugal).

This overall panorama reveals that the post-war realignment between capital and labour, enhancing the position of labour and labour unions, in terms both of collective bargaining and of 'political citizenship'[6] was largely confirmed. Two mutually opposing tendencies were observable, however. On the one hand, the return of democracy in Spain and Portugal extended the potential, if not immediately the substance, of the realignment. But, on the other, the structural conditions that had made this realignment possible throughout Europe showed signs of strain, of manifest or latent tensions that were the harbingers of the end of the long post-war period of expansion and progress.

In terms of the achievements of union action and the state of industrial relations, the most advanced countries were those where there had been some development of concertation and of the co-ordination of bargaining demands, as well as of industrial democracy (Sweden, Germany, Belgium, Denmark). This group of leaders was followed by countries in which the unions had successfully relied on direct, conflictual relations (in a relatively favourable balance of strength) with the employer side (Britain and Italy).

Compared with previous decades, there was a somewhat stronger trend towards the convergence of industrial relations systems, due more to external than to internal factors. The main cause was the increasing politicization of functional interests. This meant that the interests and demands represented by the trade unions were increasingly mediated everywhere in the political and institutional arena, because of the substantial problems of compatibility between the economy, economic policy and industrial relations, though the forms and outcomes of course varied from country to country.

If we wish to distinguish between common traits and national peculiarities – fully aware, of course, that such an exercise necessarily entails some oversimplification – we can say that the features shared by the industrial relations system we have surveyed concern three main aspects: the recognition of the unions, national-level collective bargaining, and small or negligible employer interest in furthering worker participation. The areas in which national differences prevailed, by contrast, concern the procedures and workings of concertation, the presence or absence of industrial democracy, and the extent of employer strategies to diminish the power of collective bargaining to regulate employment contracts and conditions.

2 Industrial relations in the 1980s

2.1 Structural problems

The traditional pattern of industrial relations in Europe underwent profound modification in the course of the 1980s. As noted, there was a very widespread, massive challenge to the nature of labour relations, one that was already objectively inherent in the conditions of the later 1970s. Structurally, the challenge consisted in the transformation of the economy and of the labour market.

All countries, though not all at precisely the same time, faced the need to overcome recession and simultaneously preserve or improve the efficiency of their economies. While government policymakers were concerned principally with recouping lost output, curing inflation and trimming budget deficits, private firms engaged in sweeping, complicated industrial restructuring, designed chiefly to improve competitiveness through technological innovation, new, more advanced products and new standards for the utilization of labour.

The other significant change in the European economies this decade, familiar to all, has been the much faster growth of services, the multifarious tertiary sector, than of manufacturing, particularly in terms of employment, even though as a rule the condition of any single national economy is still largely determined by the efficiency and composition of its industrial production.

The countries studied here were sharply diversified in this respect in the past, and remained so at the start of the decade. Today, the outcome of the processes of economic change is in some respects similar from country to country, but some differences have persisted, while others have emerged. And this may continue in the near future, since the needs of innovation in production and in macroeconomic policy are not about to disappear. For our purposes it may be useful to draw up, with all due caution, a ranking of economic variables, from those with the greatest transnational similarity in the course of the 1980s to those with the greatest degree of divergence:[7]

1   *Export growth*   After the general slowdown of the early 1980s, it resumed in 1984–6, most sharply in Germany.
2   *Industrial output*   During 1984–6 it grew appreciably in all countries, with Germany, Britain, Portugal and Spain doing somewhat better than the average.
3   *Manufacturing value-added as share of GDP*   A steady downward tendency, shared by the United States and even, though to a lesser extent, Japan.
4   *Real GDP growth*   Annual average growth at market prices, with frequent year-to-year variations, has been 2.3 per cent for 1980–6. Faster growth, especially in 1984–6, has been achieved by Portugal, Spain, Germany, Britain, Italy and Denmark. Overall, however, divergences are less appreciable at the end than at the beginning of the period.
5   *Overall productivity in the private sector*[8]   The improvement here was sharper in the last three than in the first three years of the period, and with substantial divergences among countries

(Italy, 1.6 per cent per year, France 0.8 per cent), and the exceptional counter-trend in Sweden (– 1.4 per cent).

6 *Labour productivity in the private sector* This has risen faster than overall productivity in the same sector. The gains were sharper in 1984–6 than in 1980–3, and rates have been fairly uniform for the leading economies (2.0 per cent for Germany, Britain, France and Italy), somewhat lower in Belgium (1.5 per cent), and negative for Sweden (– 0.6 per cent). All told, the gains have been larger than those in the United States.

7 *Inflation* Consumer price inflation has slowed markedly in the last few years in comparison with 1974–8 (when the average annual rate was about 11 per cent), with substantial divergence between countries with very low inflation rates (1986: Germany – 0.2 per cent, Netherlands 0.2 per cent, Sweden 0.7 per cent, Belgium 1.3 per cent), those with low rates (France 2.7 per cent, Britain 3.4 per cent, Denmark 3.6 per cent), medium–high (Italy 6.1 per cent) and high (Spain 8.8 per cent, Portugal 11.7 per cent).

8 *Budget deficit* As share of GDP, the public sector borrowing requirement declined between 1981 and 1986 in some countries (Germany, Sweden, Denmark and Belgium). It increased in Spain and more modestly, but from very high levels, in Italy. It was relatively stable in the Netherlands and still more so in France and Britain.

The trends in these variables confirm the significant differences between the European economies. Even more cautiously than before, the performance of these economies can be sketched, designated with plus or minus signs (indicating improvement or deterioration) for the purpose of a subsequent assessment of the extent to which economic–structural conditions are correlated with the state of industrial relations. Thus, Germany has plus signs for all variables, except for the share of industrial value-added in GDP (which is negative for all countries); Sweden has many plus signs, but minus signs for overall productivity and labour productivity; Italy, performing well or excellently for the other variables, has higher than average inflation and especially a very large budget deficit; Britain is positive, or only slightly negative, on all variables; France is mixed – with respect to some variables it lags behind all major economies, with others it is outperformed only by Germany; Belgium, Denmark and the Netherlands are, all in all, in a middling position; Spain and Portugal, the former at a more advanced stage of development than the latter, have both achieved impressive growth in output from their points of departure, but with very poor performance in terms of inflation and the budget deficit.

Clearly, the other structural challenge presented to the system of industrial relations in the 1980s concerns the labour market. This involves a set of phenomena that will exert more influence, in the present and the future, than economic variables, since their effect is not cyclical. They remain present, for the most part, even in times of economic expansion. And they affect virtually all the advanced industrial economies. This indicates that these phenomena do not vary as greatly from country to country as economic variables and trends do. Moreover, those problems whose manifestations are not only structural (labour-shedding) find only partial remedies in economic policies, specifically in the labour policies enacted so far or conceivable.

Somewhat schematically, among the phenomena connected with changes in the labour market we may distinguish between those involving an unfavourable change in the relation between labour supply and demand and those that introduce new, atypical employment (that is, different from the traditional full-time, permanent job).

The former are reflected mainly in persistent high unemployment, despite the improvement in some countries over the past three years. And unemployment does not always decline when employment expands (as in Italy and Germany). For 1986, the unemployment ranking is as follows: unemployment rate 10 to 20 per cent: Spain, Italy, Belgium, Netherlands, Britain, France; 7 to 9 per cent: Germany, Denmark, Portugal; Sweden, 2.5 per cent, the only positive exception to high unemployment in Europe and, together with Japan, in the entire OECD.

Other significant modifications of the structure of the labour market comprise: the declining proportion of the labour force engaged in industrial activities (as in Britain, France, Italy and Spain, but not only there); the expansion of employment in the services sector, involving a large range of skill levels (from new, highly skilled professions to those with virtually no qualifications); the end of employment expansion in the government sector (except in Sweden and, less pronouncedly, in Italy); and the increasing presence of women in the labour market, both where women's employment has expanded (Belgium, Britain, Sweden) and where it has not (Germany, Spain).

Manifestations of untraditional forms of employment, observable in the 1970s but expanding strikingly in the 1980s (Cordova, 1986) comprise principally: precarious jobs in small manufacturing companies, in the services, and in the informal or 'underground' economy, often as part of the decentralization of production; clandestine, unreported jobs held by immigrant workers or family members; atypical employment contracts, such as part-time, temporary and trainee contracts. These do not necessarily substitute for traditional forms, as in Britain, where there has recently been an increase in traditional manufacturing employment, mainly female. Clearly the last of these three phenomena must not be seen in quite the same light as the first two. For it is not simply a reflection of firms' demand for flexibility and lower labour costs. Rather, it also responds to changes in the outlook towards work and may stem from feelings of solidarity (with young people, with the employees of ailing firms), as in the solidarity contracts found in France and Italy. A second distinctive feature of these atypical contracts is that they are generally regulated, either by law (Germany and France), by collective bargaining contract (Sweden), or by a combination of the two (Italy, for one).

Of the types of atypical employment, the most widespread, and the one with the greatest potential for expansion, is part-time work, which mainly involves the services sector and working women. In 1985, part-time jobs accounted for more than 20 per cent of total employment in Britain, Denmark, the Netherlands, and Sweden and over 10 per cent in Germany and France. In Italy, by contrast, the share is much lower (5 per cent).

Even without considering the more deleterious aspects of these phenomena, they have certainly helped modify relations between employers and the work force, and taken together tend to create problems for union action. In this regard, let us briefly recall the following factors: almost everywhere there is an emerging dichotomy between protected and unprotected workers, between those with job security and the precarious; unemployment structurally weakens the labour force (ISE, 1986) and objectively sharpens competition among working people when economic and wage policy choices must be made; the decline of the industrial workforce and of blue-collar employment strikes at the historical 'heart' of the labour movement and the trade union outlook; the growth of employment outside industry normally generates types of workers further removed from the outlook and the values of the labour movement, fosters a more self-interested, instrumental attitude to unions, and by its composition creates a workforce marked by strong divergence of interests (Streeck, 1985); segmentation, differentiation and the diversification of occupational statuses complicate the formation and management of representative structures and make the goal of generalized defence of the interests and rights of working people harder to achieve (Baglioni, 1986a).

2.2   *The actors*

2.2.1   The state   The role and initiative of the state in industrial relations being largely determined by the composition and orientation of the governing parties, the most significant development of the period covered by this study is obviously the prevalence of conservative governments. Just before or after the turn of the decade, conservative coalitions took office in Germany, Denmark, the Netherlands, and the strongly right-wing Conservatives came to power in Britain. After five years of Socialist government, the right came to power in France in 1986 (though only temporarily), and the elections of 1987 witnessed a clear victory by the conservatives in Portugal.

Except for the interrupted period in France, since 1982 leftist parties ruled only in Sweden and Spain (and with evident signs of wear and tear in the latter recently). In Italy, the ruling coalitions have been centre–left, while the electoral strength of the powerful Communist Party has gradually declined.

Two important transnational convergences in government action, concerning top-priority economic and financial policy objectives, are observable. The first is the need to curb the budget deficit, to curb inflation and to improve the international competitiveness of the economy. Accomplishments on the first two objectives, as we have seen, have varied perceptibly from country to country. The drive for competitiveness, by contrast, has apparently been pursued more consistently and more universally.

The second, closely related convergence is the effort to curb the rise in the cost of labour and to control wage rises, mainly through incomes policy. This has had one very significant consequence, namely the expansion of active, direct intervention by the state in industrial relations. However, in practice this common tendency has been reflected in a wide assortment of different approaches including some which have gone in the opposite direction. In Britain and, in some aspects, the Netherlands, unions have been weakened by a reduction in institutional protection and by intensified exposure to labour market pressure.

In the various governments' pursuit of these converging objectives, there have been significant differences in the treatment of the labour unions, the degree of recognition accorded them and the role they have been permitted to play in serving the needs of the economy: in France there has been a growth in recognition; it has been stable in Sweden, Italy and Spain; it has declined in the Netherlands, Denmark, Belgium and Germany; and in Britain policy has been explicitly hostile to unions (Clark and Wedderburn, 1986). There has been little convergence among countries in relations between the state, unions and employer organizations. Concertation endures in Sweden but with little resemblance to the classic Swedish model (Peterson, 1987); it has declined in Belgium, Denmark, the Netherlands and Germany; and it is decidedly absent in Britain. In France (Berger, 1984) and Spain (Perez-Diaz, 1986) it is reduced in importance anyway by the weakness of civil society in relation to the state. Meanwhile, Italy has been developing its own distinctive form of concertation (Baglioni, 1986b).

2.2.2 The employers First and foremost, what has emerged from the vast, diversified business community in recent years has been determination and initiative in shaping the changes that are remodelling the industrial relations system. In practice, the employers' goal is to revise and redraft the criteria governing the use, output and remuneration of labour. This trend is visible in all the countries reviewed, and, since in part it is the product of structural factors, its evolution and manifestations will presumably not be cyclical or short-term.

This powerful tendency entails changes in the behaviour of employers in the handling of industrial relations, compared with the past (Clegg, 1976). The most important of these is the very widespread diminution of the role played by central organizations in favour of more restricted associations or individual company management.

This organizational element is but one of the factors that have accentuated the diversification of the employer community, which for that matter has always been one of its characteristics. This diversity does not stem solely from structural factors. Indeed, it could be argued that these tend to forge comparatively uniform and explicit interests and objectives, while less clearly defined, heterogeneous types of behaviour emerge with respect to interests and objectives in political and trade union affairs and relations. What I have in mind, among the structural, common factors, are three typical employer tendencies of recent years, namely the demand for flexibility, the preference for decentralization in the management of employer contracts, and the renewed employer political presence. The heterogeneous area refers to industrial relations and specifically to employer attitudes to workers and their union representatives.

The drive for flexibility in the use of labour is the employers' new frontier. The intent is to attenuate or eliminate many if not all of the rigid rules, both legislative and contractual, accumulated in the 1960s and 1970s. There is a vast literature on this topic of which I shall briefly recall three essential points. First, the demand for flexibility has been raised virtually everywhere in the industrial world, and it is a crucial problem for Europe. Secondly, this employer demand has won increasing acceptance beyond the business community, especially in government. And thirdly, flexibility has a sweeping, across-the-board impact on the traditional substance and rules of industrial relations, hence on union action itself, in that it constitutes firms' ability to reorganize and adapt promptly to changes in economic variables, in an environment now characterized by substantial uncertainty and increasingly sharp competition. This is because the request is both for internal flexibility (changes in work organization, in working hours, in work performance and the evolution of job tasks, in wage system) and external flexibility (changes in number of employees, non-standard and atypical forms of employment contract, worker mobility).

The drive for flexibility is closely intertwined with management's inclination to more decentralized regulation of labour relations and employment. In those sectors, still the great majority in manufacturing, where this regulation comes about through bargaining with unions, employers have shown a clear preference for bargaining at the company level. Employers may vary in practice in their determination to pursue this objective, but all in all it represents a very widespread conviction among them, namely that overcoming established rigidity is less difficult in the individual production facility or company than in broader contexts; and concomitantly that company or local union bodies are the most sensitive and amenable to management's needs.

Employers' determination to attain and keep greater discretionary power in exercising their prerogatives over and against regulatory constraints has also taken the form of renewed, stronger presence in the political arena. The decline of concertation practices, the requirements of competition, the increasing popularity of ideological and cultural arguments for the 'vendetta' of the market-place – all this has undoubtedly enhanced the legitimacy of businessmen's demands and needs.

The extent of employer organizations' political presence varies, depending on the orientations of the parties in government. It has, for example, been less in evidence in Britain (with a stable, strongly anti-union government), and very active in countries with governments of the left (France, Spain, Sweden) (Gustafsson, 1985).

All in all, as I have mentioned, employers' behaviour with respect to unions and the needs of the workforce are not univocal or unambivalent. They seek to take advantage of the shifting balance of power, but in many cases it is not clear exactly how far they intend to go. Certainly the state of uncertainty of the international economy does not foster solid, broadly shared strategic choices, especially in industry (to which the remarks that follow are principally addressed). In addition, there are possible or probable political developments, and the effect of politics on industrial relations has never been negligible. Moreover, it appears evident that the strategic choices of employers are to some degree related to the inclinations of the unions and (actual or attributed) of workers.

Given this set of factors, it is easy to predict great heterogeneity in the employer and management community, and this is found, to a greater or lesser extent, in all the countries surveyed. Nevertheless one crucial, central fact remains: nowhere does the employers' strategy envisage a fundamental attack on the trade union movement aimed at eliminating the principle of collective contracts in governing employment relations. Nowhere do we find a determination to cancel the legitimacy of the unions as representatives of the collective interests of working people.

If there is no country in which an employer strategy of outright attack against labour unionism prevails, it is also true that employers are attracted to methods of personnel management that represent, in terms of outlook and in terms of practices, a prospective alternative to the trade union method. On this issue the degree of variation and heterogeneity is very high, embracing both the actual content of the alternative methods and the extent of their adoption.

There is an assortment of managerial styles in industrial relations, and the European panorama may be divided, with some simplification, into three types:

1 *Constitutional* In the presence of a stronger or weaker institutional framework of rules, this style views collective bargaining and dealing with the unions as fundamental to the regulation of the use of labour.
2 *Consultative* This style seeks to use institutions and procedures to achieve stronger involvement of workers and stronger identification with the company's own problems and expansion (Brown and Sisson, 1983).
3 *Deregulatory or laissez-faire* This style aims at labour relations in which regulations and the collective bargaining contract are less influential and tries to maximize management discretion and elasticity in the deployment of labour and in determining wages (Streeck, 1986).

There are significant variants within these broad styles. This applies especially to the consultative style, in which one may observe the following:[9] worker participation that coexists with or involves the unions (in this case, it may sometimes cross over into the realm of industrial democracy); worker participation through direct management–worker relations (the newest, most dynamic version of this style); worker participation involving a financial interest in the ownership or performance of the company (shares, convertible bonds, profit-sharing); a personal interest in production processes (quality circles, information groups, autonomous work groups, and so on); forms of involvement which, in exchange for flexibility, offer job security or, if the firm is having economic troubles, more simply ask for agreement in the scaling down of earlier gains (such as trade union rights).

It is worth noting, however, that many employers and managers, especially in recent times, have not made clear choices, rather acting 'pragmatically' according to circumstances and conditions and often not following any prevailing style.

The constitutional style is seen fully in a number of countries (for example, Italy, Germany, Sweden, Spain) and less widely in some others (for example, Belgium). The consultative style is now present in some contexts that formerly displayed little consensus (Spain and France) (Delamotte and Ambrosini, 1986), but also in others with strong bargaining traditions (Germany, Sweden, Britain, Denmark), sometimes with elements of the 'Japanese model'. The deregulative style is currently growing, especially in the tertiary sector. But it is not always easy to distinguish between explicit employer choices and changes in labour relations produced by developments in the labour market.

2.2.3   The unions   Of the three actors on the industrial relations scene the one with the greatest difficulties in the course of the 1980s has been the trade union movement. Unions have been forced to retreat, and their strength has declined, not as dramatically as some observers have contended, but still significantly, both in actions and in underlying conditions.[10] The trend is general, but there are nevertheless perceptible transnational differences. The tendency emerges, first of all, in the weakness of the unions in the political arena, as a group with 'political citizenship': the decline of their image, the prevailing political and ideological climate, the recognized grounds of union legitimation and representativeness.

This weakness, most evident in Britain, can also be seen in some countries with previous concertative traditions (the Netherlands, Denmark, Belgium) and, less markedly, in some still retaining strong elements of bargaining (Germany, Sweden, Italy). In France, Spain and Portugal unions have been helped by the growth in institutional recognition, but have at the same time been compromised by their dependence on the state.

Another aspect of organized labour's political difficulties has been the less 'taken-for-granted' character of relations with 'friendly' political parties, especially where these have been in government. There have been two main reasons for this: the tensions between the parties' needs for a broad base of representation and the unions' more specific situation; and the fact that the unions no longer provide (if they ever did) a compact and secure source of support for friendly parties.

Another factor in the weakened political presence of the unions has been the growth of division, contrast and divergence between different central labour organizations and, in some cases, within the same organization. There have been two principal causes of this lack of unity. The first, a long-standing one, is the impact of relations with political parties on the unions' posture and strategy. The second, more recent and multifarious, consists in the diversity of interests among the workers themselves, hence decisions of a more strictly trade union nature, such as whether to attribute greater importance to central negotiations or to decentralized bargaining.

The former cause is found chiefly in countries with more than one central confederation, with fundamentally political and ideological lines of division (France, Italy, Spain, Portugal, Belgium). The latter is found in countries with a single central labour organization (the British TUC and the German DGB) or central organizations divided essentially not by ideology but by occupational status – blue-collar and white-collar unions (the LO and TCO in Sweden). In addition, most notably in countries with a plurality of central confederations, there has been a growth of independent unions, outside the national confederations, for the most part white-collar and management unions in the private sector or separate unions in the public sector and the services (Cella and Treu, 1982). This applied to France, Spain and especially Italy.

There has been a perceptible decline in the authority of central confederations – both within the union community and in relations with outside forces – and this has further weakened union political strength. This phenomenon is found even in Sweden (Peterson, 1987). The result of multiple factors, the political weakness of organized labour is nonetheless closely correlated with the political construction of government – though the position of German unions seems little affected by the fact of a right-wing government.

A second fundamental indicator of the changing position of unions is the level of membership, which has always shown very wide divergences between countries (Clegg, 1976: ch. 2). A simple three-way classification into countries with high, medium, and low unionization (over 50 per cent of the employed labour force, 30 to

50 per cent, and under 30 per cent, respectively) gives the following ranking for the early 1980s. Countries with high unionization are Sweden, Denmark and Belgium; medium unionization, Germany, Italy, Britain, the Netherlands; low unionization, France and Spain (Cella and Treu, 1982).

This shows that the post-war realignment in favour of labour as against capital did not involve a universally high rate of unionization. This also goes for the leading non-European industrial economies, the USA and Japan, which were at this time characterized respectively by medium and low unionization.

From this initial situation, a number of trends can be observed in the present decade. First, there has been a perceptible overall decline in unionization. Secondly, however, the decline is not universal, because two countries, Sweden and Denmark, have moved against the trend. Thirdly, it has been steeper in the countries with already low unionization (France and Spain) than in those with medium to high (Belgium, Germany, Italy). Fourthly, there is certainly no lack of overt or latent causes for an erosion of the representativeness of unions (gap between bureaucracy and rank-and-file, disaffection among young workers, failure to reorganize to keep step with the composition of the labour force, and so on), but the main cause of the decline has been structural conditions, and specifically the decline in blue-collar and industrial employment (Britain, the Netherlands and Italy). Nevertheless, the countries where the decline has been least severe are also those in which, conside .ng the decline, the union presence in industry has been relatively well maintained (Sweden, Germany, Denmark). In many countries, unionization in the services has not advanced proportionally to the growth of employment in that sector, while for the most part high or medium unionization in the public sector has been maintained (as, for example, in Sweden, Italy, Britain and Portugal).

Contrary to what might be expected, the correlation of unionization performance with the economic variables discussed in the previous section is not clearly demonstrable, at least not in Sweden, Denmark and Belgium (where the trend in unionization is better than the economic conditions) or in France (where it is worse). Unionization is better correlated with the state of the labour market, especially with unemployment. In many countries this has had a negative impact on unionization, while in two cases (Denmark and Belgium) it has presumably spurred workers to join unions or retain their union membership. Unionization does not appear to be closely correlated with the nature or policy orientation of governments. Witness the comparatively good performance of organized labour in Denmark, Belgium and Germany with their conservative governments, or the poor performance under the socialist governments of France and Spain.

Later we shall look at the correlation – not a perfect fit, in reality – between unionization trends and bargaining processes. In any event, considering the correlations mentioned so far, it can be concluded that in the 1980s unionization still depends to a certain extent on the traditional factors endogenous to the labour movement and its relations with employers and political institutions.

A third significant indicator of the state of union activity is the pattern of strikes. Here there has been a substantial decline in a good many cases dating back to the mid-1970s. This has affected virtually all the countries surveyed here as well as the USA and Japan. The extent of the decline may have a variable impact on traditional conflict levels (Cella, 1979), but in the medium term (that is, since 1975) this does not appear to have altered the custom~ ~ classification into high-conflict (for example, Britain and Italy), low-conflict (Sweden, the Netherlands and Germany) and medium-conflict countries.[11] The basic conflict indicators (frequency, participation and volume) have been giving different signals, but the following can be said concerning the most important, volume (number of days lost): there has been a notable decline in Spain, the Netherlands and Belgium; stability in France and Sweden; a tendency to decline but with moments of instability in Italy and Germany; and a substantial decline in Britain and Denmark.

The overall tendency to decline has also incorporated some exceptional developments: the emergence of some large and bitter conflicts (as in the British mining strike or the German conflict over working-hours reduction in 1984); occasional years that interrupted the trend (Italy 1982–3, Portugal and Belgium 1983, Spain 1984, Netherlands 1985); the growing number and importance of conflict among workers in the public sector and public services (in Britain, Italy, Belgium, Sweden and France) (Cordova, 1985).

It is not easy to furnish a reliable account of the motivations and objectives of industrial action. Certainly there has been a diminution in the share of traditional bread-and-butter strikes over wages and working conditions in industry. Some strikes in the industrial sector have featured demands for shorter hours, but as we know this demand has a different meaning now, in view of high unemployment, from that in the past. Traditional strike aims are more commonly found in the civil service and some public service strikes.

Particularly in industry, there appears to be a prevalence – in terms of social impact if not in terms of number of strikes – of conflictual actions (not necessarily only strikes) for defensive aims. Specifically, this means strikes to save jobs in the face of labour-shedding and restructuring, as has been happening in Britain, France, Spain, the Netherlands, Belgium, Denmark and Italy.

Overall there seems to be some convergence among the various countries. Strikes seem increasingly dependent on economic variables and to be pro-cyclical. Such recession strikes take on a defensive character and, in general, tend to decline. Unemployment tends to exercise a restraint on conflict, though it is difficult to distinguish this in different countries as they all (except Sweden) have seen high unemployment. Any relation between conflict and union membership, already problematic (one thinks of Sweden) is far from clear. An association between strikes and the place of the unions politically seems to work in some countries (for example, the Netherlands) but not others (Italy, Denmark).

3   The processes

3.1   The political and institutional arena

All in all, the industrial relations process has been marked by the fact, already noted, of the greater, more active and often direct intervention of the public powers. This is a tendency common to all countries and corroborates the decline in the independence of industrial relations vis-à-vis the political sphere, and the continuing politicization of business and labour interests. Also, inevitably, this has meant a recovery and exercise of the state's authority with respect to the organizations representing the interests of the working people, though not necessarily anti-worker or anti-union measures.

On the bases of the convergent government concerns set forth above, this tendency has been manifested: indirectly in the economic policy, fiscal policy and social policy (welfare and employment); directly in measures dealing with industrial relations proper and/or unions.

Combining these two variables – measures more or less unfavourable to labour and direct or indirect intervention – we can evaluate the processes in the political and institutional sphere and chart the positions of the individual countries, ranking them according to whether conditions engendered greater or less difficulty for the labour movement. By this approach, first place (that is, the worst problems) is held by Britain, followed by Belgium, Denmark and the Netherlands; next Germany; next France, Spain and Portugal (bearing in mind, however, the instability of conditions in these countries); finally, Italy and Sweden. Let me clarify at the outset that this ranking concerns only the processes mentioned and does not coincide with the ranking according to the state of industrial relations, and specifically the unions' position in collective bargaining.

To summarize some of the main developments we might start with the UK, where a whole ensemble of legislative measures has been aimed at reducing 'union rights' (see for example Simitis, 1986). In Belgium there have been a number of strict measures, such as those limiting the price indexation of wages. In Denmark and the Netherlands most interventions by public authority have been aimed at reducing demand. There have been some legislative measures in Germany (such as that limiting unemployment pay during strikes); in general governments have favoured structural changes that would reduce the role of national contracts in favour of local negotiations.

The socialist government in France introduced measures favourable to workers and unions in the Auroux laws (Reynaud, 1984), reinforcing workers' job rights and imposing on employers an obligation to bargain at factory level. In Spain there has continued to be an abundance of new legislation, partly in favour of individual workers (such as laws to reduce working hours), but mainly to define the institutional status of union organizations. In Portugal rigid labour market controls have accompanied increased legal regulation of the structure of collective bargaining. In Italy there was a growing legal intervention in industrial relations, with frequent impact on collective bargaining. In Sweden, following previous actions (laws on industrial democracy and active labour market policy), there was the novelty of growing pressure by government on wage development.

3.2 Collective bargaining

In the collective bargaining sphere, a key characteristic of the 1980s is that the labour movement has not only lost ground in terms of the three indicators already examined but has also been driven into retreat in direct action in defence of workers' interests, not only on wage claims and working conditions but also on rules of substance governing the use of labour.

This retreat was more evident at the start of the decade than it has been in recent years, when collective bargaining has proceeded better and produced better results (ISE, 1986). Generally this improvement has been explained as the result of better economic conditions (low inflation, the drop in oil costs, and so on) and of the substantial completion of the more drastic adjustment and restructuring programmes. Still, this pattern, though to be taken with caution owing to the brief time-span covered, suggests that predictions of a strong trend towards a decline in collective bargaining practices and methods are hasty and poorly founded.

Within the general pattern of increasing difficulties for collective bargaining compared to previous years, there are very significant national differences, giving rise to different degrees of *solidity* of collective bargaining practices:[12]

1 Overall strong solidity
  Germany: The efficacy and legitimacy of collective bargaining are confirmed, no radical changes in industrial relations are observable.
  Sweden: The status of the bargaining system has been maintained; the system has considerable adaptability and now differs in a number of salient features from the classical Swedish model.
  Italy: Though influenced by relations with the institutional and political system, collective bargaining is still diversified, extensive, and far-reaching; a new feature is the increasing role of the public and government sectors.
2 Partially eroded solidity
  Britain: The reality does not correspond to the cliché of a drastic overall decline; the situation is highly variegated, within the general conditioning influence of legislation.
  Denmark: Unions have less bargaining power now than formerly, owing mainly to legislative intervention, but collective bargaining is still the fulcrum of the industrial relations system.
3 Perceptibly weakened solidity
  Netherlands: The formalized, ramified bargaining system, with the prevalence of central negotiations, is feeling the effect of centrifugal factors making for uncertainty, but these have not seriously compromised the extensive union and bargaining presence.
  Belgium: After years of declining bargaining independence owing to state intervention in industrial relations and of marked decentralization of collective bargaining, there has recently been a resumption of bargaining initiatives and general bilateral talks.
4 Traditionally poor but increasing solidity
  France: One may properly speak of the affirmation of collective bargaining (greater legitimacy and greater extension and scope), especially company-level bargaining, with the support of legislation (EIRR, 1986).

5 Traditionally poor and stagnant solidity

Spain: Bargaining is modest in scope and depth, despite the institutional recognition of the unions; nor is the extension of bargaining at all general.

Portugal: A collective bargaining system is just being built, but so far legislative regulation and state initiative prevail.

The pattern of strength in collective bargaining does correlate with the performance of the economic variables. This shows that the time of continuous progress in bargaining demands, even counter to market conditions, is past (Baglioni, 1982). Sweden is perhaps the exception, with the solidity of bargaining superior to the state of the economy.

The correlation of the state of collective bargaining with unemployment works for Sweden, the only economy in which the level of unemployment is 'physiological' and for several countries with very high unemployment (Spain, Belgium, the Netherlands). Elsewhere the fit is much worse, especially in Italy and Britain. This shows that unlike economic conditions generally, the state of the labour market can be largely overcome by bargaining initiatives and contract results. In other words, the objective competition of the jobless does not necessarily damage the unions' ability to defend the interests of employed workers.

The solidity of collective bargaining varies proportionally with the prevalence of a 'constitutional' managerial style, except in Spain and Portugal. It is impossible, at present, to gauge the degree of correlation with the 'constitutional' style, because this is only beginning to take hold and is found in virtually all countries (except Italy).

The solidity of collective bargaining relations does not correlate well with the political position and pro- or anti-labour orientation of governments. For some countries the two variables are associated, but not for Germany, Britain and Denmark on the one side, or for Spain on the other.

Correlating collective bargaining solidity with political and institutional processes (along the axis of greater or fewer difficulties for the unions) also reveals the non-correspondence of Germany, Britain and Denmark on one end, Spain on the other. These three correlations taken together reveal, among other things, that there is no necessary convergence between political variables and industrial relations; specifically, collective bargaining does not necessarily depend on political conditions, even where there is a tendency to stronger state intervention.

This apparent contradiction is explained by the fact that the relative solidity of collective bargaining practices is heavily affected by economic conditions (more pronouncedly in the 1980s than in the past) and by management style in labour relations. Also, there is a broad correspondence between the strength of bargaining and the pattern of unionization (adjusted for the decline in industrial employment). The only exceptions to this rule are Belgium (where bargaining has declined but not union membership) and France (diametrically opposite trends).

The counter-examples cited successively in examining the validity of the correlations suggested between collective bargaining and the other factors may be explained – where bargaining is well established despite unfavourable conditions – by a strong tradition of organizational and bargaining presence (Sweden, Italy, Britain, Germany, Denmark). Where bargaining is weak, the explanation often lies in the lack of such a tradition.

One of the more common, easily visible features of European industrial relations in the 1980s is decentralization. This change is bound to have far-reaching implications for the protection of workers' interests and the regulation of the employment of labour. Decentralization can be seen in Britain predominantly at company level; in Italy it is integrated with other levels; as a major change in past practice in Belgium, Germany, Sweden and the Netherlands; as favoured by legislation in France and Denmark.

Decentralization, all in all, is part of the general retreat of the labour movement. It is often a manifestation of the alteration in the power balance in favour of management, and it has created complicated problems for union strategy. Nevertheless, this trend cannot be interpreted merely as an indicator of union retreat. This goes for Italy and Britain, but also for Germany and Sweden, and in a number of respects for Belgium and the Netherlands (Albeda, 1985) as well as France. A decentralization of bargaining is perhaps the most profound challenge to previous industrial relations arrangements, in that, apart from employers' political and organizational inclinations, it corresponds to structural developments (the decentralization of employment and the increasing diversity of occupations) and at least in private sector manufacturing and services is connected with the need for flexibility and the proposals and experiments in forms of worker participation alternative to collective bargaining.

The issue of flexibility is central everywhere for the entire decade. It is one of the aspects on which the evolution of industrial relations systems is universally converging. The management demand for flexibility has been decisively imposed in countries with strong labour movements (Sweden, Italy, Britain). It is one of the main points of controversy and innovation in Germany. It has provoked clashes and general encounters among all the actors in France, Belgium, the Netherlands and Denmark. It has surfaced in Spain and in all probability will be a key issue in Portugal as well.

It may still be too early to identify definite, general tendencies. Empirically, however, three trends can be observed. First, flexibility appears to be principally dealt with in collective bargaining contracts (Britain, Italy, Sweden, Germany, Denmark) but also in legislation in some countries (France, Spain and Belgium). Secondly, in the framework of collective bargaining on flexibility, there have been a number of national-level agreements (Belgium, the Netherlands, Denmark), as well as legislation with an impact on industrial relations at lower levels, for example on the issue of external flexibility (Germany, Italy, Sweden, Denmark, the Netherlands). In any event, the greatest number of bargaining or consultative agreements are found at the company level (Cressey, 1987). In all countries, institutional provisions and agreements on flexibility have produced procedures and norms governing the confrontation between management and unions. All in all these are somewhat removed from the traditional approach of normative regulation of the substance of the utilization of labour, being more inclined to treat the processes involved with increasing involvement of the unions (Della Rocca, 1987).

Looking at these three trends, we can see that the potentially deregulatory impact of flexibility – despite the virtually universal prevalence of management initiative and of anything but negligible concrete sacrifices by workers – has been corrected by new rules, by negotiations, with the preservation of the central role of collective bargaining. Obviously, the extent and incidence of the union presence has varied from country to country, and in some cases as between industries, regions and companies.

Negotiated agreements on the application of corrections to flexibility have been facilitated by the orientation of the unions, most of which have realized how important it is to bargain over these issues, thus abandoning their earlier tendency to introduce accumulating protective work rules. This shift, which is a manifestation of convergence in union objectives and practices, has been opposed by only a few labour organizations – the Intersindicale in Portugal, the CGT and many middle-ranking union officers in France (Gaspard, 1985) for instance – but in other cases, as in Belgium, the initial rejection and diffidence have given way to a strong propensity to negotiation.

This propensity is found in Germany, where the unions are open to innovation and determined to contain the effects of deregulation;

in Sweden, where they intend to influence technological and organizational innovation in the planning stage; in Italy, where unions have exerted broad control over flexibility, giving worker representatives the right to take part, *de facto*, in the revival of industry and to gain a new type of recognition; in Britain, where the challenge of innovation has been taken up by many unions, especially since 1984, including in advanced technology firms; in Denmark, where sharp conflict between the demand for flexibility and union requests for control over new technology has not prevented frequent negotiations; and in France, where the national conflict between business and labour is often resolved at the company level.

The results of this bargaining process, which is certainly one of the salient features of the decade, have been more substantial with respect to internal than external flexibility.

Another issue that acquired great importance in industrial relations during the 1980s was worker participation. The debate on this issue, which has been reflected at the operational level as well, has pointed to the end of the traditional labour relations arrangements in which there was a sharp distinction between managerial or employer responsibilities and those of workers and their unions. This indication has been stressed by the business community, and has been viewed as a plausible prospect by observers in a number of other quarters as well. It has been considered with attention and open-mindedness by the labour movement, within which some of the strongest and most advanced organizations had already dealt with the theories of worker participation through various forms of industrial democracy as in Sweden and Germany.

Despite a favourable cultural climate and these significant precedents, however, all in all industrial democracy has not made much progress during our period, and has registered its only important developments in the public sector (France) or state firms (Italy) rather than in the private sector (Provasi, 1987).

The lacklustre performance of industrial democracy can be understood, first and foremost, if we recall three elements. First, in the 1980s collective bargaining has met with great difficulties, and seldom has it proved possible to maintain its effectiveness and also enable worker representatives to co-determine working conditions. Secondly, bargaining over flexibility has often ultimately dealt with matters and taken forms that are largely assimilable to the typical forms of industrial democracy, so that today it is harder to draw a sharp distinction between bargaining and participation. And thirdly, the prospect of industrial democracy is meeting competition in the form of management-initiated participation.

Forms of participation of this kind that include a role for union representatives have not progressed far. More usually managers deal with workers directly, ignoring or cutting across union representatives. This constitutes one of the major novelties in current industrial relations and makes a breach with the trade unions and bargaining model. It is a breach that has affected countries with varying past experience of bargaining and has been encouraged by both cultural (that is, Japanese patterns) and structural (changing labour force composition) motives.

In practice we can observe a growing demand for and experience with the involvement of workers in quality circles and the like (especially in Belgium, France, Britain, Sweden); more rarely, forms of profit-sharing (Denmark and Sweden); and the distribution of shares to employees (Germany, Britain, France).

Another issue that has significantly affected industrial relations during this decade has been the shortening or restructuring of working hours. A major preoccupation in so doing has been the maintenance or improvement of employment levels. Except in Sweden, this has been an important aim of unions (Gaspard et al., 1987); some governments have contributed (France, Spain, the Netherlands, Belgium), but there has been widespread opposition from employers.

In recent years this opposition – repeatedly justified by reference to rising labour costs, with an accompanying demand for wage compensation – has engendered a change in the terms of the question, the issue no longer being seen as 'shorter hours in order to distribute jobs better' but as 'reduction and better management of working time'. In other words, the question no longer coincides with a typical union objective but has been transformed into a matter for collective bargaining, in which the reduction in hours is traded off against the firms' ability to arrange working time in line with their own functional needs and manage schedules in this light. In practice, the shortening of working time is intertwined with the issue of flexibility and has taken on importance in bargaining over that question.

This transformation is accompanied, in convergent fashion, by changes in the level and extension of application of decisions and provisions on working hours. At the start of the decade there was legislation for generalized reductions: in France (the 1982 law shortening the legal working week to thirty-nine hours and lengthening paid vacatio: ; to five weeks) and in Spain (the government decree setting a legal working year in number of hours).

At the same time and subsequently, measures were taken at the national level, but designed to establish the legal or bargaining premises for the application of the reduction at the production level. Instances are the 1982 Hansenne law in Belgium, and, in 1986, the 'framing' agreement for the private sector; the 1982 inter-industry agreement in the Netherlands; the 1983 concertation agreement in Italy (a forty-hour reduction in the annual workload over two years), plus the 1985 public employment agreement extending the thirty-five-hour week; the reduction from forty to thirty-eight and a half hours after the militant German metal-workers' campaign in 1984 and then to thirty-seven hours as provided by the 1987 contract; the Danish agreement for a four-hour shortening of the working week over four years in 1987; and the 1986 French law on flexibility.

With these measures and others the management of working time tends to be carried on in the context of the more general decentralization of industrial relations. This can take place in a situation of a mix of provisions deriving from higher levels, with application assigned to the production level (as in many agreements in Germany, Italy, France, the Netherlands and also in Sweden), or else more pragmatically, with other objectives connected with the reduction, such as a cut in overtime (as in Britain and Spain) (Treu, 1986).

The obstacles to shortening working hours, however, are not only structural or the result of employer resistance. It cannot be ignored that employed workers do not always share the impetus of solidarity underlying actions to create or defend jobs. There have been some encouraging examples in this sphere, as in Germany, but in other instances, as in the Netherlands, workers appear sharply divided. It is quite difficult, moreover, to make a clear assessment of the employment impact of hours reduction. Optimistic and pessimistic data and opinions clash within individual countries and in the overall European panorama. There is increasing agreement on the thesis that hours reductions have been a useful defensive weapon against the decline in industrial employment in the countries where massive labour shedding appeared inevitable. Statistics, in fact, show a strong correlation between job destruction in manufacturing and the shortening of average working time. However, the gradualness of the hours reductions and the different methods of application from country to country make it impossible to check whether the reduction has had a substantial employment impact.

The final theme to be considered in the analysis of bargaining must be, of course, wages. With recession, inflation and government anti-inflation measures, and the massive heightening of internal competition trade unions have made their prime objective, in their action for employed workers' interests, the defence of real wages.

This objective has been at the centre of negotiations and agreements with management, but to a large extent it must also take account of the desires and actions of government. This happens directly when governments intervene to determine (or rather to influence) wage rises. They may, for instance, desensitize or suspend indexation machinery, as was done in countries with long-standing traditions of concertation (Belgium, Denmark, the Netherlands, Sweden), Spain and Portugal and, less decisively, in Italy.

Government measures have a direct impact on the unions' objective of defending real wages, since their help determines whether the purchasing power of earnings is preserved. Some measures (or non-measures) depress purchasing power, such as fiscal drag or rising employee social security contributions (as in Germany, Belgium and Italy); others offer fiscal compensation, household income support, discounts on public service tariffs, and so on. The defensive stance of labour organizations on wages, and especially the difficulty of actually defending real wages, emerge in all their clarity in a comparison of the present decade with the 1970s.

Our comparison will be based on a single indicator, namely the share of wages and salaries in GDP. The results are as follows: from 1973 to 1979, the share rose in all the countries surveyed (and in Japan), except for Germany and Britain (as well as the USA), where it was unchanged; in 1985, the share was generally lower than it had been in 1979, except in Italy and France where (as in the USA and Japan) it was basically unchanged (van Ginneken, 1987).

This reversal of trend is all the more significant considering that in many cases employment has not declined, at least not in the services, where the incidence of labour costs on value-added is higher, on the average, than in industry. However, the trend does not appear to be firmly established. Rather, it appears to characterize particularly the first few years of the new decade. In the three years from 1984 to 1986, alongside more efficacious collective bargaining (ISE, 1986), there was renewed real wage growth, or at least a halt in the downward trend. This upturn was observed in Britain, Germany, France, Sweden, Portugal, Spain and Italy as well as, albeit less markedly, in Belgium, the Netherlands and Denmark.

This recent upturn is particularly widespread in manufacturing, thanks to collective bargaining and other factors, such as the slowdown in inflation and government measures to curb labour costs (such as the social security tax relief for employers enacted by Germany, Italy and Denmark) (OECD, 1987). In many cases, by contrast, wage rises have not been granted to public sector employees.

With stable governments enjoying strong parliamentary majorities, anti-inflation policy and the priority of cutting budget deficits have meant severe curbing of wage increases to public employees. This has been the case in Britain, Germany, France and the Netherlands. Relative wages in the public and private sectors are a crucial problem in Sweden, where the two groups have leapfrogged over the past fifteen years. In Italy, by contrast, with its weaker, less stable governments and bargaining rivalry between national confederations and independent unions or spontaneous rank-and-file groupings, wage rises have been larger for public employees than in the sectors subject to the constraint of competition.

In short, except for some special cases, during the 1980s wages have gone back to depending on economic variables (competitiveness and labour productivity on the one hand, anti-inflation adjustment on the other). Earlier, the balance between wage claims and the performance of the economy had frequently been upset in favour of the former by union bargaining strength, but now there is greater convergence. The new practice largely resembles the traditional 'German model' of adjusting wage claims to the performance of structural–economic indicators.

It should also be noted that there is not a perfect fit between the ranking of countries by the 'solidity' of collective bargaining practices and the rate of wage increases. In France and Britain, for instance, wage increases have been larger, in comparison to other countries, than would be indicated by the solidity index. The opposite incongruity is found in Germany and Sweden. In part this stems from factors exogenous to collective bargaining (notably political and institutional events, and not just for the public sector). It also depends, however, on the indicators used in the 1980s to measure the solidity of collective bargaining in the medium run, namely its extent, scope and depth.

The panorama that emerges from these observations must necessarily be supplemented by consideration of elements stemming from the trend to decentralization of industrial relations, which have affected wages as well as the other aspects of labour relations. These include increasing wage drift, wider salary ranges (not always set by collective bargaining) and discretionary, individual salary decisions. These phenomena are just as widespread in countries with solid collective bargaining arrangements as elsewhere, and in conjunction with employer-initiated participation proposals they constitute an insidious threat to the legitimacy and the efficacy of collective bargaining and trade union action.

4 Industrial relations, pre- and post-1980

4.1 The main changes already in progress

For a comparison of industrial relations before and after 1980 I shall use the typology set out in section 1, with few detailed empirical references as these have been set out above.

First of all, the recognition of trade union legitimacy and of the unions' necessary role and function is less universal now than in the 1970s. At the same time, the practice and the institutions of concertation are perceptibly less broadly present and less relevant to the industrial relations scene.

National-level collective bargaining between the central labour and employer organizations has been significantly undermined by the general trend to the decentralization of industrial relations. Whereas in the 1970s this type of bargaining was quite widespread and important, in the 1980s there appear to be two characteristic prevailing situations. In some countries centralized bargaining has encountered difficulties or has had diminished impact (Sweden, Spain, and the Netherlands, Belgium and above all Britain). In others its role and operational importance have been preserved (Germany, Italy, France and Denmark). There has been more regression than progress in industrial democracy, especially in the private sector.

Decentralized collective bargaining and contracts, especially at the company level, are the dominant feature of the new decade, decidedly more important than in the past. In countries where company-level bargaining has been traditional (Britain, Italy and Sweden) the phenomenon has been accentuated. More significantly, it has emerged as a new trend in collective bargaining where it was formerly much less important (Germany, France, Belgium, the Netherlands). In the 1970s the position of decentralized bargaining had been the outcome of the historical evolution of the individual industrial relations systems, and there was a broad range of relations between this and higher levels of bargaining. This latter aspect is still relevant to the labour movement, but the great importance of decentralized bargaining today has been shaped primarily by the determination of the employers and in some instances by that of the government. However, as we know, this is not always a simple symptom of trade union retreat and weakness.

As in the previous decade, management and employer strategies that were aimed at encouraging worker participation through company-level union structures were relatively unimportant and their development was insignificant. Employer-initiated schemes for direct worker participation – that is without or against the unions – by contrast became a salient, though not very widespread, feature of industrial relations in the 1980s.

There were significant new developments in the decade as regards employer efforts to develop labour relations with diminished regulations and less extensive collective bargaining without any sort of worker participation. As for standard employment (permanent, full-time jobs), hiring outside a regulatory and collective bargaining framework has been most extensive in the countries where it was already comparatively common previously, such as Britain, France, Belgium, Spain and Portugal. In others, such as Italy, Sweden and Denmark, it is still relatively limited and involves mainly highly skilled employees or technologically advanced firms.

Atypical employment has continued to become more common. Here again, however, the trend is not uniform. In some countries (Britain, Belgium, France, Spain, Portugal), it has flourished, in others less so (Sweden, Italy, Denmark). In some places, such as Germany and Spain, it has been encouraged by the government; in others (France under the Socialists) it has been opposed.

Finally, we can usefully compare the two periods in terms of possible changes in the features shared by the different national industrial relations systems and in those revealing transnational divergences. Hazardous enough for the 1970s, such an exercise is all the more problematical for the past decade, if only because we are still caught up in the rapid changes taking place.

In the 1970s, as noted earlier, three main areas had been characterized by common features: strong recognition of organized labour; widespread resort to national-level collective bargaining; and the unimportance of employer-initiated participation schemes. In the 1980s, it seems to me that the areas in which common features predominated were the following: the development of decentralized collective bargaining and negotiating processes; regression, or absence, of experiments in industrial democracy, especially in the private sector; a modest increase in the extent of managerial strategies of worker participation through unions; a growing, ramified presence of worker participation schemes apart from if not hostile to the unions.

In the 1970s, the most significant divergences concerned the methods and workings of concertation, the presence (or absence) of industrial democracy projects, the prevalence and independence of decentralized bargaining, the commonness of situations in which the regulation of employment via collective bargaining was diminished.

In the past decade, the areas in which transnational diversities were most marked, I feel, are the following: recognition of the legitimacy and the function of organized labour; the presence and difficulties of concertation practices and institutions; the importance and incidence of national-level collective bargaining; the extent of deregulation in employment and in the remuneration of labour.

On close inspection, the shared features of the 1970s involved primarily political relations and the higher levels of collective bargaining, while at present they concern first and foremost decentralizing trends, bargaining and employer proposals for trade-offs, worker involvement and participation. Divergences were found in the 1970s in the mechanisms and workings of concertation and also in industrial relations at the plant level (company-level bargaining, steps towards the deregulation of employment and use of labour). At present, diversities are glaring, substantial, in political and institutional spheres and also perceptible in the general state of relations between business and labour, and hence in the national level of collective bargaining.

Does this set of tendencies and elements mean that the transnational convergence in patterns of industrial relations in Europe has increased or decreased since the 1970s? I do not believe that a clear, straightforward answer is possible. There appear to be solid grounds for holding that there has been a decrease in convergence as regards the political–institutional connections of industrial relations and of organized labour. The politicization of interests (both business and labour), which was the principal factor of convergence in the 1970s, remains relevant, owing both to the potential constraints on industrial relations and to the importance of the interests of working people that cannot be treated in the framework of collective bargaining between unions and employers. However, this factor has not resulted in any tendency towards uniform or similar solutions. On the other hand, as we have noted, there has been a strengthening correlation between the pattern of industrial relations and the performance of structural economic variables and with management initiative and the assorted management styles of labour relations. Therefore, one observes, and one can fundamentally forecast, significant convergences in the employment and use of labour, in the objective constraints on it, in the content of talks on employment regulations, and in forms of labour regulation that are not decided on through bargaining with the collective representatives of workers.

4.2   Predictions for the future

First, as we have seen, industrial relations in European countries witnessed varied and conspicuous changes in the 1980s. However, notwithstanding the overhasty or wishful declarations of many observers, the system has not been overturned or swept away, and there is certainly no justification for speaking of a drastic, radical or definitive decline of organized labour or the collective bargaining method. In some major countries, such as Sweden, Germany and Italy, there has been no great modification of industrial relations and none is foreseeable. In others, such as Britain and Belgium, the transformation has been more substantial, but the existence of unions is in no way threatened, nor is the collective regulation of employment. In some countries, notably Spain and Portugal, the problems of the unions and those of the representation of workers' interests are more serious, but they are not due solely to the challenge of the 1980s.

Secondly, this prediction of overall stability does not apply to the entire world of labour or to all jobs. Still less is it intended to apply uniformly to all types of capitalist society. Important as they are, however, these exceptions are not a recent development. The retreat, the regression, in trade union action during this decade has been quite substantial, but it must be observed that earlier the strength of union action was not truly consolidated or successful everywhere. The labour movement has never been uniform or homogeneous in ideals, and still less so in results. Even in the 1970s there were countries where trade unionism was not permanently recognized or in which it was not extensive and in which the depth and scope of collective bargaining were modest (Baglioni, 1986a).

Thirdly, the varying degree of stability and persistence of industrial relations systems and of organized labour permits an overall transnational comparison. In the 1980s, the most stable systems were found in the countries that have retained concertation and co-ordination or in which industrial relations have the requisites of institutionalization (Sweden and Germany). Those with traditionally more conflictual relations find organized labour in less or greater difficulty depending, albeit not exclusively, on whether political conditions are essentially favourable (Italy) or unfavourable (Britain). More substantial erosion, especially in the first few years of the decade, has taken place in countries such as Belgium and the Netherlands in which traditional concertation arrangements have been seriously undermined. Unions have been less successful in maintaining their positions (unionization, above all) in countries where the labour movement has been historically weak (Spain and France), although especially in France there are signs of corrective action thanks to the backing of government.

This ranking takes account of the features that have emerged in the evolution of industrial relations both politically and institutionally and in the collective bargaining sphere. However, we must recognize that the status and potential of the trade union actor always depend significantly on the previous, traditional extent and solidity of the unions' organizational and bargaining presence. Otherwise, we could never explain the increase in unionization in Denmark and its stability in Belgium. With this 'residual' requisite, we understand why the weaker European labour movements have lost the most ground, and why, outside Europe, the difficulties of organized labour are most serious in the United States (Freeman, 1987).

Fourthly, the difficulties faced by union action are attributed in part to the characteristics of union action itself or factors endogenous to industrial relations (organizational policies, contrasts among organizations, excessive or inadequate institutionalization, levels of military, and so on). However, most observers attribute more weight to exogenous factors, such as economic–structural forces, those relating to conditions in the labour market, and changes in the composition of the labour force. The centrality of economic–structural factors, intertwined with the persistence of collective regulation of labour relations, underlies the second thesis that will be argued here: namely, that there is a tendency for industrial relations to return to a state of comparative normality, which simultaneously affects the labour movement.

This thesis was formulated with reference to the preceding period, at the outset of the wave of conflict between 1968 and 1973, when there was a disparity between the modest or poor performance of many economic indicators and the steady advance in union aims, demands and achievements. In certain countries in particular, this disparity was extraordinary and harboured implicit elements of a future crisis of industrial relations (Goldthorpe, 1984). The thesis also implies a comparison, albeit a less direct one, with the earlier post-war period; in that too there was a complex process of realignment between capital and labour to the benefit of labour and the trade union movement. Clearly, in the context of a capitalist economy, this process could not be protracted indefinitely.

The 'return to normalcy', then, is in reaction to the long period of union advance in bargaining demands and work rules and has obviously been accentuated by the change in the economic and political climate. Thus, as we know, the era of progressive accumulation of work rules and union power has come to an end, to be succeeded by a series of adjustments, experiments and trade-offs based on the principle of compromise and reciprocal concessions and successive revision of the criteria for the use and valuation of labour.

Fifthly, given this state of affairs, the scenario for industrial relations tending to 'return to normalcy' can be represented in three key points.

(a) Industrial relations and union action are more decisively conditioned by the performance of the economy and by developments in the economic structure and the system of production. As we have seen, current divergences in degree of solidity of collective bargaining depend mainly on economic variables. The continuation of this correlation will not allow many exceptions from economic compatibility on the basis of political or organizational strength, while it enhances the objective foundations of collective bargaining demands and results. And this will certainly generate more transnational similarities than national peculiarities, at least in industries exposed to international competition.

(b) Trade union affairs are returning to a fundamentally cyclical pattern, as had been the case until the Second World War; this is already detectable in some countries in the present decade. The sort of general, steady advance that marked the first few decades of the post-war era cannot be expected in the future. A cyclical pattern will not only be imposed by objective conditions but will also be engendered by the relative success or failure of union action. In other words, the action of organized labour can no longer be imagined as a steady succession of victories, gains and improvements, but must rather become experiment, risk, attempts and carefully weighed choices.

(c) Management attitudes, decisions and styles in dealing with the workforce and its representatives will continue to be crucial. Of course, this factor has never been marginal. Earlier, however, with the general recognition of union legitimacy and functions, its practical effects were more rigidly contained, either by general agreements in the political sphere or by the forcefulness of union initiative in collective bargaining.

Sixthly, obviously, however, this 'return to normalcy' is not a simple restoration of the past. The experiences of the past cannot vanish without a trace; they will surely have some impact on the present and the future. The whole series of benefits for wage and salary earners achieved through collective bargaining and political action (first and foremost, welfare programmes) is bound to attenuate the economic constraints and cyclical ups and downs in industrial relations. High unemployment has not generally damped down union initiative or collective bargaining activities.

The considerable portion of the labour force now included in government employment has long been strongly unionized, and this can only be expected to continue. The industrial relations implications of the decline in industrial employment – which is a structural and ideal loss for the labour movement – should not be exaggerated. Now and for the foreseeable future, the share of manufacturing workers covered by union protection and collective bargaining is large, and in many countries the unionized sector includes the largest corporations and those which are crucial to the national economy and its international competitiveness.

Moreover, the spread of industrial activities outside their traditional sectors and the rise of old and new services has engendered an increase in relatively unskilled jobs and workers whose individual market power is modest in the extreme. Objectively, then, there is potential scope to compensate for the decline stemming from the demise of traditional blue-collar occupations.

The inadequacy of traditional union methods in representing workers with high skills and some individual market power is certainly a problem, but it is neither a fatal nor an entirely unprecedented one. The real number of such workers should not be overstated, for one thing; nor should it be forgotten that trade unions have never grouped all wage and salary earners. Potentially more intractable problems for the unions may stem from two other trends, essentially divergent both in origins and in their implications for industrial relations. These are, first, the growing segmentation of the labour market, the expansion of non-standard employment, the spread of precarious, poorly regulated jobs; and secondly, employer and management strategies for worker participation.

The first trend threatens the unions' ability to provide general protection of the interests of wage and salary earners, because it engenders division among the employed themselves, alongside the already existing division between employed and unemployed and that (very marked in some countries) between workers in industries exposed to international competition and those in protected sectors.

The second trend poses a threat not just to the extent of collective bargaining coverage but also to the very possibility of collectively negotiated regulation of working conditions through representative organizations. However, it must be pointed out that the results of this tendency will not be uniform or stable. Even today one finds a considerable range of participation experiences, going from methods that totally bypass labour unions to a good number of others that embody the spirit, if not the classical forms and institutions, of industrial democracy.

Finally, there is even less warrant for interpreting the 'return to normalcy' as a simple reversion to the past in the sphere of the public image of trade unions and the ideals and motives that inspire union action. Thanks to the historical progress made as a result of the heterogeneity of the wage- and salary-earning classes, the prevailing acceptance of the objective needs of the capitalist economy and the full social and intellectual 'citizenship' attained by employers and managers, the labour movement exerts less attraction than it once did. It is more prosaic, more pragmatic, less enveloped in an emotional aura, frequently not raising dramatic questions. Young workers themselves, except for an activist, politicized minority, make requests of the unions that are less strongly associated than in the past with social and political ideals and militancy and with analogous support for the parties of the left.

Nevertheless, the labour movement has not lost its role and function. It remains the most thoroughly tested and efficacious means of defending the interests of sizeable groups of workers. It is a method for regulating what is after all a fundamental social relationship that intrinsically, even today, harbours the potential for and reality of injustice and abuse. True, unions are not always present wherever such abuses occur, but this too is not a novelty in the history of organized labour.

The lack of overriding ideals alone does not prevent the survival and continued functioning of the unions and the trade union method. The functional interests that unions represent more than suffice to ensure this. Nor is the trade union approach exclusively or even primarily dependent on the raising of wage and other demands. The weakening of these ideals and motives – which do not necessarily guarantee successful union action anyway – is not due principally to changes in organized labour. The genesis of the change lies elsewhere, and it consists not so much in a decline in the idealism and a weakening of the concrete objectives of organized labour as in the ideological attrition and the radical restriction of the scope for reform that have afflicted the progressive political parties and movements which have traditionally been allied with the labour movement.

There are two crucial aspects, for organized labour, in this change. First, despite the present social and employment difficulties and the substantial interests of employed workers themselves in matters outside the scope of labour contracts, labour unions are having real problems in carrying out policy decisions based on social solidarity in an effort to overcome the differences among working people. The decline of tripartite concertation is a case in point.

Secondly, this tendency is intertwined with the recent evolution of union relations with the political community and of the status of trade union action *per se*. Despite government intervention in industrial relations, trade union action seems to proceed with greater, though by no means absolute, independence from politics. Save in the few extreme cases of government action (expressly anti-union), the association between events in government and politics and those in the industrial relations sphere appears more attenuated, more nuanced than in the past. In other words, a progressive government or political system does not necessarily spur or strengthen the labour movement. At the same time, however, conservative and right-wing governments do not seriously damage organized labour, and even where the trade union movement has suffered, the action of conservative political forces has not necessarily been the sole or even the main cause.

However, I do not believe that thoroughgoing changes will result. True, the phenomena described suggest that the current transition is not a contingent one, although it is impossible to foresee the effect on industrial relations for the next decade. However, it can be argued that the decline in concertation practices – and all the more so in truly neo-corporatist arrangements – does not pave the way for a clear-cut resurgence of the 'pluralist' model. Some features of that model are of course present, such as the great extent of collective bargaining contracts, the pragmatic and flexible attitudes of the actors, and the importance of rules and procedures, as well as the closer correlation between industrial relations and the economic cycle. Some fundamental requisites, however, are lacking: first and foremost the firmly established recognition of union representation and the continuity of economic growth. Moreover, certain conditions and pressures that cannot be comprised in pluralism remain, above all the end of the sharp distinction in function and division of responsibilities between employers and workers and unions; and a trend towards industrial relations arrangements variously marked by the prospect of worker participation, albeit not only the sort of participation proposed and sought by management.

With the progressive diminution of concertation, and particularly given the unlikelihood that pluralist optimism will prove warranted, our thesis that industrial relations are returning to 'normalcy' is to be understood as an argument that the golden age for labour relations in the first twenty years following the Second

World War is over, and that the situation in the years 1968–75 was exceptional. For the future, we must not be tempted to try to map out a linear, single pattern for the development of the entire complex of industrial relations. The essential nature of this permanent, significant feature of industrial society, indeed, appears to lie in its ability to evade or disconfirm the hopes and fears of those who cannot wait to decree its destiny.

Notes

This essay is based on the national reports plus other sources, some of which are referred to in the notes. The responsibility for many of the judgements and conclusions, especially in the concluding section, is my own.

1 The judgements relative to the 1970s are drawn from Baglioni, 1986a.

2 It may be useful at this point to recapitulate our typology of industrial relations systems:

A Full recognition of the legitimacy of trade unions and their functions:

    A(a) through national concertation practices

    A(b) through national (or industry or regional) relations between unions and employer organizations
        – with bargaining and/or
        – with experiences and institutions of industrial democracy.

B Industrial relations based mainly on decentralized collective bargaining, especially at company level.

C Employer strategies for forms of worker participation and involvement:

    C(a) utilizing company-level union structure

    C(b) without or against union structure (that is, direct management relations with employees).

D Employer strategies to diminish bargaining regulation of employment, without forms of worker participation:

    D(a) with traditional, full-time employment

    D(b) with atypical employment (part-time, temporary, secondary jobs).

3 Concertation takes place in processes, which may be more or less strongly institutionalized, of co-operation between the state and business and labour organizations. In concertation, specifically, unions moderate their short-term demands in exchange for more general, longer-run compensation and the concession of a role in economic and social policy decisions.

4 The term 'industrial democracy' refers to practices and institutions involving the more or less extensive participation of worker representatives and/or unions in determining, principally but not exclusively, working conditions.

5 'Pluralist' industrial relations designates an ideal type, based on voluntary associations and the free action of those associations, with little or no state intervention. In the pluralist model the employment relation and the use of labour will be regulated mainly by collective bargaining, with a good degree of pragmatism and autonomy for the actors, on the basis of recurrent, continuous opportunities to revise and satisfy their respective interests.

6 'Political citizenship' for organized labour means that its functions and legitimacy are recognized by the state, whose administrative and legislative measures on economic and social affairs are ordinarily pro-labour.

7 Almost all data come from OECD sources, specifically *Perspectives économiques de l'OCDE*, 41(June 1987), and *Main Economic Indicators*, August 1987.

8 The data on overall and labour productivity refer to only six European countries (Germany, Britain, France, Italy, Sweden, Belgium).

9 For a typology of worker participation, see Baglioni, 1986c.

10 This process (in Britain, Germany, France, Spain, Sweden and Belgium) is described in a series of volumes prepared by CESOS (Baglioni and Santi (eds), 1982a; 1982b; 1984; 1985; Baglioni and Squarzon, 1987).

11 Data and information based on the separate national reports of this study; overall, from ILO, 1986.

12 This term is used to indicate the sum of the following elements: the recognition of the unions as actors and of union structures as representatives of the workers; the bargaining power of the unions (that is, the relations between these actors' claims and the eventual results); and above all the extent, the scope and the depth of collective bargaining (that is, respectively, the percentage of wage and salary earners covered by collective bargaining contracts; the aspects of the employment relationship governed by collective contract; and the degree of company-level union representatives' participation in the application of contracts) (Clegg, 1976: ch. 1).

References

Albeda, W. (1985) 'Les tendances récentes de la négociation collective aux Pay-Bas', *Revue international du travail*, 124(1).

Baglioni, G. (1982) 'Il sistema delle relazioni industriali in Italia: Caratteri ed evoluzione storica', in G.P. Cella and T. Treu (eds), *Relazioni industriali*, Bologna: Il Mulino.

Baglioni, G. (1986a) *La politica sindacale nel capitalismo che cambia*, Bari: Laterza.

Baglioni, G. (1986b) 'Il destino delle pratiche concertative', *Prospettiva sindacale*, 60(17).

Baglioni, G. (1986c) 'Valutazioni dell'azionariato dei dipendenti nella logica della partecipazione', *Prospettiva sindacale*, 62(17).

Baglioni, G. (1988) 'Problemi e scelte nell'analisi comparativa delle relazioni industriali', *Giornale de diritto del lavoro e di relazioni industriali*, 10(37).

Baglioni, G. and E. Santi (eds) (1982a) *L'Europa sindacale agli inizi degli anni '80*, Bologna: Il Mulino.

Baglioni, G. and E. Santi (eds) (1982b) *L'Europa sindacale nel 1981*, Bologna: Il Mulino.

Baglioni, G. and E. Santi (eds) (1984) *L'Europa sindacale nel 1982*, Bologna: Il Mulino.

Baglioni, G. and E. Santi (eds) (1985) *I sindacati europei fra il 1983 e il 1984*, Bologna: Il Mulino.

Baglioni, G. and C. Squarzon (1987) *Stato, politica economica e relazioni industriali in Europa*, Milan: Angeli.

Berger, S. (1984) 'Il conflitto sociale nella Francia socialista', *Stato e mercato*, 12.

Blanpain, R. (1982) 'Comparative Analysis of Labour Law and Industrial Relations', in R. Blanpain and T. Treu (eds), *Comparative Labour Law and Industrial Relations*, Deventer: Kluwer.

Blanpain, R. and T. Treu (eds) (1982) *Comparative Labour Law and Industrial Relations*, Deventer: Kluwer.

Brown, W. and K. Sisson (1983) 'Industrial Relations in the Next Decade', *Industrial Relations Journal*, 14.

Cella, G.P. (ed.) (1979) *Il movimenti degli scioperi nel XX secolo*, Bologna: Il Mulino.

Cella, G.P. and T. Treu (1982) 'National Trade Union Movements', in R. Blanpain and T. Treu (eds) (1982) *Comparative Labour Law and Industrial Relations*, Deventer: Kluwer.

Clark, J. and Lord Wedderburn of Charlton (1986) 'Juridification in British Labour Law', in G. Teubner (ed.), *Juridification of Social Spheres: A Comparative Analysis in the Areas of Labour, Antitrust and Social Welfare Law*, Berlin and New York: de Gruyter.

Clegg, H.A. (1976) *Trade Unionism under Collective Bargaining*, Oxford: Basil Blackwell.

Cordova, E. (1985) 'La grève dans la fonction publique: origines et évolutions', *Revue international du travail*, 12.

Cordova, E. (1986) 'From Full-time Wage Employment to Atypical Employment: A Major Shift in the Evolution of Labour Relations?', *International Labour Review*, 6.

Cressey, P. (1987) 'New Technology: An Overview of Regulation', *European Industrial Review*, 157(February).

Delamotte, Y. and M. Ambrosini (1986) 'Innovazione tecnologica e relazioni industriali in Francia', *Giornale del diritto del lavoro e di relazioni industriali*, 29(8).

Della Rocca, G. (1987) 'Improving Participation: The Negotiation of New Technology in Italy and Europe', in C. Sirianni (ed.), *Worker Participation and the Politics of Reform*, Philadelphia: Temple University Press.

European Industrial Relations Review (1986) 'France: Collective Bargaining Trends', 153(October).

Freeman, R. (1987) 'Una società senza sindacato?', *Il progetto*, 7(40).

Gaspard, M. (1985) 'Tempo di lavoro e occupazione in Francia dal 1981', in Fondazione Brodolini (ed.), *Le politiche di lavoro in Europa agli inizi degli anni '80*, Venice: Marsilio.

Gaspard, M., J. Loos and D. Welcomme (1987) 'Gestione e riduzione del tempo di lavoro: Analisi comparata di 11 paesi industrializzati', Milan: IRES Lombardia, mimeographed.

van Ginneken, W. (1987) 'La politique des salaires des pays industriels à économie de marché de 1971 à 1986: de la réglementation à la libre négociation', *Revue international du travail*, 126(4).

Goldthorpe, J.H. (1984) 'The End of Convergence: Corporatist and Dualist Tendencies in Modern Western Societies', in J.H. Goldthorpe (ed.), *Order and Conflict in Contemporary Capitalism: Studies in the Political Economy of Western European Nations*, Oxford: Oxford University Press.

Gustafsson, B. (1985) 'L'esperienza svedese della cogestione e dei fondi dei lavoratori', in *I limiti della democrazia*, Bari: Laterza.

ILO (1986) *Yearbook of Labour Statistics*, Geneva: ILO.

ISE (1986) *Négociations collectives en Europe Occidentale en 1986 et Perspectives pour 1987*, Brussels: ISE.

OECD (1987) *Perspectives économiques de l'OCDE*, 41, Paris: OECD.

Perez-Diaz, V. (1986) 'Politica economica e patti sociali in Spagna durante la transizione', *Stato e mercato*, 16.

Peterson, R.B. (1987) 'Swedish Collective Bargaining: Changing Scene', *British Journal of Industrial Relations*, 27(1).

Provasi, G.C. (1987) 'La negoziazione sindacale: strategie e procedure', *Prospettiva sindacale*, 66(18).

Reynaud, J.D. (1984) 'Francia: una esperienza sindacale con vincoli e potenzialità dovuti al quadro politico', in G. Baglioni and E. Santi (eds), *L'Europa sindacale nel 1982*, Bologna: Il Mulino.

Schregle, J. (1981) 'Comparative Industrial Relations: Pitfalls and Potential', *International Labour Review*, 1.

Simitis, S. (1986) 'Juridification of Labour Relations', in G. Teubner (ed.), *Juridification of Social Spheres: A Comparative Analysis in the Areas of Labour, Antitrust and Social Welfare Law*, Berlin and New York: de Gruyter.

Streeck, W. (1985) 'Le relazioni industriali neo-corporative e la crisi economica in Germania', in M. Carrieri and P. Perulli (eds), *Il teorema sindacale: flessibilità e competizione nelle relazioni industriali*, Bologna: Il Mulino.

Streeck, W. (1986) 'Il management dell'incertezza e l'incertezza dei managers: imprenditori, relazioni sindacali e riequilibrio industriale nella crisi', *Prospettiva sindacale*, 59(17).

Teubner, G. (ed.) (1986) *Juridification of Social Spheres: A Comparative Analysis in the Areas of Labour, Antitrust and Social Welfare Law*, Berlin and New York: de Gruyter.

Treu, T. (1986) 'Nuove tendenze e problemi del tempo di lavoro', *Stato e mercato*, 18.

2

Trade Unionism in Belgium: The Difficulties of a Major Renovation

Armand Spineux

1 The context

The Belgian trade union movement is not the only one to feel the repercussions of the economic and social upheavals generated by the global restructuring of industrial activity. Organized labour throughout the industrial West has felt the impact of this development. Two significant elements testify to the extent of the changes and highlight the cross-national similarity of conditions. First, the European labour movement has been having difficulty for several years now in defending the real wages of employed workers. Wage bargaining is unquestionably the main feature of collective bargaining contracts, but the contracts themselves are harder and harder to come by. The substance of the agreements, at both the industry and the national level, reflects the weakened state of working people, bargaining power with respect to employers being heavily influenced by the economic recession and crisis, with a pronounced narrowing of the scope for bargaining.

Secondly, the change in relative power is also reflected in the political and ideological difficulties encountered by the labour movement. Unions have often been accused before public opinion by employer organizations, political parties and other opinion leaders and groups publicized in the media of being the cause of part of the crisis.

These two elements, the curbing of wage bargaining and the emergence of an ideology attributing major blame for the emergence of recession to the unions, justify talk of a crisis of organized labour.

In Belgium, since the end of the war the 'social compact', the joint declaration on productivity and the so-called 'social planning' system of collective bargaining contracts have been the foundation and the most significant products of the great industrial relations compromise that took place between employer and worker organizations and came to form part of the nation's political system.

The compromise can be viewed as covering five major themes: union recognition of the market economy and the legitimacy of the employers' management powers; employer recognition of exclusive rights of representation and bargaining for the most representative unions; sharing the benefits of economic growth through independent collective bargaining; the creation of an all-encompassing system of social security based on universal right to benefits and funding via transfer payments; the institutional participation of employer and worker organizations in decision-making processes in all spheres of social and economic policy.

The scope of the areas covered, together with the official participation of the unions in the main organs of the economic and social world, has given Belgian unions enormous bargaining power and capacity for surveillance and control of the nation's economic activities. This specifically Belgian situation, further bolstered by a unionization rate approaching 75 per cent, has had two key consequences that have determined at once the development of organized labour and the evolution of the system of industrial relations. The first is the overall orientation of Belgian unions, which have clearly opted for a participatory model as against a strategy of radical protest against the foundations of the economic system. The second is the decisive position assumed by the unions not only in the corporate world, in both the public and private sectors, but also in the formulation and administration of social policy, as well as their substantial influence on both Christian-inspired and socialist political parties in both the north and south of the country.

Thanks to this highly particular situation, the trade unions cannot be considered a negligible or moribund actor on the Belgian economic and social scene, even though, in line with what has been happening in most of the countries of Europe, the Belgian labour movement is faced with major questioning of its legitimacy and credibility.

True, for a number of years now the compromise described has been inoperative. Frontal attacks against organized labour have been proliferating, and the unions' right to consultation and to administration in economic and social affairs has been seriously threatened. The institutionalized presence of union power at all levels and at all times, strengthened by the legal monopoly on the representation of employees and contract protections for union rights, is considered an illegitimate abuse. The unions' real representativeness with respect to working people is questioned.

Belgium's very broad social security protections are threatened by the disarray of public finances, the increasing share of social

Table 2.1 *Employment by sector, Belgium, 1980–5*

	Wage and salary earners (private sector)					
	1980	1981	1982	1983	1984	1985
Primary sector	11,456	11,113	11,152	11,400	11,688	12,173
Secondary sector	1,156,985	1,081,093	1,027,449	989,776	966,419	952,194
Energy	50,241	49,768	48,071	48,071	47,676	45,431
Non-energy, mining and chemicals	212,614	201,040	193,800	185,886	182,277	175,704
Metal industries	304,620	287,065	273,286	267,295	262,222	259,855
Other manufacturing	349,736	331,935	322,055	317,958	317,870	315,737
Construction	239,774	211,285	189,003	170,566	156,374	155,557
Tertiary sector	1,046,203	1,038,521	1,035,516	1,038,621	1,047,933	1,077,791
Distributive trades	423,684	415,943	412,911	407,883	411,573	414,922
Transport and communication	89,086	86,793	86,508	85,838	86,871	89,827
Banking and finance	189,353	187,434	186,388	194,637	199,551	214,081
Other services	344,080	348,351	349,709	350,263	350,938	358,961
incl. domestic service	101,168	101,149	99,289	97,593	94,922	93,981
'Back-to-work' programmes incl. trainees	20,678	18,976	21,798	24,866	29,486	27,245
Total	2,214,644	2,130,727	2,074,117	2,039,797	2,026,040	2,042,158

Table 2.1 *contd.*

	Wage and salary earners (public sector)					
	1980	1981	1982	1983	1984	1985
Secondary sector	14,014	14,042	13,764	13,186	12,550	12,226
Energy	11,775	11,867	11,773	11,578	11,215	10,900
Non-energy, mining and chemicals	39	40	38	36	34	44
Metal industries	1,254	1,266	1,094	827	740	689
Other manufacturing	579	563	535	528	434	400
Construction	376	346	324	217	127	94
Tertiary sector	944,926	954,598	963,302	953,919	958,909	963,087
Distributive trades	1,140	1,066	1,106	1,080	1,741	1,659
Transport and communication	171,656	173,322	172,011	165,075	160,052	156,073
Banking and finance	21,597	22,151	22,489	22,875	23,242	23,339
Other services	750,533	758,159	767,696	764,889	773,874	782,016
administration	214,767	216,994	226,560	227,162	224,598	226,196
armed services	90,345	93,386	92,646	90,814	89,423	89,300
education	272,471	276,560	280,803	279,431	278,275	277,728
'Back-to-work' programmes incl. return to work of unemployed	0	69,134	62,304	60,079	74,769	85,484
CST	37,277	35,989	32,594	29,039	28,526	31,031
TCT	29,945	24,927	21,166	14,685	15,465	16,583
	0	0	0	7,028	19,427	25,748
trainees	8,635	8,218	8,544	9,327	11,351	12,122
Total	958,940	968,640	977,066	967,105	971,459	975,313

benefits in final labour costs, and the steadily rising amount of taxes and contributions in proportion to disposable income.

The cessation of economic growth deprived collective bargaining of a traditionally crucial part of its function, namely deciding the distribution of income. The inability of the actors to manage other types of conflict of interest via collective bargaining has raised questions about the relevance and autonomy of the system. And finally, the political system is less willing than previously to accept business and labour organizations overlapping or criticizing its decision-making process for social and macroeconomic policy.

As a consequence of simultaneous destruction and rationalization of the industrial fabric, the rapid growth of the advanced services sector and the rearrangement of production methods to hasten the introduction of new technology, the structure of employment has been radically altered (see Table 2.1). At the same time, there have been major modifications in the pace of growth and the components of the labour force: the explosion of women's participation, which is still rising; a popular age structure that is generating very large net labour-force increases, a significant increase in white-collar employment, and the appearance of a large number of more or less precarious employment conditions. All of this has permanently modified the make-up of the labour market.

The emergence of new leading sectors and foci of growth, and the consequent shifts in world trade flows, the huge budget deficits of some states, monetary disorder and the multiplicity of crisis areas and scenes of confrontation worldwide were all elements of insecurity, hardly propitious to a return to sustained economic growth. Moreover, when signs of recovery have appeared, we have usually found a real increase in the demand for labour but no expansion of employment.

2 Structural problems

2.1 *The evolution of employment and unemployment*

Between 1973 and 1981, the unemployment rate rose from 2.9 to 9.0 per cent in the EEC and from 2.9 to 12.4 per cent in Belgium. On the morrow of the second oil shock, Belgium represented the most acute form of the general European malady. Still the most affluent country in the EEC in terms of per capita income, it was nevertheless the one in which least work was available. It was the most gravely paralysed by its welfare system and the hardest hit by the crisis of some traditional industries (coal, steel, and so on), but Belgians were so heedless of the crisis and of the government's yawning budget deficit that they preferred to amuse themselves with their linguistic squabbles. Belgium was a sinking ship. (Albert, 1985)

Between 1974 and 1982 Belgium lost 150,000 jobs (the result of varying trends in agriculture, industry and the services sector). Moreover, between 1975 and 1979 there was a net increase of about 30,000 per year in the number of job-seekers; the pace of this increase slowed down from 1980, but there were still 17,000 new job-seekers each year. In absolute terms, the labour force increased from 3,998,700 in 1975 to 4,234,700 in 1985, almost a quarter of a million persons in a decade. The baby boom of the 1960s resulted in a substantial increase in the number of young people reaching working age in the late 1970s and early 1980s. At the same time, steadily increasing numbers of women were interested in finding jobs.

The roots of Belgian unemployment are thus twofold. Just when it became urgent to create tens of thousands of jobs for an expanding labour force, the economy was losing tens of thousands of jobs as a result of the constraints imposed by recession. Sectoral analysis shows that the bulk of the job loss came in industry – indeed, for many years now Belgian industry has been suffering a severe manpower haemorrhage.

Government measures helped slow the advance of unemployment in 1983, and in 1984 even reduced it. Since then, though, the statistics show a steady rise. The net balance of jobs to be created thus remains impressive (531,400 job-seekers at the end of August 1986), and many of those who found jobs under the 'back-to-work' scheme are in a very precarious position.

2.2 The unemployed

Table 2.2 suggests two principal observations: first, the sharp rise in the number of jobless persons between 1980 and 1984 and its subsequent levelling off or slight decline; and secondly – the most serious indicator of the increasing precariousness of some occupations – the steady increase in the share of the long-term jobless among the unemployed. Whereas in 1980 those unemployed for more than two years constituted 38.2 per cent of the jobless, by 1984 this had risen to 47.4 per cent.

The main causes of long-term unemployment are the poor education and low skills of the workers who suffer it; 45.9 per cent of the unemployed had no more than an elementary-school education, and the least skilled workers constituted over 64 per cent of the long-term jobless (unemployed for more than two years). And the changes in the make-up of the labour market should make us duly aware that those holding only a lower secondary school diploma are practically certain to experience the same insecurity.

The steadily increasing need for better educational credentials if

Table 2.2   *Unemployed receiving benefit, by average annual unemployment, Belgium, 1980–6*

	Duration of unemployment						Total	
	Less than 1 year		1–2 years		More than 2 years			
	(No.)	(%)	(No.)	(%)	(No.)	(%)	(No.)	(%)
1980	147,043	45.7	51,883	16.1	122,969	38.2	321,895	100
1981	185,396	47.3	70,335	18.0	136,053	34.7	391,785	100
1982	191,015	41.8	97,912	21.5	167,550	36.7	456,577	100
1983	192,126	38.0	100,631	20.0	211,955	42.0	504,961	100
1984	170,499	33.3	98,676	19.3	243,225	47.4	512,400	100
1985[1]	144,075	32.2	78,066	17.4	225,315	50.4	447,456	100
1986[1]	142,513	32.5	74,837	17.0	221,826	50.5	439,176	100

[1] For 1985 and 1986 statistics as of 31 October. Also, in 1985 and 1986 some elderly unemployed were exempted from the registration requirements and thus do not appear in the table. This explains the decline since 1985. They numbered 62,267 as of 31 October 1986.

Source: Ministry of Employment and Labour

they are to have any hope of getting a job dooms whole strata of workers to prolonged confinement in the sphere of inactivity. This is especially dramatic for young people. Now 30 per cent of the totally jobless are persons younger than twenty-five. Nearly half of them have no professional experience whatever, and more that 65 per cent of these young unemployed have no more than a lower secondary education.

3   The actors in industrial relations

In the last few years Belgium has witnessed a significant shift in issues and bargaining demands by organized labour. During the years of economic expansion all efforts were focussed on improving working conditions, establishing new collective rights and social and welfare rights for working people. Now, by contrast, the energies of a significant portion of the labour force are directed exclusively to finding or keeping a job. The idea of bargaining over the terms and conditions of employment appears as a luxury available only to a highly qualified elite whose social and educational capital is far above average.

How have Belgium's leading social, economic and political actors responded to this situation?

3.1 The state

'We all give speeches about "less government" and the result is that there's more' – Mark Eyskens, Minister for Economic Affairs (*VIF*, 1985).

The rupture of the great compromise between business and labour organizations, the shift to a contracting market, and the new challenges have unquestionably been causes of a paralysis of the system of concertation with the state and direct nationwide bargaining, whose very existence and whose content, albeit limited, constituted the manifestation of a consensus. This consensus was the foundation both for political decision-making and for the development of collective bargaining at other levels.

With few exceptions, since 1975 all efforts to reach compromise via direct talks at the summit between business and labour have failed. And the same goes for the countless, long-drawn-out tripartite talks (some enlarged, others restricted) called mainly at the initiative of successive incoming cabinets.

Convinced that independent collective bargaining was no longer compatible with the economic and financial constraints imposed by the state of the economy, the government did not hesitate to limit or do away with that independent sphere. As early as 1976 the authorities introduced heavy sanctions against workers and employers agreeing on additional benefits. At the end of 1980, after the failure of the conference on employment, the Social Christian–Socialist coalition submitted to Parliament a recovery plan calling for a total, unindexed wage freeze. A nationwide agreement for voluntary restraint, agreed to by business and labour negotiators under the threat of this legislation, saved the appearance of independence.

Since late 1981, throughout the new legislature, there has been a proliferation of authoritarian interventions. The Social Christian–Liberal government called on employer organizations and unions to try, via bilateral or tripartite talks, to reach the compromise made indispensable, in the government view, by the changes engendered by the contracting market. Faced with numerous obstructions, the government did not hesitate to take painful measures, preceding them with discrete bilateral consultations with the unions closest to the governing parties (essentially, the Flemish and Walloon wings of the CSC, Confédération des Syndicats Chrétiens).

Government intervention has become so common and so far-reaching that one may reasonably speak of a transformation of the Belgian system of industrial relations. The delegation of power has been withdrawn, and independent collective bargaining has been restrained if not quite done away with. The state sets limits and changes the conventional wage indexation mechanisms; it imposes parafiscal levies on these cost-of-living allowances. It has made draconian restrictions on collective bargaining over real wage levels; at the same time it has installed a virtual obligation to bargain on other, specified issues, such as working time and compensatory hiring. Government retains a discretionary power to evaluate the results of such bargaining.

Other aspects of the institutional framework have also been profoundly modified. The sphere covered by industry-wide contracts has been sharply narrowed by the exclusion of small and medium-sized businesses. Collective agreements not ratified by one of the sides have been approved. The hierarchy of sources of law has been altered, in that agreements at company level can modify the scope of binding provisions of the law or the national contract. Finally, the unions' monopoly on worker representation has been broken. New legislation providing for separate electoral colleges for lower management and technical personnel in balloting for the company councils makes possible the direct representation of the workforce outside union structures.

Also worth noting are the countless changes in labour and welfare legislation at government initiative. And while it is true that in most cases the new provisions were the object of prior, institutionalized consultations, it is no less true that the opposition or refusal to bargain on the part of one or more important actors did not prevent the government from going ahead with its designs.

What has happened constitutes an out-and-out shift of power in Belgian labour relations. Yet the negotiations for the contracts of 1985–6 apparently comprised some manoeuvres aimed at circumvention by the major participants. It is widely known that 'secret' or 'unwritten' agreements were struck, in a kind of black-market bargaining. Is this the sign that government is being repulsed, that worker and employer organizations are attempting to regain bargaining independence?

In the present stage of Belgium's institutional reform, the regional governments do not have sufficient autonomous decision-making powers to commit themselves to fundamentally different social or economic policy options. The very nature of their powers under law and the limited financial resources and fiscal powers put at their disposal still represent insuperable obstacles to a diversification of the national policy approach. Nevertheless, regional reform has already had certain effects on the system of labour relations. New institutional actors have appeared, so that at regional level, in both Flanders and Wallonia, we have witnessed the development of tripartite concertation among unions, employers and the regional authorities of each linguistic community.

Some of the institutional actors have adapted their structures. The statutes of the Confédération des Syndicats Chrétiens (CSC) and of the Fédération Générale des Travailleurs de Belgique (FGTB) have both been revised to provide for an inter-regional structure, while 'regional wings' have been formed within some nationwide union and employer organizations (Bleeckx, 1985).

3.2 The employers

Under the great compromise, Belgian employers' strategy was based fundamentally on give-and-take. Their recognition of the unions' monopoly on worker representation and of the strict obligation to proceed by way of this mediated representation was granted in exchange for the maintenance of the employers' sole authority and management power. Bargaining rights and the linkage of wages to the cost-of-living index were compensated for by effective freedom to set prices. The planning and introduction of new benefits and active support for the unions were the price of ensured labour peace.

The conditions and terms of this trade-off having changed radically, the employers too have sharply changed course. Union mediation, if tolerated, is nonetheless resented as a hindrance and unrepresentative, and employers are turning resolutely towards 'direct communication' and 'participatory' personnel management. Collective bargaining with the union 'apparatus' is circumvented by direct consultation with worker delegates on the conditions specific to the company. There is a rejection of collective rules as too rigid or unsuited to the constraints and the plans of the single firm. And there is a clear desire to give priority to company-level bargaining at the expense of broader social solidarity. The modification of acquired rights and guarantees is suggested as a bargaining item. And finally, new elements in the employer strategy are to be found in resort to politics and the appeal to public opinion.

Quite defensive until recently, the Belgian employers' strategy is now openly aggressive. The omnipresent theme over the last few years is the demand for more flexible management of firms. This flexibility is considered indispensable if Belgian enterprises are to recover their lost competitiveness, undermined by high wages and shackled by what Belgian employers have come to call the 'almighty' trade unions. For the employer organizations, the need for flexibility concerns first and foremost wages and the terms of employment, adjustment of working time and work reorganization.

In view of the sweeping restructuring of key sectors of the economy worldwide, there is no denying that adjustment and innovation at the national level must be accomplished very quickly. The new technology at once demands and permits rapidity. Thus what must be jettisoned are legislative, administrative and union constraints on the employers' full freedom of manoeuvre. In practice this means greater insecurity and the pulverization of previous contract conditions. In general, through a substantial decrease in the overall volume of employment and the replacement of workers by machines; in hiring, by wage and contract discrimination (trainee contracts for young people, and so on); in dismissal, with shorter notice and, in the meantime, with the imposition of different contract terms on the employees who replace those having decided to take temporary leave.

'Greater flexibility frequently means greater precariousness and more insecurity for working people . . . Unchecked, unnegotiated flexibility is a source of anxiety for those who do not have better than average intellectual, physical and moral resources – that is, for half the economically active population' (Delcourt, 1985).

3.3   The unions

All the trade unions, whatever their orientation or tendency, have accused management of refusing to take into account the human dimension of the problems stemming from the new international division of labour. In their view, the 'technical–production imperative' claimed by management is greatly overrated. Its only use is to conceal the divisions sown within the working class by employer action (the retrenchment of social and welfare rights, the proliferation of non-standard employment contracts and the rupture of worker solidarity).

According to the unions, employer talk of the fragility of Belgium's economic machinery, company failures and the loss of competitiveness is nothing but an ideological smokescreen designed to mask the capitalist class's designs to strengthen itself against the workers and increase its power to determine economic and social policy choices. In these circumstances, the goal of the unions is to get decision-makers to take the labour and social dimension of the problems into account. The human consequences of policy options, the impact of working conditions and employment should obviously be taken into consideration as the economic and financial aspects are.

One cannot help noting the weakness of the union response, though. Necessary partners in a system of social concertation based on collective bargaining, they are at the same time victims of the impasse the system has reached, and they appear incapable of offering credible alternatives. Their demands, usually defensive, relate only to their traditional constituency, that is workers who enjoy stable, secure jobs.

The unions are also going through a crisis of representativeness. The old labour aristocracy, withdrawn into defence of its own self-interest, has lost the capacity to provide leadership for other groups of workers less well armed for struggle, to say nothing of totally precarious workers, who usually opt for out-and-out withdrawal from the battle or for isolation.

The exacerbation of society's division into opposed groups has shattered forms of solidarity that once seemed natural. For instance, there is the gulf that has opened up between public sector employees and those in the private sector. Public service members account for 25 per cent of total FGTB membership (about 300,000 persons) and 20 per cent of the CSC (some 260,000) – for both organizations, then, far from a negligible force. Yet there, too, the mechanisms of solidarity, of one group's stepping in for another in the struggle, have disappeared. Several times strike movements among civil servants have failed to elicit the hoped-for response among private sector workers. These strikes (in transport, pension services, the post office, schools, and so on) then engendered considerable resentment among the public, which viewed them as further demands by groups already well-off, or at least secure in their jobs. In the end, the state–employer, the necessary bargaining counter-party, could not significantly alter its position, given the budget restrictions it had been obliged to impose on itself. The internal and external influence of the public services unions was perceptibly diminished.

The unions have to deal with the fragmentation of the working-class community which results in part from the diversification of employment contracts and in part from labour-shedding in industry. In other words, the main difficulty but also the challenge faced by the unions can be expressed tersely as 'think globally and act locally', while maintaining between these two poles a coherence of strategy and affirmation of solidarity that makes sense within the world of work.

4 The processes

4.1 Social security

It is clear that economic restructuring and the decline of a good number of industries, such as steel, engineering and glass, have significantly eroded the social gains of the 'golden sixties'. Cuts were made in social security, according to the Social Christian–Liberal government coalition, in order to ward off the generalized bankruptcy of the welfare system. But they have also been required in order to reduce the public debt, which on a *per capita* basis puts Belgium unhappily ahead of its neighbours.

It must be said, however, that the basic social security benefits acquired, and the principles underlying them, have so far been maintained. Illness and accident insurance now calls for increased contributions from the insurers, but the fundamental principle has not been called into question. And the same goes for unemployment insurance, which despite severe restrictions remains more advantageous for its beneficiaries than the systems of neighbouring countries. As regards pensions, finally, the system has been put back on a sound footing after serious problems – not without drastic restrictions, but at least avoiding the abusive, discriminatory and unequal resort to privatization. The government's desire to redress the disequilibria (the recovery plan of May 1986) entails sharply higher fiscal contributions by those covered – an increase of 84 billion Belgian francs in 1987 as against FB60 billion in 1986. This additional revenue stems mainly from a number of wage-moderation measures, the introduction of a new method of calculating unemployment benefits, and the limitation of some health-care expenditures.

Meanwhile, the financial contribution of the state to the social security system has declined significantly, after an increase as rapid as it was unsustainable in the wake of the first oil shock. Between 1981 and 1986 the state contribution in absolute terms decreased by 14 per cent, while the quotas and other levies on those subject to the system (mainly workers) rose by about 46 per cent over the same period.

4.2　Wage agreements 1983–6

Figures on the evolution of wages offer a series of interesting indications. They cover wages and salaries agreed under industry-wide collective bargaining contracts, excluding any of the various types of bonus. The figures sum up both the overall evolution of hourly wages and that of the factors that have determined it, that is the influence of the indexation system, of contract rises and, for manual workers, of reduced working hours. For white-collar workers, there has been no gain in real wages since 1985, and even for blue-collar workers there has been only a scarcely perceptible 0.1 per cent rise. This increase in hourly wages, moreover, has been due essentially to the shortening of working time, which has not affected white-collar workers. The deceleration of wage gains from 1981 onwards has thus become an out-and-out wage freeze.

The two principal causes are so-called wage-moderation measures and the decline in the inflation rate. It must be observed, however, that these figures represent a sharp decrease in the purchasing power of working people as a whole. For, as we have seen, they have had to bear the burden of many of the extra fiscal levies called for by the government's financial recovery plan; what is more, the official inflation rate has been heavily influenced by the decline in oil prices, while the prices of many consumer items have not stopped going up.

Finally, there has been no rise in contract wages through a negotiated increase in industry contracts since 1982 — the visible sign of the government ban prohibiting business and labour organizations from agreeing to wage increases.

4.3 Employment policies

4.3.1 The back-to-work scheme For some years now Belgium has shown considerable ingenuity in devising policies both to facilitate putting the unemployed to work and to ease rigidity on hiring terms and enhance the flexibility of work organization. Such neighbouring countries as France, with its TUC programme (socially useful jobs for young people), have borrowed from Belgium's array of measures. There would be little point in a detailed description of each of the measures. A brief list of the main ones will be enough to show the proliferation of legislative efforts to put numerous classes or workers to work or back to work – especially young people and the long-term unemployed.

Trainee periods for young people in a firm give them some initial contact with an occupation while relieving the firm of the burden of regular contract wages and diminishing employer social security contributions as well. When the trainee contract expires, the firm may hire the trainee on a standard contract.

Back-to-work measures. The unemployed given work by government are for the most part long-term jobless given socially useful jobs (local government, social services centres, and so on).

Special temporary projects, enabling charitable, non-profit organizations engaged for the most part in social and cultural activities to hire staff whose salaries, at the start, are paid almost entirely by the state.

The third labour market is a measure similar in intent to the temporary projects. It too is intended to create jobs in socially useful but not economically profitable sectors. Here, however, the employment contracts are standard, not temporary.

Self-employment. This programme gives some unemployed workers an opportunity to go into business for themselves through a subsidized loan that does not have to be repaid if the business fails; in this case, the loan is considered as an advance on unemployment benefits.

The measures, and the list is not exhaustive, have created more than 125,000 jobs. Their great disadvantage, however, is that they are always *ad hoc*, stop-gap devices that do not generate any more fundamental recovery in economic activity. Their main purpose is to hold down the number of unemployed, and the jobs they create are usually temporary, less desirable and much more insecure than classic, standard jobs.

4.3.2 Adjustment of working time In this sphere, too, the Ministry of Labour has shown both determination in ending some rigidities that impeded the creation of more jobs and imagination in the substance of some of the measures taken. But again the results, though positive, have not always been commensurate with the expectations that had been aroused. The measures include: shortening of hours and work-sharing, the outcome of an agreement between employers and unions, but the terms were virtually dictated by government – 5 per cent shortening of working time and 3 per cent compensatory hiring, failing which the amounts that would have gone to the salaries of the extra workers must be paid into a job-creation fund; such government-encouraged traditional measures as early retirement and mid-career leave; significant subsidies to small and medium-sized companies hiring additional workers; the Hansenne, or Ministry of Labour, experiments designed to permit, in some circumstances (and with approval both by the Ministry and by the workers involved), companies to operate with work schedules radically different from those legally admissible (ten- or twelve-hour days, weekend work, and so on); part-time jobs. The latest European statistics show a significant spread of part-time jobs. In this area, Belgium is far behind such countries as France and the Netherlands. The growth of part-time work is in response to the needs of employers, who see it as an additional element of flexibility; it corresponds only in part to the wishes of employees. Most of those involved, in fact, take part-time jobs because they cannot find full-time positions.

This array of employment policies has unquestionably fostered the creation of a good number of jobs. First the rise in unemployment was curbed, beginning in April 1985; subsequently, continuing through to the start of 1987, the number of jobless began to decline. Many of the jobs are in no way permanent, however, and all the less so in that their preservation depends in part on state subsidies. The most recent annual report of the Fédération des Entreprises de Belgique (FEB) nonetheless states that 'in terms of employment, the decline in unemployment corresponds to a stabilization over the last two years in the number of persons employed. Though this stabilization can still be attributed in part to the effects of the agreement on employment, it is also due to real hiring by some firms, thanks to a better economic environment and quite independent of any regulatory constraints' (FEB, 1986: 13).

4.4 The trend in industrial conflict

To understand the pattern of industrial conflict in Belgium since the mid-1970s, one must take account of the institutional and sociopolitical context. The state of the economy can only explain a change in the type of demand (jobs rather than wages, for instance), while other differences are probably connected with the evolving institutional context.

It is our hypothesis, then, that the decline in strike activity is linked to two interrelated phenomena: the diminution of the 'negotiable' (not an exhaustion of the possibility of income redistribution, but its neutralization in the wake of a reallocation of resources) and the paralysis or impasse of the machinery for managing labour relations. This impasse developed gradually, starting in 1975, and was confirmed in 1981 with the signing of the business–labour agreement dictated by government, which drastically limited the scope for wage rises.

The characteristics of industrial conflict in the 1980s have therefore been strongly marked by the state of bargaining. The amount of strike activity dropped sharply – especially in 1982, but even 1981 was well below the average for 1976–80. Official strike statistics were not published between 1981 and 1985 and one has to rely on union sources; even after the resumption the base of calculation is not fully comparable with previous years. However, the number of days lost due to strikes (of all types) fell from 241,452 in the first half of 1981 to 71,230 in the first half of 1985. The number of wage strikes dropped perceptibly, in direct relation with the paralysis of bargaining, but there has been a relative increase in the number of strikes over jobs. Union publications put them at about 40 per cent of the total in 1981–2, as against 17 to 31 per cent in 1976–80.

The turn of the decade was thus marked, in Belgium, by a most peculiar relation between bargaining and industrial conflict. The strict limits on bargaining weighed heavily, virtually stifling industrial action. True, there were significant attempts during these years to revive industrial action, but most of them failed.

5   Levels of bargaining

5.1   The instruments of concertation

Apart from the key event, namely the loss of collective bargaining independence by business and labour, and the consequent extension of state intervention in this sphere, there was an appreciable shift in the levels at which bargaining was carried on. Major agreements ceased to be reached on the economy-wide level, and the number of *conventions* concluded at the National Labour Council also diminished as a result.

Several explanations of this state of affairs have been put forward. According to Blanpain:

> For one thing, the crisis accentuated the difference between strong and weak sectors, union leaders in the former thus being less inclined to agree to an overall *convention* that threatened to do away with the advantages they had over the latter. Also, economy-wide agreements tend to cover matters not suitable to bargaining at lower levels, which would better meet the needs of individual industries and firms. Third, there has been a hardening of both union and employer positions. And finally, a fourth factor may be the decline in authority of employer associations and central union organizations with respect to the rank and file. (Blanpain, 1984:134)

Difficulties have arisen at industry level as well, for similar reasons. Here too the number of contracts signed has declined, as is shown by the number of agreements deposited with the registrar of the labour relations office of the Ministry of Labour. The trend towards decentralization has thus shifted bargaining towards the regional and company level. Of course, there are exceptions to the trend. The textile industry has continued bargaining mainly in its joint commission, and in contrast the chemical industry has always done the bulk of its bargaining at the company level.

As to the substance of the negotiations, the unions have presented traditional sorts of demands: higher wages, shorter hours, supplementary social security benefits. Their fate has varied from case to case, but depending primarily on the economic situation in which the demands have been made. Since the mid-1970s, and especially in the 1980s, wage cuts have also been negotiated at the company level, frequently in exchange for maintaining jobs.

The importance of welfare and social security has increased significantly in the course of these years. Thus in metal and engineering, for instance, the 1975 contracts covering the various sectors (engineering, installation, garages, commerce in metal) included a recommendation that can be summarized as follows: do not resort to collective dismissals before trying all other solutions; keep worker representatives suitably informed; preferably, favour temporary or partial lay-offs; when necessary, use transfers of personnel from one enterprise to another; ban overtime, except where absolutely necessary; limit temporary employment.

6 Interpretation and analysis

6.1 Fundamental change or adjustment to new conditions?

The title of this chapter indicates the direction of my answer to this question. In speaking of a major renovation I have in mind a familiar architectural technique. This most definitely does not involve razing the building to the ground, but it does involve major structural work to conserve it (see Table 2.3).

No one in Belgium dreams of expelling the trade unions from the concert of economic and social decision-makers. Belgian unions, unlike those of some other European countries, are fully integrated, included in every important policymaking body in the country (see Figure 2.1). Similarly the union organizations, whether Christian or Socialist, are representative of Belgian workers, at least numerically, since their membership is high (about 75 per cent). The worrying sign for organized labour is young workers' marked lack of interest in either active or passive membership.

Thus the real problem is posed. It is the credibility of the unions that is in jeopardy. If the Belgian labour movement views itself more as a system of guarantees and protections than as a combative movement, it is nonetheless true that in recent years it has waged a series of defensive battles for the preservation of acquired benefits that ultimately concerned only workers who still had their jobs.

Their ability to mobilize working people has been greatly weakened, and several efforts to restore some sort of overarching solidarity among various groups of workers have visibly failed. Worse still is the inability of union leadership to offer public opinion any real alternative to the economic and industrial policy pursued by Belgium's successive governments.

The fundamentals of the Belgian industrial relations system have not come under question, nor have the importance and the role of organized labour. Concertation is still sought, and collective bargaining at all levels remains the best way to achieve it. What is

Table 2.3 *Changes in the industrial relations system, Belgium since 1980*

Type	Pre-1980	Post-1980
A(a) National concertation	Keystone of entire industrial relations system, fostered by all governments for its economic and social regulatory and planning effect	Since 1975, virtual impossibility of reaching agreements at this level Loss of significance of substance of the few agreements reached, either because made under state compulsion or because modest in social and economic impact
A(b) Industry-wide bargaining	The level preferred by organized labour and employers' organizations, because it enables strong sectors to lead weak ones (union advantage), because it puts all firms in a given industry on an equal footing (employer advantage)	Still an important bargaining forum. But clearly losing ground (drastic decrease in number of contracts signed at this level) Loss of homogeneity of traditional industries Diversified corporations New dimensions of labour market and of the workforce Marked tendency to decentralization of bargaining
B Decentralized-company level bargaining	Bargaining at this level was significant, but it was viewed as designed to improve upon national and industry contracts	Failing significant agreements at higher levels, often the only way of reading any contract at all Fostered by employers Scope for bargaining limited by government (that is, legal wage freeze)
C(a) Worker participation with union involvement	Rare, except in some small and medium-sized firms and troubled firms with substantial state shareholdings	Tending to expand either owing to sectoral features (need for competitiveness) or regional reasons (union involvement in regional development)

Table 2.3 *contd.*

Type	Pre-1980	Post-1980
C(b) Worker participation outside union control	Exceptional, given the strong union presence in the great majority of Belgian enterprises	Develops under the impulse of some modernizing employers that combine the economic growth and social progress of the firm, despite union reluctance and opposition
D(a) Individual bargaining	Extremely rare among subordinate workers and white-collar workers. Common among managers and technicians	Extension to virtually all managers and technicians and some extension to other ranks Encouraged by the flexibility measures of labour law reform
D(b) Individual contracts in the secondary labour market	The labour regulations of the 1960s and 1970s outlawed such practices save in very exceptional cases	Increasing, notably because of the proliferation of different types of employment contract (temporary, part-time, weekend, sub-statutes, back-to-work, trainee, and so on) diverging from the recognized norm of full-time jobs with a standard employment contract

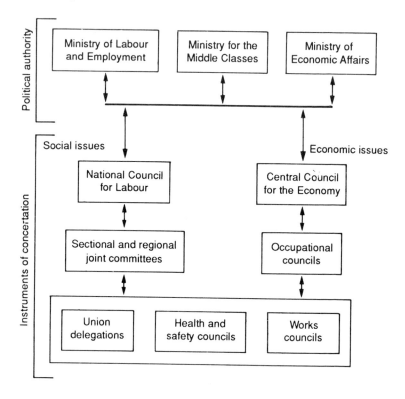

Figure 2.1   *Institutions and concertation, Belgium (based on David 1981: 140)*

questioned, however, is the substance of union action, the way unions act, and their desire to preserve a bargaining framework that the new economic issues have made obsolete. The innumerable attempts by employers to install direct relations between management and company personnel, together with the attention many workers have paid to such efforts, show clearly enough that if they are to retain their credibility and representativeness the unions will have to make a success of this 'major renovation', though this will be an arduous task.

6.2   Belgian labour's strategy
The key factor that will force Belgian unions to make adjustments that are as difficult as they are essential is without doubt the change in the organization of production and the modifications this induces in work content and working conditions. The enterprise can no longer be viewed by unions as nothing but an

undifferentiated cog in a complex economic system. The flexibility demanded by employers actually corresponds to a determination on the part of each firm to position itself as best it can, to distinguish itself from the others in confronting the multiple constraints of a changing, heterogeneous environment.

The changes in the organization of production and in the content of work stemming from the massive introduction of new technology (information technology, robots, office automation, and so on) are little by little doing away with the characteristic traits of worker solidarity, most particularly the craft of occupational culture. That was the foundation upon which the unions were built and upon which their most significant actions were conducted.

Today, the disappearance of the occupational outlook is being offset by the rise of new values, a system in which *savoir-être* is at least as important as *savoir-faire*, in which technical skills count for little without the social and educational capability of applying them.

Many firms try to define their own identity, their own culture and outlook. In doing so, they naturally create information, communication and conflict-management structures – in a word, structures for concertation and bargaining of their own, which are intended to be sharply distinct from those deriving from the classical model of industry-wide or economy-wide bargaining. This assertion of individuality is accompanied, in the minds of many company executives, by a reluctance to invest in the traditional business–labour bargaining models whose effect is to relegate the firm to anonymous status in industry-wide or other agreements.

Acknowledging the specificity of bargaining at the company level also means, for the unions, giving worker representatives some scope for independent action and sufficient technical training. The reserved, not to say defensive, attitude of organized labour to this type of bargaining reveals the latent contradiction between traditional union practices, trapped in the collective defence of acquired rights (but unable to prevent their massive erosion), and the recent rise of new social and cultural modes of representing work and the worker. These new, mainly qualitative issues overlap and at times actually conflict with those that unions have historically addressed. In their bargaining practices and their demands the unions have stressed the principle of collective advance in a framework of continuity, but now the problems posed concern the advancement and promotion of individuals and redistribution in a context of change and discontinuity.

Two other factors may amplify the impact of those cited so far. These are the changes in the make-up of the labour force and of the labour market and changes in political actors, which in our view are directly affected by economic changes and the restructuring of industrial and service activities as a whole.

Employers' stiffening requirements together with the steady spread of automation bring both higher skill levels and a smaller volume of employment. Unions are thus faced with a twofold problem, the fragmentation of the traditional occupational groups and the exclusion of a good number of workers from the job market. This entails a review and revision of practices and strategy to win the confidence and effectively defend the interests of the better qualified; and at the same time broader action, beyond national frontiers, to devise and negotiate forms of income redistribution, which is more and more necessary for those excluded from the job market.

The state is faced with the same dilemma, though the terms in which it is posed differ: namely, providing incentives and eliminating some rigidities to enable Belgian corporations to get the best possible position in international competition, and on the other hand providing significant social security for those who have to pay the price, the numerous victims of economic upheaval. On pain of fostering ever-sharpening conflict between those who might enjoy the fruits of selective growth and those who would be quasi-definitively marginalized, no government, regardless of political ideology, can shirk the indispensable task of social regulation, a role which it is harder and harder to perform.

In this perspective, the waning of practices of concertation between union and employer representatives must be viewed as a sign of the discrepancy between traditional bargaining habits and the new exigencies of the economy rather than as the sign of an outright abandonment of the principle. What needs to be modified, and profoundly, is the substance, the fixed frameworks, and the levels of bargaining; but the principle of concertation must not be emptied of content. On the contrary, precisely because of the new issues that unavoidably confront all the socioeconomic actors, the principle of concertation is more crucial than ever.

Obviously, the unions uphold this principle, and some of them have declared their willingness to make the necessary adjustments. Employer organizations call for the conduct of talks and bargaining in which the decision-making autonomy of the two sides is not limited by state intervention.

6.3   Contingent or structural causes of change

By now it is clear that the economic changes described in this chapter are permanent, structural, much more than temporary or contingent. It is equally clear that Belgian employers will seek to shift the balance of power still further to their advantage. Some employer spokesmen, described as the modernizers, do not hesitate to say that if a product depends on the men who make it, it is more important then ever to pay the greatest possible attention to the human factor in the firm and to its complexity. Labour must no longer be thought of as in the tow of production. In the life of the firm the social must no longer be dependent on the economic. Rather, the two must be perfectly interwoven. This had led some company managements to 'invest in social relations', thereby, in their words, 'filling a qualitative void that the unions have left vacant'.

These trends, which engender individual bargaining and which segment the labour market into innumerable categories defined by their specificity before they can recognize common traits, can only be offset by two elements. The first is societal. For these trends will lead ineluctably to a dichotomization of society, hence a more conflictual opposition between two social groups, namely those who are integrated into the labour market and those who are excluded. The second is within the province of the unions. They cannot refuse to take account of the new economic developments and the values connected with them. Nor can they be content with representing only those who ultimately keep their jobs. To take the former attitude would forfeit part of their legitimacy with those who are integrated in the labour market and who accept, willy-nilly, the values it imposes; to take the latter would forfeit credibility with those who are struggling to find a place in an increasingly selective market.

This is a fundamental question for organized labour in Belgium. The unions still have considerable strength, even if they are now worried by economic restructuring. Without presuming to predetermine the possible response by the unions, it seems clear enough that they need to seek to construct a twofold approach. That is, they need to strengthen their capability for action and for bargaining at two levels simultaneously: first, at the supranational level, most specifically at the European level, and concerning macro-economic developments (bargaining on the conditions for introduction of new technology, the machinery for distribution of the benefits, adjustments of working time, the development of centres of industrial and economic growth, mobility and working conditions, and so on); secondly, at the company level, concerning all aspects of the application of outline contracts. This presumes enlarged bargaining powers for worker delegates at the company level and agreement within supra-firm bargaining processes to consider the special interests of particular groups (junior management and technicians, for instance).

Politically, it would be an illusion to think that a change in the administration could greatly change the terms of the problem. First, all governments in Belgium are coalitions: this rules out any radical change in direction. And secondly, the sweeping restructuring of the economy stems from trends that go far beyond national boundaries, and regardless of the political situation there is hardly any European country in which the economic situation differs significantly.

6.4   Employer initiatives: union responses

Employers in Belgium are far from a homogeneous, united block. There are several varieties of employer, and their strategies are different, at times conflicting. First, there is the traditional management of long-standing Belgian industrial firms. These face problems of adjustment that in many cases have proved insurmountable. They are therefore inclined to resort increasingly to state subsidies to maintain their activities. And they remember to preserve a certain number of jobs in districts hard hit by unemployment. This group of employers is relatively anxious to retain the model of concertation and highly centralized bargaining, but exhibits its most unattractive elements: a generalized wage freeze, abolition of automatic wage indexation, rejection of social innovations, a very lukewarm interest in more flexible work organization, and so on.

The owners of small and medium-sized businesses most often feel that any sort of bargaining that goes beyond the firm and whose results can affect the firm's activities is not just a waste of time but a forced imposition of additional constraints.

Foreign-owned corporations are heavily influenced by an American model of industrial relations that concentrates primarily on company-level bargaining and cannot conceive of any industrial action on demands that transcend the individual firm.

The most innovative firms are probably those, both Belgian and foreign-owned, that invest in human resources or personnel management and consider that this too is an economic investment aimed at improving the firm's performance. These are the employers most eager to see the end of some rigidities in order to be able to begin *à la carte* bargaining on wages, hours, fringe benefits and so on, but without going so far as to reject out of hand the practice of economy-wide employer–union bargaining.

In this composite employer community, it seems to be this last group of firms that is leading the way, both in argument and in practice, in changing the traditional bargaining model. The primary, crucial position at stake is the adjustment of firms to the new constraints imposed by the economic environment. Technical adjustment is influenced by the appearance of new technology, and it implies changes in the organization of production. As a corollary, the adaptation of the labour force involves the question of motivation and increasing worker identification with the company's goals and purposes. Thanks to a mobilization of all its human resources and their integration into the firm's 'culture', the firm intends to defend and improve its profitability.

Both types of adjustment require greater flexibility, both to meet production imperatives and to satisfy the wishes of a substantial portion of the labour force. This mechanism entails not only greater emphasis on company-level bargaining but also an accentuation of the individual character of the negotiations: flexible working time, performance ratings, sabbatical leave, early retirement, and so on. These firms therefore want to leave the strait-jacket of industry-wide or economy-wide collective bargaining in order to devise their own ways of bargaining. They stress the possibility of offering workers a chance to share in the profits of the enterprise, to involve them in part in the firm's management, vastly to enlarge the opportunities to make workers responsible in exchange for a share in the fruits that fuller integration will certainly bring to the whole firm.

How have the unions responded to these overtures? They are faced with a dilemma: 'assume continuity or adapt to change'. Retaining the principle of overall solidarity between those with jobs and those without frequently appears to conflict with the individual advancement sought by workers, which some can actually obtain thanks to the new forms of personnel management introduced by the best-performing firms. Belgian unions are beginning to realize that they cannot continue to 'do everything', or at least cannot do it well. They see that the position of sole, obligatory bargaining partner of the employers, no matter what the level of the problem, has perverse effects that result in stalled bargaining and a loss of credibility in action. It is therefore necessary to give up certain 'monopoly' powers and practices and leave to workers more independent powers of decision. And it happens that they are demanding just that.

On the other hand, only unions can represent labour as a whole in the struggle over such social issues as rising unemployment, the redistribution machinery to ensure general solidarity over welfare and social security, and the procedures, substance and level of bargaining over the introduction of new technology. These macroeconomic and macrosocial issues affect the employed and those seeking a place in the job market alike. If organized labour expects to be a historically significant actor at this level, it cannot risk losing its role either as a negotiating partner with employers or as a mediator between different groups of workers.

The issue of flexibility reveals the sharply increasing awareness of these problems on the part of Belgian labour unions. At first the unions rejected the various formulae for flexibility in work organization, hours and the manipulation of protective legislation, but were unable to prevent them. Then they tried a new strategy. They abandoned the trenches where they were dug in to defend established rights and began to bargain over the terms of flexibility. They admitted that the new systems made possible quicker, more supple adaptation by firms to changing market exigencies. But they combined this recognition with a second goal, expanding employment.

To ensure that this second objective – top priority for them – was respected, they demanded that all derogations to the 1971 labour law be subject to union approval. This monitoring is to be performed by the joint employer–labour commissions if it is an industry-level agreement; otherwise, it will be done at the company level. In the latter case, the agreement must be between management and *all* the unions represented. In other words, there is to be no possibility of an employer playing one union off against another to impose new work schedules. Finally, in a firm in which no union is present, all plans for greater flexibility must be communicated in writing to each register, which is subsequently submitted to the industry's joint committee, which will have the last word.

Fewer legal fetters for employers, an enhanced role for union locals, and greater decision-making powers for working people – this agreement is a good harbinger of the new method of bargaining between business and labour. It exemplifies the principle of give-and-take, in which the main guidelines and trends are set at the national (or perhaps the European?) level, but in which the most touchy points, for employer and workers alike, are negotiated at the company level.

6.5   The implications of the rise of white-collar work

There is no doubt that the evolution of the labour market will mean steadily rising skill levels and higher qualifications, which go hand in hand with the rise in the number of working people who can lay claim to white-collar status. And these workers are much more sensitive to such needs as independence and rewarding work, more concerned with participatory management, involvement, the ability to negotiate individually or by small work groups their own contribution to the enterprise. However, the implications for this for the unions will be limited, because in Belgium unionization is very strong both among white-collar workers in general and in the public service occupations in particular. So there is no need to discover new demands to supplant the traditional blue-collar worker demands – they are already known. Nor do those traditional demands need to be relinquished in order to attract a new union constituency. The thorough overhaul that Belgian unions must undertake involves blue-collar and white-collar workers alike, the private and the public sectors alike.

Everywhere throughout Belgium the trade unions have sizeable membership and substantial local branches. And the temptation is correspondingly strong to dig in, to defend only those who still have the right to union benefits and to ignore the changes under way. Yet everywhere these changes pose serious questions for the labour movement. Young people, for instance, whether blue- or white-collar workers, no longer see unions as the main institutional protection of their interests.

Today, the two currents confront one another within organized labour. On the one hand purely defensive, protectionist actions, and on the other serious thought and the search for an alternative, a way of attaining both the general goals of a solidarity-based society and the specific ones of workers' rights to information, inspection and monitoring of economic activities, public and private alike. Significantly, it is the white-collar federations, both Christian and Socialist, that are most heavily engaged in this critical reflection and in the search for alternatives credible to the majority of working people.

Trade unionism will certainly continue in Belgium. The question is, what kind of unionism? A service-oriented unionism emphasizing security and the defence of established rights, but unable to resolve internal conflicts and rise to working people's emerging expectations? Or a labour movement that, despite the diversification of working people into distinct groups with distinct interests, intends to act as the legitimate representative of these interests?

In either case, the institution of trade unionism will not be shaken. It is too strongly rooted in the social and economic history of the country. On the first supposition, however, the unions run the risk of shutting themselves off, separating themselves from the foundations of their credibility in action. This would mean the asphyxiation of the labour movement due to the traditionalism, the conformity, of union organizations.

The second scenario postulates openness to the main changes, both for the lives of working people and for the conduct of enterprises, that will stem from the global redistribution of economic activities. This implies on the one hand that the assessment of these trends and bargaining over them will take place at a supranational level, in concert with labour unions in other countries; and on the other, that in the overall framework thus established due attention will be paid to the specifics of application in each firm.

These are the problems of major renovation, and they unquestionably concern both the structure and the functioning of Belgian labour unions.

References

Albert, M. (1985) 'Preface' to M. Hansenne, *Emploi: les scénarios du possible*, Paris: Duculot.

Blanpain, R. (1984) 'Les tendances récentes de la négociation collective en Belgique', *Revue internationale du travail*, 123(3).

Bleeckx, F. (1985) 'L'évolution des relations industrielles en Belgique', *Dossier de l'institut des sciences du travail*, 7.

David, G. (1981) 'Les syndicats: une crise dans la crise', *Trends Tendances*, 22 November.

Delcourt, J. (1985) 'La flexibilité: une source des droits nouveaux pour les travailleurs', *Cahier 18*, Institut des Sciences du Travail.

FEB (1986) *Rapport d'activités de la FEB 1985–1986*, Brussels: FEB.

VIF (1985), interview with Mark Eyskens, Minister for Economic Affairs, December.

3

Development and Crisis of the Scandinavian Model of Labour Relations in Denmark

Bruno Amoroso

1 New trends in the Danish system of labour relations

Danish society has participated in all stages of the economic and political cycle of the Western European countries during the period 1970–87. The significance of the events that have taken place seems to go beyond the importance that can be read out of economic, political or social indicators. They have affected the political culture as well as economic and social relations in such a way that the specific form of development model (the Scandinavian Model)[1] existing there can survive only if there is radical change; otherwise it will disintegrate into a form of welfare state similar to that dominating in other Western European countries (Amoroso, 1980).

The contradictions between a private market-oriented economy and a socialized and democratic welfare state were kept under control during the 1950s and 1960s. The classic division of the Scandinavian Model between the social actors – the economy (production) to the capitalists and the state (redistribution) to the labour movement – was properly interpreted as one of the main forces beyond social and economic development.

Growing difficulties emerged in the early 1970s due to the changing character of the process of accumulation, partly reflected in a new employment structure. The tertiary sector, including administration, trade and transport, employed more than half the labour force of about 2.5 million people; the manufacturing sector (including building and construction) employed about one-third; and agriculture less than one-tenth.

The main contradictions between employers and employees were joined by those between the institutions of the capitalist economy and of the welfare state because of their different cost–price systems and labour markets. Furthermore industry developed a dualist form with a few big enterprises relatively independent of national institutional control and many medium or small enterprises. At the end of the 1970s about one-third of Danish private companies with about 16 per cent of total employment (excluding agriculture) and 26 per cent of total turnover were totally or partially controlled by foreign groups (Vangskjær, 1986: 29).

Increasing international competition, the oil crisis in the 1970s and the accelerated introduction of new technologies gave rise to environmental and social costs, with unemployment moving from 0.9 per cent to 7.0 per cent in 1980. The tensions produced among social and political actors by this development could not but deeply affect the industrial relations system and collective bargaining.

The state questioned the autonomy of the economy, setting up institutions for more effective planning and control (for example, creation of the new ministries for industry and for energy in 1979), and actively interfering in collective bargaining in order to implement income policies. The labour movement questioned the traditional right of the employers, sanctioned in the Basic Agreement between labour and employers' confederations, to 'direct' and 'distribute' work, claiming representation on the boards of firms, and asking for the realization of economic democracy as a collective means of influencing investments and economic development. The bourgeois parties openly questioned what had previously been the common culture of political and governmental activities, that is, capability of the Social Democratic Party and the welfare state to deal with problems of a modern industrial society (such as the positive links between equality and efficiency). The employers openly used the obligations of the welfare state to pay for the social costs of private business, socializing in this way an increasing part of their production costs. Tax deductions, unemployment support, public care of the environment, public health and education became a part of entrepreneurial strategies to externalize production costs.

A review made at the beginning of the 1980s of the changes in political and industrial relations in Denmark that had taken place in the previous decade, concluded:

> The recent trends reveal the appearance of something which viewed from the past may seem a paradox, but which is actually the reflection of a new institutional reality about to find its shape: the state intervenes more and more in the economy and in the settlement of the wage level (that is, the trade unions' responsibility area), while the trade union movement still more actively produces political reform proposals which are going to affect the economic policy, planning, energy policy, fiscal policy, and in the end the governing of society. (Amoroso and Windmuller, 1982: 19)

2 Economy and economic policy during the 1980s

The new decade inherited from the 1970s all the main economic problems. Eight years later they are still unsolved and have even worsened. They are reflected in the unchanged situation in unemployment (9 per cent), the worsening of the current account deficit (− 5.4 per cent of GDP), and foreign debt (40 per cent of GDP), and in the unsatisfactory trends in investments and export. All this shows that the fundamental structural problems remain. They may be summarized as follows:

First, the size of the industrial base is small. The manufacturing sector share of GDP in Denmark is about 17 per cent compared to a 25 per cent average in EC countries as a whole.

Second, the size of firm is small. About 80 per cent of all firms have less than 50 employees. This adds to flexibility for production changes but also reduces possibilities of co-ordination and original R&D efforts. Small firms become dependent for R&D on big and multinational firms. The tendencies are stronger in Denmark because of a traditional negative attitude towards industrial policy and planning.

Third, the Danish R&D effort is weak. Denmark devotes about 1 per cent of GDP to R&D, which is considerably less than other industrial countries like Sweden, Japan, West Germany, Holland and Italy. This gap is confirmed by the deficit in the trade balance in high-tech goods.

Some major changes have occurred as a result of the strict austerity measures taken by the new centre–right coalition government since 1982 and of some positive trends in the European economy. Inflation trends and public budget deficit have shown a better performance. Some socioeconomic indicators illustrate the factors behind this development. Total taxation has increased from 43 per cent of GDP in 1980 to 50.5 per cent in 1986. Total public expenditures (consumption, investments and transfers) have been reduced by 0.1 per cent during the period 1983–6, while they have increased by 2.5 per cent in OECD countries. This is the result of a general stoppage in public expenditure and especially of cuts in central government and social security expenditure. The outcome of this policy is that many functions have deteriorated or have been neglected, resulting in rising social and environmental disaster, the costs of which will put serious constraints on economic policy for years ahead. These problems range from extremist movements of marginalized youths to pollution from illegal chemical dumps.

The wage share in the private sector has decreased since 1980, and in 1985 it fell to the 1960 level. While profits have increased by 80 per cent between 1980 and 1985, wages have increased by only 55 per cent. It has been shown that this 'dramatic redistribution' has only partially resulted in an increase in investments. The analysis of the relation between profits and investments does not lead to categorical answers, but it is a fact that there has been a *real* increase of about 18 per cent of profits that have not been reinvested, while wages have increased in real terms, during the same period by 4.5 per cent (Amoroso and Jespersen, 1986).

The changes that have taken place in the labour market during the past five years are partly due to the continuation of tendencies developed during the 1970s (the demographic factor, youth unemployment, increasing female participation, new technologies) and partly to the adaptation to the new requirements of the 1980s (stronger competition and selection in the labour market, a more permanent demarcation line between people inside and outside the labour market, the process of marginalization).

The distribution of the labour force with regard to employment form and economic sector has changed significantly. Employment for self-employed and unskilled workers has decreased, while it has increased for white-collar and skilled workers. The share of employment in the public sector, covering about one-third of the total labour force, has decreased as a result of government cuts in public expenditure. Employment in the public sector rose 4.3 per cent a year in 1972–82, 1.9 per cent in 1982–4 and 0.5 per cent in 1984–5. Industrial employment has increased by more than 1 per cent, especially in the energy sector (oil activities in the North Sea and natural gas transport-distribution net) and in the credit sector. It has decreased in the construction and building sector and in the retail trade. In 1983 the distribution of the labour force in relation to employment form was as shown in Table 3.1.

The perseverance of mass unemployment and the restrictive economic policy adopted by the Danish government since 1982 have created the basis for a new labour market and social structure differentiation. Recent Danish research has identified three different social groups, graduated according to the degree of marginalization: (1) workers in stable employment, unaffected by the economic crisis in their work and income position; (2) workers in unstable employment position, affected by the economic crisis with periods of unemployment and consequent wage losses; (3) unemployed workers on long-term assistance, early retirement schemes, early retirement pensions, social assistance (Bøje, 1986).

An attempt to measure the extension of the marginalization process by the number of people belonging to the labour force depending on transfer incomes results in Table 3.2. These figures

Table 3.1 *Distribution of the labour force, Denmark, 1983*

	%
Self-employed	9.4
Assisting spouses	2.1
Salaried employees in upper levels	7.1
Salaried employees in middle levels	11.1
Salaried employees in lower levels	22.5
Skilled manual workers	10.2
Unskilled manual workers	19.8
Not identified	8.6
Unemployed	9.2

Source: Danmarks Statistisk: Statistiske Efterretninger (1986: 2), Copenhagen: Government Printing Office

Table 3.2 *Labour force, persons depending on income transfer*

Schemes	(No.)
Permanent	
Disability pension	150,000
Early retirement pension	80,000
Voluntary retirement schemes	75,000
Total	305,000
Temporary	
Unemployment benefits	250,000
Welfare disbursement	100,000
Job creation	40,000
Rehabilitation measures	25,000
Total	415,000

Source: Auken, 1985: 64

show that 720,000 people in the productive age group are today (1984) depending on income transfers schemes (more than one-quarter of the total labour force). The same group was: 6 per cent in 1960–1; 10 per cent in 1972–3; 17 per cent in 1979; 22 per cent in 1982–3.

3   Disruption and continuity in the system of industrial relations

In analysing Danish society two interpretative schemes are adopted: one that asserts the prevailing 'liberalism' in economic policy and one that sees 'corporatism' in industrial relations. They both miss catching the peculiarity of form and content of these systems.

In reality, what has been called 'persistent liberalism' has been a way of managing the national economy by administrative/ bureaucratic means, thanks to the high level of cohesion in interests and cultural–political agreement. The 'missing' planning institutions simply aren't needed.

The demands made during the last decade for a more effective industrial policy and planning must not be interpreted as a transition from liberalism to planning, but as a transition from one type of government of the economy to a new one corresponding to the requirements of a complex post-industrial society more vulnerable to conflicts.

The corporative interpretation overlooks the dominating role and ideology of the labour movement in the building up of the Danish welfare state system. National interests have been formulated and represented by the Social Democratic Party and its right to formulate and administer state policy has been unquestioned. Even in periods of bourgeois governments the main lines of state policy and administration have been kept on the rails laid down by Social Democratic traditions and culture.

At the same time, even inside the functional division of tasks between the Party and the trade unions, the latter have developed their social consciousness concerning the understanding of the links between economic and political demands, their specific economic interests in the framework of a more general welfare development.

3.1   The state
A major change has occurred during the 1980s at state level. The minority Social Democratic government gave up in 1982 because it was unable to obtain parliamentary support for a crisis policy aiming at: restoring accumulation (investments), maintaining at the same time a balanced social policy; combining the need for economic growth with a development plan and reforms for the middle–long term.

The new centre–right government came into office with a programme of restoring the accumulation process by fully subordinating the welfare state system to it and by strengthening the market. The general elections of 1984 and 1988 confirmed the political change.

The former government (1979–81) elaborated its economic policy programme with a high degree of involvement of labour organizations. All the programmes presented and approved during this period had been approved by the LO (Landsorganisationen i Danmark) and discussed and co-ordinated with the other sectors of the labour market. Economic unobtrusiveness should have been compensated for by stronger efforts to improve the employment situation, by increasing workers' participation and control in the production process, and by investments. The reinforcement of the legitimacy of all labour market institutions was undoubtedly the goal of the Social Democratic government, based on perhaps a dogmatic belief in a still existing strong consensus on the principles of solidarity and social equity in all sectors of social and political life.

The rapidity with which the new bourgeois government, sustained by a centre–right coalition, has reformulated the contents of economic policy and reoriented the system of industrial relations shows that the consensus for the previous policy must have had some weaknesses and contradictions. The previous privileged relations and involvement between government and trade unions have been rapidly cooled down. Different issues concerning the legitimacy of the trade union system have been taken up at political level, for example the right of organizing alternative unions, the efficiency of unions' administration of some of the public functions (unemployment funds), and their financial support to the Social Democratic Party.

While relations between trade unions and government have been cooled down since 1983, the government has established more privileged relations with the employers' organizations. The target of the current policy seems to be the weakening of the unions by supporting new, breakaway groups and by reducing participation by the established unions in the political decision-making process acquired during previous decades. The outcome should be a weakened trade union movement bargaining with a strengthened employers' organization, within an economic framework dictated by the government.

At the beginning of the 1950s Walter Galenson wrote in his study of labour relations in Denmark: 'The political history of twentieth-century Denmark has been characterized chiefly by the rise of social democracy to power' (1952: 25). It appears that the 1980s are characterized chiefly by the rise of bourgeois parties to government.

3.2   Trade unions

Besides a high degree of self-regulation the Danish labour market presents a high degree of unionization. About 85 per cent of Danish wage-earners are organized in trade unions, with a structure predominantly based on crafts. The three main workers' federations on the labour market are, first, LO (Landsorganisationen i Danmark), Danish Federation of Trade Unions, which is the largest organization with more than half of all Danish wage-earners. The number of affiliated national unions has decreased from thirty-five in 1980 to thirty in 1986, due to the tendency towards amalgamation, while the total membership has increased from 1,277,748 (of whom 42 per cent were women) to 1,411,753 (of whom 46 per cent are women) during the same period. About 300,000 of LO's members are employed in the public sector. Second is FTF (Fællesrådet for Tjenestemænd og Funktionærer), Federation of Civil Servants and Salaried Employees, with more than 300,000 members, mainly public employees (teachers, nurses, and so on). Third is AC (Akademikernes Centralorganisation), Central Organization of Professions, with twenty member organizations (nineteen in 1980) and 118,583 members of whom 30 per cent are women (101,127 members in 1980).

The increasing unionization is due both to some structural changes and modernization of the organizations (tendencies from 'trade' to 'industry' unions), to the increasing risk of unemployment and to the role of the unions in administering unemployment benefit. The strengthening of the unions in terms of membership does not mean that their strength in terms of influence or decision power on policy and industrial relations has also increased. The weakening of the unions' influence on the collective bargaining process and on economic policy is a general trend in this period.

A number of problems have arisen during the past period both within LO and in the relation between it and the other central organizations. These problems will be discussed here: 3.2.1, political aspects of labour movement organization; 3.2.2, organizational changes; and 3.2.3, new trends in the major tasks of union organizations.

3.2.1   Political aspects of labour organization   The LO was established in 1898 as a part of the organizational process of the labour movement. The close links with the Social Democratic Party have been strengthened since then and they have become part of a functional distribution of tasks between the party and the unions. This finds expression in close links at the organizational level and in the material/financial support the unions give to the Social

Democratic Party every year. These relations have been questioned in the past by small leftist groups, but the new white-collar federations have of course taken a completely different attitude, eschewing political involvement.

During the 1980s these links, and especially the financial support to the Social Democratic Party and press, have been internally questioned in some of the main national union organizations. At the 1987 congress the main members' organization inside the LO, the SID (Specialarbejderforbundet i Danmark), General Workers' Union, decided to support both the Social Democratic Party and the Socialist People's Party, that is the second largest workers' party. At the same time a vivid discussion arose inside the HK (Handels- og Kontorfunktionærernes Forbund i Danmark), Commercial and Clerical Employees, in which a neutral political standpoint has been sustained in order to withdraw economic support from the Social Democratic Party.

There are many reasons for this development. First are the changes that have taken place in the composition of the working class and of employee groups in general The increasing number of white-collar workers and an increasing segmentation of the labour market make it more difficult to maintain the principles of social and political solidarity that have always been important features of Social Democratic policy in the Party and in the unions. This can also be seen in the political behaviour of wage-earners. Recent polls have shown that only 54 per cent of the LO members vote for Social Democracy at the political elections, 30 per cent of the votes go to the bourgeois parties and 16 per cent to other left parties.

In this context the main historical conflict inside the LO, which has dogged the organization throughout its existence, remains the one between the SID and Metal (Centralorganisationen af Metalarbejdere), the Central Organization of Metalworkers, the third largest member organization. During the 1980s this conflict has acquired a more general character than before, and it reflects two very different ways of understanding and acting in relation to almost all problems, political as well as economic (solidaristic wage policy, new technology, atomic energy, transport, peace movement, and so on). While the SID reaffirms socialist positions on both traditional and new ecological issues, Metal is close to the economistic and growth-oriented culture of the white-collar unions.

3.2.2 Organizational changes Traditionally the structure of the unions is based on craft unions in accordance with the particular skills of the workers, with unskilled workers joining separate organizations. A need to move towards industry unions was first discussed in 1913, as a political necessity to strengthen solidarity among industrial workers and develop their class consciousness. A more consistent decision was taken during the congress of the organization in 1971, where a big majority approved a resolution that called for 'the constitution of a co-ordinated system of nine industry unions'. Since 1970 the number of unions has decreased from fifty-seven to thirty-two (1987), and different unions have been grouped in cartels.

Again in 1979 the LO congress approved a resolution aiming at establishing a new general structure of the LO, articulated in nine industry unions. This radical structural change has not been realized yet, but the number of unions is decreasing because of the amalgamation process.

The topic of industrial organizations has been constantly discussed during the past six years at all the unions' congresses. It has become clear that the proposed solution tries to solve simultaneously both the need for a new articulation and modernization of the union structure in order to make it more suited to the existing and changing economic structure, and to preserve and reinforce the principle of collectivity and solidarity of the trade unions.

A different approach and solution to the same problems has been sustained by the SID. Since 1977 this organization has emphasized that the radical change in the labour market caused by the new technologies and the growth of new service sectors will make it difficult to operate with the distinctions and demarcations involved in the nine industry-union structure. The SID argues that a wage-levelling solidaristic policy and sufficient union strength at the central and local level require the unification of all trade unions in one great organization. The proposal presented by the SID at the 1979 LO congress called for the setting up of one unified union, articulated in eight branches. The basic idea is to organize all the employees of the same working place in the same local organization of the union. At the same time a decentralization should take place at regional level. The collective bargaining process would be influenced in the direction of an increasing homogeneity and co-ordination of collective agreements for the different groups and inside the single working place. The process of democratization would also be reinforced because of the greater clarity and comparativeness of the demands and the results obtained.

The necessity for a new organizational structure has been underlined by several demarcation conflicts between unions and the achievement of new demarcation agreements between unions in recent years (printing industry 1976–8, steel and engineering industries 1981).

A different picture appears if we look at the white-collar unions especially the AC and the FTF. Here the main tendency in collective bargaining strategy is to increase segmentation and differentiation, not as a necessity but as a choice. If the ideological character of the LO, its socialist inspiration, lies behind the proposed solution and the collectivist and 'solidaristic strategy',[2] the AC and the FTF strategies of differentiation and professionalism can also be understood through their bourgeois ideological background. Because of the slowness of the unions' response to the problem of structural change, opposite trends are manifesting themselves. There is likely to be both a movement to stronger industry unions within LO and a growth of independent ones; both a strengthening of the more powerful unions and a weakening of the movement as a whole, with increasing conflict among unions.

3.2.3 *Extension of union tasks and activities*

The major task of the trade unions is to bargain for proper wages, social benefits and better working conditions with the employers. This has been done by the industrial relations system, with special emphasis on collective agreements. During the last decade more politically oriented bargaining forms have been introduced, such as income policy and tripartite bargaining.

But the new links that the development of the welfare system has established between workers' living (and working) conditions and the political system require a more active participation of the unions at the political/legislative level. They have participated in the Economic Council since 1936, and have recently strengthened their activity there. In 1984 LO published a programme for industrial policy (LO, 1984), and it has also been active in promoting a number of *ad hoc* studies in which it elaborates its own view on economic and political development (LO, 1983). An increasing number of proposals for new legislation has been produced by trade unions during this period concerning employment and economic policy, the pension system, housing policy, environment, education and vocational training, foreign policy, cultural policy, new technology, tax policy and economic democracy.

The stronger engagement in economic policy has also affected the position of the unions in regard to the investment decision-making process, because of the possibility in this field rendered by union control of pension funds. The recent decision to allow these funds to invest in industrial activities, an idea which trade unions have been supporting, has been followed by a more political investment preference system.

A recent inquiry (*Børsens Nyhedsmagasin*, 1986: 14–16) has shown that a number of pension funds refuse to invest in firms that reveal in their economic activities an attitude different from the trade unions on major issues like co-operation with South Africa, pollution problems, production of military equipment, anti-union policy, and so on. This policy is not, however, pursued by the white-collar unions.

In 1983 LO established an investment company, Danish Industrial Investment Ltd (A/S Dansk Erhvervsinvestering). The initiative is meant as a contribution to the increase of production and employment. During the 1980s risk-bearing capital was needed to contribute to the establishment of new dynamic enterprises and to the development of existing ones. The LO initiative can transfer employees' funds into trade and industry. But it has been emphasized that the aim of the investment company is not to give 'first aid' to any firms which run into short-term problems.

3.3 Employers

Danish employers are organized in two main types of interest organizations: DA (Dansk Arbejdsgiverforening), the Confederation of Danish Employers, which is in charge of collective agreements concerning wages and industrial relations; and IR (Industrirådet), the Council of Industry, and HR (Håndværksrådet), Council of Smaller Firms, engaged in industrial policy, sector problems, economic policy, educational and information activities, and so on.

3.3.1 The Confederation of Danish Employers

The DA is the primary employers' organization for collective bargaining with the trade unions, and its power and influence is unchanged even if its organizational strength has been reduced during the last decades. The traditional weakness of the organization is caused by the fact that neither the big companies nor a large number of small enterprises are members. These employers make their own collective agreements with the trade unions.

The growth of the public sector and the tertiary sector has developed a labour market outside the manufacturing sector traditionally organized by the DA. For this reason the DA's enterprises today employ less than 20 per cent of the total labour force, and 32 per cent of the private sector. Unlike LO, the DA's membership has remained nearly unchanged over the past two decades. It has 22,642 member firms with 519,800 employees, of which 316,000 are manual workers and 203,200 white-collar (31 December 1986). There are 151 member organizations, assembled in a number of main sectoral organizations.

During the 1980s there has been debate about the DA's organizational structure, for reasons similar to those already mentioned for the LO. The DA's traditional organizational strength is concentrated in the manufacturing sector. During recent years attention has been focused on the unorganized sectors and on the sectors organized outside DA. The former sectors are the ones where white-collar employment prevails: commerce, the professions and the traditionally unorganized chemical and pharmaceutical sectors. The latter are the banks, building industry, road hauliers and agriculture. The tendency toward organization has increased in the metals employers' sector, especially among consulting and service firms dealing with high technology. The tendency toward larger organizations is also increasing within DA, and an increasing number of employers' organizations of professionals (lawyers, auditors) is joining.

The DA organizational structure is still very centralized and in collective bargaining with trade unions no single organization can sign agreements concerning essential aspects of wage and working conditions without DA permission. This right of veto is not claimed by the LO.

After a period of experiments in better co-operation and management during the 1960s, Danish employers have shown during the last five years a more rigid attitude towards all kinds of institutional relations. The innovative measures employers have supported are more oriented to counteract LO proposals, such as the introduction of individual forms of workers' profit-sharing in order to avoid the labour movement's demand for economic democracy in a general and collective form, and flexibility and decentralization in the collective bargaining process in order to weaken unions' strength and solidarity among the workers. The influence that the new centre–right coalition has had in producing these new attitudes since 1982 appears unquestionable (for a summary of these changes, see D in Table 3.3).

3.3.2 Other employers' organizations The other employers' organizations all function mainly as pressure groups for the different interests they represent, but the most important and influential lobby, apart from the Agricultural Council (Landbrugsrådet), is the IR (Industriråd). Its members include the biggest and most influential Danish companies. They are not always members of DA, but in recent years co-operation between these two organizations seems to have improved. IR has taken up all problems concerning economic, industrial and technological policy and it functions as a strategic centre for employers' policy. IR is

Table 3.3 *Changes in the industrial relations system, Denmark since 1980*

Type	Pre-1980	Post-1980
A(a) National concertation	Encouraged by successive governments but never stably established	Almost complete disappearance
A(b) Industry-wide collective bargaining	Widely established tradition under the leadership of central confederation or unions' modification by local bargaining	Endeavours from employers (private and public) to promote decentralization and differentiation
B Decentralized collective bargaining	Local modification of national sector agreements	Increasing decentralization of the entire collective bargaining system, both at the horizontal level and at the vertical level. Employers and some trade unions support it
C Worker participation via unions	Promoted by law and collective agreements	Increasing inefficiency of its control on managerial decisions and working relations
D Worker participation without unions	Unimportant; mainly among non-manual workers	Some growth related to employers' introduction of different kind of 'private' profit-share systems
D(a) Simple contracts without union	Rare	Some growth
D(b) Simple contracts (no union) in secondary (black or grey) labour markets	Occasionally but of relative importance in some sectors like painting, building repairs, and so on	Some growth tendencies but limited

represented, as will be mentioned below, in some of the tripartite institutions.

4 The industrial relations system

4.1 Economic policy and labour-market organizations

Government interventions in industrial relations in general and in collective bargaining on wages in particular have also taken place in the past. But they have always been motivated by emergency or crisis. During recent years they have become an integrated part of stabilization and economic policy in order to solve the structural imbalances and planning problems.

4.1.1 The organized state mediation system: relations between government and LO　An economic programme, based on reform and structural policy, was elaborated by the Social Democratic government, with the full support of the trade unions (LO), in December 1979. This programme was reformulated in spring 1980, owing to lack of parliamentary support, with a stronger emphasis on increasing austerity measures. The unions' support was due to the government's acceptance of the LO request for a three-year employment plan integrated with a comprehensive industrial policy programme based on selective principles for new investments (energy saving, alternative energy, urban recovery, public transport, development of trade and professional education), and with special emphasis on youth and female employment programmes, especially at local level.

During the period January 1980 to September 1982, following a well-established tradition, the government maintained close relations with LO and tried to strengthen tripartite institutions in order to obtain the involvement and support of DA.

The new bourgeois government, supported by a centre–right coalition, presented its economic programme on 1 October 1982; it was mainly based on wage cuts and public expenditure reductions. This was a clear and declared intrusion in the collective bargaining system and in industrial relations in general without any kind of consultation or negotiation with labour market organizations. The ideological basis of this programme was a radical challenge to the welfare state system and to Social Democratic policy.

Real contact between government and unions has not existed since 1983. After many protests from the LO side some meetings were held (August 1985 and February 1986), but without any content or efforts for real negotiations. Instead, meetings between government and DA have strengthened.

4.1.2   The organized state mediation system: tripartite relations   During the period 1979–82 great efforts were made in order to increase the involvement of employers' organizations in economic policy through the development of tripartite institutions (see the summary of institutional developments in Table 3.3, A(a)). The Tripartite Commission for Industrial Policy (Det Industripolitiske Kontaktudvalg) was created during the elaboration of the 1979 economic programme and was constituted by representation of trade unions and the Economic Council of the Labour Movement on one side, and the IR, HR, LR (Landbrugsrådet), the Agricultural Council, and so on on the other side. The Chairman of the Commission was the Minister of Industry, and its main activity has concentrated on the elaboration of tax reductions, industrial policy, technology programmes and the employment plan. The Commission took the initiative in the creation of a Mediation Secretariat (Formidlingssekretariat) under the Ministry of Industry, in order to ensure that larger public purchases and investments would be of advantage to national enterprises. Similar initiatives were the creation of an Information Centre for Technology at the regional level, and the Mediation Council (Formidlingsråd).

A very different attitude to tripartite relations and institutions has been demonstrated since 1982 by the bourgeois government. On many occasions this negative attitude to real negotiations and exchange of information has been registered as a problem at the political level. For example, in May 1983 Parliament approved a Social Democratic resolution that required the Ministry of Labour to prepare a report on the reduction of working hours, to be carried out in co-operation with the labour-market organizations. The report was presented to the Parliament at the beginning of 1984, but it was rejected because the contents reflected only the government view of the problem, since no contact had been established during its elaboration with labour market organizations. In fact, because of the existing links between government and employers' organizations, the trade unions were the only ones really excluded.

On 20 March 1984 the Parliament approved a further Social Democratic resolution requiring the government to re-establish tripartite contacts in order to negotiate income policy, reduction in working hours and industrial and employment policy. The tripartite meetings that took place after this saw exchanges of different points of view, but without any real dialogue or co-operation.

The government intrusion in collective bargaining in April 1985 did not reduce the tension among the parties. This situation continued unchanged in 1986. After the tripartite meetings in November 1985 the DA expressed, in the same terms as LO had done before, albeit for different reasons, its disappointment over the lack of information coming from government during these meetings.

4.2 The organized system of mediation: relations
between labour-market organizations

The economic crisis and technological development have accelerated the process of conflict and institutional change in co-operation between employers and wage-earners during the 1970s (see C in Table 3.3). The unions have increased their pressure by transforming their demands from consultative co-operation to co-determination and economic democracy and, as already mentioned, including new fields of activities under their care, such as technical and social matters.

The Basic Agreement between LO and DA, regarded as 'the constitution of the labour market', has been unchanged since 1973. At the end of the 1970s many trade unions called for a revision of it in order to obtain a change of clause 4, section 1, in which the employers' management rights in 'directing' and 'distributing' work and 'employing appropriate labour' are stated – and to achieve a more effective protection for the employees against an 'arbitrary action' in connection with dismissals.

Negotiations started in autumn 1980 and ended with a New Basic Agreement from 1 March 1981. Protection for individual workers and shop stewards against arbitrary dismissal was strengthened, but the New Basic Agreement continues to contain a 'peace clause' by which the two sides undertake to co-operate and avoid work stoppages. Any strike action requires a 75 per cent vote in favour and must be announced to the employer fourteen days in advance of its preparation and seven days before its start. The procedures in case of breach or disputes about interpreting the agreement follow the previous rules, dictating an arbitration by 'joint meeting' of both sides at local and central levels, and finally at the Labour Court. The main demand of the unions which questioned the managerial right of the employers was frustrated and slightly reformulated.

After about two months' negotiation the Basic Agreement was revised again in December 1986, coming into force from 1 March 1987, but the existing tension between LO and DA did not permit any significant change.

An innovative measure at the institutional level concerning labour market relations has been the Technology Agreement from

1 March 1981, between LO and DA. During the 1970s the introduction of new technology had caused several conflicts in individual firms and between unions and employers' organizations, and a number of initiatives and local agreements had been made at company level at the end of the 1970s to ensure job security. The agreement between LO and DA stated the right of the workers' representatives to be informed in advance about changes 'of major significance' and their likely impact on jobs.

This agreement was followed by corresponding ones for banking and the public sector. Common to all of them was that they were supplementary to the existing Co-operation Agreement, where emphasis is put on the role of shop stewards.

The LO/DA Technology Agreement was kept within the framework of the Basic Agreement, without challenging co-operation and the employers' prerogatives. Some organizations, like the Printers' Union, demanded a more radical change, including the right of veto for workers.

The Technology Agreement was renewed, together with the Co-operation Agreement, on 9 July 1986. The two agreements were transformed into a new Co-operation Agreement and their administration is now the task of a Co-operation Committee existing in all enterprises employing thirty-five persons or more within the same geographical region (against fifty or more employees in the previous agreement).

Co-operation Committees are composed of equal numbers of representatives of management and employees. LO and DA agree that improvement in the firms' competitiveness and in employee job satisfaction are joint aims. In this context attention is directed to the introduction of new technologies, and the employers' duty to inform employees is emphasized.

Since 1974 employees of companies with more than fifty workers have been entitled to elect two representatives to the companies' boards of management. In 1981 a new law increased this participation. The employees in joint-stock companies with more than fifty workers are entitled to elect from among themselves a number of representatives equal to half of the shareholders' representatives on the board, with a minimum of two seats (three seats in banks, plus one board member appointed by the government to represent public interest), provided that at least half of those entitled to vote are in favour. Nevertheless scepticism persists about the real efficacy of these reforms as a means of controlling the firm. The most important decisions taken by enterprises on the introduction of new technologies or the closing down of units are still taken on grounds that the employees' representatives can only ratify.

The general climate of co-operation at the general organizations level (DA/LO) and at the local level has deteriorated in recent years. DA has become very critical of many public and collective institutions that govern or control the job environment. In 1986 and 1987 co-operation between DA and LO reached a very critical point with regard to the functioning of Safety Committees and Service (BST-Centre). The DA's strong criticism of the Directorate of National Labour Inspection (Direktoratet for Arbejdstilsynet) is developing along the same lines. The Directorate has increased its interventions against poor environmental conditions in many enterprises and has supported extending the powers of Safety Committees. The DA regards this as an intrusion into managerial prerogatives.

4.3 The collective bargaining process
The collective bargaining process and collective agreements are still the core of the entire system of industrial relations, even if their importance has been weakened because of the increase in legislation and political regulation in this area. During the 1980s, these processes have undergone significant changes that will be examined with regard to three main aspects: forms, contents, conflicts.

4.3.1 The forms
Up to the 1980s the two main features of the Danish system of collective bargaining were the centralized bargaining form and the free bargaining right of the organizations. The centralized bargaining form implies that the labour market organizations organize, negotiate and co-ordinate the entire process with the help and participation of the different unions involved. After having collected the proposals elaborated from the respective member organizations, the LO and DA normally agreed on the timetable and the agenda for the negotiations. For many decades it was a tradition that LO and DA negotiate on all the 'general' proposals (wages, working hours, holidays, and so on), while the respective branch organizations negotiate on 'special' proposals.

Since 1981 this system has been changed. The collective bargaining process has become decentralized, the member organizations negotiating all the bargaining demands, both the 'general' and the 'special'. A revival in centralized negotiations took place in 1985, but it ended in a bargaining collapse and in the government intervention already mentioned. The decentralized form has been sustained by DA and by some of the stronger unions that feel their wage level is kept down by the strong emphasis LO has always put on the protection of the lower wage groups.

As long as the centralized system was functioning it was possible to maintain an egalitarian strategy that was able to influence other sectors. In this context the LO/DA sector had a leading function in collective bargaining. But with the diffusion of the decentralized bargaining system this leading position has been taken over by single branches of activities, for example the metal sector, which influence negotiations both in the private sector in general and in the public sector. In this way the principle of solidarity in the wage structure and labour conditions has become untenable (see A(b) and B in Table 3.3).

The constantly emphasized 'freedom of negotiation' in the Danish system of labour relations seems to be a myth rather than reality. Co-ordination between labour market organizations' demands and economic policy targets began in the 1920s. As already mentioned (4.1) the main links between government and labour market during more than fifty years was with LO, but since 1982 this function has been taken over by the DA.

The 1985 state intervention in collective bargaining was the twenty-eighth since 1933. The peculiarity of this last intervention was that for the first time both the labour market organizations and the Conciliation Board (Forligsinstitutionen) were excluded from the process. Furthermore the government has by this central-ized solution created the formal institutional structure that seems likely to become the foundation of future decentralized collective bargaining. The 1985 law indicates both the total level of wage increase and its distribution among the different sectors of the economy during the entire period of validity of the collective agreements.

By settlement of the level of wage increase in the main sectors the government has introduced priorities substantially different from 'solidaristic wage policy' claimed by the LO and converging with 'flexibility in wage policy' claimed by the DA.

The 1985 law also introduces a fundamental change in the formal position of the labour market organizations. Their function becomes that of realizing and administering the basic government decisions: it is 'a position that is not very different from the executive one of a decentralized organ in public administration' (Pedersen, 1986:110). Recently the claim for free bargaining rights has revived inside the trade unions, in order to contest the bourgeois government's intrusion in labour relations.

On the other side the government and the DA also seem to claim freedom of negotiation, although with a different interpretation from that sustained by the LO, namely from a deregulation and anti-unionist point of view. They refer to the single worker's right to be non-organized, the right to choose between different unions by creating new ones, and the right to extend local bargaining to the enterprise level.

4.3.2   The contents   During the 1970s the contents of collective bargaining developed from wage-oriented negotiations to broader ones including economic policy measures and industrial and economic democracy. The opposite seems to have become the case during the 1980s. The contents of bargaining have increasingly been reduced to wage problems, and the maintenance of a limited degree of protection for lower wage groups has been weakened by allowing increased wage differentiation and the prolongation of collective agreements to a four-year period (with limited re-bargain possibility after two years).

The working-hours reduction, introduced in 1985 (with validity from 1 December 1986) with one weekly hour, and in 1987 with two more hours during a period of four years, will, because of its very gradual application, be absorbed by productivity increases and the intention of strongly influencing unemployment and labour market structure will not be realized.

Collective bargaining in 1987 brought some increase in wages, estimated to be about 6–7 per cent per year within LO/DA sectors, and an increase in the contributions to the ATP pension system and to the vocational training fund. The DA obtained the prolongation of collective agreements to a four-year period. While the first result, in favour of workers, will be easily reabsorbed by economic policy measures, the second will probably be maintained.

This situation is insoluble for the trade unions because the rules of the labour market do not permit any pressure from the workers' side during the period of validity of a collective agreement in case of government intervention on wage incomes. Today the stabilization function exerted by economic policy in order to guarantee the results of negotiation reached by collective bargaining seems transformed into a destabilization function of the latter in order to maintain the primacy of the former.

4.3.3   The conflicts   Conflicts in the Danish labour market are regulated and limited by a series of norms which labour market organizations have negotiated and agreed upon. Among them the law on the Industrial Court, the Basic Agreement and the 'Norm' applied to regulate industrial conflicts must be recalled. The general commitment of the labour market organizations to create and maintain co-operation also contributes to the avoidance of conflicts, although both the trade unions and the employers' organizations maintain large strike/lock-out funds.

Table 3.4   *Industrial conflicts, Denmark, 1970–85*

	Total conflicts (with more than 100 lost working days)	Workers involved	Working days lost (000s)
1970	77	55,585	102.0
1971	31	6,379	20.6
1972	35	7,601	21.8
1973	205	337,100	3,901.2
1974	134	142,352	184.2
1975	147	59,128	100.1
1976	204	87,224	201.3
1977	228	36,305	229.7
1978	314	59,340	128.8
1979	218	156,589	173.0
1980	225	62,073	186.7
1981	94	53,463	651.6
1982	180	53,185	92.7
1983	161	40,919	78.8
1984	157	50,764	131.7
1985	820	581,297	2,332.7

Source: Danmarks Statistisk: Statistisk Tiårsoversigt (1985 and 1987),
Copenhagen: Government Printing Office

The main tendencies during the 1980s have been described as an 'institutional trap' for the labour movement because of the limitation to their negotiation power imposed by government intervention on one side, and by a more rigid interpretation applied by the DA and the Tribunal of Labour to the 'organizations' responsibility' in maintaining law and order in industrial relations.

The whole picture of the conflicts can be divided in two parts: conflicts that have arisen in the context of the negotiations for new collective agreements and within the mentioned norms (official conflicts); and conflicts that have arisen during the period of validity of the new collective agreements because of sectoral or local conflicts caused by anti-union measures, dismissals, government policy, and so on (unofficial conflicts).

The former have been increasingly provoked by falling real wages and increased wage differentials between the private and the public sectors. The latter have been increased by growing rigidity in employers' attitudes toward co-operation, anti-unionist initiatives consisting in employing non-organized workers, the creation of a pluralist system of workers' representation (by creating Christian unions) and, finally, by dismissals and shutting-down of undertakings.

Table 3.5 *Number of disputes submitted to the Industrial Court, Denmark, 1978–86*

1978–9	1979–80	1980–1	1981–2	1982–3	1983–4	1984–5	1985–6
295	444	332	243	256	274	340	606

Source: Pedersen, 1986: 114; and DA, 1985–6

Beside these two types of conflicts directly related to labour market relations, others should be recalled concerning social movements and protests provoked by unemployment and marginalization processes in the labour market (a squatters' movement among young people, absenteeism, and so on).

With regard to official and unofficial conflicts the classical indicators (for the private sector) are the strike statistics and the number of industrial disputes submitted to the Industrial Court. Table 3.4 shows the level of industrial conflicts (working days lost because of conflicts) during the fifteen years to 1985.

The large increase in the number of conflicts in 1985 can be understood both as a signal that the upper level of the applicability of austerity measures has been reached, and as the reaction to the state intervention demonstrated in the figures illustrating the number of industrial disputes submitted to the Industrial Court (Table 3.5).

5 Types of unions and industrial relations: new trends

As already mentioned, the important changes in union organizations and in the industrial relations system that have taken place during the 1980s were foreseen. Nevertheless, the most realistic predictions were dealing with the timing of the change and its different alternatives within the same system and goals. While analytical care prevents us from drawing firm conclusions based on a period the length and events of which trace a path but do not indicate for certain the point of arrival, we can nevertheless conclude that the character of the changes and a comparison with the development of a similar system during the same period (Sweden) reveal the radicalism of the transformation that has taken place with regard to the system and its goals.

During the 1980s trade unions suffered a loss both in bargaining power and in political citizenship rights. The new potential conflicts, although (as already mentioned) kept under control by the institutional network of the labour market, have started to manifest themselves in forms that will deeply affect both the institutions and the trade unions. They show a parallel path of development, although in different forms and contents, among both the manual and non-manual workers. It can be summarized in the formation of a double dualistic structure: one between the employed and the non-employed (comprising the unemployed, early retired, and so on) and one between A-employed and B-employed, which distinction is based on the different level of job protection and security (Bild, 1985). This could well lead to internal division in the trade union movement and to major changes in its organizational structure. These possibilities will be evaluated after we have considered the internal and external factors affecting its development.

The internal factors concern mainly: the breaking up of the tight links between the trade unions and the Social Democratic Party; the boomerang effect caused by the institutional function taken up by the unions in many areas. In a time of increasing demand for institutional reforms and changes, the trade unions are exposed to the same criticism and ruptures as public institutions, because of this role; and the increasing contradictions between the structure of the trade unions, organized according to traditional vocational training criteria, and the restructuring of the vocational training system due to technological development.

These internal factors are, of course, related to the following external factors and reinforced by them: the existence of a 'bourgeois' government for a period of four years and in a political contest that shows the penetration of liberal–conservative ideologies and administrative practice in local and central administration; an increasing 'Europization' of the Danish welfare state, expressed by the dismissal of full employment and social equality as main policy goals; an increasing structural dependence of the Danish economy on foreign capital, industrial groups and political interests.

5.1   Is there a future for the 'Danish' system of union and industrial relations?

All these processes and events are producing a perceptible shift in the system of union and industrial relations towards a more pluralistic and decentralized form of collective bargaining, and towards increasing use of employers' strategies to implement forms of workers' participation, workers' involvement in and identification with the company. The result of 1987 collective agreements and the persistent support of the bourgeois government by a parliamentary majority seem to confirm and reinforce these trends. The achievements of the government and employers can be seen in

the great difficulties experienced by the LO and the Social Democratic Party in restoring the unity of the labour movement.

A point on which the different positions of the DA and LO and
of the trade unions reveal the complexity of the contradictions in
the Danish labour market is that of flexibility concerning the
employment situation, the wage system and working hours. A
particularity of the Danish system of labour relations has long been
a high degree of flexibility in employment. It has always been very
easy, both in the private and in the public sector, to fire people
because of a reduction in activities, productivity measures or any
other reason. The trade unions' concern on this matter was more
directed at the protection of employees from income losses and the
establishment of a well-functioning system of job mobility. Behind
this attitude lay a period of full employment and optimism about
the maintenance of this situation.

Today the situation is radically changed and the trade unions are
very divided because of the different degree of unemployment risk
to which their members are exposed.

The only area in which LO has claimed protection against
'unfair' dismissal is the one related to the introduction of new
technology but this protection has been almost non-existent. This
lack of job protection is today a powerful instrument in the hands
of the employers who, without significant resistance, are free to
decide on dismissals and restructuring matters.

The Danish wage system has always incorporated a certain
degree of flexibility in industrial activities in order to stimulate
productivity, and this attitude has been supported also by the
unions. The novelty in recent developments is the extension of
wage-flexibility criteria to all sectors, both in the private and in the
public sector, with the abolition of the principle of the same wage
for the same job.

Because a flexible wage system related to productivity implies a
concept of 'production' and 'productivity' that differs from sector
to sector, the extension of the criteria adopted in the 'export'
sectors and in the 'commodities' sectors to all other activities raises
the problem of the 'commercialization' of the entire welfare system
(in the sense of the 'commercial society' recalled from Polanyi)
and, therefore, its transformation into a very different system.

Also on this very crucial matter, with huge implications for
Scandinavian society in general, the trade unions are divided. The
principle of flexibility in wages along these lines, extended to the
public sector, has been introduced in the 1987 collective
agreements.

Flexibility in working time has met a greater resistance from the trade unions, in order to prevent overtime work and night work being paid at the same rates as ordinary work. But the resistance of the unions has a more general motivation because of the demonstrated negative effects that shift-work hours can produce both on the general level of employment and on the living conditions of the workers and their families.

The latest development has not affected this attitude but it has made it possible to reach local agreements at the plant level. In the context of increasingly decentralized negotiations this will become a further cause of division among unions and workers.

Notes

I am grateful to the participants of this research group for their comments on the first drafts of this paper. I wish to thank in particular Guido Baglioni, Gösta Rehn, Colin Crouch and Jesper Jespersen for their detailed comments and suggestions.

1 The concept of 'Scandinavian Model' applied here has been elaborated in Amoroso (1980).

2 In the Danish labour movement 'solidaristic wage policy' expresses a policy combining the collective strength of the trade union movement in achieving an egalitarian wage policy by collective bargaining and by improving the status of those who are worse off (by bargaining and by law).

References

Amoroso, B. (1980) *Rapporto dalla Scandinavia*, Rome: Laterza.

Amoroso, B. (1985) *1. Socialøkonomisk Rapport om landets tilstand*, Roskilde: RUC.

Amoroso, B. and J. Jespersen (1986) (eds) *2. Socialøkonomisk Rapport om landets tilstand*, Roskilde: FS&P.

Amoroso, B. and J. Windmuller (1982) *Labour Movement and Socialism in Scandinavia: Ten Years' Development: A Review*, Roskilde: RUC.

Auken, G. (1985) *Døgnet skal hedde to dage*, Copenhagen.

Bild, T. (1985) 'Hvad skal der gøres ved arbejdsmarkedets stigende overskudslagre?' *Samfundsøkonomen*, 3:16–20.

Bøje, T. (1986) 'Labour Market Segmentation and Social Welfare Programmes: The Divided Society', paper to the XIth World Congress of Sociology, Delhi, India.

Børsens Nyhedsmagasin (1986) November 14, Copenhagen.

Galenson, W. (1952) *The Danish System of Labour Relations*, Cambridge, Mass.: Harvard University Press.

LO (1983) *Det kan gå to veje: økonomisk politik for 80'erne*, Copenhagen: LO.

LO (1984) *Erhvervspolitisk Program*, Copenhagen: LO.

Pedersen, O.K. (1986) in B. Amoroso and J. Jespersen (eds) *2. Socialøkonomisk Rapport om landets tilstand*, Roskilde: FS&P.

Vangskjær, K. (1986) *Multinationale selskaber og deres indflydelse i Danmark*, Copenhagen: SID.

4

Recent Changes in France

Denis Segrestin

1 Introduction: industrial relations in France in 1980

At the turn of the decade, French industrial relations were marked by four elements.

First, the country was in the throes of recession. The depth of the economic crisis can be gauged by the level of unemployment, which had already reached 7.2 per cent of the labour force. Two other indicators are equally striking: inflation (13 per cent) and the chronic balance-of-payments deficit. On the positive side, however, government authorities could point out that overall there had been no decline in wage-earners' purchasing power.

In a pre-election year, however, the 'real wage taboo' had a high and symbolically charged price. It prevented the restoration of overall economic equilibria, as economic policymakers themselves admitted. And it eliminated virtually all scope for collective bargaining – the only 'bargaining room' lay outside the field of economic constraints, and in a climate of incipient recession. Thus 1979 and 1980 were years of widespread discussion of job insecurity, of part-time and temporary employment, and of unregistered jobs. Bargaining involved such items as dismissal compensation, unemployment benefits, resource guarantees, and the regulation of short-time working.

All this indicates that government, employers and the workers themselves realized that the crisis was a structural, long-term one. But they had not yet squarely faced the issue of industrial restructuring, conversion and the regaining of lost market shares. Even the question of working hours, though officially on the order of the day for public discussion (an official white paper was published at the behest of the government, with no consequences), had not clearly emerged as an issue in industrial relations. It had given rise to no broad union strategy. This question would emerge only very slowly.

Secondly, the turn of the decade was a time of great political uncertainty. True, the right was in power and was intent on accentuating the free-market orientation of the regime. France was engaged in price liberalization and the reduction of the budget deficit (consisting mainly in curbing energy costs and measures to improve industrial competitiveness). The eighth five-year plan called for stepped-up efforts on behalf of the strategic industries of the future (electronics, aerospace, telecommunications, and so on).

Yet all this was exceedingly fragile. For one thing, the majority coalition was weak and divided. For another, since 1974 (which saw Giscard d'Estaing's election as President of the Republic but also the onset of the economic crisis) the left appeared as a credible alternative, despite an impressive array of weaknesses and divisions of its own, notably the rupture of the unity pact between the Communist and Socialist parties in 1977. Ultimately, of all the major trends confirmed under Giscard's seven-year term, only one was not called into question by this highly uncertain political situation: the opening of the domestic market to foreign competition and the irreversibility of the impulse effects coming from the EC. The opposition of the Communist Party and of a part of the Socialist Party to this opening would never achieve true credibility in France, despite the acute unemployment problem.

Thirdly, the recession and the uncertainties of politics established an entirely different social context, as the 1980s got under way, from that which had underlain the 1960s and 1970s. The level of strike activity had already declined considerably, despite a number of strong, localized actions involving the most disadvantaged workers (immigrants, workers not covered by labour law or contract). The unions were clearly on the decline (with only about 15 per cent of the eligible workforce enrolled), although at the same time workplace elections demonstrated their continuing representativeness. The balance of power within organized labour appeared to be shifting towards the 'reformist' unions. Thus in the *prud'hommes* elections[1] at the end of 1979 the 'reformist front' of Force Ouvrière, CFTC and CGC could boast of being as popular, taken together, as the more radical CFDT (23.1 per cent as against 22.4 per cent), while the largely Communist CGT, though losing ground, still took 50.2 per cent of the total ballots.[2]

Although originally working-class consciousness in France had been constructed around the theme of unity and although fifteen years had elapsed since the historic pact for 'unity of action' between CGT and CFDT in 1966, the division within organized labour appeared deeper than ever, involving not so much tactical matters as fundamental, long-term differences over such issues as the concept of trade unionism and the relationship with the rank and file, the definition of the 'working class', and relations between organized labour and government.

Whether as the direct effect of this state of affairs or as a parallel development throwing it into starker relief it is hard to say, but employers were strengthening their power. Most notably there was a revival of employers and firms at the grassroots, as the source of authority and initiatives in industrial relations. Against the weakened unions, management increased its sway, whether it was a matter of resolute implementation of collective dismissals or proposing new forms of concertation on hours and working conditions.

Fourthly, in this relatively unstable political and economic context, one nonetheless discerns a number of elements having all the hallmarks of being virtually irreversible points of reference as early as the end of the 1970s. We have already mentioned some of them, such as the opening of the French market and the restoration of union pluralism against the backdrop of de-unionization. More generally, one is tempted to recall three fundamental tendencies often mentioned by the commentators of the day.

The first is the crisis of ideology, doubt as to the political system's ability to provide resources for the society or to resolve the most sensitive problems of the moment. The unions were caught in the vicelike grip of this widespread scepticism towards all social projects of any sort.

The other two tendencies are more immediately relevant to the industrial relations system and the social 'rules of the game'. First, developments in the 1970s had established a state of affairs in France that cannot perhaps, strictly speaking, be termed neo-corporatism but that nevertheless did help to organize social regulation of a complicated, indeed inextricable, entanglement of matters governed by contract and by law, by bargaining policy and public policy. One example among dozens is the question of unemployment benefits. Along the same lines, the 1970s generated a multifarious but extremely dense network of communications between business and labour organizations. Consultation and discussion came to be the rule, and the institutions that lent an official character to this practice (planning commissions, the collective bargaining council) were virtually obscured by the welter of occasions in which unions, employers and government could meet.

Finally, one trend was already firmly established, namely the diversification of forms of bargaining, both as regards parties and levels and as regards issues. The branch or industry-wide agreement remains the foundation of the system, but it is eclipsed by a series of highly variegated initiatives fostered by numerous laws, the main source being traceable to the creation of company-level union locals in 1968. In a word, a major risk had arisen, whose evolution in subsequent years bears close examination: the threat of a widening separation between centralized regulation and highly decentralized union–employer regulation, most especially at the company level.

2   Structural problems: the search for a crisis equilibrium

2.1   An overview

Before the 1980s, the French economy had been excessively slow in adjusting to the changing international environment and the new requirements of competition. French economic and industrial strategy had been insulated from major economic development outside Europe. In 1980, it was still very poorly prepared for the 'economic world war' waged by Japan, the United States and the entire group of newly industrialized countries, which was reshaping the established international division of labour. France suffered from a number of structural weaknesses that had been evident since the inception of the crisis and that the developments of 1980–5 would only confirm.

France experienced two significant policy phases in the early 1980s. In 1981 François Mitterrand was elected President and the left came to power. The new government experimented with an expansionary economic programme aimed principally at stimulating demand and as a consequence output and employment. The experiment, not the first of its kind, failed. It resulted in a record trade deficit and a serious deterioration in the balance of payments on current account, while inflation held above 10 per cent. Productive investment stalled. In 1982, for the second time, it contracted sharply.

Thus began the effort to reach a new equilibrium, marked by two successive 'austerity plans' and a Cabinet reshuffle, Laurent Fabius replacing Pierre Mauroy as premier in 1984. France brought its economic policy more closely into line with those of its main trading partners. Political voluntarism gave way to a recognition of the structural constraints under which Europe operated. The government set out to reduce the trade deficit and restore international credibility of the French economy. Very severe measures were taken to curb wages, incomes and prices. The rise in workers' purchasing power was halted, the government pledging only to maintain average real wages, which amounted in practice to encouraging the steady narrowing of disparities among wage-earners. The acceleration of prices was reversed, inflation declining from 13 per cent to 3 per cent between 1980 and 1986.

Two central, interrelated options accompanied this economic policy reversal. On the one hand, despite the pronouncement that 'employment remains the priority of priorities' the structural handicaps of the economy and their short-term implications were acknowledged. Growth prospects were revised downwards, and French economic growth averaged 1 per cent per year between 1983 and 1985 against an EEC average closer to 2 per cent. Policymakers resigned themselves to steadily rising unemployment (10 per cent of the labour force in 1985 as against 6 per cent in 1980), at the cost of a return to the 'social treatment' of the problem, mainly in the form of new avenues of entry into economic life for young people, the so-called TUC (*travaux d'utilité collective*), or state-subsidized 'socially useful jobs').

On the other hand, a long-term policy to correct the weaknesses of the French economy was sketched out. The officially endorsed prospect was 'restructuring' and 'modernization' as the only way to right the situation. France began a period of transformation of the industrial apparatus, which entailed a corresponding transformation in social behaviour. The crucial themes were not just industrial change but also mobility and flexibility as conditions for social progress.

What made the French situation particular was that the call for transformation was not just late and abrupt but also made at a poor time, in a highly contradictory political situation. This partly explains the trauma that the change in course would entail for industrial relations and then for political life itself.

2.2 The limits of modernization

One apparent consequence of the turnabout in 1983 was the strong recovery in industrial investment, which expanded by 9 per cent in 1984–5 against the 6 per cent contraction of 1982. Yet in essence, indeed by definition, a programme of industrial conversion and transformation is a process whose fruits can be reaped only in the long run. Its most immediately visible effects are social problems – a rise in collective dismissals. In the French case, things were made all the more difficult by a number of tendencies and rigidities that constituted so many stumbling blocks for the modernization effort.

In the labour market, modernization is commonly associated with an enormous increase in the flexibility of forms of employment. Yet between 1980 and 1985 the trend to more flexible forms of employment remained comparatively marginal. Temporary employees in the private sector numbered 110,000 in 1985, appreciably fewer than there had been in the wake of the boom of the 1970s (200,000 in 1979). The number of term contracts did grow steadily, but the growth was curbed by regulatory constraints. Such contracts covered 315,000 employees in 1985 and 380,000 in 1986 (not counting central government employees) out of 18 million wage- and salary-earners. Part-time jobs also increased rapidly, but by 1985 they still involved no more than 11 per cent of the labour force; most part-time workers were women, and 22 per cent of economically active women were in part-time jobs. Overall, it was estimated that in 1986 about 6 per cent of the French labour force were in 'interim' employment while waiting to obtain a steady, stable job (*Economie et Statistiques*, 1986).

Moreover, these figures are to be viewed in conjunction with gross trends that in some respects contrast with a more flexible labour market. For instance, the available labour force has been rising, and will continue to rise, by some 200,000 a year until the end of the decade. Equally remarkable is that the increase in unemployment did not prevent the constant rise in the women's participation rate to 65 per cent in 1985.

The general trend is also quite clear in the modernization of the industrial apparatus. The order of the day is technical change, the spread of numerically controlled machines, the 'flexible workshop' and production islands. But it is not at all easy to find any overall gauge of the actual impact of these changes unless it is the index of labour productivity. Yet in France, as in the other industrial countries, one still observes the slackening pace of productivity increases consequent to the long-lasting slackening of economic growth since 1973–4. Rates of productivity increase in industry were no higher than 3 per cent per year in 1980–5, compared to a 5 per cent rate from 1951 to 1973.

Industrial restructuring and the shift of manpower towards expanding sectors (the services) also have contradictory effects. Against a recessionary background manpower flows have been especially large. They show the vitality of small and medium-sized firms (one out of every two French wage-earners now works in a company with fewer than fifty employees). More generally, the figures reveal an appreciably better employment trend than in Britain or Germany. Despite strikingly high job destruction (1.5 million in 1984) and the steady increase in collective dismissals (23 per thousand wage-earners in 1980, 32 per thousand in 1984), the actual net loss of jobs has been quite modest – just 450,000 in the four years, half as many as in Germany or the UK.

Yet at the same time intersectoral manpower mobility has remained very poor. The average length of unemployment has increased from 275 days in 1980 to 360 in 1985. Efforts by the government of the left to orchestrate, accelerate and humanize industrial restructuring proved ultimately chaotic, falling far short of the stated objective of industry-by-industry negotiation of restructuring and conversion. The only effective measures were the creation of *pôles de conversion* (liberalized enterprise zones enjoying special subsidies for training and job creation) and some timely action affecting the nationalized corporations (for example, the restructuring of the telephone network). On the painful issues of steel, coal mining, shipbuilding and even the motor industry, the government temporized rather than cut the Gordian knot.

3 The position of the participants: the '1981 effect'

3.1 Government
From June 1981 to March 1986, after the election of Mitterrand as President in May 1981, French politics featured what can only be called a most singular experience: the executive power virtually monopolized by the left flanked by a National Assembly in which the Socialist Party held the absolute majority. The rejection of the plan for the Union of the Left in 1977 was compensated for, in the three years beginning in 1981, by the presence of Communist ministers in the new Cabinet. The new government incarnated the hopes of the labour movement. The first measures taken by the Mauroy Cabinet were the immediate fulfilment of the left's promises to its constituency: pro-worker and anti-unemployment reforms (shorter work time, a fifth week of paid vacation, retirement at sixty); a far-reaching programme of nationalization in large industry and banking; more industrial democracy in the public sector; the drafting of a reformed charter for civil servants, the extension of union rights in firms (the 'Auroux Laws', named after the Minister of Labour, in 1982); new policies on health care, immigration, equal rights for women, and so on.

The new government's economic and social activism was especially pronounced at the outset. It was manifest not only in the decrees on retirement and working time but also in the '100 per cent nationalizations' and the great scope of the 1982 laws on worker rights within firms, which reformed a very substantial portion of French labour legislation. The spontaneous tendency of the successive Mauroy Cabinets of 1981–4 was to take upon themselves full 'social legitimacy' and to dispense with the reformulation of the rules dividing power and responsibility between legislation and bargaining. In 1983, on the matter of industrial restructuring, the government continued to offer only a simulacrum of negotiation and took a series of delicate decisions with no concertation whatever with the unions. In retrospect, this appropriation of social legitimacy by the government appears to have been something of a blunder, with detrimental effects on relations with unions and employer associations.

The change in the economic policy course in 1983–4 intensified the disputes with social forces that had originally favoured the left. Following the thinking outlined above, the measures taken from now on would be designed essentially to benefit companies, supplemented by long-term social measures and companion measures for dealing with unemployment: youth training schemes, socially useful work projects (involving 350,000 young people in 1985), and legislation, in 1985–6, on the issue of adjustment of working time (the Delebarre Law of 28 February 1986).

During this period, the government's activism changed in nature but was even more hostile than before to concertation. Only the CFDT backed the government's plan for the restructuring of working hours. The Communists were no longer in the Cabinet, and the CGT began to attack the government more and more harshly. The '1981 effect' had just about petered out.

3.2 Employers

These years brought major changes for the employer organizations as well, taking concrete form in the designation of Yvon Gattaz as President of the leading employer association, the Conseil national du patronat français (CNPF). The new President broke with the technocratic, contractual approach established by his predecessor, François Ceyrac. His is a down-to-earth personality and he is concerned above all with the defence of the enterprise and the high-stakes process of its adjustment. In his view, relations with the unions are conditional upon these priorities. The opposing approach is incarnated by Yvon Chotard, the CNPF's Vice-President in charge of union relations, who provides some continuity with the Ceyrac era.

All in all, the CNPF's image was clouded; its unity and its authority were not unquestioned. The economic crisis, followed by the political upheaval of a leftist government, confirmed the precariousness of employer unity, given the diversity of the particular interests to be advanced. The employers of the small-business association (Confédération générale des petites et moyennes entreprises, CGPME) were torn between their feeling of agreement with the line taken by the CNPF and the concern with preserving the autonomy of the small-business interest group. A more marginal small-business group, the Syndicat national des petites et moyennes industries (SNPMI) gained in influence, demonstrating the continued presence among French employers of far-right, anti-union elements. The difficulties of summit negotiations and the gravity of the problems of individual industries led the major branch organizations to act with greater independence. Finally, the sudden extension of state control to a series of new enterprises further divided the employers' front.

This destabilization of the leading central employers' organization stood in stark contrast to a new grassroots dynamism and vitality. Spurred by new technology and new trends in management, a significant portion of large and medium-sized enterprises had gone over to truly large-scale experimentation and innovation. Production processes were recombined and rearranged, 'participatory management' was practised, autonomous and self-responsible micro-groups proliferated. New forms of personnel management emerged. Multiple skills and internal mobility were fostered. Individual-based earnings were adopted. Career programming was extended downwards, no longer being the exclusive attribute of supervisors, technicians and managers. Employers began to familiarize themselves with the 'symbolic management' of the collective life of the enterprise: a 'company culture', the formulation of company projects based on group dynamics, company newspapers and video displays, on external advertising and patronage of the arts.

While the movement for the improvement of working conditions of the 1970s had been a relatively restricted affair, the most advanced employers now adopted the 'quality circle' technique. More than 150,000 employees in 2000 firms participated in 1985. Employees' right to direct collective expressions of opinion concerning working conditions and work organization, established by the law of 4 August 1982, did not encounter significant resistance at the grassroots level. Forty per cent of the firms covered (those with more than 200 employees) signed agreements on schedule; more than 60 per cent had engaged in negotiations before the promulgation of the definitive law on 3 January 1986.

Another, perhaps equally significant development was that while waiting for the work-hours adjustment talks (1984), and then for the proclamation of the measures announced by the government, many firms signed 'deregulation agreements' on their own without reporting to their industrial associations. The decree of 16 January 1982 establishing the thirty-nine-hour week allows derogation from the regulations, and many employers (more than 600 in 1985) took advantage of this provision, at the risk of non-compliance with the law. These are just so many signs of the new independence on the part of entrepreneurs, emboldened by the need to meet the challenge of competition and by the widespread feeling that it is now up to the enterprise and it alone to find a way out of the crisis.

3.3   *Unions*

Like most other European labour movements, French trade unionism has of late suffered a steady decline in mass mobilization and in unionization. This dates back to the onset of the economic crisis in 1974–5, and ironically the political events of 1981 had no effect whatsoever on the regression of unionism, except perhaps to confirm it. In 1974–5 the number of man-days lost as a result of strikes in France was 6.3 million. In 1985 it was a mere 1.2 million, virtually the same remarkably low figure as that of 1980–1, which was followed by a modest recovery in 1981–2 to 2.4 million. At the same time, in these years the constituency of the unions, as measured by unionization rates, shrank continuously, from about 20 per cent of wage- and salary-earners to 15 per cent. The decline, which is obviously difficult to evaluate precisely, was sharper in industry and in the private sector, so much so that the metallurgical employers' association could declare in 1985 that in its branch 'the real unionization rate has fallen from 25 to 5 per cent.'

Some '1981 effect' is observable, however, at the level of individual unions. Those most active on the side of the left (the CGT and CFDT) clearly suffered from their new relations with the government, while the so-called 'reformist' unions (FO, CFTC and CGC) kept or even enhanced their membership. In 1985 the number of active CGT members was estimated at around 1 million (a loss of about a quarter of its membership in three years) and that of the CFDT at 700,000, while FO retained its 600,000 members and the CGC its 150,000 managers and technicians, and the Catholic CFTC expanded to about 200,000 members. These figures tally with the relative strength of the unions as reflected in various work-related electoral consultations (company councils, *prud'hommes*, social security funds). Elections for company councils in the private sector show the decline of the CGT (29 per cent) and the CFDT (21 per cent) and the joint growth of FO (13 per cent), of non-union candidates (21 per cent), and abstentions (over 30 per cent).

Another paradoxical effect of 1981, then, was to have helped do away with any drive toward unity among the French trade unions. Twenty years after the historic 1966 'unity of action' pact between CGT and CFDT, and apparently irreversibly from 1981 on, the unions renounced all forms of institutional alliance. Now when there is convergence of action or tactical alliance on a particular question, the unions are always careful to specify that it carries no broader, strategic implications. Each union is intent, in practice, on building an image of independence from government and from the other unions. Since 1981–2 French trade unionism appears to have moved effectively into a situation of pluralism and competition, the CGT having lost is former hegemony.

The changes in union strategies proper can be summed up in three fundamental observations.

The first concerns the tendency of all the unions, in one way or another, to establish their distance from politics. At the outset of the left's experience in office the unions' confidence in the new administration was accompanied by a unanimous, natural syndicalist reflex in the form of the assertion that 'political power is not everything' and 'nothing can be done without action by working people.' After the policy turnabout of 1983, the distance between unions and political power lengthened significantly. The pressure of recession, the ineffectiveness of calls to mobilization, and disillusionment with political change fuelled the process. The unions gave the impression of no longer seriously trying to affect political decisions, any more than they sought to counter the employers' new-found ability to take the initiative. Even the efforts of the CGT to continue nationwide action and rank-and-file bargaining pressure appeared more symbolic than operative (the 'commando' actions in troubled industries in 1984–5 are a good instance). All in all, the unions' attitude echoed the general depreciation of politics and political action. In some respects the change was enormous – on the occasion of the parliamentary elections of 1986, neither CGT nor CFDT endorsed any party.

Second, there is the unions' inability to make any significant progress towards a strategy of action alternative to politics. The CGT rejected any compromise that threatened acquired rights. The CFDT, and FO as well, by contrast, took the risk of direct involvement in economic responsibility; but they did not succeed. In the course of the broad business–labour talks in 1984 on the reform of working conditions, these unions agreed with the employers to take steps even without prior 'integrated negotiations'. The objective, clearly, was to regain some control, via negotiations, of the unemployment problem, even at the cost of a piloted deregulation of acquired labour rights. Yet these symbolically charged talks failed. This failure reveals the reluctance of middle-level union officials to engage in practices out of their control as well as the very limited spread of 'recession thinking' among the rank and file. The average union member is not convinced, *a priori*, either of the need to view jobs as the absolute top priority, or of the need to make concessions involving past gains by labour.

Finally, there have been the perverse effects of the institutionalization of unions, which was accentuated after 1981 with nationalization of a number of enterprises and the extension of union rights in companies. In a climate of weak mobilization, the rise of such institutionalization posed three major problems at once. It widened the disparity between large firms and small ones, where the unions are most often completely absent. It increased the distance between the rank and file and the union hierarchy, which was inclined to intervene in economic and social policy matters regardless of the real state of mind and consciousness of the workers and the labour movement. And it highlighted France's deplorable lack of any real tradition of contract bargaining and the need for organized labour to reformulate the foundations of its legitimacy.

4   The outcome: conflict between legislation and bargaining

The administration that took office following the elections of 1981 had occasion in 1985–6 to offer a balance-sheet on its economic and social policy actions. It could point to some economic recovery, reflected in a fall in inflation, the elimination of the external payments deficit, and some success in reining in the public sector deficit (embracing the central government, the social security system and local authorities), which despite rapid growth was nevertheless less than the average for the other industrial countries. Another accomplishment to which the leftist government could point was the first signs of industrial recovery: a breakthrough in investment, the expansion of the research effort (2.3 per cent of GNP in 1985 as against 1.8 per cent in 1980), a return to corporate profitability, most especially in the nationalized industries, and the buoyant stock and bond markets (a tripling of bond issues, a doubling of share prices).

Citing the importance of medium-term adjustment, the government pointed out that its policy of austerity, begun in 1983, had not fundamentally harmed either economic growth (the GDP had risen by 5.9 per cent between 1981 and 1985) or real purchasing power (average disposable income had risen 5 per cent in those same years). It had also not reduced the value of households' savings, and had been accompanied by a rise in unemployment less pronounced than that in most of France's neighbours.[3] At the same time, households enjoyed a rise in family allowances, a reduction in income taxes, and an increase in retirement pay and pensions. The policy of 'modernization' also featured reform of the educational system, the 'computers for everyone' programme (120,000 computers in the schools with 100,000 teachers trained to work with them), and some opening as regards teaching designed as preparation for work.

The policy of 'new rights for workers' has already been mentioned. In 1982, persons covered by social security were given the right to elect representatives to social security councils. The Auroux Laws established employees' right to be consulted over the content of work, working conditions and work organization. They extended trade union rights, enlarged the powers of company councils and employee delegates, and instituted compulsory annual negotiations at company level on wages, working hours and technological modernization.

On the whole, however, it must be said that the Socialist government's economic and social activism diminished the autonomy of industrial relations and hindered the progress of national business–labour negotiations.

At first, the government chose to foster centralized bargaining on several key issues, such as working time. It thus pressed for the rapid conclusion of a framing agreement on the matter (17 July 1981), which was to be followed by negotiations at the industry level. But the process soon got bogged down. The issue was taken up again by legislative decree at the injunction of the President: the legal working week was shortened to thirty-nine hours with no reduction in weekly wages. This precedent marked the beginning of a period in which, despite the renewed effort to achieve flexibility in 1984, legislation increasingly displaced collective bargaining in the resolution of such questions.

In 1982 and 1983 especially, labour and employer organizations dealt with a number of important issues, but for the most part they were technical questions or items put on their agenda as a result of government decisions. The first was, once again, the working week. Talks at branch level were resumed after February 1982 to decide how to implement the government decision. The second item was the right to retirement at sixty. Here too the initiative came from the government, but the reform entailed 'downstream' revision of the supplementary pensions managed jointly by employers and unions. After talks lasting months, agreement was reached in February 1983. The third issue was unemployment insurance. This was a problem raised by the employers, who wanted to re-examine a 1958 agreement that had become ruinously expensive and to distinguish between employers' responsibilities and those of the state. In other words, they wanted to separate insurance (joint employer–employee responsibility) from solidarity (at government expense). The negotiations were delicate, because they affected acquired rights, but they were eventually concluded without great difficulty in January 1984, to be followed immediately by tripartite talks with the government on the machinery for funding the new system.[4]

In the meantime, at the request of the employers' side, the major negotiations on flexibility got under way (June–December 1984). The unions mistrusted the employers' desire to deregulate, but they hoped to shift the substance of the talks towards what they considered to be the real core of the employment problem: controls on dismissals, training and retraining, technological innovation, shorter hours. In view of the unions' substantial concessions on hours flexibility, temporary and insecure employment and threshold levels for application of labour-law guarantees within firms, the compensation ultimately offered them was much too small (the right to advance notice on technological change and on collective dismissals). No agreement was reached, which demonstrates that the government had removed from the control of business and labour organizations a matter in which a major, innovative agreement was possible. The issue of flexibility had to be taken up again in legislation (in 1986), while that of working-hours adjustment had to be dealt with more explicitly at the branch level.

The impulse to bargaining imparted by the state was much less ambiguous and much more innovative at a different level: that of company-by-company bargaining, which was stimulated especially by the 1982 Auroux Laws. Specifically, the right to direct freedom of expression affected the pattern of industrial relations in at least two sensitive ways: first, by leading to joint definition, at the company level, of procedures for the application of the right; and second, by generalizing concertation on working conditions and work organization at the most highly decentralized level and *outside union control.*[5]

Although one cannot term this a veritable new model of industrial democracy, it nevertheless presented a remarkable contrast between the problems of centralized bargaining (either it is only technical in scope and subordinated to government, or else it is too ambitious to be successful) and the innovative approach taken at plant level, in widespread and informal fashion. Between 1980 and 1985, no provision for centralized regulation was introduced that can be described as tending to the modernization of industrial relations. But the new plant-level practices, such as the obligation to bargain and the right of expression, offered a most significant, alternative model of modernization. This analysis was shared by a good number of trade union officials, such as those of the CFDT, which sought to mobilize its local branches on the theme.

5 Levels: the scope and limits of decentralization

In the context described above, the French industrial relations system has unquestionably accentuated the trend, observable since 1980, to decentralization of bargaining to the company level. As we have seen, this development has clearly been affected by the labour legislation of 1982 and 1983. In another way, it has been encouraged by innovative employers and a part of organized labour. The CFDT has been the most favourable, FO the most hostile.

The growth of company-level bargaining is reflected in official statistics. In 1983, the first year in which the Auroux Laws were in operation, there was bargaining on effective wages, working hours and work organization in 42 per cent of the enterprises covered. In 1985 the percentage rose to 71.5 per cent. This did not mean that the share of companies successfully concluding at least one agreement diminished; on the contrary, fewer than 2000 firms had signed at least one agreement in 1983, compared to over 5000 in 1985.

The phenomenon appears even more significant if one takes into account the sharp rise in the other forms of contract or 'infra-bargaining' that have accompanied technological changes and new forms of labour relations at the grassroots: the negotiated plan for computerization in banking; the creation of informal work groups on hours adjustment either in addition to, alongside or in place of consultation with the official institutions at the company level (company councils and health and safety committees and committees on working conditions); 'progress groups' assigned to solve specific problems; 'expression groups'; broader consultation with employees as part of 'corporate project' operations; and so on. The development of these forms of 'company-level infra-bargaining' is now an established fact in France's altered industrial relations scene, and it has not failed to raise the issue of the very uneven role of the unions in the process.

It would be a mistake, however, to leap to the conclusion that traditional industry-by-industry bargaining has been swept aside. To understand its evolution several different measures must be adopted.

First, the percentage of employees covered by collective bargaining contracts at branch level has continued to rise, steadily approaching the objective set by the law of 13 November 1982, namely universal collective contract coverage: 92.5 per cent in industry in 1985 as against 90.5 per cent in 1981; 85 per cent in the services, as against 72 per cent.

On the other hand, it is true that the pace of industry-wide bargaining has slackened; 1370 contracts were signed in 1982 and only 930 in 1984. There are two countervailing factors, however. First, the decline is observable mainly in *regional* branch contracts, while national branch contracts have increased their share. And second, the status of this type of bargaining has changed. Formerly acting primarily as 'safety nets' on wages and job classification, they have tended to become regulatory frameworks for multifarious union–employer relations that are then extended at the company level. Hence the extension of new bargaining demands such as technological modernization, work-time adjustment and vocational training, at the expense of past issues (including job classifications, on which the average age of the sector contracts in effect reached fifteen years in 1985).

Of course, the combined pressure of employers and the parties of the right for independent company-level bargaining has more and more directly questioned the function of branch contracts. But this has had the paradoxical effect of transforming such agreements into symbols of resistance to 'deregulation'. Thus in 1981 on working hours, and in 1984 on flexibility, all the unions set as a precondition for more flexible hours and employment terms the preservation of the control exercised by branch agreements. And this position prevailed again in 1985–6 with the Delebarre Law on more flexible hours, which retained the compulsory industry-level agreements.

6   Addendum: the shock of March 1986 and its consequences

The results of the parliamentary elections of March 1986 produced another upheaval in French politics. Jacques Chirac, the leader of the right, replaced Fabius as premier. A regime of 'cohabitation' was thus begun, with Mitterrand presiding over a Cabinet made up entirely of members of the late opposition.

The new government's programme was deliberately liberal, free-market in orientation. It announced a radical turnabout in economic and social policy. Its intention was to enact – thanks to the accelerated procedure of administrative orders – a series of strikingly spectacular measures: the privatization of sixty-five public-sector enterprises, plus economic and social deregulation. High priority was assigned to the liberalization of prices and interest rates, and to tax reform to favour corporations. The government announced the abrogation of the requirement that firms secure official authorization for dismissals made for economic reasons.

Nevertheless, the persistence of economic constraints, the unprecedented circumstances of 'cohabitation' and the pragmatism of the new minister for social affairs, P. Séguin, were not conducive to an immediate upheaval in labour relations. Until 1987, the impact of the March election shock remained quite modest on this front.

Privatization, which was planned in a leisurely series of stages, stirred no significant mobilization among either the rank and file or union officials. Nor, despite its highly charged political and ideological symbolism, did the July 1986 law repealing the requirement for authorization for dismissals provoke violent reaction. Despite the reiterated opposition of the CGT, central-level talks actually got under way on the manner in which the law's provisions could be implemented. The negotiations led in October to a 'balanced compromise' that appreciably strengthened judicial monitoring of dismissals.

Bargaining at branch level on the adjustment of working hours, as called for by the legislation passed by the Socialist government in February 1986, began in several industries, although the new government had announced that the provision was to be reformed. An agreement was signed for basic metals in July and another for public works in November. The metallurgical agreement, however, was not ratified either by the CGT or by the CFDT, and it gave rise to opposition within FO as well. Meanwhile, the reform of the Delebarre Law on working time had been deferred until the spring of 1987 after a procedural battle involving the President of the Republic. Agreements on the conditions for introducing technological changes were reached in banking (May 1986) and metallurgy (February 1987).

Social protest and mobilization reappeared in the winter of 1986–7, but surprisingly it took forms and involved issues that had little if anything to do with the broad thrust of economic and social policy. The point of departure was the massive, victorious mobilization of secondary-school and university students against the planned university reform (November 1986). In December and January a series of major strikes disrupted several large public service corporations (railways, the Paris public transport system, Electricité de France). Wage claims were not absent from the strike demands, but they were less important than fears of amendments in the personnel regulations and promotion rules of these bodies.

In each strike the unions appear to have been left behind by the rank and file. 'Co-ordinating committees' outside the control of the union organizations played a significant role for the first time in years.

These developments delayed the implementation of the government's programme, and at the same time pushed into the background efforts to resume bargaining dialogue, which only began to take shape in February. At the same time, on the employers' side, Gattaz's decision not to ask for another term as President of the CNPF gave rise to unusually sharp conflict: there were two candidates to succeed him! The victor, François Périgot, elected in December, made an extremely discreet, low-key entrance on the social scene.

7   French trade unionism and the crisis of centralized regulation

7.1   The effect of the Auroux Laws and their limits

The late 1970s had already provided the material in France for a debate on the 'crisis of unionism', apparently best summed up in the decline in unionization rates. A deeper analysis, however, views the crisis as a more complex phenomenon. It was not so much de-unionization that constituted the crisis but its paradoxical association with the institutionalization of trade unionism. Another typical distortion of the late 1970s was the tendency on the part of some employers – more or less openly supported by the CNPF – to install highly decentralized forms of concertation, in parallel with the temptation to short-circuit the unions in favour of the existing hierarchy at the workplace.

In the 1980s, an important turning point was marked by the passage and implementation of the Auroux Laws. Their virtually explicit intent was to resolve the problems of the previous period. Specifically, they were designed to redirect the institutionalization of the unions *towards the company* through such provisions as compulsory bargaining and enhanced powers for worker representatives and to encourage the unions to deal with 'real' problems, that is those experienced on the ground: bargaining on real wages and working conditions, joint installation of machinery to implement the right to employee expression. Implicitly, the aim was also to revive unionization and 'active bargaining' at the company level, working obliquely through the restoration of the unions to a position at the core of the actual working community.

What, then, has been the actual effect of the laws? In 1985–6, just three years after their initial application, they had already worked a far from negligible change. But on a series of issues, discussed below, results were not up to expectations. The chief positive achievement was the massive revival of company-level bargaining, which was indeed accompanied by a new recognition of the legitimacy of union action on the shop floor. But the beginnings of reunionization and renewed mobilization of the rank and file were not wholly achieved. With few exceptions, the workforce did no more than accept the new agreements or express their reservations: they did not work actively for them. And the unions that engaged most actively in the new types of company-level bargaining, such as the CFDT, derived no special benefit from it. They expanded no more than the CGT, which was steadfast in its rejection of 'crisis management' and signed agreements much more seldom than the CFDT.

The 5000 or 6000 agreements signed in 1985–6 certainly renovated the state of French unionism. Yet they did not fundamentally narrow the distance between unions and workers, any more than they basically altered the balance of power, which remained heavily favourable to the employer side. A certain degree of 'coexistence' came to be accepted between areas of union regulation and others that gave employers discretion, even direct concertation between management and the workforce.

7.2 A new relationship between unions and the shop floor

How can this paradoxical situation be explained? The best approach would appear to be to interpret it as the sign of a highly problematical redefinition of the relationship between unions and working people. On the one hand, it was said, organized labour managed to shore up its image and its role among working people. From another standpoint, however, the new situation is one in which organized labour tends to have recognition only in its strictly *regulatory* role, that is maintenance of the recognized collective rights of working people; or, given the context of crisis, the management of compromises involved in adjusting to the changed economic environment at the least possible cost to workers as a group.

In such a perspective, two of the traditional functions of trade unions are wiped out. One is that of collective actor with the task of directing social change. The other is that of representative of social groups, if by this concept one understands the representation of *real* groups and the traditional processes of social identification that have so far given meaning to the act of joining the organization.

It can thus be argued that concrete social groups of workers compete with the union in the sphere of action proper, leaving to the latter the work of institutionalization of the compromise reached and the monitoring of the rules instituted. A number of observations can be cited to corroborate this tendency, such as the major strikes of the winter of 1986 – especially that of the railway workers. In an occupation that is normally strongly regulated by statute and the union presence, an acute crisis had the paradoxical effect of marginalizing the unions, as if at crucial moments the 'true actors' (the real social groups involved) were naturally inclined to take over from union organizations.

7.3   The last gasp of the labour movement for social transformation

After the failure of the extensive bargaining over flexibility in 1984, the progressive transformations in the social and political outlook of French trade unions came to an end. A complicated process of political disillusionment has resulted in union leaders now having no more faith than ordinary workers in the idea of radical political change as a way out of the crisis. What the unions concluded from the experience of 1984, more particularly, was the ineffectiveness of needlessly all-embracing concertation procedures, which duplicate the perverse effects of the traditional political culture. That culture has been brought up to date and the ideological space available to the labour movement drastically narrowed. This has unquestionably brought the French social and political situation more closely into line with that found in the rest of Europe.

Still, it cannot be said that the French unions' horizon was restricted at a stroke to a purely defensive stance and to short-term projects. The issue of job security certainly weighs very heavily indeed. But to deal with it the unions have agreed to a new kind of economic and social action, for the most part at company level via decentralized bargaining. The thesis, adopted notably by the CFDT, was that this change in approach meant not a retreat to defensive positions but the announcement of 'new frontiers for organized labour' (Maire, 1987). It still needs to be demonstrated that such a strategy is viable. The current state of mobilization and of the unions' relations with workers has not yet made such a demonstration possible.

7.4   The end of a cycle: what are the explanatory factors?

French unions are no longer seen by working people as a powerful force for social change, and even union leaders no longer see organized labour in such a role. Given today's realities, and without necessarily prejudging the future, French unions tend to act as agents of economic and social regulation, grappling first-hand with crisis and recession and the problems gripping companies in the crisis.

The suddenness of the turnabout can be explained as follows. Essentially, a number of factors helped conceal the consequences of the objective transformation of work and work organization for longer in France than elsewhere. Among these factors were the ideological polarization generated by French politics, the strength of the anarcho-syndicalist and revolutionary heritage of the French labour movement, the enormous inertia of the prevailing model of class-industrial relations and the paradoxically 'conservative' effect of union pluralism with respect to all these elements. The shock therapy of the crisis of the 1970s was needed to spur a change in consciousness and, albeit to a lesser extent, in union practices – an initial return to reality and an awareness of the constraints imposed by the real world. The advent of the leftist government in 1981 did nothing but confirm this new collective consciousness and hasten the questioning of the model of labour action that had prevailed until then. It is the swiftness of this 'revolution' that gives us our best insight into the intensity of what has come to be called the crisis of French trade unionism, which has indeed been more profound than in the rest of Europe, judging, for example, by the decline in unionization rates.

In brief, then, the economic crisis and the political developments of the early 1980s are of crucial importance, but only in that they *disclosed* deeper-lying dysfunctions, which must be traced in reality to the sweeping and thoroughgoing transformation of the French economy, French technology and French society that took place in the 1960s.

The *underlying causes* – held at bay for an extraordinarily long time-span – bring us back to the start of the 1960s: the transformation of the labour force with a steady shift towards the services sector and towards small and medium-sized companies; the growth of women's employment, the expansion of insecure employment and the more general diversification of forms of employment along a continuum ranging from secure lifetime jobs to unemployment; a new mobility in the structure of firms, their territorial structure and their management of human resources; far-reaching changes in technology, in organizational models, in the methods of job place-ment and in the transmission of skills and qualifications, and so on. The cumulative effect of these changes involved the diversifica-tion of occupational cultures and outlooks and of the modes of belonging to the working class; there emerged phenomena of *exclusion*, competing more and more strongly with the inclusive model upon which the traditional labour outlook had been founded. This was reflected in the strikes by unskilled workers – frequently immigrants, younger workers or women, rather than the usual French striker – in the early 1970s.

Over against this, the dominant union outlook still stressed unity over diversity, basing its conception of solidarity on the archetype of the craft worker in the metal industry or the railways. In short, it was a worldview that postulated that, in the dynamics of a system of social relations, institutional and political factors always prevail over economic, organizational and cultural ones. Yet at the company level the experience of the right to expression demonstrated the contrary. Perhaps unexpectedly, it was not the desires of Parliament or of the unions that ultimately left their mark on concrete practices; rather, the state of internal relations within each company prefigured the form and the real scope of the innovation.

8   The change in the French industrial relations system

8.1   *The outburst of concertation and its limits*
Our earlier inventory of the diversification of types of bargaining in France in the early 1980s justifies talk of a veritable outburst of concertation practices. As noted, the development of company-level bargaining fostered by the Auroux Laws of 1982 was but the catalyst of a much more complex process that is not easily circumscribed. Behind the shift in levels of bargaining one can observe the multiple processes of the proliferation of actors, the enlargement of the spheres of concertation, and the diversification of procedures.

Must we conclude, then, that the French industrial relations system is in the process of changing from one model to another? That is, are the shifts described above to be seen as part of a general tendency to downplay France's traditional centralized regulation in favour of a new 'pluralist' model, less dependent on the state and more consistent with the image of a complex fabric of local contracts? (This would correspond to a shift from Model A to Model B in our A–B–C–D typology – see Table 4.1.)

This hypothesis can only be put forward with extreme caution and with due regard for all the factors that inhibit such a change. One of the most important of these is the fact that France lacks a true tradition of collective bargaining contracts and a commitment to bargaining by business and labour. In the past the inability to conclude contract bargaining was justified, up to a point, by an ideological 'rejection of the working class's integration' into the system. But this argument is very largely outmoded, which reveals the more tangible reason for this shortcoming, namely the weakness of labour unions, and also the demand-leapfrogging stemming from union pluralism.

The unions' weakness also works in another way to impede the growth of a 'pluralist' system in France. There is actually a great risk that the systematic encouragement of company-level regulation will spontaneously produce a kind of 'non-institutional concertation' (that is, without union representation); as a practical matter, deregulation without real concertation rather than a state of affairs in which the norm of collective bargaining contracts has really made progress. Thus the unions have very little influence on the issues dealt with in the meetings of workers' direct expression groups. Hence the danger that this supposed shift to pluralism will translate in practice into a state of anomie in French industrial relations. (This would correspond to a shift from Model A to Models C and D in our typology – see Table 4.1.)

However, the risk of 'pluralist deregulation' so conceived seems to have been perceived and rejected in France by virtually everyone, not just the unions and the political parties of the left. Even if some employers are arguing for radically more flexible bargaining procedures, there are no grounds for holding that the ideology of labour deregulation is now prevalent among French employers. The fragility of the French economic fabric, the sharp competition between small and large firms, and the uncertainty of markets rather lead the management of ordinary companies to press for stability in the rules of the game, if not for stronger state intervention in social and labour matters.

This state of affairs explains why even at the end of the 1981–6 experience of Socialist government some consensus was observable among business, labour and government for a halt to the regressive trend of centralized regulation. Business and labour organizations do not appear to have any intention of breaking openly with the original model of centralized regulation that has been forged in France over the past twenty years.

France has not clearly gone over from one model to another. New experiences are accumulating, but no real transformation appears to be on the horizon. The situation is unstable, and certainly not favourable to union representation. But it does not admit of any accelerated slide into social deregulation, which would come at the cost of the objective marginalization of organized labour.

Table 4.1 *Changes in the industrial relations system, France since 1980*

Type	Pre-1980	Post-1980
A(a) Recognized unions, concertation at summit	Heavily institutionalized tripartite concertation (government, unions, employer organizations) on general issues going beyond employer prerogatives. For example, joint union–employer management of unemployment insurance system	New goals (for example, industrial restructuring, flexibility) but incommensurate results. Less scope for summit accords; conflict between legislation and bargaining; competition from decentralized bargaining
		'Joint management' of unemployment benefits continues, but with difficulties
A(b) Recognized unionism, tradition of centralized collective bargaining agreements	Industry-wide contracts are the foundation of the system. Sectoral talks (metal and engineering, for example) have a pivotal role	In a context of decentralizing concertation, industry-wide contracts survive; extended to universal coverage; the industry contract becomes the regulatory framework on working hours, flexibility, technology (under the pressure of unions and government)
	Yet at company level, the enforcement power of the industry agreements is poor	
	Very marginal experiments with industrial democracy	At least from 1986 on, government abandons the industry contract for the company level
B Pluralist system, decentralized bargaining	Decentralized bargaining but mainly in the largest corporations (and not all). (Typical issue: real wages)	Spectacular growth in the number of company agreements and in their importance, based on the new legislation of 1982
	Elsewhere, it arises where the relative strength of the employer is great	Nevertheless, this trend is dominated by employer initiative passively submitted to by unions under the club of unemployment

Table 4.1 *contd.*

Type	Pre-1980	Post-1980
C(a) Encouragement of worker participation, with union consent	Very rare experiments: – legal right to profit sharing, very marginal; – limited experiments in improving working conditions and technological change	Institutionalization of this approach on working conditions and work organization: 1982 law giving the 'right to direct expression' to all employees. Unions called on to bargain over rules of the game within company Limits: practice escapes union control. Opposition in principle by FO, CGC, employers
C(b) Encouragement of worker participation without union involvement	Diversified, unequally distributed experiences on hours adjustment, working conditions, technology Experiments blocked where union power is significant	Experiments become more common and are less regularly condemned by unions (quality circles) However, there is a consensus that this does not lead to deregulation: unions hold back the movement, rank-and-file workers approve and legitimize union intervention, employers remain 'legalist', government provides a framework
D(a) Direct employer–worker relations in framework of standard employment contracts	Typical model in small companies (under fifty employees). This is under the threshold for labour legislation, and usually there is no union.	Now the model applies to various kinds of firm in which unions are weak (four types described in section 8.2)
D(b) Direct employer–worker relations with insecure contracts	Typical model in small firms in some industries (apparel, construction, civil engineering)	Extension to more industries. Law and government intervention significantly hold back its spread, however

8.2   *Pockets of deregulation*

There is nevertheless an undeniably real need to investigate the existence of significant 'pockets' in the labour market where the formula of unionless concertation, or the temptation to circumvent the law to the detriment of workers' rights, is supposedly becoming the rule even today, since the balance of strength between employers and unions appears to give the former a comparatively free hand. Four typical situations can be identified. But, as we shall see, the tendency to 'deregulation' differs from case to case, and it often needs to be nuanced.

The first typical case is that of the large corporations that have explicit strategic plans to weaken the unions and to integrate and co-opt the workforce through new personnel policies encouraging direct relations between the individual employee and the management hierarchy, his identification with the firm and its economic performance, the development of quality circles, and so on.

On first inspection, this pattern would seem to be characteristic of the private rather than the public sector. Yet what is remarkable is precisely the observable fact that under the impact of the crisis neither the individual 'company outlook' nor the private–public cleavage is decisive any longer. In the corporations with a 'social tradition' but in which unions have been greatly weakened and economic conditions are critical (such as steel and even the nationalized Renault group), strategies for the involvement and mobilization of the workforce are emerging that explicitly do without union mediation.

The second typical case is that of medium-sized firms that use small, unrepresentative unions and/or important unions driven by the state of the labour market to a highly conciliatory stance, to carry out more or less dissimulated projects of 'deregulation'. The projects consist most notably in the individualization of wages and the adjustment of working time. Earlier we mentioned that 600 firms had been surveyed as engaged in such projects in 1985. In reality there were undoubtedly many more.

The third typical case is that of a good many growing companies in the services sector (service companies proper, chain stores and hypermarkets, and so on) where industrial relations traditions have little importance and where employers as a matter of practice have great freedom to experiment with the reorganization of working hours, personnel motivation, the diversification of personnel status, and so on. In a sense, these firms are the most typical representatives of the tendency to active deregulation of industrial relations, because in this instance it involves a set of explicitly innovative policies pursued in a context of growth and expanding markets, with the more or less explicit acquiescence of at least part of the workforce.

Finally, there is the case of smaller firms. In firms with fewer than fifty employees, unions have very little foothold. Labour legislation is applied only in part, the obligation to bargain on wages and working conditions no longer affects more than a minority. Where skill levels are low, the employers enjoy virtually untrammelled discretion in exercising their power, under the very intermittent surveillance of inspectors from the Ministry of Labour.

This, ultimately, is where the true blind spot in French industrial relations is located. This is where we find the persistence of the most archaic conditions of dependency, confrontation and exploitation.

9 Conclusion: the paths of integration between old and new norms

The dramatic extension of the practice of concertation at the company level, the proliferation of company-level agreements introducing provisions for internal flexibility, and the much more recent measures taken by the government to encourage external flexibility (the July 1986 abrogation of the former requirement on dismissals) have brought significant changes to the French industrial relations system, but they have not altered the basic model, which remains that of centralized regulation. The relative lack of a bargaining and contract mentality means that all sides tend to hold back the pressure for sweeping deregulation, which, *prima facie*, would not be difficult given the present weakness of French trade unions.

From this circumstance stems a major paradox that strongly marks the conditions in which the traditional system of industrial relations is adjusting to change: namely, that it is almost always the state that takes the initiative in innovations in bargaining between business and labour. Even more so, and specifically with respect to the so-called 'internal' and 'external' flexibility measures, it was the state – partly under employer pressure but mainly owing to its responsibilities in matters of employment and unemployment – that led the way in reforming French labour legislation to provide for substantially greater flexibility in manpower management.

State intervention in substance as well as to establish the rules of the game would appear, at present, to be the procedural form on which business and labour have implicitly agreed in order to find an acceptable compromise between the employers' demands for more flexibility in manpower management, the general interest in reducing unemployment, and the unions' appeal to safeguard workers' rights and to retain their own powers in the labour relations system.

However, this *de facto* state of affairs cannot conceal a grave shortcoming – the fact that it utterly prevents any thoroughgoing modernization of the system, which would require both greater freedom of business and labour from state tutelage and the large-scale use of collective contracts responding to the two major needs of the day: more flexible forms of employment (if not the abrogation of acquired rights) on the one hand, the defence of workers' moral and economic interests on the other. In this regard, we have seen that the crop of company agreements since 1983–4 has had some success, where the national-level negotiations of 1984 failed. But this success, it must be said, has been semi-clandestine, denied in practice by the union confederations themselves, which tend rather to stress the shortcomings of the agreements and the pressure exerted in most cases by the problem of jobs. At the industry level as well, the precedent represented by the agreement on the restructuring of working time in metalworking reached in July 1986 has remained highly controversial.

There has been more general recognition of agreements on the conditions for technological innovation in some large corporations and in some industries (banking, engineering) starting in 1986. It is no accident, though, that the matters covered in such agreements do not touch directly on either jobs or working time.

This signals the unsolved problem which means that on the most sensitive issues the method of concertation is doomed to an irreducible dichotomy for many years to come: a dichotomy between the sphere of centralized regulation, of key strategic importance for the unions, and the sphere of company regulation, much less well monitored except in the case of major, trend-setting corporations; and a dichotomy between the types of issue instinctively felt by all concerned to be under the jurisdiction of government, collective bargaining and/or the unions (such as wages, employment and *general* rules on the restructuring of working time) and those perceived as ultimately under the jurisdiction of the employer or, in some cases, to be regulated by agreement directly with his employees (working conditions and work organization, specific arrangements on work hours and terms of employment).

Overall, as is shown by the failure of the 1984 negotiations, the disputes engendered by the clash between the traditional rules of the game and the development of new loci and issues for business–labour bargaining are far from settled. Behind the curtain of the unions' pronouncements, the salient feature for appreciating what is going on on the ground is strategic uncertainty. Except to call for government arbitration, no French union has yet produced a set of theses functioning simultaneously to safeguard acquired rights and to monitor the 'new policies in human resources management'.

The historic difficulty is above all that of moving from an occupational mode of contract regulation and bargaining to a company-linked mode. If an apprenticeship is needed, for many what must be learned is a new way of experiencing the social relations of production within the company, assuming and accepting that the latter has become a human community, whereas until recently it was viewed, ineradicably, as the locus of exploitation in which interests could only clash. The economic crisis and the decline of Manichaean ideology have certainly weakened such concepts. But it will still be some time before the enterprise as such can become a definitive part of society in France.

Notes

1 Labour 'courts', elections for which, following a recent reform, offered a very broad survey of the representatives of the various organizations. The figures given here are for wage-earners in industry (excluding technical and managerial personnel).

2 Force Ouvrière emerged from an anti-Communist split in the Confédération Générale du Travail (CGT) in 1947–8. The Confédération française des travailleurs chrétiens (CFTC) is a Catholic-inspired union that survived the creation of the Confédération française démocratique du travail (ex-CFTC, changing name to CFDT) in 1964. The Confédération générale des cadres (CGC) is the largest union among technical and lower managerial personnel. For the last ten years it has sought to broaden its recruiting towards the lower ranks; hence its new name CGC–CFE (Confédération française de *l'encadrement*, not just *cadres*, which implies a higher rank, such as middle managers, engineers, and so on).

3 On salaries, the wage-freeze decreed by the government from June to November 1982 was followed by a period of 'bargaining guidelines' (*négociation encadrée*) during which the primary objective was to hold wage rises behind prices. On the whole the wage-moderation directives issued by employers and government were respected.

4 Among the other 'technical' matters dealt with in business–labour bargaining between 1983 and 1985, the more significant were the status and treatment of management personnel and technicians (agreement of April 1983), in-service training for young people (October 1983), and then again the unemployment benefit system (July 1985).

5 In 1983 these measures were supplemented by a law for industrial democracy in the nationalized sector which created 'shop councils' – with slightly more extensive powers than those given to the expression groups of the private sector – and permitted elected worker representatives to sit on firms' boards of directors.

References

Economie et Statistiques (1986) 193(November), 194(December).

Maire, Edmond (1987) *Nouvelles frontières pour le syndicalisme*, Paris: Editions Syros.

5

West Germany: Continuity and Structural Change

Otto Jacobi and Walther Müller-Jentsch

In West Germany as elsewhere the 1970s could be regarded as a decade of the unions. Now it seems that, in turn, the 1980s became a decade of the employers. This is mainly due to the facts that the conditions of the labour market have deteriorated remarkably since the mid-1970s and that a serious political change took place in the early 1980s: the Social Democratic–Liberal government was replaced by a Conservative–Liberal one.

Four main developmental tendencies can be observed during the period under consideration, producing substantial problems for the unions' power position. First, there is enduring mass unemployment that negatively influences the bargaining power of the trade unions and their representatives in the firms. The sensitive shift from a sellers' market to a buyers' market has enlarged the room to manoeuvre for management concerning allocation, remuneration and qualification of the labour force. Secondly, the employers are launching various strategies to combine labour more flexibly with new technologies. Their attempts at more flexibility have their political counterpart in the deregulation measures taken by the neo-conservative government. Flexibility and deregulation are attacks on the traditional functions of trade unions. Thirdly, the question of shortening the working week has become a crucial issue in the power struggle between employers and unions, culminating in 1984 in the biggest industrial dispute of the post-war era. Fourthly, relationships between the trade unions and the employers' associations are by and large still characterized by a relatively high level of co-operation and willingness to compromise.

The future of the unions will heavily depend on how they cope with the new problems in the organization of production, and in the economic and political environment. Have they to adjust their strategies and politics to the new facts? Can they defend their dominant role in regulating working life? Either way, a new union realism is in demand.

1   Structural problems

The West German economy has been the most efficient in the European Community for many years. The country's share of the national product of all members of the Community – measured in US dollars at the exchange rates and price levels of 1980 – was, in 1984, little less than 29 per cent, while its proportion of the population amounts to 19 per cent.

The overall economic situation was first characterized by the worldwide recession of the early 1980s and then by a sustained economic upswing (see Table 5.1). Industrial production had stagnated for some years and the pre-recession level could not be exceeded until 1985. In 1986, real GNP was 10.2 per cent higher and the volume of manufacturing industries 7.5 per cent higher than in 1980. The labour market has undergone important changes in many respects. The number of persons in employment dropped between 1980 and 1983 by 1 million, a reduction which took place almost exclusively in manufacturing. In contrast to the 1970s, the reduction of employment in the industrial sector has no longer been compensated for by an extension of employment in the private service sector and in public administration.

The social composition of the labour force now includes a higher proportion in the tertiary sector and with higher qualifications. The developments in the labour market have been an acceleration of long-term changes (flexibilization, differentiation, segmentation) which conflict with the traditional forms of trade union interest representation. Until now the unions have not been very much affected by this since the skilled workers forming the core of their membership have to a large extent escaped unemployment.

There have also been some remarkable changes in wages and income distribution. The incomes of those in employment – earning an average gross income of 46,000 DM per year in 1986 – followed the development of growth and employment in a surprisingly flexible manner. The old wage formula of the dual adjustment of wages to the rates of inflation and productivity could not be maintained by the unions. As a result of a constantly and considerably stronger increase of incomes from profits as compared to wage incomes since 1982, the wage share showed a strong decrease. The unions' income-distribution successes achieved in the 1970s have been completely eliminated. The trade unions' wage policy became the victim of the dampening effects of the 'industrial reserve army', although it was also a captive of its own decision not to block the technological modernization of the economic production apparatus from the costs side.

Table 5.1 *Economic growth, employment and wages, FRG, 1980-8*

Item	Unit	1980	1981	1982	1983	1984	1985	1986	1987	1988
Gross National Product[1]	Percentage change from previous year	1.9	-0.3	-1.0	1.5	3.0	2.4	2.5	1.9	3.4
Manufacturing	Percentage of GNP	32.5	32.0	31.6	31.3	31.3	32.0	32.0	31.9	32.5
Exports of goods and services	Percentage of GNP	28.4	30.8	32.0	31.3	33.0	34.5	34.4	33.9	33.8
Employment										
1 Dependent labour force	Millions	23.0	22.9	22.4	22.1	22.1	22.2	22.5	22.8	22.9
2 Unemployed	Millions	0.9	1.3	1.9	2.3	2.3	2.3	2.2	2.2	2.2
3 Unemployed rate	Percentage of total labour force	3.3	4.7	6.5	8.3	8.3	8.3	7.9	7.9	7.7
Wages distribution										
Entrepreneurial and property income	Percentage change from previous year	-1.9	0.0	5.5	13.5	9.4	8.8	9.7	4.0	8.5
Wage and salary income	Percentage change from previous year	8.6	4.6	2.2	2.0	3.5	3.8	5.0	3.9	3.8
Wage share	Percentage of national income	73.5	74.4	73.8	71.6	70.5	69.5	68.2	69.0	68.0
Prices										
Cost of living index for all households	Percentage change from previous year	5.4	6.3	5.3	3.3	2.4	2.2	-0.5	0.2	1.2

[1] At 1980 prices.

Sources: OECD, 1988; Deutsche Bundesbank, 1988; Sachverständigenrat, 1988

The increasing internationalization of the German economy, while on the one hand reflecting its high competitiveness, includes on the other hand an extreme dependence on global developments and therefore has a high external vulnerability that could develop into a dangerous structural problem. The international integration of the overall economy is the result of the export-oriented production structure of the industrial sector. Up to now the Federal Republic has benefited from its international industrial competitiveness but a setback is not impossible.

The securing of industrial efficiency and international competitiveness are closely linked and have brought about extensive efforts to encourage technological innovations in order to be able to offer highly advanced goods. The German Council of Economic Experts (a government advisory body) has summarized the objective of this modernization strategy as follows:

> The improvement of competitiveness must be achieved through the adoption of new products into the product-range, i.e. of those products whose production requires special technical knowledge available only to a few suppliers. . . . Such products are competitive not because they are particularly cheap, but because of their high utility for those who use them; in short, because they are particularly expensive. . . . A high-wage country cannot afford to fall back on the role of follow-up competition. (Sachverständigenrat, 1981)

The FRG had some difficulty in keeping pace with technological developments. The expectation that it will overcome the gap in innovation and thereby eliminate the technological lead of the US in certain areas (biotechnology, office communications, computer technology, satellite technology) is based on the comparatively high levels of R&D expenditures in the Federal Republic. The advantage of the German economy over the US lies in its higher investment rates, and over Japan it rests on the diversity and specialization of its industrial goods. German industry is particularly successful in the application of process engineering, especially in the capital goods sector, and its ability to resolve problems of individual customers. To avoid innovation competition with the US and productivity competition with Japan, German industry can make use of its great experience in refining and applying new technology to mature industries to generate products with high value.

This problem determines the union movement's perspectives of action, since IG Metall (metalworkers' union), its strongest individual union, is exclusively engaged in industries depending on exports and working with the most advanced technologies. As in the past it will be part of its strategic calculation to consider carefully the costs and benefits of a co-operative and of a conflict-oriented interest representation. The whole country is one single export lobby and the skill of the unions consists in getting as much as possible for their contribution toward a secured continuation of production and technology.

2 Actors and their relationships

2.1 State

The decisive political change was the replacement of the Social–Liberal government in 1982 by a conservative alliance formed by the two Christian sister parties (CDU–CSU) and the Liberal Party. The governing coalition between the Social Democratic Party (SPD) and the Liberal Party (FDP) installed in 1969, which had its most powerful ally in the trade unions, broke up because the Liberals decided to change their government partner primarily for reasons of their economic and sociopolitical strategy.

Although German conservatism is intellectually less ambitious and less rigid than foreign variants – clearly a result of the less pressing political, economic and social problems – the ideological affinity is nevertheless obvious. The Federal Republic too has witnessed the emergence of an alliance of *Wertkonservative* (referring to traditional conservative values) and *Strukturkonservative* (referring to doctrines of economic liberalism, laissez-faire policy, and so on) that differs fundamentally from the interventionist, integrating and co-operative intentions of the Social–Liberal alliance.

Between the Social Democratic and the conservative power blocs, there exists a fundamental difference in their respective assessments of the market and the role of trade unions. Whereas the former emphasized the inherent imperfections of the market and supported corporatist relations between government and union, the latter blames excessive union influence for the market's failure to secure prosperity and employment. Theoretically these positions may be incompatible; but in practice manifold ways of mixing them can be found. The change in government has not entailed a fundamental political about-turn; instead there has been a high degree of continuity. In terms of economic and social policy, the new administration was able to follow the course adopted by the former government, since a partial abandonment of Keynesian strategies in favour of a supply-oriented policy had already taken place in the Social–Liberal era.

The aim to reduce the state's share in the national product could not be realized. Public revenue and expenditure – measured against the share in GNP – remained constant. Public sector borrowing even continued to rise so that the rate of indebtedness increased to 44 per cent (1986). A retrenchment of government subsidies did not take place either. However, there was in relative terms a slight decline in social services. The government saw no necessity for employment-promoting programmes and trilateral arrangements. The basic effect of the budgetary practices of the Conservative–Liberal government is that they have brought to a standstill the predominant trend of the Social–Liberal era of an over-proportional expansion of public revenue and expenditure.

Like its predecessor, the current government has explicitly declared that its aim is to increase the innovative capacity of the German economy by promoting investment in promising technologies. Whereas the Social–Liberal government tried to include the trade unions as a partner in managing the process of modernization, the new administration dispenses with trade union co-operation. It can, however, afford to do so, since the trade unions – owing to their strong self-interest in safeguarding jobs by securing international competitiveness – cannot boycott the modernization of the economic production apparatus.

2.2 Employers

During the recent period management and employers have seemed to be more innovative than trade unions. Changing labour market conditions granted them more room to manoeuvre; the changing product market forced them to use the flexible potential of new technology; and the political change provided them with new opportunities for more flexible personnel management.

In general, during the last few years there has taken place an extensive restructuring of the labour and production processes with more automation and electronic equipment, with far-reaching information networks and control systems. Social scientists speak of processes of 'systemic rationalization' with great impact on the character of work in factory and office. Flexibility of production and flexible personnel management are key objectives of the employers. New models of organization and employee involvement are the main instruments for reaching these goals. There is a shift away from Taylorist work tasks to a reprofessionalization of industrial and clerical work, but this holds true only for particular strata of the workforce, a kind of 'new labour aristocracy'. There are still large groups of blue- and white-collar workers with restrictive and routinized jobs. These 'losers in the rationalization process' are less skilled, older, female and foreign workers who are furthermore under the threat of being made redundant by the ongoing processes of rationalization and automation.

Table 5.2 *Enterprises with quality circles, FRG, 1979–86*

	No.
End of 1970s	30
1982	200
1986	1,200–1,400

Management and employers' associations have pressed for more flexibility of working time, personnel transfer and working arrangements. They have pursued their goals on different levels. At factory level they refined their human-resources policies and introduced more flexible working schemes, diverse working-time schedules and opportunities for the internal retraining of the core workforce. They did this partly unilaterally, partly in co-operation with the work councils. At industry level they reached collective agreements on variation and differentiation of working hours by conceding to the unions a reduction in the working week. These general collective agreements formed the basis for negotiations with the works councils and the works agreement on flexible working time. At state level employers' associations succeeded in pressing for the relaxation of protective labour law.

The introduction of new models of employee involvement and employee participation is part of sophisticated human-resources management. Quality circles and other forms of employee involvement supplement and support the flexibility strategies. They are designed to stimulate workers' productive and creative resources and secure their compliance. Quality circles have greatly expanded since the 1970s. By now 45 per cent of the hundred biggest firms have introduced this Japanese device. (See Table 5.2.)

Volkswagen was one of the companies that introduced quality circles relatively early. After initial opposition from the works councillors and shop stewards of IG Metall, management and works council signed a works agreement on the introduction, agenda and proceedings of quality circles. Another company, Hoesch steelworks on the Ruhr, started even earlier with participatory groups as part of a 'humanization of work' project (sponsored by the Federal Ministry of Research and Technology). Being a company under the jurisdiction of the strongest model of co-determination (equal representation on supervisory board) the management was inclined to strive for the works council's co-operation from the earliest drafts. The unions and works councils have accepted participation because they then stand a chance of turning them into instruments for extending co-determination while if they abstain managements may introduce them without any union or council participation.

2.3   Trade unions

With the coming of the Conservative–Liberal government the trade unions have lost their partner in the political arena, and with the rise in unemployment their bargaining power against the employers has been weakened considerably. Structural change in the economy and in society has continued apace. The unions have found only initial tentative answers to the technicization of everyday life and working life with its inherent tendencies to destandardization and deregulation in the field of industrial relations; they still lack a convincing alternative concept to a flexible capitalism.

From the point of view of organization policy, the trade unions have proved to be extremely stable. Their status as a party to collective bargaining has up to now remained unchallenged because of the high degree of juridification and centralization and their monopoly-like legal privileges in collective bargaining and in calling strikes. Whereas the 'institutionalization of class struggle' could be seen as a fetter on the unions' development of power in the years of sustained high employment, institutional protection now constitutes a bulwark against labour-exclusion strategies.

The results of works council elections can be seen as an indicator of unions' continuing strong support among the labour force. Union candidates gained in the industrial sector 85 per cent of the votes and in the private service sector almost 60 per cent. As shown in Table 5.3, the loss of membership has been kept within limits. The unions have lost most members among male blue-collar workers in the industrial sector; however, in comparison with the reduction of employment, this loss has been below average. On the other hand, an increase in female white-collar employees can be observed. Although some unions could improve their membership in the service sector, they have in general been only modestly successful in recruiting new members among technical employees and personnel in private administration.

Table 5.4 on union density clearly illustrates the current organizational situation of the unions. For the overall economy, the proportion of the labour force belonging to the seventeen unions affiliated to the DGB has remained unchanged. Union density has increased among blue-collar workers, stagnated among white-collar employees and dropped among civil servants. In all categories of the dependent labour force the unionization of women could be improved; the politicizing effect of the women's movement has increased the readiness of women to join trade unions.

Table 5.3 *Deutscher Gewerkschaftsbund (DGB) – membership 1986 and 1980*

Union	Manual	White-collar	Beamte[1]	Men	Women	Total 1986	Total 1980
			(1986 in 000s)				
Metal industry	2,203	395	–	2,211	387	2,598	2,622
Public service	577	537	85	831	368	1,199	1,150
Chemical industry	527	127	–	528	126	654	661
Construction	445	40	–	454	31	485	533
Post	143	39	281	318	145	463	450
Trading, banking, insurance	50	327	–	158	219	377	351
Mining and energy	308	47	–	348	7	355	368
Rail	167	14	170	321	30	351	407
Food, drink, tobacco	212	54	–	176	90	266	253
Textile, clothing	227	29	–	109	147	256	294
Education, science	–	51	142	92	101	193	184
Police	9	17	137	149	14	163	166
Wood-processing, plastics	133	10	–	124	19	143	157
Printing	108	35	–	109	34	143	144
Leather	46	2	–	27	21	48	56
Agriculture	37	3	3	37	6	43	42
Arts	–	28	–	17	11	28	45
DGB 1986	5,192	1,755	818	6,009	1,756	7,765	
DGB 1980	5,377	1,658	848	6,286	1,597		7,883

[1] Permanent civil servants with life-long job security who have no right to strike.

Source: Deutscher Gewerkschaftsbund

Table 5.4   *Union density,*[1] *FRG, 1980, 1985 and 1987*

	1980	1985	1987
Men	43.4	43.8	42.9
Women	18.8	20.0	20.3
Blue-collar workers	48.7	51.6	51.4
Male	56.9	60.5	59.4
Female	27.3	29.2	30.4
White-collar workers	17.2	17.6	17.3
Male	22.3	21.6	21.2
Female	12.6	14.0	14.0
Civil servants	36.4	33.9	33.3
Male	38.1	34.9	33.6
Female	29.3	30.2	32.0
Industrial sector	46.4	50.0	–
Private service sector	9.5	9.2	–
Public administration	53.3	51.2	–
Total	34.2	34.7	34.2

[1] Union density ratio $= \dfrac{\text{Members of unions affiliated to DGB}}{\text{Dependent labour force}}$

Source: Federal Republic of Germany, Statistisches Amt (annual)

Table 5.5   *Social composition of labour force and trade union members, FRG, 1987*

	Blue-collar workers	White-collar workers (percentage share)	Beamte
Labour force	44.4	44.9	10.7
Trade union members	66.8	22.8	10.4

Source: Federal Republic of Germany, Statistiches Amt (annual)

Density ratios in the industrial sector and in public administration are about 50 per cent. It is important to note that unionization in the metalworking industry, and particularly in the regional bargaining units where IG Metall normally conducts its strikes, is – even among white-collar workers – significantly above the industrial average. In sharp contrast to that is the very low density in the private service sector. The result is that some relevant service industries are virtually union-free.

Another aspect is that the gap between the social composition of the labour force and that of trade union members could not be bridged (see Table 5.5).

3 Processes in the political and state arena

It is a basic pattern of the state's economic policy that measures promoting employment have nothing to do with Keynesian employment programmes but are aimed at adapting the labour supply to labour market conditions by training, flexibilization and provision of cheaper labour. The government sees in the unduly high unemployment of low-skilled or unskilled labour and in the partial excess demand for skilled workers and technicians an indicator that the bottleneck of highly qualified labour – which it also expects on the basis of the demographic development – can only be avoided by a long-term drive to increase skill levels. It has therefore introduced an array of initiatives for the training of young people, further training of those in employment, and retraining of unemployed persons. In order to get efficient workforces used to working with modern computer technologies, a pre-retirement law was passed. This provides financial subsidies to companies when a vacant job is given to a younger employee. The government also considers the flexibilization of working hours extremely important. There is clearly a trend to destandardize the working hours in public administration (for example, changed visiting and opening hours) while at the same time offering more part-time jobs. With its Employment Promotion Act the government wants to contribute to a flexibilization of employment. In the case of new recruitments it allows employment contracts for a fixed time so that the companies can part from such employees without expensive dismissal notices.

Measures affecting the status of trade unions are aimed in a much more direct way at the structure of industrial relations; they have subsequently given rise to extremely sharp conflicts with the unions.

With the statutory new regulation concerning the granting of unemployment benefit for striking or locked-out employees (para. 116 AFG – Labour Promotion Act), the government intends to impede the union 'pinpoint strike' which is the typical form of labour dispute in the Federal Republic. In order to underline the significance of this measure it should be pointed out that IG Metall, although concluding industry-wide collective bargaining agreements, does not conclude such agreements for the entire Federal Republic but reaches formally separated agreements for different regional bargaining units. When there is a labour dispute in a regional bargaining unit leading to a strike and a lock-out, the union provides its members with a high level of strike pay while non-members come away empty-handed because the state, as a result of its neutrality obligation, does not grant unemployment benefit. What has also been retained is the regulation that those employees who are indirectly affected by a strike in other industries are paid unemployment benefit. A new rule, however, provides that employees working in the same industry but in a bargaining unit other than the one involved in the strike are no longer granted unemployment benefit when indirectly affected by it. This new regulation is applied only if the trade union in this bargaining unit has the same main demand (for example, reduction of weekly working time to thirty-five hours) as in the bargaining region which is on strike. This provision was the government's reaction to a production process which has become more and more interdependent as a result of tightly scheduled production or the logistic integration of the entire production chain from order to delivery.

It obtained its illustrative material from the strike in 1984 on the reduction of weekly working hours when IG Metall succeeded in bringing the whole car industry to a standstill by the skilful selection of a relatively small number of firms playing a strategic role in the production of cars. However, the government is taking the risk that the predominant type of a periodically recurring, calculable labour dispute led on behalf of the whole economy will no longer occur. As the trade union pacemaker in collective bargaining, IG Metall not only went out on strike at intervals of four to five years on behalf of the entire trade union movement but it also launched pinpoint strikes which concentrated on one collective bargaining objective and on one regional bargaining unit. These strikes were always model confrontations in which IG Metall had to stand the test required by the employers to prove its ability to engage in conflicts and which in the end produced results which could subsequently be transferred with only a few exceptions and partial modifications to the entire metal industry and other sectors of the economy. The periods of peace in the interim phases, the almost strike-free conditions in other industries, that is the extremely low conflict-proneness in comparison with other countries, prove the high efficiency and legitimacy of the German pattern of conflict settlement and regulation. To maintain this type of strike is now made more difficult for IG Metall. If it adheres to it, it will be expensive since the union would have to provide strike pay to its members outside the strike area who are indirectly affected. If it decided to bypass the law by putting forward and imposing different main demands for each bargaining unit (wage increases or reductions of working time or rationalization safeguards and so on), the model character of collective bargaining results would be put in question. This could lead to an extreme differentiation of working conditions in which neither the unions nor the employers are interested. The unions, for reasons of social solidarity, aim at the greatest possible degree of equality in living conditions for their members. For their part the employers, for reasons of similar competitive conditions and thus of the unity of their association, are intent on achieving labour costs and flexibility potentials as uniform as possible. It is therefore not surprising that the new law was met with widespread scepticism. Thus a leading representative of the CDU who had been a government member in the 1960s and later became the President of the German Federal Constitutional Court (Bundesverfassungsgericht) furnished the SPD-led government of the *Land* of North Rhine-Westphalia with a legal opinion outlining the faulty design of the new legislation (Benda, 1986). Moreover, this expert considers the new regulation to be unconstitutional on the basis that the government is not allowed to deny the individual employee his right of benefit which had been acquired by his contributions to the unemployment insurance; the *Land* of North Rhine-Westphalia therefore made an application for a constitutional review of the law. At the time of writing, the matter has still not been decided.

A similar problem will inevitably arise if the government goes ahead with its announcement of changing the Works Constitution Act (Betriebsverfassungsgesetz). Under this act, the works councils, which are formally independent of the trade unions, become the institutions for representing the interests of the various groups of employees at the level of the works. They have the right neither to engage in collective bargaining nor to call a strike. They have many co-determination rights in personnel matters, and they are in charge of checking whether the provisions in collective agreements are applied. Interest representation in matters of collective bargaining by the union and the representation of interests at workplace level by the works council have led to a dual structure which has provided the German system with flexible problem-solving capacities.

The influence of trade unions on the works councils consists, on the one hand, of the right to nominate candidates; on the other, in the fact that the union lists are as a rule elected by overwhelming majorities. Through this 'lever', the unions could expand their institutional collective bargaining and strike monopoly by adding a monopoly of representation on the works councils. What is more, responsibilities in the trade unions and in the works councils are concentrated at the top, among representatives on headquarters-level councils and on supervisory boards. This facilitates a close co-operation. The government intends to give minority groups in the works councils, which have hitherto rarely played more than a powerless opposition role, a share in the administration of industrial relations. The result would be a fragmentation of interest representation at workplace level on which neither the unions nor the employers are keen. Whereas the unions are afraid of losing their monopoly-like representative position, the employers fear losing competent, reliable and predictable bargaining partners.

Since there is no law in the FRG regulating strikes and lock-outs, the valid norms of labour disputes are based entirely on judicial decisions. Two court-of-last-instance judgements were delivered on this in the 1980s. First, employers are allowed to take defensive lock-out actions, but cannot lock out for offensive reasons. In a supplementary judgement the Federal Labour Court developed for the first time binding legal regulations concerning the (pre)conditions of the employers' right to impose lock-outs. Going back to competition law and taking account of the competitive relationship prevailing between the enterprises organized in an employers' association, the highest labour court laid down the following norms: in the case of a 'partial', pinpoint strike, which encompasses less than 25 per cent of the wage- and salary-earners in a collective bargaining region, the employers' side is permitted to expand the scope of the dispute by up to 25 per cent of the wage- and salary-earners affected. In this way, not only should the parity between the parties to collective bargaining be restored, but also the employers' solidarity should be guaranteed. The latter is endangered in the case of pinpoint 'selective' strikes by the fact that individual enterprises must resist the trade union attack on behalf of the entire association and run the danger of losing market shares to competitors not affected by the strike. If more than 25 per cent of the wage- and salary-earners are brought into a strike, lock-outs of up to 50 per cent of wage- and salary-earners are deemed not to be out of proportion. If more than 50 per cent are affected, the imposition of a wider-ranging lock-out is held to be out of proportion. The court's intention was to ensure the readiness of the trade unions to offer compromises through the employers' lock-out rights, but also, by limiting these rights, to limit the risk of the unions being more than 'appropriately' weakened by excessive financial costs arising from their high payments to striking or locked-out members.

Secondly, in the entire public service, including railways and post, there are three categories of public sector employees: about half the approximately 4.5 million state employees are blue- and white-collar workers who have the right to strike and the other half are permanent public servants (Beamte) with life-long job security and without the right to strike.

During a minor post-office strike in 1980, the then Social Democratic Minister gave an official order that public servants had to do the work of the 25,000 striking employees. The union concerned contested this measure by arguing that the ban on strikes for public servants included their being neutral in a labour dispute and that they could thus not be forced to act as strike-breakers. The action, which lasted several years, was temporarily ended by a judgement of the Federal Labour Court pursuant to which the transfer of public servants to workplaces of striking employees was declared lawful. Since this judgement had the effect of virtually nullifying the public service union's ability to strike, the union concerned has lodged a complaint of unconstitutionality which has not yet been heard.

4 Processes in industrial relations

The following survey of the most important results of collective bargaining shows that both parties to collective bargaining are still very much willing to compromise.

Loss of income: During the 1980s, the trade unions accepted wage agreements which led – for the first time in the post-war era – to a considerable loss of real net income (see Table 5.6). There was no single strike in which wage demands were the main issue of the conflict.

The development of wage policy was a result of the unions' weakened bargaining position, but it also reflected their unwillingness to block the modernization process through their wage policy; it was, further, an effect of their emphasis on the reduction of working hours rather than achieving wage increases.

Reduction of working time: Trade union efforts to achieve this centred on the demand for a thirty-five-hour week. In 1984 this led to the biggest industrial dispute in the history of the FRG. IG Metall achieved a trail-blazing breakthrough. The employers, who had laid down in a so-called 'taboo-catalogue' that the forty-hour week was inviolate, had to accept a reduction to thirty-eight and a half hours. In the following years, the forty-hour week was broken on a wide front in many sectors of the economy (Table 5.7). Including agreements already concluded but which have only become effective in 1987, almost half the labour force have a

Table 5.6 *Development of wages, FRG, 1980–7*

	Actual gross wages per employee		Actual net wages per employee		Real net wages per employee	
	1	2	1	2	1	2
1980	100	6.7	100	5.2	100	−0.1
1981	104.9	4.9	104.5	4.5	98.3	−1.7
1982	109.2	4.1	107.5	2.9	95.9	−2.4
1983	112.7	3.2	110.0	2.3	95.2	−0.8
1984	116.0	3.0	111.9	1.7	94.5	−0.7
1985	119.4	2.9	113.5	1.5	94.0	−0.6
1986	123.9	3.8	118.2	4.1	98.0	+4.3
1987	127.6	3.0	120.4	1.9	99.8	+1.8

[1] Index 1980 = 100.
[2] Percentage change from previous year.

Source: Wirtschafts- und Sozialwissenschaftliches Institut des DGB

Table 5.7 *Collectively agreed weekly working time, FRG, 1980–7*

	Under 40 hours	40 hours	More than 40 hours
		(As a percentage of all employees)	
1980	–	94.0	6.0
1984	1.1	98.9	–
1985	26.6	73.4	–
1986	40.6	59.4	–
1987	50.0	50.0	–

Source: Bundesministerium für Arbeit und Sozialordnung

regular working week of thirty-eight and a half hours as a collectively agreed weekly working time. In April 1987 a new agreement was settled in the metalworking industry. IG Metall achieved an additional reduction: in two steps the thirty-seven-hour week would be introduced by April 1989.

Other forms of reduced working time worth mentioning include changes in holidays. In the late 1970s six weeks' holiday was agreed for important sectors of the economy. IG Metall was again the pacemaker, so that during the 1980s this holiday regulation became generalized throughout the economy. In addition, as one form of shortening life working time, older employees have been given the opportunity of an early retirement (in most cases at the age of fifty-eight). This regulation entails a loss of income but guarantees the pension level.

The question of working time has been the predominant issue of industrial relations. In contrast to the introduction of the forty-hour week in the 1960s, it was motivated by considerations of improving the employment situation rather than of providing more leisure. The employment effects of reduced working time have been estimated by IG Metall at more than 100,000 additional jobs in its sphere of organization alone.

Flexibility of working time: Employers made flexibility of working time an item of negotiations on the agenda of collective bargaining. Their objective was to utilize in the best possible way the flexibility and thus productivity potentials inherent in new technology through a destandardization of uniform working hours. A flexible adjustment to a changing level of orders and changing sales prospects as required by the market is, according to the employers, incompatible with rigid working hours. In particular the separation of potential machine hours and working hours of the employees is seen by employers as a flexibility reserve.

Whereas employers had to make concessions on the question of reduced working hours, IG Metall gave way on the issue of flexibility. This was the compromise which ended the labour dispute in 1984. The weekly working time of thirty-eight and a half hours is merely an average figure to be observed by firms, since the flexibility regulation allows different working hours for different groups of employees or different sectors of employment within the range of thirty-seven to forty hours (in the 1987 agreement between thirty-six and a half and thirty-nine hours). This was the first collective bargaining agreement which included the option of the introduction of flexibility. It is part of this agreement that the power of deciding whether and how to use the opportunity to introduce diversified working hours was delegated to the management and the works council. The agreement thus includes a tendency toward decentralizing industrial relations, implying a shift of competences in collective bargaining from an industry-wide to a company level.

The increase in other forms of destandardized working hours can be observed in many cases, including the following: Agreements on shorter working weeks for older employees in some sectors of the food industry (reduced working time to twenty hours with full wage adjustment) seem to be expanding. Reductions in working time have occasionally been negotiated on conditions that the gain in time ought to be used for vocational retraining and further training. In general, one can say that unions have intensified their efforts on issues such as training and retraining. In the chemical industry for instance both parties to collective bargaining established a Council for the Promotion of Vocational Training with equal representation; in the metalworking industry a totally new schedule for the training of school-leavers has been settled. Reduced working hours for shift-workers which have frequently been agreed have led, as a rule, to an additional shift so that the trade unions could successfully increase employment while the companies could fully utilize their expensive machinery. Agreements on a fixed working year which can be flexibly spread over the whole year are still rare; but the chemical workers' union is demanding the introduction of a working year and considers this to be the big new initiative in working-time policy. And in spring 1987 the first industry-wide collective bargain for part-time work has been concluded in the chemical industry.

Degree of conflict: The pattern of conflict which has been followed since the mid-1950s is that of major disputes at intervals of about five years with almost strike-free periods in between (see Table 5.8). This rhythm was determined almost exclusively by IG Metall (see Table 5.9). It has never called a nationwide strike but has taken action only in one regional bargaining unit at a time, choosing the form of a limited strategic strike in selected companies. The employers' answer to that since the early 1970s has usually been a lock-out. Since the metal industry (4 million employees) is the main sector of the German economy with the strongest employers' association and the strongest trade union facing each other, these disputes have always been conflicts for power fought on behalf of all and have always produced model collective bargaining compromises.

This pattern has been basically maintained in the 1980s. A renewal of the arm-wrestling took place in Baden Württemberg (Stuttgart–Mannheim) in the metalworking industry's hours-reduction strike in 1984. The dispute lasted seven weeks. It began with approximately 10,000 employees in the supply firms of the car industry. IG Metall extended the strike to approximately 60,000 employees and the employers locked out 140,000 more. The strike was carried mainly by blue-collar workers, salaried employees being involved only in some companies.

What was special about this conflict was its scale. Never before had so many companies outside the strike area become involved. Many put their workers on short time or shut down plants, arguing that they could not deliver their products to the strike area or had been forced to stop production because of an absence of supplies from the strike area. More than 300,000 employees, primarily in

Table 5.8 *Total labour disputes, FRG, 1978–87*

	Workers involved (in 000s)	Days lost
1978	487	4,281
1979	77	483
1980	45	128
1981	253	58
1982	40	15
1983	94	41
1984	538	5,614
1985	78	35
1986	115	28
1987	155	33

Source: Müller-Jentsch, 1989

Table 5.9 *Major labour disputes, FRG, 1978–84*

	Economic sector	Number of workers		Demand
		Strikers	Locked out	
1978	Printing industry	20,000	55,000	Job and earnings protected
1978	Metalworking industry	85,000	120,000	Earnings protection
1978/9	Steel industry (also IG Metall)	60,000	40,000	35-hour week
1980	Post office	25,000	–	Additional leisure time for shift-workers
1984	Printing industry	45,000	–	35-hour week
1984	Metalworking industry	57,000	140,000 315,000 (additionally affected by 'cold lock-outs')	35-hour week

Source: Müller-Jentsch, 1989

the car industry, were affected by these measures, which were termed 'cold lock-outs' by the trade unions. These effects, for which IG Metall had planned in its so-called 'mini-max' strategy, were only partly a result of economic–technological integration; they were also a manoeuvre by the employers aimed at putting IG Metall in a mood for compromise by extending the scope of the struggle.

The strike was ended after conciliation by a high-ranking Social Democratic politician who had formerly been the President of the construction union and then Minister of Defence. By suggesting a combination of both reduced and flexible working hours, he made a compromise possible for both parties. As shown by developments in the following years, an attractive agreement had been reached which was copied in many other sectors of the economy.

5 An interpretation of changes

The industrial relations system in West Germany has changed less dramatically than those in other European countries. Nevertheless, new elements have been brought into the system which, without challenging the basic principles, provide the foundation of several new emphases. These changes are mainly due to the initiative of industrialists and managers as well as to the deregulatory measures of the Liberal–Conservative government coalition.

To begin at the highest level, national concertation had already come to an end during the late 1970s (see Table 5.10). Industry-wide collective bargaining continues to play a decisive role in the regulation of working conditions and terms of employment. This is especially valid as regards global wage increases and general reductions in working hours, whereby the powerful bargaining agencies in the metal industry continue to be, without doubt, the pace-setters and wage leaders. The shifting or transfer of collective bargaining competence to the negotiators at company level – management and works councils – represents, however, a loosening of the typically centralized system of negotiation which has existed until now in West Germany; others speak here of a necessary and suitable 'completion' of the system.

Company-wide negotiations have been strengthened, especially within the framework of qualitative collective bargaining policy and the working-hours policy. If one considers that flexibility and decentralization are accompanied by a destandardization of employment contracts (work for a fixed period, agency employees, part-time work and other forms of precarious employment) and that an increasing specialization of work-tasks can be observed, it becomes clear that work is increasingly characterized by a tendency towards heterogeneity and differentiation. The form of interest policy with a universal orientation and the objective of achieving uniform working conditions for as many employees as possible which is a typical feature of modern mass trade unions becomes increasingly more difficult. A new demand arises for regulation specific to one workplace which is no longer covered by extensive agreement negotiated on an industry-wide level. The scope of workplace industrial relations on the plant level has been

Table 5.10 *Changes in the industrial relations system, FRG since 1980*

Type	Pre-1980	Post-1980
A(a) National concertation	Tripartite 'Concerted Action' 1969–77 effective only during the first years	Only some verbal proclamations in favour of re-establishing tripartism
A(b) Industry-wide collective bargaining	Most important bargaining level in all industries (in some bigger industries also regional bargaining)	Loosening by transferring some functions to negotiators at company level
B Decentralized collective bargaining	Only in a few companies not affiliated to employers' associations (among them, Volkswagen)	Works councils increasingly adopting some complementary bargaining functions
C(a) Worker participation via unions	Co-determination at supervisory and management boards (coal and steel since 1951, remaining industry since 1976)	Further decline of the 'strong model' in coal and steel (full parity, strong union representation) as result of declining number of enterprises in this industry
C(b) Worker participation without unions	Unimportant	Increasingly important: quality circles
D(a) Simple contract (no unions)	Only important in some multinational companies and in small firms	Slightly more important in computer industries
D(b) Simple contract (no union) in secondary labour markets	Limited to some employments	Spreading after recent deregulation in labour law

expanded, and it is possible that they will play a key role in the future.

We may also expect modifications from the numerous initiatives in the field of employer-sponsored participation. Just how seriously these initiatives will change the industrial relations system has yet to be seen. However, it is certain that the trend towards quality circles and group-work with delegated responsibility is not just enjoying more popularity within management and personnel theory but also has caused a growing number of companies to introduce new forms of participation. When 'enlightened' personnel and organization managers show increasing interest in group concepts, it looks as if they are poaching; after all, the subject of group-work and partly autonomous groups was always an essential part of the unions' programme of 'humanization of work' in the 1960s and 1970s. These new management-initiated models, however, deal with participation of an instrumental character, whose aim is to mobilize the productive and motivational resources of the employees, or, to be more exact, the resources of the privileged core labour force. Whether or not management can practise workers' involvement and workers' participation inclusive or exclusive of the institutionalized representation of interest is dependent on the embodiment of the trade unions within the company and the power of the works council. In expanding industries and white-collar occupations one tends to pursue managerially controlled and flexibly manageable forms of participation of a consultative nature. Where management cannot ignore the institutionalized workers' representation it will attempt to use it as an instrument for its own purposes and try formally to involve the works council.

The unions' initial rejection of quality circles has meanwhile given way to a differentiated opinion. They see the danger that collective employees' representation could be sapped by employer-sponsored participation, and therefore try to ensure, on the one hand, that the works councils have influence on the quality circles and, on the other hand, that they have raised their claim for co-determination at the workplace, something the union left has been demanding for years.

Employer-sponsored participation is a major part of the extensive personnel management strategy that aims to develop and strengthen the core labour force. This strategy is supported by the deregulatory labour legislation of the government coalition. A direct consequence of this has been the expansion of the secondary labour market: that is, the number of people with employment contracts unaffected by collective industrial relations has increased and continues to increase.

The question of whether West German unions have lost some of their bargaining power in the 1980s is less easy to answer than it may seem in view of the worsened socioeconomic and political framework. As organizations equipped with the potential to negotiate strategically and with the ability to learn, the unions can adjust to new situations with changed concepts and bargaining strategies, instead of simply reacting to them. The following are the main issues that confront the unions:

First, the substantial number of unemployed, and the increasing proportion of long-term unemployed, represents a major burden for their solidarity functions. The question for the unions is: towards which interests should their collective bargaining policy be oriented, and with which groups can they carry through their collective bargaining objectives? The reduction of the working week has been established by them as a collective bargaining objective, above all, in the interest of the unemployed or those employees threatened by unemployment. The trade unions have used industrial action to enforce this objective.

Secondly, socioeconomic structural changes are leading to a long-term restructuring of the labour force. A crucial issue is the altered composition of union membership and therefore union security. For the unions, the decline of the older industries means the loss of a significant membership sector, namely the 'born trade unionists'. Expanding employee groups tend to be those that have a more distant relationship to union organization: white-collar workers in private sectors, engineers, employees in the new, so-called future industries. Between the traditional industries and the new there are other sectors (like the auto industry, the mechanical engineering, chemical and electronic industries) which have been through spates of modernization and are now equipped with the most up-to-date technology. In such industries, the unions still receive much support, especially from skilled workers. Nevertheless, it cannot be expected that this 'new type of skilled worker' (flexible employees with extensive, polyvalent and multi-subject related qualifications) emerging in such industries will still, as a matter of course, join the trade unions as the classic industrial workers did. It is even more difficult to organize the fluctuating and heterogeneous group of peripheral employees that is currently growing in size.

Thirdly, the increasingly heterogeneous nature of union membership and, at the same time, the need to recruit and represent groups in strong as well as weak positions on the labour market do not only aggravate the recruitment efforts of the unions but also challenge inherited, centrally practised and universally oriented collective bargaining policy. The traditional union objective of standardizing wages and working conditions through 'common rules' (S. and B. Webb) is in a dilemma, because of both the divided interests of the various employee groups and management's diverse efforts towards flexibility. A possible solution may be found in the decentralization of interest representation and the transfer of collective bargaining competence to company negotiators.

Fourthly, other serious problems for the unions stem from management's offensive. Increasingly popular concepts of flexible group work and offers of participation compete with the institutions of 'industrial democracy'. What is called 'human resources management' nowadays also strives for the personal loyalty and normative integration of the core workers, for a policy which aims willy-nilly at the alienation of employees from union organizations and officials. For, after all, the basis of the trade union bond until now was that the working masses were relatively indifferent to work and the employer; in other words, they were instrumentally oriented towards their work so that their emotional commitment and personal loyalty could be devoted to unions and to informal groupings on the shop floor. Contemporary management strategies tend towards an 'ideological subordination' of the core blue- and white-collar workers; they are expected to commit themselves emotionally and totally to company objectives in order to ensure their security and integration into the company.

Fifthly, the party political composition of the government is a very significant, influential factor for those unions with a pronounced state orientation and a centralized collective bargaining policy. This statement is even more valid given that it is unlikely in the short term that political power will be reclaimed by social democracy. If the conditions for the 'political exchange' between government and trade unions have thereby deteriorated, the unions no longer need to take government policy into consideration and can frontally attack all those measures they are not in favour of.

Sixthly, changes in labour and social security laws have, on the one hand, restricted the unions' financial scope concerning industrial disputes (para. 116 of the Labour Promotion Act) and, on the other hand, strengthened the tendency towards a segmentation of the labour market and peripheralization of employee groups. Whereas the changes in individual labour legislation have led to a cumulation of disadvantages for the peripheral workforce, unionized core groups and core labour forces have until now remained relatively unaffected by them. One can even say that their jobs have been made more secure because of these; external barriers have been erected to entry on the internal labour market.

The present condition of West German trade unions can be characterized as 'new realism'. After the strong setback with the union-owned house-building group Neue Heimat (whose financial crisis had accumulated a mountain of debts of 17 billion DM) the unions have not only separated themselves from their companies (among them one of the largest banks and one of the largest insurance companies in the FRG) but have also set aside their concepts for common ownership and a 'commonweal economy'. The election victories by the Liberals and Christian Democrats persuaded the unions to press on by themselves and to concentrate on the objectives which can be achieved through collective bargaining. The generational change which has taken place in the leadership of many of the trade unions has definitely helped acceptance of the new realism and the pragmatic pursuance of collective agreements. The DGB and IG Metall have started an intense debate with intellectuals and social scientists in order to reach an adequate interpretation of the transformations taking place in capitalist societies and to gain new perspectives for a redefined strategy. Worthy of mention is a series of conferences on 'The other future' organized by IG Metall in 1988.

The prediction that the unions will continue to play an important role in the working and social lives of the Federal Republic in the near future is justified not only by this 'new realism' but also by their stable position in society. They proved their ability to oppose vigorously and to succeed in the important question of the reduction in working hours, despite unfavourable circumstances and without at the same time giving up their willingness to compromise and to co-operate. In view of this, informed employers will have to be careful not to drive the trade unions into isolation and radicalism through non-cooperation and the rejection of compromises.

A generational change in the leadership has also taken place in the most important employers' associations. Integration problems between big and small businesses, between prosperous, stagnating and shrinking industries have become larger rather than smaller, due mainly to the reduction in working hours and to flexi-time. The dissatisfaction in the medium-sized company with the most recent bargaining compromises has not diverted the officials of the employers' associations from their efforts to come to terms with this new realism of the unions during negotiations. Indeed, it may be that the employers' proposals for a peace treaty between the negotiating parties will be rejected by IG Metall. However, it can be expected that interest disputes and industrial conflicts will in future be executed with less ideology and with more understanding of the organizational constraints on integration and action that each side is respectively experiencing. No more will they be drawn out into 'ideological battles'.

If one dares to make a forecast for the near future, this would be: a readjustment in collective bargaining is probable, through the co-operation of the parties, which will pay more attention to the increased tendency towards flexibility, segmentation and decentralization, with the result that agreements will limit their universalistically oriented interest representation more and more according to the procedural rules and average norms. Further, providing services for both management and works councils could become the most important function of employers' associations and trade unions. This prediction includes the consequence of the company negotiators becoming the actual key figures in the regulation and administration of industrial relations. In this event, West German industrial relations would naturally lose some of the transparency which has prevailed thanks to the dominant centralized negotiating structures.

Already the private sector at least is offering a diversity of industrial relations patterns at the factory level ranging from companies with a strong union representation and unionized works councils with a structure of bilateral (be it co-operative or adversarial) industrial relations; through companies with a dual structure of institutionalized workers' representation (works councils) and employer-sponsored participation (quality circles); to union-free companies with sophisticated human-resources management. These three types of industrial relations are found mainly in big companies; in the small and medium-sized companies there is even more diversity, because here informal and *ad hoc* regulations are the rule. In future the factory level will have to be more actively included in empirical research than at present, if a more precise forecast is to be made of the future of the West German industrial relations system.

References

Benda, E. (1986) *Sozialrechtliche Eigentumsposition im Arbeitskampf*, Baden-Baden: Landesregierung Nordrhein-Westfalen.
Deutsche Bundesbank (1988) *Report*, Frankfurt am Main: Deutsche Bundesbank.
Federal Republic of Germany, Statistisches Amt (annual) *Jahrbuch für die Bundesrepublik Deutschland*, Stuttgart: Kohlhammer.
Müller-Jentsch, W. (1989) *Basisdaten der industriellen Beziehungen*, Frankfurt am Main: Campus.
OECD (1988) *National Accounts*, vols 1 and 2, Paris: OECD.

Sachverständigenrat (1981) *Sachverständigenrat zur Begutachtung der gesamtwirtschaftlichen Entwicklung, Jahresgutachten 1981/82*, Bonn: Deutscher Bundestag, Drucksache 9/1061, Ziffer 459.

Sachverständigenrat (1988) *Jahresgutachten*, Bonn: Deutscher Bundestag.

6

Industrial Relations in Italy

Serafino Negrelli and Ettore Santi

The system of industrial relations that took shape in Italy in the wake of the 'hot autumn' of 1969 featured the following: a strong, ramified organizational and bargaining presence of the unions, based on large corporations at company level; as a rule, no separation between the economic and the political bargaining demands of the unions, within a primarily conflictual, antagonistic cultural perspective; a high level of conflict, especially at the company level, with a heavy stress on spontaneity; a union approach to relations with government linked closely to ongoing disputes at all levels; a highly militant and united rank and file, encouraged in part by a weakening of traditional organizational divisions and union identities.

In the later 1970s, the alteration of important aspects of both the economic and the political situation favoured the emergence of trends that significantly modified each of the above features.

The massive threat to worker incomes and to employment that materialized in the wake of the recession of 1974–5, with a slowdown in growth and soaring inflation (17.2 per cent on average for 1974–8) imposed upon the unions increasingly defensive preoccupations and concerns in deciding their goals. A process was thus set in motion whose main stages were: the agreement between Confindustria (the private industrialists' association) and the united union confederations CGIL–CISL–UIL in February 1975 to strengthen and reform the wage indexation system (*scala mobile*); a complex negotiating process among government, unions and employers on the reduction of labour costs in the winter of 1976–7; the unions' re-examination and revision of the relationship between bargaining demands and reform strategy, beginning with the programme approved by the three confederations at their congress in Rome in January 1978.

This process worked profound changes in the previous pattern of industrial relations. It brought about a decided, albeit gradual, centralization of collective bargaining and organizational relations. At the same time it encouraged a steadily increasing stress on union initiatives in the political arena, favoured and endorsed now for their implicit regulatory functions in the social and economic system rather than as a mere extension of bargaining action.

Together with the deterioration of the economic situation, the latter half of the 1970s witnessed the emergence of new political conditions as well. After a period of great instability, in the summer of 1976 co-operation among all the major political forces got under way, in which, for the first time in nearly three decades, the Italian Communist Party (PCI) was invited to participate.

The unprecedented breadth of the party-political support enjoyed by the 'national solidarity' governments until 1979 fuelled explicit expectations, both in the political community and in the country at large, of the installation of stronger social consensus. Ultimately, this climate of opinion led to the full legitimation of the reduced autonomy of industrial relations engendered by the dynamics of the political and institutional system and by actions in response to the unavoidable need to achieve effective management of the key macroeconomic variables responsible for the crisis. A clear sign of this reduced autonomy has been the marked change in the relative importance of collective bargaining and legislation.

In any event, the changes in the economy and in political equilibria had a differential impact on the organizational and bargaining arrangements of the industrial relations system. Countering the trend found in some European countries, for instance, unionization continued to expand in Italy in the second half of the 1970s, rising to over 9 million members for the three major confederations in 1980. The overall unionization rate peaked in 1978 at 49.3 per cent and then began to decline slowly, essentially because of a poor organizational response by the unions to the growth of employment in non-union sectors and industries.

The new relationship between bargaining and political action, moreover, helped generate perceptible changes in the configuration of the actors themselves. The three confederations, for instance, after years of discussion and debate, agreed in 1979 to begin a broad organizational restructuring, the objective being to achieve a more highly ramified union presence in the community and to simplify industrial representation. At the same time, however, inter-confederal relations saw the re-emergence of cultural and ideological pluralism and antagonism that for fifteen years had seemed to be superseded by the unification process.

Employer associations also further established themselves, and began an initial process of renovation in organizational form, spurred primarily by the growing importance acquired during these years by small and very small businesses.

Despite the central role of action at the national (confederal) level, however, the independence of branch and especially of company contracts was not formally called into question. Thus even while in practice bargaining claims proved to be 'regulated' by agreements at the central level between CGIL–CISL–UIL, employer organizations and the government, the highly diversified bargaining contract structure inherited from the earlier period remained operative. And this, together with the unions' increasing difficulties in using revised forms of what had once been a decisive tool, namely the national industry-wide employment contract, fostered the emergence of a certain polarization in bargaining arrangements towards the end of the 1970s.

Finally, the model of industrial conflict that had marked Italian labour relations following the 'hot autumn' was also modified. There was a substantial decline in the number of strikes (hence of decentralized, company-level industrial conflict) and also in the number of days lost (which is the prime indicator of the bitterness of labour conflicts). By contrast, adherence to industrial action by the workers remained high. And the timing of the strikes continued to depend principally on the three-yearly renewal of nationwide branch and industrial contracts (1976, 1979). Industrial action tended most definitively to shed the spontaneity of the earlier phase, typical of a collective movement, and to be transformed into a highly organized form of struggle, with primarily demonstrative purpose and directed at a bargaining partner found first and foremost in the 'political market'.

1 Economic and structural factors

Since the start of the 1980s, the Italian economy has evolved rapidly, with new elements emerging. After a modest expansion in the wake of the second oil shock, the economy suffered one of the worst recessions since the Second World War from September 1981 to May 1983, and then began a long, and strong, expansion that is still under way (see Table 6.1). The factors that influenced economic developments throughout the industrial West (high oil prices, the uncertain growth of world trade, exchange rate volatility and the massive introduction of the new computer technology) certainly had profound effects in Italy, producing in just a few years a very sharp transformation in cultural outlook and in the behaviour of social and political actors.

Thus the first half of the 1980s saw the emergence of an unheard-of consensus converging on measures to achieve macroeconomic priorities such as disinflation, industrial modernization and the recovery of international competitiveness. On

Table 6.1   *Main economic indicators, Italy, 1981–6*

Indicators	New series (percentage change on previous year)					
	1981	1982	1983	1984	1985	1986
GDP	1.1	0.2	0.5	3.5	2.7	2.7
Private consumption	1.5	1.1	0.4	2.2	2.7	3.2
Public consumption	2.7	2.9	2.8	2.0	3.5	3.0
Gross fixed investment	−2.3	−5.7	−1.6	4.4	3.3	1.2
Imports of goods and services	−3.8	−0.7	−1.6	11.3	5.3	5.1
Exports of goods and services	7.5	−1.1	2.3	7.6	4.0	3.1
Industrial production	−1.6	3.0	−3.2	3.4	1.2	2.8
Capacity utilization	−2.6	−1.5	2.0	3.4	1.8	2.0
Total employment (full-time equivalent)	0.0	0.6	0.5	0.5	1.4	0.8
Mfg employment (full-time equivalent)	−3.6	−2.6	−4.2	−4.2	−1.0	−0.9
Inflation rate	18.7	16.4	14.9	10.6	8.6	6.1

Source: Ministero del Bilancio e della Programmazione Economica and Ministero del Tesoro, 1986; ISCO, various years

closer inspection, it was in reality this last that was the true 'governing priority' – acknowledged by public opinion as a whole – that was operative in practice for the entire period.

As the overall data clearly show, the Italian economy was distinguished from the broader international, and especially European, context by a number of striking peculiarities: its singular employment trend (especially as regards youth employment), the uninterrupted expansion of output in virtually all sectors of the economy throughout the period; the quick and dramatically successful resolution of the financial troubles of many of the large industrial corporations; and, more recently, the economy's buoyantly renewed growth and the simultaneous re-emergence of long-standing territorial disparities.

According to many observers, these specificities are largely the result, for good or ill, of the peculiar ways in which Italy began to deal, in the early 1980s, with the economic and industrial situation inherited from the previous decade. And it should not be forgotten that the social climate underlying these economic conditions had long been profoundly shaped on the one hand by ever-rising expectations of welfare and affluence, yet deeply marked on the other by recurrent outbreaks of political violence and terrorism.

In part, however, these Italian specificities have been rightly considered as indirect effects of the new approach to handling the external constraint that shaped the crucial economic policy decisions of successive governments after the turn of the decade – especially the intervention in this sphere by the Bank of Italy, the country's powerful, independent and well-respected central bank. This refers above all to the exchange-rate policy adopted by the monetary authorities for the first half of the 1980s. Unlike that of the 1970s, the new course rejected recouping competitiveness vis-à-vis Italy's European trading partners by devaluation, at a time of progressive, excessive depreciation of the lira against a steadily rising dollar. The necessary complement was high interest rates, enabling Italy to achieve and keep a competitive stance in the international capital market despite the very wide inflation differential with respect to other industrial economies.

Both of these options, which were kept in force for the entire period under study here, fostered an accelerating internationalization of the Italian economy. Between 1980 and 1986, imports and exports expanded by 15.8 and 25.4 per cent respectively in real terms, while real GDP rose 13.3 per cent. And, together with the factors mentioned earlier, these policy options helped produce a most particular framework of constraints and incentives, which had a highly selective influence on the trend of the various economic aggregates, especially the modernization choices made by Italian industry.

Thus while inflation has slowed greatly since the turn of the decade and many economic indicators (in particular those reflecting international competitiveness) have shown regular improvement since 1984, the government budget deficit has remained enormous (still 6.5 per cent of GDP in 1986, after peaking at 7.2 per cent two years earlier). And above all, unemployment continued to increase, while regional disparities were exacerbated.

1.1 The labour market
Since the turn of the decade, the Italian labour market has undergone very substantial changes (see Table 6.2). Developments have largely continued – with greater dynamism – the trends of the 1970s: for instance, the steadily increasing incidence of the services sector in total employment. In part, however, the changes reflected newly emerging trends connected with Italy Ltd's adjustment to the world economic cycle, the introduction of computer and information technology and the achievement of great flexibility in the use of the workforce in many branches of the economy. This refers most particularly to the new structures of employment brought into being by large corporations.

The overall scene was dominated, in any event, by the steady

Table 6.2 *Employment by branch and sub-branch, Italy, 1980–6*

Branch and sub-branch	Full-time equivalent employment (000s)							Percentage change
	1980	1981	1982	1983	1984	1985	1986	1980–6
Agriculture	2,994	2,845	2,663	2,746	2,677	2,595	2,571	−14.1
Energy products	190	192	190	187	189	191	191	0.5
Manufacturing	5,966	5,750	5,603	5,366	5,143	5,090	5,043	−15.5
Construction	1,762	1,792	1,791	1,786	1,715	1,678	1,683	−4.5
Industry	7,918	7,733	7,584	7,339	7,045	6,959	6,916	−12.7
Distributive trades	4,161	4,273	4,426	4,534	4,701	4,830	4,877	17.2
Transport and communications	1,257	1,293	1,318	1,351	1,357	1,367	1,391	10.6
Finance and insurance	350	360	367	374	384	389	399	14.1
Misc. services	1,736	1,823	1,994	2,074	2,335	2,588	2,725	56.9
Market services	7,505	7,748	8,105	8,333	8,776	9,174	9,392	25.1
Government departments	3,194	3,260	3,303	3,323	3,368	3,397	3,417	7.0
Other services	453	473	508	549	596	651	667	47.3
Non-market services	3,646	3,734	3,811	3,873	3,964	4,047	4,084	12.0
Total	22,062	22,060	22,182	22,292	22,463	22,775	22,962	4.1

Source: Ministero del Bilancio e della Programmazione Economica and Ministero del Tesoro, 1986 (observation of full-time equivalent employment)

Table 6.3 *Labour market indicators, Italy, 1980-6*

Indicator	1980	1981	1982	1983	1984	1985	1986
Participation rate	39.8	40.2	40.3	40.6	40.7	40.9	41.5
Men	54.4	54.7	54.6	54.6	54.5	54.6	54.7
Women	26.0	26.5	26.7	27.3	27.6	28.0	28.9
Employment rate	36.8	36.8	36.6	36.6	36.6	36.7	36.9
Men	51.8	51.6	51.3	51.0	50.9	50.9	50.7
Women	22.6	22.7	22.7	22.9	23.0	23.3	23.8
Unemployment rate	7.6	8.4	9.1	9.9	10.0	10.3	11.1
Men	4.8	5.4	6.1	6.6	6.6	6.8	7.4
Women	13.1	14.4	14.9	16.2	16.5	16.7	17.8

Sources: Istate, 1986a (sample labour force surveys to 1983); Ministero del Bilancio e della Programmazione Economica and Ministero del Tesoro, 1986 (sample labour force surveys, 1983-6)

and apparently irresistible growth of unemployment: from 7.6 per cent in 1980 to 11.1 per cent in 1986 (see Table 6.3). However, the development of unemployment itself needs qualification by two observations. First, with the passage of years, unemployment in Italy has become progressively 'younger' more 'feminine' and 'southern'. In 1986, 73 per cent of all unemployed persons seeking jobs were younger than thirty, while the unemployment rates for women and for the south (17.8 and 16.5 per cent respectively) were far above the national average. Secondly, the growth of unemployment has not been accompanied, in the 1980s, by a decline or perceptible contraction of total employment, as has happened in many other industrial countries.

In other words, during the recession powerful 'shock absorbers' were at work, while the recovery has witnessed the resurgence of the structural constraints that are now blamed for the persistence in Italy of an additional quota of unemployment attributable to 'economic and social underdevelopment'.

By major aggregates, employment in agriculture and in industry has declined considerably (by 22.7 and 11.4 per cent respectively), while that in services has grown appreciably (19.3 per cent). This variegated, diversified sector has actually accounted for more than half the total Italian employment since 1982. The productivity drive of the early 1980s in large manufacturing concerns produced massive labour shedding, especially of blue-collar workers (− 29.6 per cent). Meanwhile the civil service, traditionally the 'protected' sector par excellence, showed employment growth of 7 per cent over the same period. Among the shock absorbers which have been highly effective, especially in the middle years of this period, the most important in many respects, including certainly the institutional side, has been the Short-Term Earnings Compensation Fund (Cassa Integrazione Guadagni, CIG).[1]

During the early 1980s, resort to CIG by manufacturing industry and above all by large firms rose precipitously, peaking in 1984. This was because the Fund was not used primarily as a countercyclical device by employers and unions, but as a way to take care of the massive redundancies produced by restructuring. On the basis of the number of hours of wage compensation paid by CIG in 1984, for instance, it has been estimated that the number of 'redundant' workers laid off in CIG amounted to some 10 to 12 per cent of the entire workforce in the engineering industry; it was even more extensive in chemicals (12 to 16 per cent) and in basic metals (16 to 19 per cent). At this time, 9 per cent of the employees of all Italian firms with more than 500 employees were laid off, working zero hours and drawing their entire earnings from CIG (Dal Co, 1986). While the use of CIG certainly helped greatly to maintain the level of employment during these years, it also entailed significant costs, both economic (increased government expenditures) and social (weakened solidarity among workers).

A buffer against the social and economic impact of unemployment was work in the 'underground' economy. The largest class of such employment, namely 'irregular' employment (which comprises a portion of 'off-the-books' jobs, clandestine, unreported jobs, moonlighting, part-time and seasonal work, and so on), involved no fewer than 4.7 million persons in 1984 (23 per cent of the number of 'regularly' employed workers).

Next there is 'precarious' work, a smaller class consisting of workers with temporary employment, which involved some 2 million persons in 1984, according to the Central Statistical Institute (Istat). Another 2 million people, according to a Labour Ministry estimate in 1985, were engaged in off-the-books work (minors, foreigners without work papers, unregistered workers without contracts, and so on). 'Undeclared workers' numbered about 700,000 in that year. Finally, there are moonlighters, a group that has been extensively studied in recent years and variously estimated at between 15 and 25 per cent of the regularly employed.

Though no one is rash enough to offer a precise estimate of the total number of people affected by this highly variegated phenomenon, these remarks show that 'underground' work has expanded substantially in the course of the 1980s and now comprises literally millions of workers, many of whom, however, are still officially counted as unemployed.

1.2   *The corporate recovery*

In the first half of the 1980s the Italian corporate sector gradually returned to sustained, substantial profitability. This completed a process that had begun on the morrow of the deep recession of 1974–5 and continued essentially without interruption even through the recession of 1981–3. Unlike the 1970s, however, when the main factor behind the profit recovery had been inflation, the more recent period has seen an enormous improvement in Italian firms' financial position and profits with massive investment and rising real interest rates. Certainly this achievement has been the fruit of a complex set of factors, including macroeconomic trends; but equally certainly a crucial role has been played by the steady gains in overall productivity, first and foremost the productivity of labour, made in these years (see Table 6.4).

Even allowing for the variety of the processes in individual firms and industries, there appear to have been three general factors at work helping to produce this rise in productivity: profound changes in the use of the workforce (including the elimination of the 'excessive manpower' mentioned earlier); investment and technological innovation; and industrial and marketing reorganization and the related decentralization (CER–IRS, 1986). Taken altogether, however, while the far-reaching restructuring of the early 1980s has enabled Italian firms greatly to improve their flexibility and adaptability with respect to the business cycle, increasing efficiency and cutting costs, it has not so far produced any real expansion of the productive base.

The uninterrupted development and growth of small firms warrants a different series of observations. As the industrial census of 1981 showed, the 1970s witnessed a dynamic, buoyant expansion in the number and in the output and employment of small and very small businesses. And the trend appears to have continued in the 1980s, even though some indirect indicators, such as electricity use, suggest that there has been some selection in this sector.

Most observers agree, in any case, that in the last few years the spread of small firms in Italy has been decreasingly the result of decisions by large firms and increasingly the outcome of the independent progressive spread of an industrial model that has successfully raised the profit rate of small firms by highly flexible organization of work, technology and marketing. On the other hand, looking at the main indicators of firms' economic success, one finds that during the first half of the 1980s large firms regained a great deal of lost ground with respect to small ones in virtually all spheres.

Table 6.4 *Productivity, labour costs and profits in industrial enterprises, by size (annual average rates of growth), Italy, 1974–84*[1]

	Small and medium-sized (20–100 employees)			Large (more than 200 employees)		
	1974–7	1978–80	1981–4	1974–7	1978–80	1981–4
Labour productivity[2]	3.2	5.6	3.4	1.7	3.6	7.2
Labour income per employee[3]						
Nominal	25.6	19.3	16.9	21.3	16.5	15.9
Real[4]	6.9	2.8	1.8	3.0	0.4	0.5
Unit labour costs[5]						
Nominal	21.7	13.0	13.1	18.9	12.3	7.7
Implicit value-added deflator[6]	19.9	15.9	13.8	18.9	13.5	10.7
Profits						
Real value[7]	– 1.0	10.8	6.2	1.4	2.5	5.5
Percentage of value-added (average percentage value)	32.1	34.0	36.8	24.5	25.6	30.2

Source: Banca d'Italia, 1987: 45
[1] Compound growth rates. [2] Value-added per employee at 1980 prices. [3] Labour income equals wages and salaries plus employers' social security contributions, appropriations for redundancy payments, pensions, and so on. [4] Deflated using the general retail price index. [5] Labour costs per unit of output, expressed as a ratio between labour income and value-added at 1980 prices. [6] Calculated from the national account deflators of value-added. [7] Adjusted using the implicit price deflator of gross fixed investment.

2 The evolution of industrial relations

2.1 *Industrial relations and politics*

The relations between business and labour on the one hand and the political–institutional system on the other intensified progressively throughout the early 1980s in Italy, owing primarily to the universally perceived need to take effective action in three main problem areas. There was, first, the decisive, but not sufficient, role of government initiative in 'regulating' the Italian economy and productive base as a function of the state of the world economy. Secondly, there was the direct management by the public sector of an increasing share of overall output and its ever more decisive role in determining income distribution. Thirdly, as the social and cultural upheavals generated by the persistent state of economic crisis accelerated, the 'internal' consensus of business and labour organizations proved more and more clearly insufficient to establish and run a stable system of industrial relations.

Even more than in the 1970s, then, the interlinkage between

industrial relations and the government and political system emerged in a variety of contexts and forms and with multiple issues of substance. The most significant developments came in two spheres: first, centralized, tripartite concertation of economic and social policy measures; and second, the changing nature of institutional conflict mediation.

2.1.1   Concertation and economic and social policy   The involvement of the unions in centralized political bargaining took place in three relatively distinct phases.

The first, from the autumn of 1979 to the end of 1982, consisted in a long, discontinuous and fruitless negotiating effort at the central level between government, business and labour, intended to devise a hypothetical 'anti-inflation pact'. The five different cabinets that came to power one after another in rapid succession during these three years took the initiative in the negotiation, putting heavier and heavier pressure on employers and unions to get their consensus – and consistent behaviour – with respect to various macroeconomic policies aimed at disinflation. This course of events was also favoured by the role assumed by the employers, as is shown for instance by Confindustria's disavowal of the 1975 agreement on the *scala mobile* in June 1982. This was a decisive step in the politicization of collective bargaining.

The unions, by contrast, confronted this phase both unsure about objectives and internally divided. Assessments of the earlier experience of concertation during the 'national unity' governments were divergent and controversial, and this weighed both on inter-union relations and on the relationship between leadership and rank and file. Another important factor was the establishment of a system of governing alliances with the Communist Party in opposition.

In this situation, agreement on the proper policy initiatives, though required by the worsening economic crisis and the narrowing of the scope for collective bargaining solutions, was increasingly difficult. And each time it required laborious talks between the various union confederations, which ultimately, especially when rank-and-file ratification was needed, created a climate of tension and ambiguity.

The second phase ran from the start of 1983 to the summer of 1985. It saw an attempt to install the first formal arrangements for the practice of centralized concertation to make possible the success of the government's macroeconomic policy course in an explicit, mutually agreed incomes policy framework.

In January 1983 government, unions and employer associations signed an agreement that unexpectedly brought the long-drawn-out negotiations of the previous phase to a successful conclusion. The agreement focussed on short-term anti-inflationary measures, and in particular the curbing of labour costs. But it also set forth a good number of other areas for action, some of them involving medium- to long-term implementation and requiring the continuation of concertation and its extension to other levels. Finally, the agreement ended the impasse in bargaining for the renewal of contracts in the major industries, which had been stalled for months.

A new stage in political negotiations opened towards the end of 1983, but by now the climate of relations between business and labour had been profoundly transformed and embittered. A fierce dispute over the interpretation of the 22 January agreement had arisen (the employers refusing to pay accumulated fractions of points in the rise of the cost-of-living index). The unions too had ample grounds for dissatisfaction, both in the government's slowness in carrying out its obligations under the agreement and in the steady worsening of the employment picture.

The public sector interlocutor for business and labour at this time was a new coalition government – the first headed by a Socialist Prime Minister since the Second World War – formed following early elections in June 1983, which was resolved to pursue the incomes policy experiment that had just got under way, but equally resolved to take all necessary measures to ensure 'governability'.

The negotiations still centred on disinflation and economic recovery, and this time they were concluded, in February 1984, after a comparatively brief period of bilateral talks, with a 'protocol of understanding' which the Prime Minister presented to business and labour and which was potentially legally binding. Though covering roughly the same terrain as the 1983 agreement, the new protocol was distinctive both in the more highly specified diversification of actions and some new operative ideas (the legislative 'predetermination' of *scala mobile* points and a one-year freeze on indexed increases on housing rents) and in its more markedly unequal impact on business and on labour.

The opposition of the Communist majority of the CGIL, the largest union confederation, prevented the protocol, which was agreed to by all the other union components and employer associations, from being converted into another formal agreement between the two sides in industry. Thus the government decided to enact the main points of the protocol immediately as decree-laws.

This anomalous conclusion to the second phase of political

bargaining had a complicated series of consequences both within and outside industrial relations. First, it caused the definitive rupture of the united CGIL–CISL–UIL federation, with high tension in the factories and public demonstrations organized mainly by Communist militants and supported by the majority of the CGIL.

Moreover, the subsequent months saw a long, paralysing parliamentary dispute between government and opposition, the opposition's objective – pursued not entirely without success – being to block the passage of the legislation implementing the protocol in its full version, and in particular to prevent the so-called 'cut' in *scala mobile* points. Later, with the passage of the decree legislation, this clash would shift to another terrain, namely a popular referendum for its abrogation. The referendum, called at the initiative of the PCI and held in June 1985 in a climate of acute tension between the two political–union alignments, resulted in definitive defeat for the Communist position, 54.4 per cent voting 'No'. At the same time it helped restore the conditions for a return to independent industrial relations practices at the central level, which could thus be detached from the internal dynamics of the political system.

The third phase, which began in mid-1985 immediately following the referendum, did register major agreements between government and unions and employer organizations on economic and social policy measures, but it also saw a progressive contraction of the role of political bargaining. This was due, more than anything else, to the steady, substantial improvement in all the main indicators of economic health and output – except for the employment picture – which forced each of the actors to revise its strategies. Each took advantage of the new manoeuvring room to improve the balance between costs and benefits in its bargaining activity at all levels. A part was unquestionably also played, however, by such 'subjective' factors as the need to consolidate the unity of action among the union confederations that had resumed following the referendum, burgeoning disengagement from the political arena by many entrepreneurs, and the activism and stability of the Socialist-headed government.

Thus the resumption of political bargaining in the autumn entailed the establishment of separate negotiating tables for the encounter between business and labour, while the main unresolved questions were still those raised in the previous phase, whose solution continued to demand, in practice, simultaneous commitments by all sides, including government.

When the talks between unions and employers reached an impasse, once more it was the government that, with a surprise move, broke the deadlock. As the employer of millions of workers in the civil service – hence in a strictly collective bargaining role – the government signed an agreement with the three confederations in December 1985 that, among other provisions, laid down a new wage-indexation system. Within a few weeks, under pressure from the government, the private employer associations agreed to the public sector solution, thus opening the way to the passage of the 'fiscal compensation' measures that were eventually agreed. Meanwhile, special legislation extended the agreement to cover all working people.

The definitive conclusion of the entire dispute over the *scala mobile*, however, was not reached until some months later, after further direct negotiations between the unions and Confindustria. The May 1986 agreement, which included a significant provision to foster youth employment, was the first truly bilateral pact in about a decade. The problem of wage reform thus settled, talks between government, business and labour continued more fragmentarily and irregularly over succeeding months, although they remained virtually concertative on a number of issues. Nevertheless, it was evident that political bargaining had lost its role as the catalyst, the central element in industrial relations.

It is anything but simple to draw up a detailed list of the individual measures taken in the 1980s as the 'output' of more or less formal concertation between government, unions and employer organizations. For our purposes, it will suffice to relate the actions taken on three major themes: the cost of labour and inflation; employment and the regulation of the labour market; and the control of social and welfare spending.

The objective of curbing the rise in the cost of labour was unquestionably the one most heavily emphasized in these years by employers and by government. The unions, for their part, while accepting the top priority for disinflation in the negotiations, sought constantly to reconcile labour-cost measures with the defence of real wages.

If at the start of the decade the administration only asked business and labour organizations to observe programmed inflation 'ceilings', the main issue soon became the desensitization of Italy's widespread indexation mechanism, first and foremost the *scala mobile*.[2] The January 1983 agreement did not alter the fundamental elements of the wage indexation system that had been in effect since 1975 – namely, quarterly adjustments and equal across-the-board rises for all employees, regardless of salary or rank. It did, however, make a substantial change – a 15 per cent reduction – in the size of the cost-of-living adjustment for each one-point (adjusted) rise in the price index.

Over the next year, the goal of further moderating automatic wage increases was pursued without any formal change in the indexation machinery, but simply setting, in advance, a ceiling on the number of *scala mobile* points that would be recognized, in accordance with the planned inflation rate.

The December 1985 agreement between government and unions – later extended to the entire economy by law – radically modified the very structure of the *scala mobile*; it also changed wage adjustments from quarterly to semi-annual. The new cost-of-living mechanism abandoned the old, strongly egalitarian absolute figure system in favour of a percentage-based one depending on earnings brackets; and it further decreased the average degree of coverage provided by indexation.

Concerted action to curb labour costs was also furthered by other major initiatives, which were often straight bilateral agreements (in form) or even simple administrative decisions, but which were nonetheless considered by all participants to be integral parts of the tripartite negotiations. The issue of social security tax relief for employers, for instance, was crucial to every successive stage of the centralized, tripartite talks. And while the size of the 'discounts' granted in this sphere may have been alternatively raised and lowered, no year passed without an extension of the programme in time or its enlargement to additional beneficiaries.[3]

On the union side, the concern to defend real wages as automatic indexation was progressively reduced led to repeated negotiations aimed at income-tax reform or readjustment in parallel with those on reducing labour costs; comparatively significant results in this sphere were achieved in 1983 and 1986.

Finally, the successive stages of the tripartite negotiations also comprised commitments to curb price increases as well. Specific procedures for doing so, however, were devised only where the legislative or institutional tools already existed, as in the case of public service tariffs and so-called 'regulated' prices. A significant measure, in this framework, was the decision, incorporated in the protocol of understanding of February 1984, to suspend index-linked rent increases on rent-controlled apartments (theoretically, all rented apartments).

In the early 1980s, employment issues were only fragmentarily included in tripartite negotiations, and their handling was largely shaped by an 'emergency' outlook. Indeed, most actions focused on employment crises connected with industrial restructuring, especially that of large corporations. There was a substantial body of legislation (sometimes clearly designed to aid particular firms in

Table 6.5 *Coverage of new employment contract forms,*
Italy, 1984-6

No. of workers	1984	1985	1986
Solidarity contracts		11,640	7,663
Trainee contracts	32,600	108,434	229,384
Part-time (new)	51,000	111,198	108,105
Part-time (formerly full-time)		24,805	27,867

Source: Ministero del Bilancio e della Programmazione Economica and Ministero del Tesoro, 1986

trouble) both to extend the applicability of CIG and to provide new subsidies for early retirement plans.

The agreement of January 1983 signalled a new stage, marked by a series of measures instituting an effective 'active labour policy'. Various though the commitments embodied in the accord were, three major areas for action are identifiable: a special programme for the south; a more active employment contribution on the part of the government sector; and a number of projects for youth employment. The proposal of a Solidarity Fund for employment, on the model of the one suggested several months earlier by the unions, was also part of the overall employment approach.[4]

This set of commitments, reaffirmed and spelled out in greater detail by the February 1984 protocol, generated a vast array of legislative and administrative measures over the next three years whose individual importance was accentuated in many cases by supplementary bilateral accord between employers and unions. Certainly among the most innovative measures were those permitting and regulating employment contracts different from the standard, full-time contract: 'solidarity contracts' (shorter hours with reduced pay, either to prevent redundancies or to foster new hiring); 'trainee contracts' (temporary hiring of young people under thirty, for training purposes, at entry-level salaries lower than the union minimum, and at the employer's discretion, that is not bound by the government employment agency rankings); and part-time work (which was regulated in terms of interchangeability with full-time employment). These measures very quickly produced significant, though unequal, employment effects, as Table 6.5 shows. Other new regulations also enhanced the flexibility of the labour market.

Finally, in the area of job creation proper, a number of truly innovative measures were enacted in 1985 and the first half of 1986 to implement the clauses of the 1984 protocol concerning public sector hiring and development of the South. This confirms that political bargaining has proved productive in job terms as well, albeit only after a considerable delay.

Although the progress of political negotiations was repeatedly interrupted by unresolved problems connected with social policy, the substance of the tripartite agreements touched on those issues only indirectly. The direct encounter between government and unions – which was certainly much more significant in this regard than the tripartite talks – was nonetheless more selective and pragmatic than in the past. In practice, the new approach focussed on curbing social spending rather than trying to improve the quality of public services. Where income redistribution proper was concerned, the bilateral talks touched only intermittently on problems of security and fairness.

At the same time, the operative implementation of government agreements with business and labour was more and more heavily modified in the course of parliamentary passage of the relevant legislation, even though Parliament's amendments, owing to the absence of a clear, shared outlook for reform on many issues, were often contradictory. In the end, this heightened the tension in the confrontation between employers and unions and helped produce major inconsistencies in the outcome of the negotiations themselves.

A significant example is the story of pension reform measures. In the first three years of the decade, a series of measures were enacted, all in one way or another increasing either the number of beneficiaries or the size of pension benefits. The result was a widening divergence between the revenues and the expenditures of INPS (Istituto Nazionale della Previdenza Sociale), National Institute for Social Security. Starting in 1983, however, faced with the system's worsening financial troubles, the union confederations agreed to austerity measures on pensions. It was thus decided to toughen disability pension eligibility standards.[5] The pension advantages enjoyed by women civil servants (eligible to become so-called 'baby pensioners') were abolished. And the Finance Act for 1984 radically revised the automatic cost-of-living adjustment of all pensions.

Even during these years, however, some measures enlarging pension outlays were taken, such as the extension of the early-retirement provisions to specified troubled industries (mining, publishing, docks, steel) and, following union pressure, increases for some types of pensioners. In 1986, moreover, six-monthly cost-of-living adjustments to pensions were restored, just two years after they had been made annual.

This legislative and negotiating pattern was largely duplicated in the other spheres of social policy. In the case of health, as serious problems of efficiency and health-care quality arose in connection with the inception of the National Health Service,[6] the early 1980s witnessed ballooning health outlays. To deal with this problem, which was attributed chiefly to increased demand for health services, successive governments concentrated mainly, on the expenditure side, on monetary disincentives based on prescription charges.[7] Obviously, such a policy repeatedly ran into vigorous union opposition. The story of the family allowance payments was somewhat different, in that the talks between government and unions focussed not primarily on cutting expenditure but on revising the income redistribution role played by these benefits in the framework of welfare policy. The egalitarian reforms of the 1970s and the failure to index these benefits meant that the family allowance had gradually lost virtually all importance as a household income supplement. The reform, enacted in 1984 but anticipated in part in the tripartite agreement of 1983, completely revised the eligibility rules and payment procedures. It also introduced means testing for the 'base' allowance, with different thresholds depending on the number of dependants.

Following the introduction of significant adjustments in threshold income levels by the Finance Act for 1986, however, it became apparent that if on the whole the new regulations were having a perceptible redistributory impact in favour of the less affluent single-income households, it had also radically reduced the number of family allowance beneficiaries. The need to put this situation to rights – it was seen as especially unsatisfactory for wage-earners and pensioners – thus became one of the central issues in union–government negotiations in the autumn of 1986, and the agreement reached provided for a very substantial rise in the threshold levels for means testing that had been set just months earlier.

2.1.2 Institutional initiatives and conflict mediation As noted, the involvement of Italian employer and labour organizations in the political arena in the 1980s consisted principally in a series of negotiations around the main issues of economic and social policy. In practice, these talks entailed the participation of government institutions as one 'party' to the many-faceted interaction among private and public interests. At the same time, however, and sometimes tightly interwoven with this negotiating role, the function of the state as industrial conflict-mediator also expanded and changed. The most significant aspects of this development were, first, the systematic prevalence of the political over the technical dimension in mediation; second, against this backdrop, the large-scale decentralization of mediating forums; and third, the use of new 'techniques' and instruments of mediation.

The model of dispute settlement that gained currency in the aftermath of the 'hot autumn' of 1969 and strengthened throughout the 1970s involved the intervention of public authority to mediate and resolve major industrial disputes on the basis of its own solutions, which were often felt to be inequitable, or at least not to the liking of one side or the other. The 1980s saw a further extension of this tendency concomitant with the new issues brought into industrial conflict by the recession (specifically, redundancies and reductions in manning levels, and the narrowing of the scope for effective bargaining on economic issues) and with the emergence of a specific government interest in broadening the conflict-prevention function itself to avoid jeopardizing economic policy goals.

The effect and embodiment of the spread of political mediation was the progressive decentralization of the institutional forums of mediation. This occurred first at the ministerial level, where efforts to settle industrial disputes now involved a good number of other departments, alongside the competent technical–institutional body, the Ministry of Labour. As a rule, the situations in which this kind of decentralization took place were of two types. First were the most seriously troubled firms, often burdened with problems of restructuring common to an entire crisis-struck industry. This covers the bulk of mediation efforts by the Ministry for State-Controlled Companies and the Ministry of Industry. The second type consisted in mediation in industrial disputes involving spheres or groups of personnel falling within the 'jurisdiction' of the individual ministries.

The decentralization of public mediation activities also affected local levels of governmental authority. The studies available indicate that the shift from the technical forums (the provincial and regional labour offices) to more properly political forums (local and regional governments) almost always came in conjunction with grave market or financial crises affecting firms in the area and carrying a potentially massive threat to local employment. Rarely, however, did regional mediation prove conclusive. It turned out to be only a step – albeit a significant one – in the settlement of the dispute, whose final resolution was reached either at local government level (where the mediation efforts were almost always launched) or at ministerial level.

The increasing politicization of government mediation activities also affected the 'techniques' and instruments for the settlement of disputes used by public authority. A multiplicity of responses was offered to the employment problems posed by corporate restructuring and financial ills. They included the simple extension of CIG benefits in time; the revocation of dismissals, converting them into lay-offs, and subsequent recourse to CIG (First in 1980, Montedison in 1981); the dispensation of special *ad hoc* assistance in the framework of sectoral policy (Telefunken); the employment of redundant manpower by the formation of new companies (the Zanussi–GEPI affair in 1981); the extension to specified industries of early-retirement legislation (the most important case being that of the steel industry in 1984). In the worst cases, the Ministry drew up actual industrial salvage plans, with the intervention of banking consortia on the one hand and pools of companies on the other (the most recent case was that of Indesit in 1985).

Finally, with a view to more active involvement of business and labour in conflict-prevention, the government has made ample use during the 1980s of the 'Committee' formula.[8] In a number of different cases, committees have been formed and given a primarily informational mandate, although often the proposals ultimately made by these expert working-parties have substantially influenced the subsequent negotiating stances of the two sides.

2.2 Processes and results of industrial relations

2.2.1 Real wage trends The figures supplied by the *Relazione generale sulla situazione economica del paese* (issued annually by the Ministry of Budget and the Treasury) show that on average real wages in Italy have essentially maintained their level in the course of the 1980s. This is the end result of contrasting tendencies both from year to year and between sectors.[9]

The strategy pursued by Italian unions in the 1980s has often been described as if a single part were the whole – namely, an exclusive effort to defend the earnings of industrial workers. True enough, the constant rise in the real earnings of all employees in industry (an annual average rise of 0.9 per cent in 1981–5) is the result of rising wages for blue-collar workers (+ 1.28 per cent) and a significant decline for white-collar workers (− 0.64 per cent), although the latter began from a higher level. There are other sectors, however, with even higher average annual wage increases: agriculture (+ 1.74 per cent), the distributive trades (+ 1.24 per cent), and the civil service (+ 1.62 per cent). The least advantaged sectors were transport and communications (+ 0.42 per cent per year, 1981–5) and banking and insurance (– 0.18 per cent). Here again, however, the starting pay levels were higher.

Moreover, these figures must be treated with extreme caution in establishing a ranking of gains (or losses) by sector. For the data, provided by Istat, do not include rises won in bargaining at the company level, which was especially vigorous towards the end of the period and perhaps earlier as well, though less overtly and explicitly.

No analysis of overall wage trends in Italy in the 1980s can ignore the chief innovation of these years, namely the return to wider wage differentials, both between industries and between firms in the same industry, produced by the restoration of differentials in industry-wide contracts and company policies to reverse the wage levelling of the 1970s. Obviously, this trend was accentuated by the modification of the *scala mobile* in the central agreements of 1983 and 1984. Even more significant in this regard was the December 1985 agreement covering all civil service employees, which radically reformed the wage-indexation system. This reform was later extended to the rest of the economy by law. In 1982, for instance, of overall gross wage increases of 16.7 per cent, the cost-of-living allowance amounted to 14.5 per cent, leaving just 2.2 per cent for increases not provided by the *scala mobile*. A study by Centro Europa Ricerche (1985) found that thanks to the cut of four *scala mobile* points in 1984, in that year indexation accounted for only 40 per cent of overall wage growth, as against 60 per cent in the years following the 1975 agreement that established the system.

According to the *Relazione generale*, the renewed spread of intersectoral salary differentials worked to the advantage of public sector employees as against the private sector. If we treat the average earnings of employees, economy-wide, as equal to 100, the wages of employees in industry slip from 104.3 in 1980 to 100.8 in 1984, while those of civil servants rise from 104.9 to 113.3. This constituted a sharp recovery for the latter from the equalizing trends of the 1970s, and it has continued with the latest civil service contract renewals.

After the reform of the *scala mobile*, industry-wide contracts showed a stronger tendency to increase pay differentials by rank. Now, the dominant approach is to reward higher skill levels and the new skills required by changes in technology, production processes and work organization, in sharp contrast to the previous strategy of egalitarianism and wage-levelling. The nationwide contracts in industry, renewed in 1986 a considerable time after their expiry, widened the base pay spectrum substantially in printing and publishing from 100–200 to 100–225 and less substantially in the private chemical industry and in textiles, while the spread in public and private engineering remained unaltered (100–200). Another instrument for making pay structures more flexible is the recognition of 'managers and technicians' with a special bonus (outside the regular pay scale).

The revision of the base pay scales was much more substantial in the state sector: for civil servants, from 100–233 to 100–323; for semi-governmental agencies, from 100–262 to 100–342; for the school system, from 100–213 to 100–260 (Ufficio Studio delle Relazioni Industriali SIP, 1987). The state sector also saw such innovations as the suspension of seniority rises, in anticipation of a thorough restructuring of this wage component; the institution of a productivity incentive fund; and provision for higher career levels.

Recently, wage drift has been accentuated by the new company salary policies, by bargaining at company level, and by the change in the structure of employment, as has been shown by a number of studies sponsored by the Industrialists Association of Lombardy and by ASAP, the public petrochemical employers' association (see for example ASAP, 1987).

ASAP in particular notes an acceleration of wage-drift in 1986, especially for white-collar workers and the higher grades, but also for blue-collar workers. This is a sign of a return to management practices of incentives and individual wage determination. It can thus be predicted that in the last few years of this decade the scope for salary increases, generated in part by productivity gains, will be the object of intensifying competition, more or less aggressive, between company-level collective bargaining and direct dealings between management and individual employees.

2.2.2 Employment and working hours Virtually all the bargaining platforms drafted by Italian unions for industry-wide contract renewals in the late 1970s included the demand for a generalized shortening of the working week. More than as a means to preserve jobs, this demand seemed originally intended as a way to improve the quality of working life and to give working people more free time. Only during the 1980s did this demand become a pressing one, as in other countries, in relation to the problem of structural unemployment, changes in the makeup of the labour force and in the organization of work (Treu, 1986b).

The serious economic troubles of Italian industry in the early 1980s forced a moderation of the demand for a shorter working week, owing in part to vigorous employer opposition. In the platform drafted late in 1981 the goal of a thirty-five-hour week was reaffirmed by the metal and engineering union, but it was now to be achieved in diversified fashion and gradually over successive contracts. In the event, even the forty-hour reduction in annual working time called for by the contract in 1982 was suspended, because of the industry's troubles. Only printers at daily newspapers achieved the thirty-five-hour week. Elsewhere, except for industries with continuous production processes (steel, chemicals, paper) and those in which new formulae were established (six six-hour days in the textile industry, for instance), the forty-hour barrier was not broken even in the contract renewals of 1983.

The idea of a generalized or industry-wide shortening of the working week thus having run aground, in the years that followed the question of working hours was increasingly dealt with, as the economic situation improved, either at the macroeconomic level or at the company level. Industry-wide bargaining was more and more commonly oriented to annual hours-reduction packages or to the implementation of the forty-hour reduction in yearly work hours called for by the agreement of 22 January 1983 for the second half of 1984 and the first half of 1985.

In company-level bargaining, working hours have been the most commonly negotiated item since 1984. Union representatives have now agreed to concede, in exchange for shorter hours, the types of flexibility particularly requested by management. This trade-off has been made most notably in mass merchandising chains and supermarkets (GS, Esselunga, Rinascente). But it has also developed in textile firms, in connection with flexi-time and part-time, and in chemicals, over the question of shifts and the distribution of working time. Pragmatically, in these cases the unions have agreed to concur in flexibility practices, not only because this creates fewer problems than would a reduction in wages, but also because it offers the opportunity for a significant monitoring role over work schedules, bargaining on annual working hours, flexi-time periods, part-time, the introduction or extension of shift work, the application of the reductions in the working week – all crucial in a time of rapid technological and productive change.

The improved state of the economy in recent years has again spurred Italian unions to demand a substantial shortening of working hours, inspired partly by the momentum of the major agreement in the civil service sector in December 1985. This accord lays down the standardization of the working week in the entire public sector at thirty-six hours, with decentralized, diversified programming of hours and flexibility, shifts, the off-premises availability of employees, part-time and temporary employment, a limit to overtime, and the earmarking of a substantial portion of turnover for part-time jobs. The objective, more realistic now than in the past, is to make conditions within each category uniform, by means of annual or weekly hours-reductions. And this objective was also endorsed by the nationwide business–labour agreement of 8 May 1986, calling for hours-reduction plans adapted to the specific situation of each industry, that is consistent with the need for competitiveness, flexibility and plant utilization.

At the industry level, however, employer opposition soon arose, based mainly on the fact that the reduction in labour costs would be smaller, proportionally, than the reduction in hours and a fear of conceding a competitive advantage to other countries. In the nationwide contract renewals in 1986 only the textile unions won substantial agreement to their bargaining demands (an annual reduction of fifty-six hours for day-labourers and fifty-two hours for those working in teams). In other industries, demands for shorter hours won only very minimal acceptance: half the reduction demanded by the engineering and chemical unions (sixteen as against thirty-two hours yearly); a third in printing and paper (twenty-six hours and forty minutes instead of ninety hours). There was less trouble with extension of flexibility, specifically part-time work and work schedules in which the working week is conceived of as an average that can be achieved over a number of weeks or even the entire working year. But flexi-time, which fits the needs of individual workers better, is still restricted to the civil service.

On the whole, then, Italian employers, even at a time of economic expansion like that during the 1986 bargaining round, have proved more willing to offer wage increases than a shortening of work hours.

2.2.3 Industrial restructuring and work flexibility Italian industrial restructuring accelerated noticeably in the 1980s. Automation and computer-controlled production processes, robots, CAD–CAM, numerically controlled machines and so on were progressively incorporated into the new production models based on flexible systems, with integrated design, manufacture and marketing of products. Two kinds of firm capable of responding successfully to external market and technological upheavals seem to have emerged in Italy. First, there is the transformation of the large corporations, which as in other Western countries has deverticalized and adopted new management strategies, agreed to a greater or lesser extent with the various social actors involved, to enhance the flexibility of corporate structures and of the employment of capital and labour resources. Thus Fiat, Montedison,

Olivetti, Pirelli, Italtel, Dalmine, SIP and many other large Italian firms, in all sectors of industry and the services, have weathered the crisis of the 1970s to achieve corporate growth and success in the international arena despite fiercer competition.

Second, there is the extraordinary success of small enterprises in certain industrial areas of what has been dubbed the 'third Italy' (Carpi, Prato, Ancona and so on). They have succeeded in launching a 'flexible specialization' based on constant innovation, versatile technology, skilled labour and local governments interested in the creation of true 'industrial communities' (Piore and Sabel, 1984).

There was a shift in union strategy itself, marked by greater attention to measures to protect jobs and bargaining on restructuring and flexibility, in contrast to a strategy in the 1970s that had aimed chiefly at 'opposing the capitalistic organization of production'. Very likely the unions' relative inability to control or monitor the substance of restructuring stemmed in part from the essential failure of Law 675/1977 on industrial conversion (which had been passed thanks to union pressure), and the ineffectiveness of a number of tools for union participation, such as the CGIL's 'company plan' and the 'solidarity fund' proposed by the CISL. This was all the more so since the recession had shifted the balance of strength in favour of management, whose initiative required a certain deregulation both internally and externally. The start of the new decade dramatically signalled this shift with the defeat of the metalworkers' unions at Fiat in October 1980 (after the so-called 'march of 40,000' supervisory and managerial personnel who opposed the continuation of the all-out strike). And the engineering employers' association, Federmeccanica, assumed a rigid position, denying any and all union involvement in technological restructuring and maintaining at a Florence conference on 'Men and Machines' in June 1981 that the organization of production was 'not negotiable'.

This ideological conflict on the management of restructuring and innovation was much more common at the macro level, between confederations, industrial unions and associations, than at the company level. From 1983–4 on, one begins to see signs at just this micro level of more pragmatic attitudes in bargaining over industrial change and labour flexibility. Agreements of technological innovation are still found mainly in the mass-production industries based on blue-collar labour, not the services, public employment or white-collar employees in industry, as a 1982 survey by the European Trade Union Institute found, citing this as a peculiar feature of Italy. However, there were also innovative agreements, rapidly increasing in number, concerning work at video terminals, in the pharmaceuticals industry and in banking and insurance, on new integrated technology in publishing (Biliotti and Della Rocca, 1986). In some companies, such as Italtel, Montedison and Pirelli, the management strategy and industrial policy itself was the object of discussion, and of bargaining with the unions. In the industrial districts of central and north-eastern Italy, local governments were also involved in such negotiations, offering resources and having the power to prevent unfair competition between small firms.

Almost everywhere, the unions accept bargaining over labour flexibility, if not as a proper 'programming strategy' (as proclaimed in a conference sponsored by the CGIL's research institute in 1982), at least as a pragmatic way to take part in the industrial recovery and gain renewed recognition from management. For it was in fact management which made explicit demands on the unions in this sphere in order to achieve its array of objectives: adaptation to market fluctuations, higher plant utilization, improvement of quality, greater productivity, optimal introduction of new technology, and the linking of earnings to performance and skills. All this required greater labour flexibility in terms of hours, tasks, mobility, employment contracts, turnover and wage incentives. More than a trade-off between labour flexibility and jobs, what was introduced was a significant degree of union control of the deregulation requests made by employers – or, more accurately, the sort of utterly unilateral management control of the process that has occurred in other countries was avoided.

2.2.4 Bargaining and participation The Italian industrial relations system is still based primarily on collective bargaining. In the early 1980s the new tripartite talks between unions, employer organizations and government on inflation, the cost of labour and related income-distribution matters seemed to hold out the prospect of new types of regulation. On the morrow of the agreement of 22 January 1983, many observers believed and stated that Italy too was finally moving towards a neo-corporatist, or at any rate a more strongly institutionalized, system of industrial relations. But this did not happen. The main reason was that the agreement itself, except for a few matters relating to industrial conflict and bargaining, made no provision for more formal industrial relations procedures at the central level (Santi, 1985).

Still less did the central-level agreements of 1984 and 1986 diverge from the established framework of industrial relations. The main innovations came at the micro level, in individual companies, but always in the framework of collective bargaining, not via legislation. These were all experiences that enlarged the sphere of union rights to information and to consultation that have been a feature of the industry and branch contracts since 1976–7. Most significantly, firms that must engage in lengthy programmes of recovery, restructuring and renewed productive expansion have taken advantage of the opportunity to involve unions and workers in the pursuit of company objectives in exchange for a limitation of management prerogatives in personnel management. In some cases, joint committees have been formed, at the group or company level, for consultation on specific issues: work organization, vocational training, affirmative actions. The committees' recommendations are not formally binding, but they often work in practice as if they were, in that agreement on certain issues is often transcribed into the contract. In other cases an *ad hoc* joint committee is brought into being informally, not by written agreement, to deal with a specific problem, such as the geographical mobility of employees or personnel job classifications, or yet again the effect of new technology on work organization.

This development entailed changes in the scope and nature of union representation and activity. Based in Italy on a single-channel method, representation now developed a 'technical' function, performed by members of the joint committees at company level, and also a territorial role, which sometimes clashes with the traditional 'political' role of the unions owing to mutual incomprehension or material incompatibility between the consultative role and the bargaining/conflictual one.

The introduction, by contract, of new procedures has been quite common in Italy during the course of the decade. In July 1984, for example, government, employers and unions signed a protocol on a new bargaining code and self-regulation of the right to strike in public transport. An agreement between IRI (the state Institute for Industrial Reconstruction), and the unions in December 1984 concluded negotiations that had lasted two years and offered some formal institutionalization of the practices, cited above, that had arisen at the company level in the wake of the new information rights, as well as embracing the new contract principles incorporated in the tripartite agreements of 1983 and 1984. It established a series of committees and procedures for sectoral, company and local consultation; instruments for an affirmative employment policy; procedures and negotiating forums to prevent company-level strikes or keep them from spreading. The new bilateral committees for information and consultation must assess and give a compulsory, but not binding, opinion on the industrial policy objectives, development and restructuring orientations of the group's firms in various industries, and on the management of human resources. They remain, however, a forum for technical expertise, with functions distinct from the union and management bodies that wield final decision-making authority.

The civil service agreement in December 1985 also strengthened the institutionalization of industrial relations by according broader information rights at the local level and enhancing the participation and consultation of workers and the unions during the introduction of new information technology.

Finally, all the nationwide industry contracts renewed in 1986 embody the substance of the IRI and civil service agreements and extend them organically to their respective industries. Some broaden and diversify information rights (tourist industry, banking, petroleum); some constitute sectoral and territorial observers, run jointly by employer associations and unions, on new technologies, the labour market, training and hours (private metal and engineering industries, private chemicals, textiles), some create joint committees at various levels for joint assessment and consultation on firms' industrial plans, the employment impact, and the technological consequences (public metal and engineering, public chemicals, the distributive trades).

3 Bargaining levels

Collective bargaining in Italy has historically been bipolar. From the 1960s to the mid-1970s the main loci of bargaining were the national industry-wide level and the company level; since 1975, the confederal (that is, national inter-industry) level has come to replace the single-industry level as a key bargaining level. The reasons for this arrangement stem from Italy's uneven industrial structure and the character and behaviour of unions, employers and government.

As the 1980s got under way, it seemed as if the effort to achieve compatibility between industrial relations and the state of the economy, and the consequent narrowing of economic room for bargaining gains or concessions, would be bound to change this structure. Union activity focussed more and more heavily on the political arena, the prime forum for talks on the dynamics of wage growth and the management of the labour market.

In subsequent years, formal tripartite negotiations were abandoned altogether, while even bilateral negotiations, which finally produced a union–employer agreement only in May 1986, were marked by a steadily worsening informality that often prevented the control or even predictability of the bargaining process (Cella, 1986).

What seems to be emerging, then, is a tendency to end the centralization of Italian industrial relations, as has happened in other countries with conservative governments in power. Yet one must be cautious in offering such a judgement. True, the May 1986 agreement between Confindustria and CGIL–CISL–UIL paid less heed to macroeconomic matters than the centralized agreements of 1983 and 1984. And it is more adapted to the needs of individual firms, creating additional room for decentralized bargaining on wages and hours. However, the more flexible negotiating approach depends on the support, albeit indirect and informal, of the third, public actor, which continues to make available to the other two such indispensable resources as a curbing of fiscal drag, social security relief for employers and active employment policies.

Thus the decline of centralized industrial relations in Italy has not been an uncontrolled process, though it can certainly be said that since 1984 the decentralized company-level pole of bargaining has become predominant. Factors working for decentralization have been the recovery of the economy, technological innovation, the necessary diversification in line with divergent sectoral and company restructuring and renewed expansion of output, and the constant management request for labour flexibility, as well as the strengthening of management initiative in company-level industrial relations. Yet this bargaining decentralization did not take place in fragmented fashion, with the typical 'shop' action of the 'hot autumn' and its aftermath. The resumption of company-level bargaining was marked by a capacity to observe, as far as possible, the limits set at higher levels and by its orderly diversification within the firms themselves. The growing propensity for company-by-company bargaining is particularly striking, for the years 1984–6, in large engineering and food-processing firms (over 500 employees), but also in smaller firms in a context of industrial adjustment. The number of group or area-level company agreements is on the increase (from a sixth to a fifth of the total), while there has been a perceptible decline in shop or office-level accords.

All in all, then, though with some conflicting tendencies, the bipolar structure has been preserved in the 1980s, tilted more towards the centre in the early years, then moving more substantially toward the periphery. If these two trends, apparently conflicting, have paradoxically helped produce a more equal balance between the two poles, they have also speeded the waning of importance of the intermediate and industry levels.

However, this conclusion too, broadly shared by Italian labour-relations specialists, needs to be made less generic and summary. True enough, branch-level contracts have several times been renewed only after lengthy delays in the 1980s, and since 1979 bargaining at this level has been rigidly subordinated to centralized talks. Yet in the public sector the leading role of the services, especially the health service and the education system, emerged right from the start of the decade. The public service agreement of December 1985, while on the one hand making the bargaining and contract structure more rational in this sector, on the other relegated certain issues to lower bargaining levels: employment planning (shorter hours, part-time, turnover), flexible management of services (manning levels, work organization, mobility), productivity incentives (planning of objectives, earmarked financing).

In the distributive trades, private services, construction and agriculture, branch or industry-wide bargaining has also altered its role, from the exclusive concentration on contract demands that had marked it in the 1970s to a co-ordination of the new, decentralized levels. And this search for balance was a concern of employers and unions in manufacturing as well. Thus, despite the drawn-out renewal process, proposals to do away with industry-level bargaining have always aroused vehement opposition. The preferred idea is to convert these contracts from pacts covering categories of workers to agreements covering specific economic sectors. In part, this transformation has already been made. The purpose of the contracts would be to sift and standardize certain questions (hours, job classifications, wages, minimum worker rights and guarantees, supplementary pensions, industrial relations procedures, and so on). The more specific questions, especially those connected with productivity, are felt to be the proper sphere of company-level bargaining (Cella, 1986).

Equally important is the local level territorially. Here, tripartite institutions exist for dealing with labour-market issues, the impact of company restructuring, training and retraining. This level administers public funds for employment policies and the related flexibility of the local labour market. At first, up to 1983–4, action here eased the excessive incidence of central-level tripartite negotiations, and subsequently it attenuated the risk for unions entailed in bargaining decentralization, the diversification of industrial relations and labour flexibility (Treu, 1987). Moreover, the unions' presence in these local bodies gave them an otherwise unavailable means of monitoring and controlling the small firms dispersed throughout the regions, which offered the possibility of significant bargaining victories.

4   The actors

4.1   The state

Traditionally, the chief limits to the Italian state's action within industrial relations have been seen to be the low degree of institutionalization of relations between government and organized interest groups, scanty instruments for promoting collective bargaining contracts, and the lack of ability to enact reforms. Nor does this picture appear to have been altered by the way the state has intervened in collective bargaining during the 1980s.

The main feature of the years around the turn of the decade was the continuation, or better resumption, of the concertation that had begun in the later 1970s, transforming the government's role from the indirect one of spectator or referee to the more direct one of active mediator between business and labour. The experience of the national unity governments of 1976–8 had helped delineate the potential and the limitation of incomes-policy accords. The trade-off between wage moderation and public action on jobs, in a time of economic recession and rapid inflation, had worked to some extent, at least in curbing unemployment. But the unions' difficulty in guaranteeing continued moderate wage claims, together with the disappointing outcome of the legislation that had been 'contracted' for – on industrial restructuring, youth employment, vocational training and pensions – led to the collapse of this political bargaining. Some observers argued that this was due in part to the unions' growing awareness that they had overestimated the benefits of involvement in economic policy choices (Regini, 1983).

In the early 1980s the resumption of concertation came in an economic situation that had degenerated further in the interim. There was general agreement to abandon employment objectives for the moment as simply unrealizable, and to concentrate instead on lowering the inflation rate, which was viewed as indispensable for a return to economic growth. The agreement of 22 January 1983 specified that the success of this accord would depend on the amount of resources that the state would be able to provide.

The subsequent agreement, of 14 February 1984, also involved an exchange that was advantageous, in substance, to workers. The rejection of the accord by the Communist majority of the CGIL and its consequent implementation by decree, however, made any further resort to this explicit tripartite concertation out of the question. It thus failed even though the cost–benefit balance was not unfavourable to any of the three actors.

To understand the obstacles to an explicit policy of tripartite concertation in Italy, one must look at the characteristics of the political system. First, the exclusion of the party most representative of labour, the PCI, from a potential governing role. Second, the skewing between the political and the trade union representation of the workers, at once involved in political bargaining carried on by the unions and for the most part kept out of political decision-making. And third, consequently, the absence of any particular advantage for the PCI in participating in concertation practices, which worked much more to the benefits of the other parties (Baglioni, 1986).

According to some observers, political reasons extraneous to industrial relations proper are what lay behind the failure to achieve unanimous approval of the agreement of February 1984, in that the new Socialist-led government had actually exacerbated the divisions within the left and thus made more evident the skewing in the representation of workers' interests, making a rupture virtually inevitable (Cella, 1987).

Others, however, argue that the decline of concertation in Italy, which fits in relatively well with the broader European context, also stemmed from the inadequacy of the agreements themselves, in substance. In dealing with the governments of national solidarity, the unions offered wage moderation in exchange for future benefits, mainly in terms of jobs. In the 1980s, in a riskier context for the unions, because disinflation had been accepted by all sides as the priority objective in the agreements of 1983 and especially 1984, the revision of a key institution like the *scala mobile* assumed political significance, quite transcending its concrete economic effects, and in order to be accepted would have had to be compensated for with equally symbolic elements (Regini, 1985).

In practice, the government adapted itself to the new situation, which required lower-profile concertation practices. The state was there, but it could not show itself. Talks, formally, were bilateral, although the negotiating 'table' may have been 'laid by the government' (Baglioni, 1986). Yet the new objectives, that is the reform of the *scala mobile* and the shortening of working time, could hardly be attained without state intervention and state financial support. Indeed, for the *scala mobile*, which was more problematic due to its highly charged symbolic content and Confindustria's revocation of the 1975 pact, it was the government itself which signed its own 'separate pact' with the civil service unions in December 1985. And in the May 1986 agreement between national business and labour organizations, the first such bilateral accord since 1975, the 'independence' of dealings between the two actors was assured by the government commitment to introduce the new trainee employment contract.

The practice of concertation, then, has not totally disappeared in recent years; it has simply developed more pragmatic and flexible forms. Governments have been more careful to avoid the dangers of skewed representation for workers, while continuing to provide the resources (chiefly, correction for fiscal drag and social security relief) that are indispensable in the present phase of 'inconspicuous concertation' (Baglioni, 1986).

4.2   The employers

The number of associations representing Italian employers' interests is large, and actually rising of late. This multiplicity is due not so much to traditional ideological reasons as to such factors as type of ownership, firm size and industrial differentiation. Despite this diversity, however, Confindustria has retained the decisive role throughout this decade, most notably in its unilateral revocation of the *scala mobile* agreement. Confindustria's industrial relations strategy has shifted from the search for centralized tripartite agreements in the late 1970s and early 1980s to the more recent move towards decentralization and company-level bargaining. But this is only apparently contradictory, for actually businessmen's preference for the market as the main form of regulation is obvious. Political action is only a second-best solution, to be taken pragmatically when the economic and social conditions for the preferred market-place formula are lacking (Chiesi and Martinelli, 1987). From 1975 to 1984, Confindustria's main goal was to obtain for its members (among which Fiat, the largest private sector enterprise in Italy, naturally played a key co-ordinating role, with its Chairman of the board, Gianni Agnelli, acting as President of the association for several years) a curbing of both labour costs and industrial conflict. Through political bargaining it succeeded in attaining these objectives, with the revision of the *scala mobile*, social security relief and greater labour flexibility, without having to concede much of anything in return (Lange, 1987).

Like the other actors, employers have sought, in the implementation of concertation, to maximize their own advantage. A good instance is the refusal to pay accumulated fractions of *scala mobile* cost-of-living index points, on the pretext that the central agreement did not explicitly lay down that they must be paid. Yet paradoxically, it is precisely this highly utilitarian grasping of advantage that explains the sustained success of concertation in Italy. And this is what we really have to explain, because it is what distinguishes Italy from the rest of Europe – from France and Britain, where legislative decree and market-place prevail, as much as from Germany and Sweden, where concertation has had crises, albeit transient ones. The present Italian situation is not unlike that of the years of economic difficulty in the late 1940s or the mid-1960s. The recession over and firms successfully restructured, the market principle was restored to the centre of the employers' worldview. Beginning in conjunction with the economic recovery of 1984, then, Confindustria began to attack tripartite collective bargaining agreements, and the pressures for decentralization and flexibility in industrial relations gathered strength. There was also increasing employer opposition to any further government intervention, state action being viewed as too advantageous to the unions, which Confindustria felt were weaker on the market than on the political terrain (Treu, 1986a). This was no definitive neo-liberal detachment from all relations with the state, however, since such dealings were and are instrumental in obtaining some subsidy of the cost of labour and in gaining the improved flexibility of the labour market both centrally and locally. Nor was this strategy adopted without some internal dissent within Confindustria. Many people saw the breaking off of bilateral talks at the end of 1985 as a defeat for the unions at the hands of a groundswell of employer opinion that was increasingly hostile to centralized industrial relations. The Federmeccanica had been pushing this line for years, having issued a sort of 'manifesto' postulating the relegation of collective bargaining to a residual role with respect to the desired expansion of direct employer–employee relations.

Employer organizations for the chemical and textile industries sharply criticized this strategy, however. ASAP and the public employer association for the metal and engineering industries, Intersind, also showed a decided inclination to involve the unions, especially in dealing with the question of the *scala mobile*. The IRI group, by signing the protocol of agreement with the unions on joint consultative committees and on cooling-off procedures, actually counterposed a more participatory industrial relations model of its own to the unilateral approach taken by Fiat at the turn of the decade.

In practice, divergent styles in industrial relations management emerged among firms, and not just as between public and private corporations but even among the latter. The fact is that the economic recovery highlighted the existence of differentiated strategies at the association level depending on sector or industry, ownership structure and size. The diversification of firms' industrial relations strategies had been going on for some time, thanks to the increased competitiveness and turbulence of markets as well as to the differential impact of technological innovation on both processes and products (Negrelli, 1987).

Table 6.6   *Union membership, Italy, 1977–86*

	CGIL		CISL		UIL		Total	
	No.	%	No.	%	No.	%	No.	%
1977	4,490,105		2,809,802		1,160,089		8,459,996	
1978	4,527,962	0.8	2,868,737	2.1	1,284,716	10.7	8,681,415	2.6
1979	4,583,474	1.2	2,883,097	0.5	1,326,817	3.3	8,793,388	1.3
1980	4,599,050	0.3	3,059,845	6.1	1,346,900	1.5	9,005,795	2.4
1981	4,595,011	−0.1	2,988,813	−2.3	1,357,290	0.8	8,941,114	−0.7
1982	4,576,020	−0.4	2,976,880	−0.4	1,358,004	0.1	8,910,904	−0.3
1983	4,556,052	−0.4	2,953,411	−0.8	1,351,514	−0.5	8,860,977	−0.6
1984	4,546,335	−0.2	3,097,231	4.9	1,344,460	−0.5	8,988,026	1.4
1985	4,592,014	1.0	2,953,095	−4.7	1,306,250	−2.6	8,851,359	−1.5
1986	4,647,038	1.2	2,975,482	0.8	1,305,682	0.0	8,928,202	0.9
Change, 1977–86	156,933	3.5	165,680	5.9	145,593	12.6	468,206	5.5

Source: internal union data

4.3   The unions

One of the essential sources of Italian union strength in the post-war period has proved to be the prevailing organizational model, based on a combination of vertical (industrial) and horizontal (territorial) structures. If centralization and a very strong horizontal component in the early post-war period were signs of union weakness and political dependency, between 1968 and 1973 there was a progressive far-reaching shift of power and resources to the industrial structures. Recession brought this trend to a halt after 1975, providing more room for local and central forums.

All in all, the two dimensions appear to have bolstered one another in the course of the 1980s, well balanced and showing no signs of incompatibility. Thus the unions' response to Italian employers' recent drive for decentralization and flexibility could be an essential pragmatic adjustment. If the new tendency constitutes an objective challenge to the established union power that grew up in the 1970s, above all in the political arena, today the unions still have the power to bargain over the new management demands, obtaining in exchange the right to participate in decision-making at company level. One reason for this is that decentralization in Italy has not been an explicitly anti-union move, and the effort to install direct management–worker relations has been more preached than practised, except for the higher ranks of employee.

The indication of crisis for unions and union action in many industrial countries over the past decade, with the simultaneous decline in unionization and strike activity, are seen more modestly

Table 6.7 *Membership share of main union confederations,*
Italy, 1977–86 (%)

	CGIL	CISL	UIL	Total
1977	53.1	33.2	13.7	100.0
1986	52.0	33.3	14.6	100.0

in Italy. Unionization has remained at medium-to-high levels, as a result of the great successes of the 1970s and the public safety net provided by the 'Workers' Charter' (Law 300/1975), CIG, welfare measures in agriculture, and relations between charitable institutions and health and social security systems (see Table 6.6). Overall membership in the three principal confederations has actually increased slightly in the past decade, from 8,459,996 in 1977 to 8,928,202 in 1986, an increase of 5.5 per cent. There was fairly substantial growth until 1980, with a historic peak of 9,005,795 union members, then a slight decline followed by stagnation (Santi, 1987a).

There has been only a very slight change in the distribution of total membership among confederations (see Table 6.7).

Active membership alone (that is, not counting retired and unemployed members) declined by 1,117,242 in the course of the decade, or 15.5 per cent. The unionization rate, based on active members, dropped by 9 percentage points, from 48.4 per cent in 1977 to 39.5 per cent in 1986 (see Table 6.8). But outside farming the decline was less steep, from 44.3 to 36.6 per cent, a level comparable to the rest of Europe, putting Italy in an average position among the major industrial countries (above average if we include membership in other unions, outside the three major confederations, which is still hard to quantify). By sector, the data show that the unionization rate in industry declined by 6.5 points over the decade, from 50.3 to 43.9 per cent; in the services, public and private together, the decline was 7 points, from 38.1 to 31.1 per cent.

As to strike activity, the 1980s have seen the continuation of the downward trend that began in the late 1970s for all three indicators, number of strikes, number of participants, and number of man-days lost (see Table 6.9). The declining number of strikes, the indicator most closely linked to company-level bargaining, was due first to the waning of the massive wave of decentralized disputes of 1969 and the early 1970s and to the recentralization of industrial relations between 1975 and 1983. Afterwards, the continuing decline is a sign of the more peaceful climate in which the resumption of company-level bargaining has taken place.

Table 6.8   *Union density, Italy, 1980–6*

	Overall				Non-agricultural			
	CGIL	CISL	UIL	Total	CGIL	CISL	UIL	Total
1980	23.6	17.0	7.8	48.4	21.5	15.4	7.4	44.3
1981	23.2	16.2	7.8	47.2	21.1	14.7	7.5	43.2
1982	22.3	15.6	7.8	45.7	20.3	14.2	7.5	42.0
1983	21.7	15.4	7.8	44.9	19.8	13.9	7.5	41.1
1984	21.0	15.7	7.7	44.4	19.1	14.2	7.3	40.7
1985	20.0	14.0	7.2	41.2	18.3	12.7	6.9	37.9
1986	19.1	13.3	7.1	39.5	17.7	12.2	6.8	36.6

Source: internal union data

Table 6.9   *Industrial conflict, Italy, 1980–6*

	Total strikes (indices: 1977 = 100)						
Basic indicators	1980	1981	1982	1983	1984	1985	1986
Number of strikes	68	67	53	47	55	41	44
Number of strikers	100	60	76	50	53	35	26
Days lost	99	64	112	85	53	23	34
Strikes/100,000 employees	66	64	51	46	54	39	43
Strikers/100,000 employees	97	58	73	48	52	34	25
Days lost/100,000 employees	96	51	108	82	51	22	33

Source: Istat, 1986b and 1987

Moreover, in the new decade, in Italy as in some other countries, strikes became primarily demonstrative, which is to say relatively frequent, with a large number of workers involved but not very incisive or powerful. Of course strikes of this sort are no longer aimed directly at the employer as bargaining partner but at the political system and public opinion. In part this change stemmed from the simultaneous increase in conflict in the public sector and in the services. The number of man-days lost due to strikes in industry averaged 62.7 per cent of the total in 1974–83, but was just 50 per cent in 1985, while the share of the services sector rose from 29.9 to 43 per cent. The biggest contribution to this increase came from the transport and communications sectors, which in 1985 accounted for 16.5 per cent of all man-days lost, scarcely less than the 19 per cent accounted for by the engineering industry, which in 1974–83 had accounted for nearly half of all man-days lost to strikes in industry (Bordogna, 1987). In 1983–5 the government sector, services and transport accounted for just under a third.

Industrial action in the public sector and in the services is inclined to be 'demonstrative' in that it is based more on social than on economic disruption. Its effect is more to produce damage than an economic cost, and it tends in involve 'innocent by-standers' (Accornero, 1985). And for these reasons it causes image problems for the unions, exacerbated by the fact that in these sectors there is a relatively large membership of broad adherence to 'independent' occupational unions, often in competition with the industrial and territorial model of CGIL, CISL and UIL. The fragmentation of union representation in the public sector and in the services has grown recently precisely because of the pressure of this unionism. It is generally organized on the 'craft' model (airline pilots, train drivers) or by 'skill' (state-sector managers). There is also poor representation of the major unions among specific strata of working people, especially those most exposed to technological and organizational change: junior managers, technical staff, and the better-educated employees. This has given rise to temporary forms of worker organization, or sometimes, as in the case of junior managers, more permanent organizations, which have engendered as yet unresolved problems of legal recognition and collective bargaining roles.

Another weak point in Italian union action to surface dramatic-ally during the 1980s has been the resurgence of political ties, taking precedence over trade union identity proper. The return to ideological positions linked to the different union organizations and the deterioration of relations among CGIL, CISL and UIL eventually brought the amalgamation experiment of the united federation to an end. This led to divergent approaches on the *scala mobile* and on employment strategy in general. The CISL was more inclined to try for a reduction of both hours and wages to produce more jobs, while the CGIL was less willing to give up the advantage of wage rigidity, partly because it was sceptical of the supposed benefits offered in return.

It was in this context that the Communist Party chose to involve the majority Communist component of the CGIL in its opposition to the agreement of 14 February 1984 and the Craxi Cabinet's legislation enacting that accord. The PCI sought to abrogate the law through a popular referendum, which split the Italian trade union movement in two but failed to gain the political victory that had been hoped for.

One final problem underlying Italian unions' difficulties is relations with the rank and file and the related questions of representation and union democracy. For years now it has been clear that worker assemblies, whose function in the past was actually more to mobilize than to consult the membership, have been in crisis. But the increasingly widespread practice of holding membership or employee referendums has not yet completely solved the problems.

The debate focusses on the constitution, functions and even the unity of company-level union representative organs. In this context, emerging rank-and-file movements began in 1987 to protest against the three major confederations, most notably in the services and in government employment. The first rank-and-file committees (*Comitati di base*, Cobas) were formed in the school system. On 25 May 1987 some 40,000 teachers marched in Rome to signal their rejection of the new contract signed by CGIL, CISL and UIL. The movement then spread to the railways. The train drivers, mostly former CGIL members who had gone over to the independent state railways union FISAFS, opposed the agreement reached with management by CGIL, CISL and UIL. In the autumn, airport workers, though not forming any rank-and-file committee, refused to follow the confederation's directives on industrial action to win their new contract, and their wildcat strikes called the effectiveness of their self-regulation codes into question. Calls for the legal limitation of the right to strike were heard from many quarters, and fomented new divisions in the labour movement, the UIL favouring legislative regulation but the CGIL and CISL opposing it.

In the first few months of 1987, the confederations had successfully managed similar rank-and-file protests – such as the protests of Genoese dockers against the reorganization of the port of Genoa and the reaction of Alfa Romeo workers to the abolition of production teams provided for in the May agreement by which Alfa Romeo was merged into Lancia (Fiat). On the whole, however, precisely because of their established organizational structure the confederations are finding it increasingly difficult to deal with the excessive diversification of demands coming from the rank and file, which itself is increasingly inclined to organize in the defence of both long-standing and recent craft and group interests.

5   Conclusion

First, like all or nearly all of Europe, Italy has witnessed far-reaching changes in the industrial relations system. More than a profound, decisive 'turning point', however, the changes constitute an adaptation to new conditions. Though diminished, concertation practices have remained, after their thorough establishment in the early 1980s. The unions have not lost their 'political citizenship', although their practical influence in the political and industrial sphere has diminished. Their bargaining power has declined, but this has not engendered substantial innovations with respect to the earlier period. The national, industry-wide contract continues to be viewed as essential by employers. Decentralization has thus been controlled. Management strategies are designed to decrease the scope and impact of union action, but not as a rule to eliminate it entirely. Outside public corporations, the forms of union participation are weak (information, consultation), are introduced by contract, and almost always involve union bodies at the company level.

Secondly, though it is not easy to determine the relative importance of the diverse factors causing these changes, it can very plausibly be argued that causes external to the trade unions have outweighed internal ones. In part these factors have been economic and structural (crises in the traditional manufacturing sectors, international competition, new technology); in part they have been related to the makeup of the labour force (segmentation, relative decline in the importance of the labour factor, new types of unemployment, and so on); and in part they have been political (above all, the impossibility of forming an explicitly pro-labour government and the tensions between the majority coalition and the Communist opposition).

Among the internal factors, which must not be thought marginal, the following are of particular significance: the problems of unity and united action among the three confederations; the competition from 'independent' unionism (in government employment and some public services); hesitancy and uncertainty in establishing procedures for either direct or representative democracy within the unions; and the relative lack of formal industrial relations procedures. This last factor, together with insufficient institutionalization of industrial relations, has played a particularly important role in the diminution of Italian unions' bargaining power.

Thirdly, in terms of concertation, Italian trade unions do appear to be interested, now, in overall agreements. This does not prevent efforts to reach more restricted accords, either at the national or at the local level. In such agreements the unions generally seek defensive, short-term objectives, since these are more readily obtainable in tripartite talks than bilateral dealings with the employers. There are essentially two reasons for the unions' renunciation of overall agreements. The first is to avoid reproducing the acrimonious conflicts of the political party system (with their impact within the labour movement). The second is to try to enlarge the scope of more independent, decentralized collective bargaining (at the company and industry level).

Fourthly, Italian industrial relations and union action have been conducted in a comparatively stable political framework, and this seems likely to continue for the foreseeable future. The centre–left coalitions produced a period of overt concertation under the Socialist premiership of Bettino Craxi in the early 1980s, but this is unlikely to recur. Both before and afterwards, the majority, though not having all the characteristics of a pro-labour government (the PCI being in the opposition), continued to support the full recognition of the trade unions and to negotiate with them, finding it to its advantage to win the consent or at least the neutrality of organized labour. On the other hand, these governments have made a number of significant concessions to employers (the moderation of wage indexation, social security relief, the legalization of trainee contracts, and so on).

Fifthly, in a comparatively pluralistic industrial relations system like Italy's definitive changes are naturally, by definition, not possible. It can be maintained, however, that Italian employers have obtained considerable advantages in recent years, most especially gaining the initiative in the use of labour. This has taken place mainly at company level, with a return to flexible management of the workforce and the rise of wage policies involving higher than union rates for selected individuals (an increase in wage drift). Despite intensive bargaining and contract activity, then, there has been a relative growth of non-union participation and potentially deregulated employment contracts, for the higher-than-average ranks and in small firms. Yet it cannot be said that this is a real strategic line adopted by Italian employers for worker involvement outside or against the unions or for progressive deregulation in the use of labour.

Sixthly, the response of the unions to the employers' demands and to the needs of firms has been essentially defensive. This applies most notably to the CGIL, while CISL and UIL have offered more active proposals and experiments in adjustment. Bargaining over flexibility (safeguarding the economic interests of employed workers and defending the legitimacy of the unions) has proved quite successful in many cases, at least in the private sector. Even in such 'mature' industries as textiles, worker representatives have basically retained their role as bargaining actors.

On the issue of untraditional employment contracts, in practice the unions have recognized their inevitability and have managed at any rate to bargain over their introduction, at least in medium-sized and large firms. These contracts provide, for instance, for temporary employment and part-time jobs. The unions have voiced positive responses to company participation schemes, especially in firms where conditions are favourable (public corporations and the large private ones). But they have not always shown a comparable ability to handle the substance of negotiations or to bring junior managers and technicians into the process.

Seventhly, the Italian labour movement still aims at the fundamental goal of defending the interests of all wage- and salary-earners. In practice, moreover, this objective is largely attained, with two limitations. First, very little progress has been made in organizing or defending the secondary labour market (home work, small or tiny businesses, precarious jobs). And second, the unions have little purchase on the upper segments of the workforce.

All in all, the strongest point in the Italian trade union experience is the unions' ability to represent and defend their traditional constituency. The labour movement has accomplished very little indeed with its initiatives on jobs, especially in the South. Even the union programme in this sphere via solidarity contracts (hours-reductions in exchange for jobs) have mainly benefited their traditional constituencies in traditionally strong union areas.

Craft unionism exists only among the 'independent' unions, and nowhere in industry. However, the three confederations have been incapable of adjusting organizationally to the new exigencies, except for pensioners and, partially, workers in artisanal businesses. So far the potential for union advances in the new spheres of the services has been realized only quite modestly. Here again, the unions have displayed good defensive capabilities rather than an aptitude for innovation.

Eighthly, the overall impact of the changes now under way in the structure of employment may lead to a decline in Italian trade unionism. If this were so, it would in any case be a very gradual process (slowed considerably by a number of buffers and shock-absorbers) and would not be limited to Italy alone. More likely, however, is that Italian unions will make a number of adjustments and adaptations to the emerging conditions and will expand their functions. This may of course come concomitantly with a decline in the union presence in certain sectors.

Meanwhile, the organizational and political importance of Italy's traditional industrial unionism will diminish within the three confederations. And so will the decisiveness of the traditional, three-yearly industrial contract battles. Though in more attenuated forms than in some other countries, Italy too is beginning to encounter the problems stemming from the end of a long era, the era of industrial unionism centring on the representation of relatively uniform masses of workers in the key sectors of the economy. At the same time, some new features and trends are perceptible. We shall have unions with large numbers of members but fewer militants. Workers will continue to look to the unions for the defence of their material and occupational interests but will tend to invest their political and ideological hopes in them much less. There will be more marked functional conflicts in the unions' operational sphere (between active workers and pensioners, for instance). Finally, it will be harder to win broad, uniform labour regulations and to commit the entire trade union movement to battles for sweeping objectives of social reform.

Notes

1 The Fund, which is regulated by law and has been in existence for many years now, operates on the basis of an accord between employer and unions (such an agreement is an indispensable prerequisite in resorting to CIG). It is administered by the social security system (INPS), and its mandate is to give to workers in troubled or restructuring firms supplementary earnings in proportion to the number of hours not worked. Such benefits can last for very substantial periods of time.

2 The last measure strengthening automatic income adjustment was taken in May 1982, with the passage of legislation introducing quarterly cost-of-living adjustments for pensioners.

3 The measure was introduced 'temporarily' in 1977. The January 1983 agreement for the first time limited this relief to firms whose employees enjoyed economic conditions at least as good as those specified by the nationwide branch contract.

4 The idea of a fund for investment to create jobs, advanced in the late 1970s by the Christian-oriented CISL confederation, was decisively vetoed by the employers, and was openly opposed by the Communist Party as well. After years of debate, however, in 1982 the proposal was incorporated in the CGIL–CISL–UIL bargaining platform.

5 In the 1970s increasingly lax eligibility standards had transformed disability pensions into an out-and-out welfare subsidy. In numerical terms, too, the situation had clearly become aberrant: by 1982, disability pensions actually outnumbered old-age pensions (5,195,000 to 4,186,000).

6 The National Health Service, instituted in 1978 and fully operational in 1982, replaced the previous employment-based health insurance schemes with a single national health insurance system covering all citizens.

7 Prescription charges for drugs were introduced in 1978, those on diagnoses and laboratory analyses in 1982.

8 The main committees of inquiry named by the central government in these years have looked into: the regulation of the right to strike in public services (the Zangheri Committee, 1980); family allowances and income distribution (the Gorrieri Committee, 1980); the cost of labour and wage indexation (the Giugni Committee, 1982); and more recently the 1983 committee on labour policies and pension reform.

9 The analysis of these tendencies and the statistics given here rely heavily on the work of L. Di Vezza, 'Retribuzioni: andamento e struttura', in Cesos (1982–7).

References

Accornero, A. (1985) 'La terziarizzazione del conflitto e i suoi effetti', in G.P. Cella and M. Regini (eds), *Il conflitto industriale in Italia*, Bologna: Il Mulino.

ASAP (1987) *Rapporto sui salari 1987*, Milan: Angeli.

Baglioni, G. (1986) 'Il destino delle pratiche concertative', *Prospettiva sindacale*, 59(17).

Baglioni, G. and C. Squarzon (1987) *Stato politica economica e relazioni industriali in Europa*, Milan: Angeli.

Banca d'Italia (1987) *Annual Report for 1986*, English edn., Rome: Banca d'Italia.

Bilotti, E. and G. Della Rocca (1986) 'Azione sindacale e mutamenti dei processi produttivi', in Cesos, *Le relazioni sindacali in Italia. Rapporto 1984–85*, Rome: Edizioni Lavoro.

Bordogna, L. (1987) 'Conflittualità', in Cesos, *Le relazioni sindacali in Italia. Rapporto 1985–86*, Rome: Edizioni Lavoro.

Cella, G.P. (1986) 'Struttura e sistema della contrattazione', *Prospettiva sindacale*, 59(17).

Cella, G.P. (1987) 'Criteri di regolazione nelle relazioni industriali italiane: le istituzioni deboli', in P. Lange and M. Regini (eds), *Stato e regolazione sociale*, Bologna: Il Mulino.

Centro Europa Ricerche (1985) *Rapporto No. 2*.

CER–IRS (1986) *Quale strategia per l'industria?*, Bologna: Il Mulino.

Cesos (1982) *Le relazioni sindacali in Italia. Rapporto 1981*, Rome: Edizioni Lavoro.

Cesos (1984) *Le relazioni sindacali in Italia. Rapporto 1982–83*, Rome: Edizioni Lavoro.

Cesos (1985) *Le relazioni sindacali in Italia. Rapporto 1983–84*, Rome: Edizioni Lavoro.

Cesos (1986) *Le relazioni sindacali in Italia. Rapporto 1984–85*, Rome: Edizioni Lavoro.

Cesos (1987) *Le relazioni sindacali in Italia. Rapporto 1985–86*, Rome: Edizioni Lavoro.

Chiesi, A. and A. Martinelli (1987) 'La rappresentanza degli interessi imprenditoriali come meccanismo di regolazione sociale', in P. Lange and M. Regini (eds), *Stato e regolazione sociale*, Bologna: Il Mulino.

Dal Co, M. (1986) *Ristrutturazione dell'occupazione e relazioni industriali*, Bologna: Il Mulino.

ISCO (various years) *Congiuntura italiana*, Rome: ISCO.

Istat (1986a) *Sommario di statistiche storiche, 1926–1985*, Rome: Istat.

Istat (1986b) *Annuario statistico italiano*, Rome: Istat.

Istat (1987) *Annuario statistico italiano*, Rome: Istat.

Lange, A. (1987) 'La crisi della concertazione sociale in Italia', *Giornale di diritto del lavoro e di relazioni industriali*, No. 33.

Ministero del Bilancio e della Programmazione Economica and Ministero del Tesoro (1986) *Relazione generale sulla situazione economica del paese*, Rome: Government Publishing Office.

Negrelli, S. (1987) 'Le relazioni industriali nella grande impresa tra continuità e mutamento', *Industria e sindacato*, No. 20.

Olini, G. (1986) 'Orario del lavoro: assetti e problemi', in Cesos, *Le relazioni sindacali in Italia. Rapporto 1985-86*, Rome: Edizioni Lavoro.

Piore, M. and C. Sabel (1984) *The Second Industrial Divide*, New York: Basic Books.

Regini, M. (1983) 'Le condizioni dello scambio politico. Nascita e declino della concertazione in Italia e Gran Bretagna', *Stato e mercato*, No. 9.

Regini, M. (1985) 'Relazioni industriali e sistema politico: l'evoluzione recente e le prospettive degli anni '80', in M. Carrieri and P. Perulli (eds), *Il teorema sindacale*, Bologna: Il Mulino.

Santi, E. (1985) 'Le relazioni sindacali alla ricerca del circolo virtuoso', in Cesos, *Le relazioni sindacali in Italia. Rapporto 1983-84*, Rome: Edizioni Lavoro.

Santi, E. (1987a) *Un decennio di sindacalizzazione (1977-1986)*, Rome: Cesos.

Santi, E. (1987b) *La contrattazione aziendale dal 1984 al 1986*, Rome: Cesos.

Streeck, W. (1987) 'La questione dell'incertezza e l'incertezza dei managers: imprenditori, relazioni sindacali e riequilibrio industriale nella crisi', in Baglioni, G. and C. Squarzon (eds), *Stato politica economica e relazioni industriali in Europa*, Milan: Angeli.

Treu, T. (1986a) 'Tattiche e strategie della Confindustria', *Prospettiva sindacale*, 59(17).

Treu, T. (1986b) 'Nuove tendenze e problemi del tempo di lavoro', *Stato e mercato*, No. 18.

Treu, T. (1987) 'Rapporti tra sindacati e industria italiana negli anni '80: un caso di adequamento positivo?', *Prospettiva sindacale*, 18.

Ufficio Studio delle Relazioni Industriali SIP (1987) *Notiziario de lavoro, speciale contratti*, No. 24, April.

7

Continuity and Change in Dutch Industrial Relations

Jelle Visser

1 The main characteristics of the Dutch industrial relations system

The 1980s have been a period of transition in Dutch industrial relations. Coalitions between actors have shifted and policies have been revised. Union membership fell sharply. Facilitated by a slack labour market, employers gained the initiative. Income redistributions have been reversed, and the further development of the Dutch welfare state called into question.

The principal question to be addressed here is whether the result of the current shake-up will be a different industrial relations system.

The fundamental tenets of the Dutch system of industrial relations are easily summarized: the preponderant role of the government, the reliance on inter-organizational consultation, and the high level of centralization in organizational decision-making and bargaining. These were the 'mainstays' of the system as it had developed after the Second World War. Windmuller (1969:435–8) predicted that the 'order of priorities' would change, the 'weight of the government' would probably be 'less than at present' and decentralization would probably lead to 'a less precarious balance' compared with the first twenty years; but he firmly believed that the basic institutions would endure.

The end of the government-controlled central wage policies (1945–63) did not remove the state from the collective bargaining scene. The 1970 Wage Act relocated the primary responsibility for wage formation to union and employer organizations. The government gave up its preventive control over pay bargaining and the Board of Mediators was abolished. But it retained important statutory powers to freeze or limit negotiated agreements (Fase, 1980). Almost every year the government took part in lengthy negotiations with the peak organizations of unions and employers in an attempt to reach voluntary wage moderation. Between 1970 and 1982 an agreement was reached only once, applying to 1973.

The government intervened no fewer than eight times: in 1971, 1974, 1976 (twice), 1979, 1980 (twice) and 1981. Wage bargaining remained a tripartite and highly centralized affair.

Dutch trade unions and employers' associations have maintained a high degree of centralized decision-making. Relationships between them, shaped under the period of central wage policies, are institutionalized in stable structures. Between 1945 and 1979 unions organized a stable (35–40 per cent) proportion of Dutch employees (Visser, 1987), 87 per cent of them joining one of the three peak associations. In 1976 the social-democratic Nederlands Verbond van Vakverenigingen (NVV), Dutch Federation of Trade Unions, and the Nederlands Katholiek Vakverbond (NKV), Dutch Catholic Trade Union Federation, merged to form the Federatie Nederlandse Vakbeweging (FNV), Federation of Dutch Trade Unions. This now represents almost 60 per cent of total membership. The Christelijk National Vakverbond (CNV), Christian National Trade Union Federation, represents about 20 per cent. The FNV and CNV each join together seventeen unions, mainly organized by industrial sector and comprising both blue- and white-collar employees. In 1974 a federation of white-collar organizations was founded: the Federatie van Middelbaar en Hoger Personeel (MHP), Federation of White-Collar Employees, currently represents 7 per cent of all union members. Independent unions are mainly found in the civil service, among the military, teachers and nurses. Among manual workers and in industry, independent unionism is negligible.

Dutch employers are highly organized by international standards. Three out of four firms belong to an employer organization, nearly all firms with thirty or more employees being organized (de Vroom and van Waarden, 1984). Most employers' associations affiliate with peak associations following a twofold pattern: by sector and size of firm, and by religion, conforming to a widespread characteristic of Dutch organizational life. Thus we find three peak associations – general, Catholic and Protestant – in agriculture which together organize over 80 per cent of all farmers. In the small-firm sector and in the retail trade there are now two peak associations following the amalgamation of the Catholic with the general one. Together with the Protestant organization it organizes some 40 per cent of all firms in the domain. Finally, two major peak associations represent the employers of large and medium-sized enterprises. The Verbond van Nederlandse Ondernemingen (VNO), Confederation of Dutch Enterprises, covers some 10,000 firms. The Nederlands Christelijk Werkgeversverbond (NCW), Dutch Christian Employers' Confederation, was founded in 1970 by a merger of the Catholic and Protestant organizations, and represents over 3500 firms. All peak associations co-operate in the Raad van Centrale Ondernemersorganisaties (RCO), Council of Central Employers' Associations.

Obviously, in industrial relations VNO and NCW carry most weight. In matters of socioeconomic policy and in central bargaining VNO and NCW have sought co-operation with small businesses as a defence shield against union demands. But the outcomes of this co-operation, by accommodating marginal firms, may have contributed to the wide coverage of collective agreements. Within the union movement, inter-confederal co-operation was discontinued following the formation of the FNV.

1.1   The system of national consultation

Trade unions and employers' associations interact with each other and with the state in a number of statutory and voluntary institutional settings and policy areas.

Central union and employers' organizations meet in the Stichting van de Arbeid (SVA), Foundation of Labour, which originated in 1945. Here they prepare the ground for possible central agreements. A number of standing committees exists in the field of labour market policy, immigrant labour, social insurance policy, and so on. The Sociaal-Economische Raad (SER), Social–Economic Council, was founded in 1950, and is a statutory and truly tripartite body. Central union and employers' organizations occupy two-thirds of the seats, while government appointed experts take the remainder. The Council's role is mainly advisory and its Economic Expert Committee used to prepare the annual wage bargaining round on the basis of forecasts of the Centraal Plan Bureau (CPB), Central Planning Office. Another major role of the SER is to advise the government in matters of social security legislation and labour market policies. Legally the SER is the 'top' body of a three-tiered joint-consultation system. But the planned introduction of a system of industry boards failed to materialize outside the domain of agriculture and retail, and the enterprise councils long remained weak.

Independent unions are excluded from the Foundation, the SER and most sectoral negotiation bodies. The MHP acquired 'representative status' in 1977, obtaining a seat from the CNV. The agricultural and small entrepreneurs' associations are part of the employers' delegation in both national consultation bodies. In none of these national forums is representation subject to electoral competition.

1.2 The collective bargaining system

Some 800 collective agreements are negotiated each year, covering 75 per cent of all private sector employees. They are mainly negotiated nationally for entire sectors of the economy. About 400,000 employees, mainly working in multinational companies (Philips, Shell, Unilever, AKZO, and so on), are covered by company agreements. Like the sectoral agreements, these single-employer agreements are negotiated by paid union officials and supervised by union headquarters. Although conducting bargaining single-handedly, the large companies co-ordinate activity with the employers' associations of which they are normally the most important members. Many of the 600 company agreements signed each year are reached with the close assistance of employers' associations.

In the 1970s the importance of company agreements rose – mainly due to the concentration process in industry – but this should not be interpreted as decentralization (Huiskamp, 1983). Multi-employer agreements remained the norm in the same domains where they had been established in the 1950s: agriculture, printing, metal, textiles, construction, commerce, transport, banking; while single-employer agreements are predominantly found in food, chemicals and oil-refining. The large number of agreements should not obscure the fact that the vast majority follows the pattern set by a few key agreements (metal, construction, Philips). Once these agreements have been reached, other sectors and companies follow suit. The annual consultation procedures, the expiry of most contracts between January and April, and the involvement of central organizations further contribute to standardization. Inter-industry and inter-firm differentials are small and invariant. Typically, by introducing compensations for low-paid workers, government interventions in the 1970s compressed pay differentials within sectors but left inter-sectoral differentials unaltered (de Wolff, 1983). Until the 1980s, (semi-)public employees were 'wage followers', their salaries being pegged to the trend set by private sector agreements.

The typical employers' association signs one or two contracts. The largest industrial unions, on the other hand, may be involved in as many as fifty sectoral and some hundred company agreements. In nearly all agreements affiliates of both FNV and CNV are involved. Agreements signed by only one of them are rare. In about one-third of all cases they are joined by MHP-affiliates, most often its union of supervisors and clerical staff. In many industries, unions and employers' associations have formed voluntary joint bodies, in which they prepare the annual bargaining process or elaborate details. These bodies are normally staffed by the employers' federation and as a rule unaffiliated unions are excluded. In the public sector, union–employer consultation is formalized through regular meetings in which the union side is represented by four cartels, formed by unions belonging to the FNV, CNV, the MHP and an independent federation of civil servants.

Collective agreements in the Netherlands regulate a wide array of issues in addition to wages, including working hours and conditions, employment security, safety and training, and consultation procedures. The legal basis of collective agreements has not changed since the 1927 Collective Agreement Act and the 1937 Collective Agreement Extension Act. Under these laws collective agreements have acquired public recognition and protection against outsiders. Agreements are legally binding on the signatory parties and their members. Upon request of the parties, agreements may be declared binding by government decree on all employees in firms or industries regardless of membership in employers' associations or trade unions.

The Minister can also nullify agreements but this has never occurred under the 1937 Act. There is little doubt, though, that the Minister would not go along with contractual terms which would limit the constitutional freedom of association or restrict benefits to union members only. The 1937 Act discourages single-union agreements and competition between 'representative' unions by requiring the Minister to ensure that an agreement is 'representative' before making it generally enforceable. The criteria of what constitutes a 'representative' union are deliberately vague, and are monitored by the confederations represented in the SER. All unions belonging to the FNV, the CNV and, since the mid-1970s, the MHP are deemed 'representative'. Together with the high level of employer organization, the extension of agreements explains why bargaining coverage in the Netherlands is two to three times larger than the membership in trade unions.

1.3 The joint-consultation system in firms
Under the 1950 Works Councils Act, employees were entitled to representation in joint enterprise councils under the chairmanship of the employer. During the first twenty years the councils remained in a subservient role and suffered from a lack of enthusiasm on account of their limited authority. Works councils acquired a more independent but equivocal role in the 1970s, following legal changes in 1971. The uneasiness of trade unions showed especially during the 1972 and 1973 strikes in the metal

industry. In some cases the councils had attempted to conciliate, while in others they had sided with the employer. It was against this background that the FNV pressed for reform. The first proposals were put forward in 1976 when the Labour Party was still part of the coalition government, and they prompted three years of heated debate. The principal employers' organization, VNO, feared that the removal of the employer from the chairmanship deprived the works council of its conciliatory influence just at the time when their power was being extended into new areas of company policy. The CNV welcomed the change but, in accordance with its Christian philosophy of co-operation, it had reservations about council meetings without the presence of management. FNV unions in industry expressed reservations about giving increased co-determination rights to a body which was not of the unions' own making.

Under the 1979 Works Councils Act councils in firms with 100 or more employees acquired the right to meet without management. All employees, except those working few hours or 'on loan' from other companies, are entitled to vote and to stand as candidates in biennial elections. Although voting and candidature are not limited to union members, 65–70 per cent of the councillors belong to FNV, CNV and MHP unions, more than double the size of these unions among the electorate (Teulings, 1981; 1987). While far from being part of, or dependent upon, the larger union organization, the councils have become the centre of worker organization in firms.

Under the 1979 act, works councils have a large array of legally specified consultation and co-determination rights. Management must seek the council's advice with respect to major commercial decisions, including mergers, closures, takeovers, major investments and loans, hiring outside consultants and the employment of temporary staff. It is required to seek the council's approval in matters of changes in remuneration, pension and profit-sharing schemes, the arrangement of hours and holidays, grievance procedures, health and safety conditions and training. The councils are legally charged with monitoring the application of collective agreements but cannot (re)negotiate issues, in particular wages, that are settled by collective agreement.

Detailed procedures prescribe that overall there must be six annual consultative meetings between management and the council. The council is entitled to seek independent expert opinion and has a right of appeal against certain employers' decisions. The council has some influence over the composition of supervisory company boards, but the German example of extensive representation on the boards was not followed. In 1981 the legal obligation to establish works councils, with restricted powers, was extended to firms with 35–100 employees, and in 1982 a legal provision made two annual personnel meetings with management obligatory in small firms (10–35 employees).

2 Entering the 1980s: socioeconomic challenges

Table 7.1 portrays the deterioration of economic performance in the past decade. The first oil shock, in 1973 (OPEC I), had a major impact as the cost of the energy-intensive products in which Dutch industry had become specialized was pushed up considerably. However, until 1980 real wages still increased by small amounts while unemployment rose to three times the level of the early 1970s. The second shock, in 1978 (OPEC II), was followed by a sharp downturn. Output, profits and investments fell after 1980. Many sectors suffered from over-capacity and the profit share of value-added dropped from 16 per cent in 1969–73 to 9 per cent in 1980–3. The net investment rate, which declined from 7 per cent before OPEC I to 4.6 per cent in the second half of the 1970s, dropped to a mere 2 per cent in 1981 and 1982. In 1981, 1982 and 1983 the average annual labour shake-out amounted to 100,000 man-years, and unemployment rose by more than 150,000 persons yearly. Real wages fell by 9 per cent cumulatively between 1980 and 1985. The sharp rise in the public debt, from 4.3 per cent of GNP in 1975 to 7.5 per cent in 1980 and 10.7 per cent in 1982, induced the government to introduce sharp austerity measures which had a dampening effect upon domestic demand.

In the early 1980s the Netherlands experienced its worst economic setback since the Second World War. The economy is currently in a better shape. Higher demand, largely from abroad, accompanied by wage restraint and shedding of excess labour, has led to an unprecedented fall in labour costs. Between 1982 and 1985 unit labour costs in manufacturing fell by 5.5 per cent. Profits recovered and business investments strengthened between 1984 and 1986 by almost 9 per cent per year. The peril of inflation has virtually disappeared, though this is largely the result of depressed demand, deflationist policies and the continuing appreciation of the Dutch guilder. Unemployment remains exceptionally high. The level of investments is low compared to the 1950s and 1960s, and the recent fall in the value of the US dollar

Table 7.1 *Some economic indicators, Netherlands, 1964–87 (average annual changes and rates in percentages)*

	National income (real)	Labour productivity	Employment growth[1]	CPI	Nominal wage rate	Real wage rate	Unemployment rate[1]
1964–73	5.6	5.5	0.7	5.8	12.2	6.4	1.5
1974–9	1.5	2.5	0.3	7.4	10.2	2.8	5.1
1980–5	0.6	1.8	–1.1	4.6	3.0	–1.6	11.3
1980	–0.4	1.0	0.7	7.0	4.7	–2.3	6.0
1981	–1.0	1.2	–1.5	6.7	4.4	–2.3	8.7
1982	–0.3	1.1	–2.5	5.7	5.7	0	11.7
1983	0.4	2.7	–2.1	2.6	1.3	–1.3	13.8
1984	2.5	3.0	–0.5	3.0	0.4	–2.6	14.2 (13.9)
1985	2.5	1.9	0.7	2.5	1.4	–0.9	13.5 (12.9)
1986	2.5	1.5	1.0	0.0	1.5	1.5	12.6 (11.8)
1987	1.3	1.0	0.7	–1.5	1.5	3.0	11.7 (11.0)

[1] Employment is measured in man-years, but unemployment refers to persons registered at labour exchange offices and looking for jobs of twenty hours and more weekly. The unemployment rates given here are standardized according to ILO and OECD definitions. The effect of the 1984 change in registration is shown in brackets.

Sources: The average annual changes are calculated from CBS, 1985, *Vijfentachtig jaren statistiek in tijdreeksen 1899–1984*; and updated with the help of CBS, *Statistisch Zakboek*, annual; CPB, *Centraal economisch Plan*, annual; and CPB, 1986. The figures for 1987 are projected target values and subject to revision from the last-mentioned source and from Ministry of Economic Affairs, 1986; they are projected target values and subject to revision

has drained the growth prospects of the leading export sectors, despite the improvement in costs. Even before the 1987 stock market crisis, the predicted growth rate (1–1.5 per cent) was lower than for the OECD as a whole. For 1988 a growth rate of less than 1 per cent is expected. The public deficit has been brought down to 7.3 per cent in 1987, but a further reduction is hard to come by despite severe budget cuts and austerity measures. The fall in oil prices has reduced government revenue from North Sea gas fields. In sum, the recovery is frail and the future uncertain.

2.1 De-industrialization

In November 1977 the *Financial Times* wrote that the Dutch had succeeded in establishing one of the 'world's most prosperous and enlightened welfare states, with minimum wages higher than in any other industrial society, high labour productivity, remarkably few strikes, and a widely developed social security network'. In sharp contrast, however, the paper observed that the industrial base had been badly undermined. It was also noted that, within the OECD, the Netherlands had the most rapidly expanding government sector and, with public spending amounting to over 60 per cent of GNP, it ranked second only to Sweden. The incidence rate of taxes and social security charges rose from 38.5 per cent of net national income in 1968 to 52.2 per cent in 1980. Internationally, the phrase 'Dutch disease' began to spread. The government's large revenues from the gas fields permitted generous welfare programmes. The pressure on the competitive position of Dutch manufacturing goods, emanating from the continuous appreciation of the guilder and reflecting a positive trade balance due to the gas fields, was not sufficiently compensated for by bargained wage restraint. It has been demonstrated that until 1978 unit labour costs in Dutch manufacturing rose more than in, for instance, West Germany (de Wolff and Driehuis, 1980; Flanagan, Soskice and Ulman, 1983).

The importance of labour costs needs little explanation once it is understood that three-fifths of all industrial sales are directed abroad. Owing to the historical specialization in (colonial) trade, finance and transport, industry has long remained in a subsidiary role. Another result of historical 'specialization' is the predominance of upgrading industry. Dutch industry is biassed towards processing bulk goods (food, oil, chemicals), concentrated in large-scale production, highly capital-intensive, energy-consumptive, little diversified and scarcely innovative (WRR, 1980). Its competitive position used to be dependent upon cost and trading advantages, and did not generally derive from high product quality, customized design, superior engineering, efficient maintenance, sophisticated marketing or flexible specialization. These characteristics explain why Dutch industry shared so much in the 'European manufacturing malaise'. The share of manufacturing in total output fell from 27 per cent in 1970 to 18.7 per cent in 1985. By 1984 there were some 300,000 or 30 per cent fewer jobs in manufacturing than in 1970. Half of this decline took place in the early 1980s. In terms of employment or output share the Dutch manufacturing sector is now one of the smallest of all OECD countries.

2.2   The labour-market crisis

At the close of the 1970s a considerable employment deficit had developed, which showed in overt unemployment once the avenue for further expansion of public aid and relief schemes had been blocked. The number of people on the dole trebled from 1980 to 1984, and the rate of unemployment rose from 5.5 per cent in 1979 to 14.2 per cent in 1984. Between 1980 and 1984 total employment, expressed in man-hours, fell by 7 per cent.

The rise in unemployment in the Netherlands coincided with major changes in the pattern of employment and the functioning of labour markets. Employment concentrates more than ever in the prime age group. Labour-force participation of males continued to decline, from 74 per cent in 1971 to 65 per cent in 1985. The decline, from 85 to 67 per cent, was quite dramatic among older males (50–64), due to early retirement and disablement. A similar decline, from 59 to 42 per cent, occurred among younger males (15–24), reflecting more and longer schooling. Female participation rose from 25 per cent in 1971 to 34 per cent in 1985. While participation of young females declined, from 48 to 41 per cent, participation in the other age groups and of married women increased, especially in the second half of the 1970s. Female labour participation is still very low by international standards.

Unemployment in the Netherlands is heavily biassed against the young and the unskilled, while older workers bear the brunt of long-term unemployment (SAE, 1983–7). In 1985 over half of all the unemployed stayed unemployed the full year round, almost one-quarter for longer than three years. Seventy-five per cent of all unemployed aged fifty and older had been on the dole for more than one year, against 50 per cent two years earlier in 1982. Long-term unemployment increasingly affects the younger age group as well: one-third of all unemployed under the age of twenty-five against one-fifth in 1982. Long-term unemployment overlaps to a large extent with low or inadequate skill-levels. Unemployment is highest among workers with no further training: 33.5 per cent for men and 42.2 per cent for women. Low skill levels explain part of the higher incidence of unemployment among immigrant workers. Their share in total unemployment was 9.5 per cent in 1985, double their share in the labour force.

Over the past ten years the Netherlands has experienced a strong growth in labour supply, reflecting both demographic causes and the entry of more women into the labour force. Labour-force growth will not attenuate before the late 1990s. Some of the pressure deriving from labour-force growth has been cushioned by the exit of older people, longer schooling, labour-time reduction and the shift towards part-time employment. It is doubtful whether these palliatives will remain available or effective. Employment decline did affect mainly full-time jobs. At the same time part-time labour rapidly expanded. Currently, nearly one-quarter of total employment is in part-time jobs, against one-seventh in 1975. Half of all women work in part-time jobs; four out of five part-time jobs are held by women and three out of five by married women. Undeniably, in past years fewer jobs have been distributed among more people, but at present job-distributive policies appear to have lost their momentum (Visser, 1989). The decline in unemployment in 1985 and 1986 can in part be attributed to a change in registration practices, eliminating the need for older workers to register.

The government admits that its target of 500,000 unemployed by the end of the 1980s is not realistic. Even if it is conceded that the register is inflated by about 30 per cent, as recent research seems to suggest, it hardly outbalances the large number of discouraged or hidden unemployed and involuntary short-time working. The most worrying aspect is the stable number of long-term unemployed, especially in the younger age groups. With on average 250,000 freshly educated young people each year entering a labour market which is increasingly affected by technological change, the job prospects for those who took the brunt of unemployment in the early 1980s are slim. A sizeable proportion is on the brink of permanent exclusion from the labour force.

The concentration of unemployment among youths, women, older males, immigrants and ethnic minorities may also explain why unemployment has not been a greater political liability. Although less generous in recent years, the extensive provisions for social security and the relief measures provided for older unemployed males may be another factor which helped to diffuse the explosive potential of large-scale unemployment. The danger of the present situation is that people and policymakers will become accustomed to a continuing high level of unemployment. The difference from the early 1980s, when constantly lengthening dole queues embodied a real threat to many people, is that today the tendency towards segmentation and exclusion continues while public attention is less obvious.

2.3   The expansion of the social security sector

Between 1970 and 1985 the number of people depending on transfer incomes doubled from 1.6 million to 3.2 million. Recipients of one of the unemployment benefits increased tenfold between 1970 and 1985. Disability pensions accounted for the second-largest increase – from 275,000 to 713,000. Following the decision, in the mid-1970s, to widen the allowances for (partial) unemployability, the latter figure includes (older) unemployed people. The number of people receiving old age pensions rose from 1.2 to 1.6 million. Counting only the population aged fifteen to sixty-four years, the ratio of employed persons to recipients of social benefits of one kind or another has slipped from 8.4 to 1 in 1970 to 2.7 to 1 in 1985 (SAE, 1986). The sharp increase in transfer incomes has created formidable problems of cost-sharing. Under conditions of declining national income, as experienced in the early 1980s, the squeeze on primary incomes is bound to evoke tensions. Since social benefits were tightly linked to wages, these tensions are reproduced in the collective bargaining system.

In the 1970s, following the introduction of a statutory minimum wage which is biannually adjusted to contractual wages, the principle of 'net linking' was introduced: the net minimum wage was to function as the absolute minimum for all benefits. All benefits above the minimum (unemployment, sickness and disability) were calculated through 'gross linking' as a percentage of the insured person's last wage. These interconnections guaranteed that all benefits moved in line with pay rises in the private sector. Moreover, in the 1970s virtually all collective agreements included an automatic 'cost-of-living-adjustment clause'. Clearly, this tight system of upward-moving readjustments left little discretionary power to policymakers, be they governments, employers or trade unions.

3   Reluctant change

Policy revisions came slowly. Organizational hierarchies and institutions, being the result of long-term investments and the embodiment of past accomplishments, do not easily adapt. Only after external conditions had fundamentally transformed the relations of power between capital and labour, did employers gain the initiative. Once the state did retreat, unions became far more exposed to the adversity of markets, and they were poorly prepared. The large labour slack, combined with falling membership, was probably the main factor which sapped the confidence with which unions had pressed their demands in the past. As so often, trade unions had the most difficult role to play – yet the script was partly their own.

3.1 Governments and government policies

Until 1982 Dutch governments continued to play an active role in industrial relations and pay bargaining. Given the tight interconnection in pay developments they could not easily withdraw. To their dismay, governments discovered that 60 per cent of the budget was already fixed by the outcome of collective bargaining. Moreover, in the 1970s the government's share in social security more than doubled and was partly financed through its non-tax income and by increased public borrowing. This reflected two developments. First, a growing number of recipients no longer qualified for insured status. Secondly, most governments tried to slow down the rise in social charges in order to encourage wage moderation. Often this was done by subsidizing employers' contributions to social security, with the unintended consequence of lowering their resistance to pay demands. It has been shown that the rise in social charges was associated with lower after-tax wages, indicating that 'the employed did make some payment'. But from the fact that before-tax wages remained constant and the share of profits fell, it may also be concluded that there was 'a limited responsiveness of the bargaining system to pressures emanating from both an appreciating currency and an expensive welfare policy' (Flanagan, Soskice and Ulman, 1983:131).

As to the attempt to achieve voluntary restraint there was little difference between the 1973–7 government in which the Labour Party held a majority, its centre–right successor (1977–81), or the short-lived centre–left government (1981–2). In default of central agreements these governments did not hesitate to intervene and limit the outcomes of union–employer bargaining. With the passing of time the terms of exchange for bargained restraint worsened. In the early years of the 1980s it became clear that real incomes could not be maintained at their 1979 level and the issue became how the decline was to be shared out among employed workers, public employees and a rising number of social benefit claimants. Another factor, which did nothing to facilitate concertation, was the troubled relationship between most governments and the largest union confederation, the FNV. This may seem obvious for governments in which the Labour Party took no part, but relationships were hardly better in 1976–7 or in 1981–2 when Labour was in office.

From the start, the 1977–81 centre–right coalition government was troubled with rising public debt. Soon hit by the economic setback of OPEC II, it had little to offer by way of direct pecuniary compensation. Of the reform proposals of its predecessor, it eventually succeeded in enacting new legislation on works councils (1979) and on health and safety (1981). In order to make wage restraint more acceptable to the unions, it also introduced Income Guidelines (1978) applicable to higher incomes outside the scope of collective bargaining. After many compromises the proposal of a Wage-Earner Fund, to be paid out of 'excess profits', led to a stalemate in Parliament.

This government's most significant act was the publication, in June 1978, of its austerity plan 'Blueprint 1981'. The objective was to reduce public spending, via lower increases in public sector wages and social benefits, while maintaining public employment and basic social security guarantees. The proposals angered public employee unions and prevented the conclusion of a central agreement for 1979. The government went ahead with its plan to reduce the salary increases of its 800,000 civil servants by 0.5 per cent (0.2 per cent for the lowest salaries and 0.7 per cent for the highest) below the trend implied by the thirty largest collective agreements. This was repeated six times, each half year, between 1979 and 1981. Temporary legislation, starting in 1979 but extended each year until definitive legislation in 1985, prescribed the same restraint on the 500,000 employees in the semi-public sector who hitherto had 'followed the trend' voluntarily. These measures likewise affected social benefits.

In mid-1979 the government departed from its initial policy that it would not intervene in union–employer bargaining. Alarmed by a rapidly deteriorating trade balance, it placed a ceiling upon cost-of-living adjustments. At the end of the year the central organizations almost reached an agreement over wage moderation and a small reduction in working time, but at the last minute the FNV, facing opposition from its food union, withdrew its signature. The government promptly responded by imposing a freeze for the first months of 1980. When sectoral agreements over voluntary restraint proved impossible, it prescribed a reduced but equal lump-sum price compensation for the remainder of 1980. Similar interventions followed in 1981 and 1982, leaving only partial freedom to union–employer negotiators. The last of these measures was taken by the short-lived centre–left government. Early in 1982 the Labour Party, whose leader was Minister of Social Affairs and Employment, faced a major conflict with its union allies over proposals to curtail sickness pay benefits. In May 1982, the Party, not able to win consent for an employment-stimulation programme from its coalition partner, left the Cabinet. The elections of September 1982 led to the renewal of the centre–right coalition which, after completing its full term in office, returned to government office after the elections in May 1986.

In the early 1980s the economic and political climate rapidly deteriorated, preparing the ground for more drastic cures. The many varieties of income policies seemed neither to work nor to bring the improvement in employment they had advertised. Both employers and unions had grown tired of government intervention. The ultimate proof of ineffectiveness was delivered by the quarrelsome centre–left coalition, which once again curtailed bargaining freedom but could not deliver on employment. Nothing seemed to halt the rising costs associated with social security, the consequent rise in government expenditure and public debt, the implied squeeze on investments, incomes and employment, and the constantly growing dole queues.

The new centre–right government, led by Mr Ruud Lubbers, advocated a 'no nonsense' policy of severe cuts in public spending in which there was no room for half-hearted measures or side-payments to the unions. It soon withdrew some of the legislative proposals (Wage-Earner Fund, Union Representation in Firms) of its predecessors, and discontinued the voluntary Income Guidelines. Reducing public debt was seen as a prime condition for restoring private sector profitability and investments. Incomes policies of the redistributive type that hitherto had predominated did not figure in its policy toolkit. This was the first government in ten years which openly advocated a policy of widening income differences.

The government welcomed the two reports, published in 1981 and 1982, by the Advisory Committee on Industrial Policy chaired by Shell's President, G. A. Wagner. In sharp contrast to past policies these reports stressed the need for re-industrialization and a less conspicuous role for the state. In particular, the Wagner Committee recommended that the government should stay out of collective bargaining, that all automatisms (cost-of-living adjustments, minimum wages, linkage for social benefits and public service salaries) should be removed, the minimum wage be lowered and income differentials encouraged. This was largely a catalogue of employer demands, but under the new government employers stood 'a good chance of seeing their aims realized', as the former Christian-Democratic Minister for Social Affairs (1977–81), W. Albeda, drily observed (Albeda, 1985:53).

The government had a head-start thanks to an unexpectedly signed central agreement in November 1982 applying to 1983 and 1984. The union confederations conceded a reduction in real wages in exchange for lifting the employers' veto on labour-time reduction. The government could now turn its back on pay developments in the private sector, having been reassured that real wages would fall and were not conditional upon government promises or side-payments. With respect to its own employees, it immediately imposed a salary freeze for 1983. Later that year it imposed a 3 per cent cut in public service salaries, followed by similar but smaller cuts in 1985, further standstill in 1986, and a minute increase in 1987. In the semi-public sector (hospitals, welfare and social security institutions, railways, broadcasting, and so on), it prolonged the restrictive controls. Definitive legislation was introduced in 1985. Only after prior consultation with the government are employers in these institutions now able to enter into pay negotiations with the unions. The Minister of Social Affairs is empowered to nullify pay settlements and employers can be penalized by stricter cash limits in the next pay round.

The lowering of civil servant salaries likewise applied to social benefit recipients, followed by structural measures which took effect in 1987. Under the new unemployment support system insurance and relief provisions will be integrated. After having worked a prior spell of at least twenty-six weeks, the unemployed person is entitled to a standard benefit of 70 per cent (previously 75 or 80 per cent) of the last earned wage for six months (previously up to two and a half years). Thereafter one is moved on to social assistance, guaranteeing 70 per cent of the minimum wage. An interim benefit of up to two years, depending on one's age and job history, is meant to cushion older workers with longer work records from too sharp a fall in income. In 1985, people under the age of twenty-two were excluded from the right to claim under the old Unemployment Relief Act. Workers older than fifty-seven and a half years are now allowed to stay on the dole until the legal retirement age of sixty-five and in early 1984 the obligation to register for job search was lifted in their case. Unlike the old system, men and women will have equal rights.

3.2 Employer organization and policies

In early 1977 the central employers' organizations staged a major campaign to eliminate the automatic price escalator clauses; this campaign failed. Within a few weeks employers, impressed by successful union strike-calls, were forced to return to the bargaining table. Soon they signed agreements in which the said clauses were fully retained. A number of consequences followed from this defeat. First and foremost, the issue of the cost-of-living clauses remained blocked for the rest of the decade, and gradually employers grew convinced that there were no concessions to be gained from trade unions in central bargaining. It also became clear that a less egalitarian wage structure was unlikely to result from central-level bargaining or government orders. Instead, most government interventions until 1982 had a strong equalizing impact. Secondly, the larger branch-level employers' associations and multinational firms criticized the peak associations for their handling of central-level bargaining. Powerful branch organizations like the metal employers, moved towards greater independence and stressed the need for less egalitarian pay structures. Companies such as Philips, Shell and AKZO took it upon themselves to set a new trend in Dutch industrial relations, and assumed a less compromising 'free enterprise' stance, calling for less regulation, a contraction of the public sector, the abolition or at least substantial lowering of the statutory minimum wage, and decentralized bargaining. The peak associations of employers were further handicapped by the declining capacity of the FNV, in particular, to co-ordinate its affiliates and negotiate on their behalf.

Thus, employers gradually overcame their nostalgia for central bargaining. The small-firm sector remained reluctant to do without the moderation of union demands which was to come from central-level bargaining or additional government controls. Decentralization was most wanted by, and indeed least threatening to, the largest, internationally operating companies, which could vary their total wage bill by reducing employment levels at home. But wage movements in the Netherlands are highly patterned and quickly spill over to sectors and companies in which a similar strategy meant marginalization or outright closure.

To this should be added the lack of discipline of which employers often gave proof. The Mutual Guarantee Fund, which was created during the 1973 strikes in the metal industry, had been a step towards greater employer solidarity. But in 1977 employers had not been able to hold a common line, and as late as 1980, when unions safeguarded full pay compensation against rising prices at the Hoogoven steel plant, it was clear that no agreement would settle for less.

All this was changed by the extreme degree of labour slackness in the 1980s. Employers now had much to gain, and little to lose, from decentralized bargaining without government involvement. In sum, one of the major changes of the 1980s is that employers shook off their inferiority complex and grew more assertive. On a number of occasions, starting in 1980 when Shell organized a successful action of its white-collar staff against union pickets, they have challenged the representativeness of unions. Recent examples of employers' defiance are the agreements in banking (1986), at Philips (1986) or Heineken (1986), in which the FNV and CNV unions were simply asked to sign agreements already reached with staff associations or be excluded.

3.3   Union organization and policies
In the 1980s the Dutch union movement suffered a major setback. In December 1985 all unions together totalled little more than 1.5 million members against almost 1.8 million at the end of 1978. This decline was the largest ever since the early 1920s. Not even in the 1930s recession had the union lost so many members (Visser, 1987). Moreover a growing proportion – now over 17 per cent – have retired from the labour market. These are mainly members who are on old age, pre-retirement or disablement pensions, while the unemployed appear to have dropped from membership (Visser 1986). In the 1980s the union density rate dropped to 24 per cent of the labour force, or 27 per cent of employees in employment (see Table 7.2).

More than half of the FNV's losses have been borne by the Industriebond FNV, which organizes throughout manufacturing with the exception of printing. This union alone lost more than 100,000 (or one-third) of its members. Half of the losses occurred in metalworking, which is supposed to be the union's stronghold (Vos, 1987). The point should be stressed, though, that *all* unions, whatever their political colour, policy or recruitment domain, lost members. The decline in the CNV is partly concealed by the affiliation of some former independent Catholic unions in the public sector. The general nature of union enfeeblement is evidenced by the data on sectoral developments (see Table 7.3). Density rates fell in all sectors and occupational groups. We observe that only one out of five employees in the private sector is organized – one-third of manual and one-eighth of non-manual employees. The lowest rate is found in private services, with less than 10 per cent of all employees joining unions. In banking, for example, the figure is

Table 7.2 *Trade union membership by confederation (000s) and union density rates (%), Netherlands, 1976–86*[1]

	FNV	CNV	MHP	Other	Total union membership			Employees		Density rates	
					All	Pens.	Less pens.	All	Employed	All	Employed
1976	1,050.7	256.9	111.9	329.0	1,748.5	180.1	1,568.4	4,469	4,238	35.1	37.0
1977	1,069.1	294.8	113.2	306.2	1,783.3	185.4	1,597.9	4,520	4,304	35.4	37.1
1978	1,079.9	300.6	117.4	292.0	1,789.9	192.3	1,597.6	4,581	4,361	34.9	36.6
1979	1,073.7	303.9	118.5	259.4	1,755.5	200.5	1,555.0	4,729	4,512	32.9	34.5
1980	1,053.7	302.4	113.2	252.6	1,721.9	210.0	1,511.9	4,879	4,557	31.0	33.2
1981	1,008.0	346.3	113.4	246.9	1,714.6	223.6	1,491.0	5,016	4,542	29.7	32.8
1982	988.8	334.3	112.6	226.9	1,662.6	239.4	1,423.2	5,151	4,507	27.6	31.6
1983	949.5	316.0	111.2	227.8	1,604.5	256.8	1,347.7	5,211	4,355	25.9	30.9
1984	906.0	301.5	109.4	233.0	1,549.9	260.3	1,289.6	5,282	4,485	24.4	28.8
1985	893.0	298.1	106.9	231.6	1,529.3	258.2	1,271.1	5,347	4,597	23.8	27.7
1986	891.2	294.8	108.3	233.5	1,527.8	257.5	1,270.3	5,400	4,695	23.5	27.1

[1] Membership, labour force and density figures refer to 31 December of each year (data reported at 1 January have been transformed to 31 December of preceding year). The figures on employees include part-time workers and job-seekers.

Sources: Visser, 1987:371–4; as regards unemployed workers I have used the CBS figures on registered unemployment in December each year

Table 7.3 *Union membership by sector and occupation, and density rates, Netherlands, 1979 and 1985*

	Union membership			Employees in employment			Density rates	
	1979 (000s)	1985 (000s)	Change (%)	1979 (000s)	1985 (000s)	Change (%)	1979 (%)	1985 (%)
Total exposed sectors	664.4	494.0	−25.6	2,428.5	2,679.5	10.3	27.4	18.4
Manufacturing and mining	448.8	315.7	−29.7	1,097.2	1,016.6	−7.3	40.9	31.1
Manual	354.3	237.6	−32.9	692.4	636.0	−8.1	51.2	37.4
Non-manual	94.5	78.1	−17.4	404.9	380.6	−6.0	23.3	20.5
Private transport and ports	60.4	48.4	−19.9	164.9	178.6	8.3	36.7	27.1
Commerce, banking and insurance	102.5	73.3	−29.5	710.2	785.8	10.6	14.4	9.3
Commercial services	52.7	56.6	7.4	456.1	698.5	53.1	11.6	8.1
Total non-exposed sectors	863.0	779.6	−9.7	1,834.8	1,799.8	−1.9	47.0	43.3
Agriculture	24.6	19.3	−21.5	92.4	84.9	−8.1	26.6	22.7
Construction	175.4	134.2	−23.5	464.9	354.8	−23.6	37.7	37.8
Public transport and PTT	82.0	73.8	−10.0	138.9	131.9	−5.0	59.0	56.0
Public services and utilities	581.0	552.3	−4.9	1,138.6	1,229.1	7.9	51.0	44.9
Total private sector	864.4	643.4	−25.6	2,985.7	3,119.8	4.5	22.9	20.6
Manual	608.1	433.7	−28.7	1,544.2	1,422.9	−7.9	39.4	30.5
Non-manual	256.3	209.7	−18.2	1,441.5	1,696.9	17.7	17.8	12.4
Total public sector	663.0	629.0	−5.1	1,272.5	1,360.5	6.5	51.9	46.2

Source: Visser, 1987:381–4; end-of-year data

only 7 per cent (FNV, 1987). Little has changed since van de Vall (1970) wrote that Dutch unions attract only a small minority of salaried employees. Despite initial growth, the new organization of salaried employees (MHP) soon stagnated and shared in the current malaise.

The strength (or weakness?) of Dutch unions is found among public employees, nearly half of whom join unions. About half of all employed union members are now working in the public sector against 38 per cent in 1971 or 26 per cent in 1947. In the CNV this proportion has risen to 64 per cent, in the FNV to 38 per cent. Calculated over the total reported membership we find that in 1985 only one-third of all union members is in jobs exposed to international competition. The dramatic position of Dutch unions is underscored by the available data on membership by sex and age groups (CBS, 1979–85; Visser, 1986). The collapse of the youth labour market has caused a sharp decline in membership among young people. Density rates fell from 31 to 19 per cent among males, and from 13 to 7 per cent among females under the age of twenty-five. In the 25–64 age group density fell from 48 to 38 per cent among males, and remained at around 20 per cent among females. The FNV (1986) recently described its current membership as dominated by the 'full-time employed, older and semi-skilled male breadwinner' and 'to reflect best the structure of the labour force in the 1950s'.

The explanation of trade union decline must take account of several causes. The above-average losses between 1981 and 1984 suggest that the steep rise in unemployment and the reduction of manual employment played a major part. Once their members become unemployed, Dutch unions have little to offer to them by way of insurance, job recruitment or (re)training. Unemployment insurance and labour exchange are state-administered activities. Membership turnover data suggest that unions recruited fewer members, while unemployment, pre-retirement and the ageing process were causing continuing high separation rates.

The fact that union density has decreased in all sectors and occupations indicates that structural shifts can only explain part of the decline. My econometric analysis of union growth between 1913 and 1985 shows that there is a strong relationship with inflation, while in the post-war period the impact of wage increases and unemployment is small (Visser, 1987). The current deflationary climate seems to have removed some of the need to seek union protection. The absence of wage increases in the 1980s may have reduced the benefits for which workers tend to credit unions. The analysis also suggests that union growth in the Netherlands reaches its 'saturation point' relatively early. This is probably due to the high degree of institutional security of Dutch unions in the past. Recognized at the national level, unions' bargaining capacity used to be unrelated to their representation in single bargaining units, thereby removing the need to back up demands by enlarging membership. Membership drives are rare. The Dutch system offers large opportunities for 'free riding'. Collective bargaining laws prevent discrimination between members and non-members. Union attempts to make non-members pay for their services have met with little success in the past. Printing is the only industry in which a closed shop was established (in 1912) and was maintained. National bargaining, in the context of high government involvement and little membership participation, intensifies the 'public good' problem in union organization. The availability of an alternative public institution for worker representation in the works councils and the absence of a union-based system of grievance-handling within firms weakens the need for workers to join unions, and diminishes the selective benefits which might accrue from membership.

Preceding the current membership crisis, the Dutch union movement was becoming more divided. Following the foundation of the FNV and the MHP, relations within the movement were becoming more conflictual. The religious cleavage of the past was giving way to a political split, partly based on differences in membership composition. The failure to build a single organization from the three original 'pillars' led to deep-seated frustration. The FNV disengaged from all existing joint ventures and co-ordinating bodies with the CNV, and the latter organization's closer (though not untroubled) relations with most Cabinets after 1977 was regarded with jealousy (Albeda, 1986). Within each confederation the formation of large conglomerate industrial unions in the early 1970s and the growing weight of public sector unions in later years led to increased rivalry and reintroduced an element of competition over membership domains and policies. Private sector unions became less than sympathetic to the demands put forward by their colleagues in the public sector, which they felt to be a dead weight in bargaining and a pretext for government intervention. Within most unions leadership styles changed; members became less complaisant and more resourceful in pressing for particular union policies. Consequently, the confederal ability to co-ordinate its affiliates declined.

Union responses to the changing socioeconomic environment have been slow. It took until late 1982 before unions made employment their first priority. Their 1977 victory over the cost-of-living clauses proved an ambiguous one. Unions that made an attempt to negotiate higher employment levels in exchange for real wage restraint discovered that the clauses had become a symbol of firmness. Whatever their benefit in defending the real income of workers, the cost-of-living clauses prevented unions and managements from negotiating wages and differentials in response to labour market change and skill scarcities. Moreover, while the government was severing the link with social benefits, the unions found themselves in the awkward position of defending a protective mechanism which was associated with high labour costs but unable to prevent the erosion of incomes of a growing number of people priced out of their jobs.

Union demands for working-time reduction began to take shape in the later 1970s. Both FNV and CNV supported the well-known campaign of the European Trades Union Council (ETUC) to reduce working hours by 10 per cent in five years. What divided the unions was the issue of wage compensation for less hours. In 1978 the Industriebond–FNV was forced to abandon its demand for shorter hours. In 1980, this union and the CNV seemed ready to renegotiate the price compensation clauses and to accept uncompensated shorter hours. Despite cautious backing from the confederal leadership, the Industriebond–FNV failed to win the support needed from other unions. Except for the widening of pre-retirement schemes, unions were unable to make any progress until late 1982, when the union confederations agreed, for the first time, to forfeit pay increases deriving from rising prices in exchange for shorter hours. Five years later the combination of employer opposition, lack of backing from members and internal divisions brought job-sharing policies to an end.

4 Collective bargaining: processes and outcomes

Despite the fall in union membership, there has been no significant decline in bargaining coverage in recent years. The number of sectoral agreements has remained pretty constant, and the growth in the number of company agreements is not spectacular. Taken together, the figures presented in Table 7.4 do not warrant the conclusion that major changes have occurred during the 1980s. In this respect, there appears to be a significant contrast with the inter-war period when single-employer agreements were predominant, coverage was much lower than the membership in unions and was decreasing proportionate to the decline in union membership. In the post-war period collective bargaining has clearly become an

Table 7.4 Collective agreements, number of agreements, bargaining coverage and strike involvement, Netherlands, 1976–86

	Sector agreements		Company agreements		All agreements		Coverage in % of private employees	Strike involvement		Working days lost per 1000 employees
	No.	Employees (000s)	No.	Employees (000s)	No.	Employees (000s)		No. of strikes	No. of workers (000s)	
1976	184	2,117.5	462	348.3	646	2,465.8		11	15.4	3.4
1977	186	2,161.9	479	371.3	664	2,533.1	73	9	35.9	55.6
1978	192	2,311.9	510	383.9	702	2,695.8		11	2.7	0.7
1979	185	2,326.7	533	406.6	718	2,733.3		30	31.8	69.0
1980	185	2,350.0	543	412.3	728	2,762.1	75	11	20.4	12.1
1981	184	2,407.1	560	416.3	744	2,823.3		11	8.6	5.3
1982	180	2,373.2	607	414.1	787	2,787.5	76	12	69.8	47.9
1983	190	2,395.2	593	406.7	783	2,801.9		9	20.3	26.9
1984	192	2,419.0	607	410.6	799	2,829.6		11	16.2	6.5
1985	192	2,351.7	627	420.6	819	2,772.3		45	22.6	19.3
1986	191	2,284.8	590	422.9	781	2,707.7	75	35	17.0	8.3

Sources: Collective agreements: DCA (Department of Social Affairs and Employment), 1987. Strikes: CBS, Sociaal-Economische Maandstatistiek, 1977–87

institution which both parties find hard to disregard. Clearly, the high level of employer organization, the presence of joint negotiating bodies in many sectors and the legal extension of collective bargaining helps trade unions to maintain their influence even if membership is at a low. Yet beyond this apparent institutional stability changes have occurred in both the content and process of collective bargaining. I will first summarize the actual developments in pay, hours and employment conditions, and in work stoppages and industrial conflict, and then consider more 'systemic' changes in the final paragraph.

4.1 Developments in pay and incomes

One of the long-term consequences of the changes in the socio-economic environment is the decline of redistributive wage bargaining. Collective bargaining in the private sector stopped giving guidance to pay developments elsewhere. In the first half of the 1980s the real wage rate, averaged for all employees, fell by over 9 per cent (see Table 7.1). The impact of the 1982 central agreement is also clearly visible. Although agreement over shorter hours at sectoral and company levels proved difficult, in less than a year two-thirds of all collective contracts, affecting about 1.9 million wage-earners, had been renegotiated. In contrast to common practice, most settlements applied for two years, during which the payment of price compensation was suspended. By the mid-1980s the automatism of cost-of-living adjustments had virtually disappeared. In 1985 price compensation was only fully paid in less than 10 per cent of all contracts; 30 per cent no longer contained an escalator clause (FNV, 1985). With only slightly increasing contractual wages (1.3 per cent in 1983, 0.4 per cent in 1984 and 1.4 per cent in 1985), real wages fell sharply. In 1986 and 1987 real wages increased by a small amount (1–1.5 per cent). In general, rises have been larger in the higher income brackets, partly in response to skill scarcities and profitable firms' ability to pay.

The curtailment of public sector salary increases, taking effect from 1979, the 3 per cent cut in nominal pay in 1984 and the stand-still in other years have caused a greater setback. Compared to the situation in 1978, civil servant pay has lagged about 10 per cent behind pay developments in the private sector. In 1987 civil servant salaries have risen, in nominal terms, for the first time since 1982 by about 0.5 per cent on average, varying from 0.2 in the lowest scales to 1.2 per cent in the highest. Following the suspension of the 1980 Adjustment Mechanism Act and the government measures taken after 1982, the statutory minimum wage fell behind the

Table 7.5   *Percentage changes in disposable incomes: earnings and benefits, Netherlands, 1974–86*

	Minimal level			Mode	
	employed	pensioners	disabled	employed	disabled
1974–9	19.4	24.8	25.7	9.3	18.0
1980–5	− 2.1	− 2.3	− 2.4	− 1.8	− 4.8
1980	− 1.0	− 0.8	− 0.8	− 1.9	− 1.7
1981	− 2.7	− 3.5	− 3.6	− 4.1	− 4.4
1982	− 2.0	− 2.6	− 3.2	− 2.2	− 4.6
1983	− 2.8	− 3.0	− 3.0	− 3.5	− 7.2
1984	− 3.4	− 3.1	− 3.1	− 0.8	− 4.6
1985	− 0.5	− 0.5	− 0.5	1.5	6.5
1986	1.3	1.5	1.5	2.5	1.5

Source: SAE, 1986

contractual wage index by 10 per cent cumulatively between mid-1980 and the end of 1985. Incomes deriving from social benefits have fallen by the same percentage. The cuts have been made structural by lowering maximum benefits, in two steps, from 80 to 70 per cent of last earned wages.

It is fair to say that these developments witness a reversal in income developments. First, the erosion of incomes deriving from profits came to a halt. The wage quota, which measures the total wage bill as a percentage of value-added, dropped from 75.5 per cent in 1975 to 69.4 per cent in 1983. Secondly, in 1980 people depending on social security suffered a greater loss than the employed, sharply contrasting the trend of the 1970s (see Table 7.5). Finally, comparing the earnings of the employed at minimum and mode levels, income differentials widened again after 1983.

4.2   Working-time reduction and job-sharing
The bargaining round which followed the 1982 central agreement generally led to the conclusion of agreements providing for a reduction of annual working hours by 5 per cent in two years. In some agreements (printing, department stores, DAF trucks) a further reduction of 5 per cent in 1985–6 was agreed upon. But in most cases the 1985 bargaining round produced a standstill. Most larger agreements, including Philips, AKZO and metal engineering, referred the issue to joint working-parties with the predictable outcome that employers demanded greater flexibility and opposed

Table 7.6 *Change in actual hours worked and disposable
incomes of employees (average change per period in
percentages), Netherlands, 1952–85*

Period	Working hours	Disposable incomes
1952–62	− 0.75	3.5
1962–72	− 0.85	4.3
1972–7	− 1.35	2.2
1977–82	− 0.35	− 0.2
1982–5	− 1.30	− 0.9

Source: Visser, 1989

a further general hours round. The only concessions won related to
extra days off for shift workers. Between 50 and 60 per cent of all
full-time employees in the private sector have gained a standard
working week of thirty-eight hours, and 10–15 per cent a working
week of thirty-six hours. These are annual averages; most of the
reduction took the form of extra days off. In 1986 the government
introduced a thirty-eight-hour week for civil servants. During that
year no further concession was won by the unions (Visser, 1989).

The working-time reduction between 1982 and 1985 was the
result of an extraordinary situation and a surprising central agreement which was not likely to be repeated. Sharing out employment
over a larger number of people, each taking a small part of unemployment, seemed really the only thing on offer in 1982. Faced
with a choice between continued resistance against working-time
reduction and acceptance of what then seemed the only means to
stave off unemployment, employers had to consider the intractable
risk of widespread dissatisfaction caused by an unconditional veto.
They could not yet be sure that the government would not intervene and impose a standard reduction, should they refuse to co-
operate. Late in 1982 the Minister of Social Affairs and his principal civil servants voiced such threats on several occasions. The
trade unions simply could not afford to continue defending fully
indexed wages, which would price more people out of their jobs
and no longer apply to those living on benefits.

The 1980s hours movement had the characteristics of a recession-
induced campaign. This explains its moderate success and rapid
termination. Unlike past movements, unions could not build on a
voluntary trade-off of income for leisure in which workers valued
fewer working hours as a gain in individual welfare. This is highlighted by the figures in Table 7.6, which relate the average reduction
of working hours per period to changes in after-tax take-home pay.

A policy pursuing working-time reduction, not for its own sake but canvassed as a palliative for mass unemployment, must make additional recruitment the ultimate criterion by which it stands. In this respect the campaign has been less than satisfactory. The CPB estimated the refilling of vacant hours in the private sector at zero in 1983 and 25 per cent in 1984. There was every reason to believe that the real effect was in fact less. The first steps were taken in 1983 when utilization ratios in industry were unusually low and the third consecutive year of the massive labour shake-out showed that many firms were still overstaffed. Labour-time reduction primarily helped to reduce the least productive hours. Operating hours were in most cases reduced as well, thus violating the condition for additional recruitment. The 1983–4 agreements put the employers under no obligation to hire new workers for vacant hours. They successfully resisted union-specified employment targets, and unions suffered from a lack of in-plant control.

Early retirement and part-time employment have continued to be important in the redistribution of jobs. After 1979 pre-retirement clauses have become a regular ingredient of collective bargaining, following government-sponsored experiments with early retirement in the crisis-ridden docks, shipyards and steel industries and among school-teachers. Currently, most collective agreements offer a choice to take indemnified retirement at the age of sixty-one. Attempts have been made to refill jobs with trainees and young entrants.

In 1984 unions and employers in the metal industry struck an agreement to introduce jobs in the range of 25–32 hours for young entrants, relaxing the conditions concerning minimum pay and training. Other unions and the youth sections of FNV and CNV collided with the Industriebond–FNV, which had masterminded this 'Plan for Juvenile Employment'. A weaker version was agreed upon between the central organizations, inviting negotiators to arrange job-sharing schemes for school-leavers and young employed workers. The results have been disappointing, and in 1985 the engineering employers discontinued the job-sharing scheme for young workers, arguing that the industry was disadvantaged since others had not followed.

In May 1986 another central agreement was reached, inviting continued wage moderation, while the government specified a target of 500,000 unemployed in 1990 and promised extra measures concerning long-term unemployment and training. In neither the 1984 nor the 1986 agreement did employers commit themselves to working-time reduction, and even more than in 1982 they insisted that lower-level negotiators should find their own solutions.

Unions are now under pressure to concede flexible arrangements concerning different groups of workers, and some unions want first to recapture the forgone pay increases. Unions still committed to job-sharing cannot count on too much enthusiasm among their members, many of whom experience intensified workloads for fewer paid hours while few new jobs have been created. Far short of their initial aim of thirty-five hours in 1986 and thirty-two hours in 1990, the 1987 conferences of FNV and CNV dropped the issue.

4.3 Trends in industrial conflict

The retrenchment of labour and the reversal in conditions of pay during the 1980s have resulted in few overt conflicts. There was no significant break in strike trends between the 1970s and the 1980s (see Table 7.4). Dutch unions and Dutch workers are the opposite of strike-prone. Indeed, during and after the period of centrally guided wage policies the number of days lost was very low by international standards. Only once every few years did the annual number of days lost exceed a hundred thousand. With on average only eighteen working days lost per 1000 employed workers between 1980 and 1986, strikes have remained a marginal phenomenon in Dutch industrial relations.

The effects of the recession are clearer in the case of factory occupations. In the 1970s and during the first years of the past decade there was a surge in this type of activity. In two-thirds of all cases the objective was to prevent plant closures or lay-offs. Rarely have these desperate forms of action met with success. As a matter of fact, over time the failure rate rose from 50 to 70 per cent despite the fact that unions became more willing to support this type of militancy (J.C. Visser, 1986).

While the right to strike is not regulated by law, the judiciary has tended to accept its legality as far as the private sector is concerned. Generally, courts stipulate that bargaining has to be in good faith and strikes must not inflict 'unjustified costs' on third parties. Civil servants had been denied the legal right to strike since the great railway strike of 1903. However, when the government ratified the European Social Charter in 1980 its proviso excluding civil servants was justified by a promise of impending legislation, but its failure to introduce legislation led the courts to decide that the government had *de facto* intended to grant this right to its employees.

The first post-war strike, called by the FNV's union of civil servants, took place in 1978 against the trend adjustments, but still went largely unnoticed. In 1982 teachers went on strike and in 1983 the FNV cartel of public employee unions staged a major strike which lasted three weeks. In the abundance of lawsuits which accompanied and eventually ended the strike, the courts ruled that the police could not strike and did not take a lenient view on the admissibility of strikes in public services. As a rule, Dutch unions comply with court decisions. In this case the unions did so expediently, for the strikes of post-office clerks, garbage collectors, railwaymen and busdrivers had become extremely unpopular among a public which had no experience of such inconveniences (Lammers, 1984).

Dutch law stipulates that the government must consult the representative civil servant unions before making final decisions, but is under no obligation to negotiate. Given the time-honoured guarantees of the trend mechanism, civil servant unions had seemed satisfied with a consultative role; they guessed that little could be gained by independent bargaining. Suddenly they were confronted with employer unilateralism and a determined Cabinet which was not prepared to honour what civil servants' unions saw as their customary rights. Parliament has until now upheld the government's position, but probably some form of restricted bargaining over civil servant salaries will emerge, as it is unlikely that salaries will again be pegged to private sector wages.

In 1984 an expert Advisory and Arbitration Committee (AAC) was installed, which can advise or arbitrate in case of conflicts. Only if both sides seek arbitration and give prior consent are its rulings binding. Currently, employment relations in the public sector are at a low. Thus far, the Minister of Home Affairs, responsible for civil servants, has not shown the slightest tendency to negotiate, or accept final-offer arbitration. But recent events suggest that this position will not be upheld. In 1987 the Minister was ordered, by the AAC and Parliament, to 'renegotiate' a deal struck with the MHP union of higher civil servants and seek the consent of other unions. At the end of the day unions of all four cartels, including the FNV's teachers' union but not its leading union of civil servants, put their signature to a modified 'contract' for 1987–8.

5   Preparing for the 1990s

There is little doubt that the early 1980s were a watershed in Dutch industrial relations. In many areas, a departure from past policies and practices can be observed (see Table 7.7). In this section I will evaluate the changes by discussing a number of questions relating to the role of concertation, the meaning of decentralization, the

Table 7.7 *Changes in the industrial relations system, Netherlands since 1980*

Type	Pre-1980	Post-1980
A(a) National concertation	Before the 1970s, regular; in the 1970s, tried by all governments but succeeded only once	Annual consultations, but less focal role of the government; absence of side-payments
A(b) Industry-wide, collective bargaining	Firmly established, except for multinational companies; co-ordinating role of central organizations in decline	Stable, but with less or no central co-ordination; attempts of employers to promote differentiation
B Decentralized bargaining	Not very significant, only minor local modifications; wage drift not a major factor, and not institutionalized	Increased scope for additional bargaining at local level, especially over working hours, and training; further attempt of employers to increase scope for local bargaining
C(a) Worker participation via unions	Collective agreements play minor role in enhancing direct union representation in firms; law promotes worker participation and consultation via works councils; elected council members mostly union members, but unions do not control councils	Legal position of works councils and council members strengthened; tendency (of employers rather than unions) to involve councils in local bargaining; relation with unions still precarious
C(b) Worker participation without unions	Not very significant, except for managerial staffs	Some employers' initiatives; weakening of unions offers more opportunities – partly via councils; some cases of 'yellow' lists of council candidates supported by employer
D(a) Simple contracts without unions	See under C(b)	Increased scope for flexibility and individual contracting; some cases of 'buying off' union contracts via better individual terms
D(b) Simple contracts in secondary or grey labour market	Of some importance in retail and private services; Extension Law and Government Orders limit impact	As before, but more important, especially agency labour and 'zero hours' contracts

extent of flexibility and the impact on employment relations. I will finish by considering the stability of the current changes and the likely future of Dutch industrial relations.

5.1   The current realignment

The Dutch system, as it emerged after 1945, was based on a decision to co-operate. In exchange for the commitment to the goal of full employment and recognizing their partnership in the development of a nationwide social security system, unions accepted the authority of employers over within-firm production and investment decisions. Unions and employers endorsed a strategy which aimed at fostering a competitive export sector that could secure robust output and employment growth, and would pay for extensive social security. To this end they accepted that the government should have a final say in collective decision-making over wages, while governments took their decisions in matters of socioeconomic policy only after consultation. This was classic societal corporatism, based on comprehensive organization and trilateral concertation, and aimed at output growth, employment and security by ensuring higher levels of productivity and lower wages than otherwise would be the case.

Disintegrating tendencies became manifest before the external shocks of the 1970s. Co-operation became more contingent, each party had to cope with more divergence in its ranks and central authority was less easily accepted. Disenchantment with elite control showed itself throughout society and eroded the conditions for elite co-operation. Perceptive authors such as van de Vall (1970) and Windmuller (1969) rightly suspected that the initial consensus would be undermined by its very success in bringing about welfare, security and full employment. Challenged by membership disaffection and 'black wages' conceded by employers in tight labour markets, both employers and unions gradually changed strategy. Sectoral unions, employers' associations and multinational companies, whose role was enhanced by the opening of European markets, all demanded greater bargaining autonomy.

In the 1970s unions claimed a greater share in productivity gains and emphasized redistributive wage policies. Their wage formula included what one might summarize as 'productivity increases plus inflation plus redistribution in favour of the low-paid plus protection of social benefit incomes'. In all four areas unions were largely successful until the late 1970s, which is remarkable considering the faltering rate of growth, rising unemployment and the absence of a strong rise in trade union membership or strike action during these years. The lack of resistance on the part of employers, and the extended income and welfare guarantees with which governments sought to legitimate their recurrent interventions, explain in large part how the Netherlands became a 'low employment–high wage' country. Both unions and employers looked to the state for the guarantees they were unable to win from each other. The central organizations became accustomed to the fact that in lieu of a central agreement governments would intervene anyway. It helped both sides to shed their responsibility to enforce within their own ranks what would most likely be painful compromises. The far-reaching impact of a few bargaining decisions in the private sector on the national economy and, not least, on its own budget made it difficult for the government to withdraw. Maintaining the automatic linkage of social benefits to wage developments would inevitably have required the return to some sort of government-guided wage policy. But neither employers nor unions wanted a return to the central wage policies of the past.

The idea that a steadily rising income for all could be guaranteed, despite a long-term erosion of investments and a rapidly increasing number of people for whom no place in the productive process could be found, was self-deluding (Kalma and Krop, 1983). The failure to halt the trend towards rising unemployment, already manifest in the mid-1970s, was crucial. The answer at the time was an increase in public employment and welfare, and the diversion of labour slack into channels other than overt unemployment. This may have suggested that structural problems related to declining competitiveness and de-industrialization could be solved with little pain. In its 1976 survey of the Dutch economy, the OECD observed that in spite of the sharp rise in unemployment 'public concern had been less than what one would have expected only a few years ago' and attributed this to the 'highly sophisticated system of social security and income guarantees'.

In the early years of the 1980s unions could no longer accomplish their goal of real wage defence. In only five years labour's share in the national income, which had risen from 75 per cent in 1963 to 91 per cent in 1981, fell to 80.5 per cent in 1986. This reflected a major change in the distribution of power between employers, unions and governments. In the 1980s employers became the demanding party. Given a slack labour market they were in a position to defy the unions. The government needed the employers – and whatever action to stimulate investment and employment they would take – more than they could be harmed by a weakened trade union movement. Until the early 1980s governments, with or without the Labour Party, had taken for granted that they needed the legitimacy provided by extensive consultation and co-operation with the unions. The elections of 1982 and 1986 produced a new political fact: despite a sustained high level of unemployment, governments could survive without the co-operation of the trade union movement.

5.2 The end of corporatism(s)?

Foreign observers were always struck by the high degree of institutionalization and far-reaching trust placed in statutory provisions in Dutch industrial relations. Yet the 'extremely complex system of decision-making' (Windmuller) had seemed to function quite well in the development stage of the Dutch welfare state. It is paradoxical that the same institutional arrangements that had assisted in co-ordinating socioeconomic policies and broadening the welfare state, were conspicuously absent in managing its crisis and decline. Put to the test, corporatism – or should one say the remnants of corporatism? – failed.

In comparative studies of 'neo-corporatism' the Netherlands was usually ranked among the first three or four countries, along with Austria, Norway and Sweden, although many students found it difficult to judge the developments that occurred in the 1970s (see Lehmbruch, 1982), and it was noted that the organizational structure of interests, especially of labour, was very different from the others (Schmitter, 1981; Korpi, 1983). Observers writing during the 1970s stressed the 'polarization' of interests (Akkermans and Grootings, 1978) and the 'erosion' of societal consensus (Peper, 1975). The consequence was a dislocation and pluralization of interests, a development which was responded to by various incorporation strategies of the state (Geelhoed, 1983). Zimmermann (1986) correctly identified the 1970s, and not the 1950s or 1960s, as the heyday of 'tripartism'. He failed to note, however, that societal corporatism was replaced by many little corporatisms, each capturing some state agency and holding the others in check. The proliferation of advisory and consultative bodies, many emerging in the shadow of the welfare state, added to the effect of stultifying adaptation to change. In recent years the state has been trying to pull out, to reduce the area and scope of its interventions and to reshape its relation with society in a technocratic rather than corporatist fashion. There are a number of recent changes – varying from privatization to the new industrialization and labour market policies – which testify to the decline of popularity of neo-corporatism in the Netherlands.

National concertation has not disappeared, but its role has

become more ephemeral. Still, each year there is a spell of tripartite bargaining in which central organizations and the government check whether a consensus about current trends and policies can be attained. The central agreements reached in 1982, 1984 and 1986, committed neither the organizations nor the government. Lower-level negotiators were not bound by the agreements as they had been under the regime of central wage policy. The ability of union confederations to co-ordinate affiliates has weakened. Other difficulties derive from inter-confederal competition and the growth of the private–public division within confederations. In recent years, the CNV has broken with the tradition of issuing bargaining guidelines on behalf of its affiliates. The FNV is reluctant to give up national concertation, but is less capable of holding its affiliates together. Responding to changes in product markets and facilitated by a depressed labour market, employers have discovered that their current strength lies with the company and try to obtain less uniform collective bargaining arrangements. National concertation is not in their current interest. Without the government reassuming an active role in designing incomes policies, national concertation will weaken further.

Meanwhile, tripartite bodies such as the Sociaal-Economische Raad (Social-Economic Council) are going through a difficult period. The polarization of interests within the SER is one reason for its declining authority: in less than half of the fifty-three advisory statements made between 1977 and 1984 did it reach the unanimity needed for real influence (Albeda, 1986:24). Once the 'apex of institutionalized conflict-management' (Lijphart, 1968), the SER has become synonymous with 'institutional sclerosis'. Some of the most painful government decisions in recent years – for instance, the revision of the unemployment support system – have been taken without awaiting the advice of the SER and its connected bodies. Committees of independent experts, such as the Wagner Committee, have been far more influential in setting new policies in train. Not the SER but the bipartite Stichting van de Arbeid (Foundation of Labour) has become the government's interlocutor in matters of socioeconomic policies, while the once influential biannual reports of the SER's Economic Expert Committee play a much smaller role. Currently, employers – and not unions – discuss whether they should continue their presence in 'corporatist' bodies such as the SER.

5.3 Decentralization and the role of works councils
Employers want to reshape pay and employment conditions more in accordance with the particular needs of firms. This objective is

served by a destandardization of the process and outcomes of collective bargaining. The bargaining rounds over working-time reduction have added fuel to the ongoing process of decentralization of Dutch industrial relations. Collective agreements in their existing form are considered less suitable than within-firm arrangements. The question is whether trade unions will remain the principal interlocutors if additional bargaining were to take place in firms. At the time of writing, proposals abound to restrict multi-employer agreements to procedural matters and basic standards of pay and employment, increasing the scope for differentiation. Employers are much better equipped – and more 'at home' so to speak – than unions to conduct bargaining at the level of firms.

There is little doubt that, following the legal reforms in 1979, the position of works councils has strengthened (Teulings, 1985; 1987; Looise and de Lange, 1987). But it is doubtful whether it has helped trade unions to improve their plant effectiveness, as it apparently did in West Germany after the reforms in 1972 (Streeck, 1985).

While employers may increasingly turn to the councils as possible co-managers of company employment relations, unions have been reluctant to grant the councils a bargaining role, and little use has been made of the legal possibility of involving the councils in bargaining (Looise, 1985). Union members in councils tend to criticize their unions for lack of support and information, and an excess of paternalizing.

It is difficult to say where decentralization will stop. Some standardization – taking wages out of competition – at sectoral levels is in the interest of employers. Sectoral employers' organizations and trade unions will not easily surrender their central activity – and part of their raison d'être – of negotiating sectoral agreements. Yet it seems a safe conclusion that these agreements will become more like a 'menu' from which local bargainers, with or without the assistance of trade unions, must choose solutions. The limit of decentralization, from the point of view of employers, is well formulated by Streeck (1987:45) for the German case and probably equally applicable to Dutch employers: the weakening of trade unions at the national and sectoral level is welcome to employers as long as it does not result in militant shop-floor bargaining. Under the conditions of the early 1980s, it was unlikely that it would do so, but will it in the future? And there are no guarantees that conservative governments will not re-enter the collective bargaining scene should inflationary pressures re-emerge. A high level of unemployment is not going to work as a brake on pay demands forever.

5.4   Flexibility strategies

In order to match shorter working hours of employees with unchanged or longer operating hours and costlier machinery, employers have stressed the need for more flexible standards to be applied to the utilization of labour. Partly this has been achieved by introducing working hours of different length and fixed-duration contracts for particular categories of labour. Either way the variability of labour in response to changes in product demand or production requirements increases. Flexible working-time arrangements replace the traditional adjustments via overtime hours and obligatory shorter hours, both of which are subject to legal restrictions and are costly to the employer. Long-established legal norms which limit the normal working day or restrict night and weekend hours have come under pressure.

Internal flexibility, applied to labour contracted under standard conditions and protected by constraints on hiring and firing, is not only enhanced by varying the input of labour, measured in time or availability. Other strategies aiming at the mobilization of 'internal labour markets' seek to enlarge the possibility of, and to create incentives for, 'on-the-job mobility' in terms of location, tasks and skills. On the basis of a survey of annual reports of nineteen large firms in industry, commerce, banking and insurance, van Bergeijk and de Grip (1984) suggest that most of these firms have developed 'internal labour markets' for their core labour force. Between 1975 and 1983, the average length-of-service increased, and in the critical years after 1980 separation rates fell sharply. Natural wastage and pre-retirement have become the major instruments in reducing manpower levels. This conclusion must, of course, be restricted to the regular labour force employed in large firms which have remained in business, and to large parts of the public sector. With respect to these employees, measures to increase internal flexibility would seem of great importance. The precarious relations between unions and councils suggest that under present conditions Dutch unions might not be able to make councils withdraw from co-managing internal labour markets. Unions could of course try to design the antagonist strategy needed, but it is doubtful whether they would be well advised to do so. In the present circumstances, many employers may be prepared to take the risk and see how large the scope for 'unionism with councils but without unions' is.

There is no doubt that the external flexibility of the Dutch labour market has increased. The extreme labour slack has been the major factor behind this change. Currently some 15–20 per cent of all Dutch employees, not counting those involved in the 'informal economy', work under employment contracts that differ from standard (open-ended) employment contracts. Including the growing number of part-time jobs, between one-third and one-half of the 4.4 million Dutch wage- and salary-earners are now employed in jobs that in one way or another deviate from the concept of a full-time job (OSA, 1986). The greater variety and individualization of time schedules and labour standards have complicated the recruitment task of trade unions. Likewise they face a greater difficulty in organizing this heterogeneous workforce around common objectives.

The greater fluidity in the labour market is confirmed by the comparison of the 1979 and 1984 Wage Surveys (Corpelijn, 1986). In 1984 people who served with the same firm as in 1979 had on average ten (females) or nineteen (males) years' service. As expected, length of service is highest among males between twenty-five and fifty. This category is clearly less subject to dismissals and enjoys more seniority-related protection against lay-offs. The short average-length data of all completed employment spells (four years in 1984) is evidence that elsewhere in the labour market turnover is high. Half of all new hirings started in 1984 terminated within the year, a noticeably higher percentage than in 1979. This testifies to the increase in short and fixed-duration contracts, and the greater importance of 'agency labour'. It will be recalled that the rise in part-time work mainly affected (married) women. Many of these jobs are precarious and involve only short weekly hours. As a matter of fact, two-fifths of all part-timers work less than fifteen hours weekly and are not covered by legal employment protection, social insurance or works council provisions. Some of these jobs, mainly held by women, are based on so-called 'min-max' or 'zero-hours' contracts which stipulate that the number of hours and the time-span of work depends on the 'call' of employers. Unions have not succeeded in obtaining a statutory ban.

Here, the unions are clearly in need of some help from the legislator, because it would be very difficult to organize the people involved. Part-time labour is concentrated in services: 45.7 per cent of all jobs in health and welfare, and 42.8 per cent in retail, against only 7 per cent in manufacturing. In some of these sectors (especially in retail), unions are extremely weak, and bargaining coverage is far from complete. In retail coverage it is only 50 per cent, against 80 per cent and more in industry, construction and transport. There is a clear relation with the size of firms: in the small-firm sector (less than ten employees) bargaining covers half the employees, while in large firms of over 500 employees collective agreements apply to 93 per cent of the workforce.

5.5 Likely futures

In order to predict the future of Dutch industrial relations we need a clear understanding of the pattern of causation leading to the current changes. We must also take into account the strategic options of each party. Are the changes that occurred primarily related to the recession in recent years, and perhaps reversible under more prosperous economic conditions? Or has the current economic recession rather seen a long-term process of transition finally surface? In the preceding pages I have argued that the latter is more likely.

First and foremost, we must assume the continuation of a high level of unemployment in the foreseeable future, even under much improved conditions of economic growth and world trade. High unemployment is the biggest of all challenges to trade unions and erodes their bargaining power. Not only is it a moral challenge because Dutch unions regard themselves as representing the whole working class, both employed and unemployed, but the failure to fight off massive unemployment and its divisive consequences has paralysing effects on the movement at large. The current reversal of policies cannot only be attributed to increased employers' opposition. There was no majority within the trade unions either for policies that could have safeguarded the social security network at its existing high level of coverage (Vos, 1987). After the mid-1970s it was clear that the unions would not, or could not, support a centrally co-ordinated policy of real wage restraint, and also that its absence would eventually lead to the severance of the tight linkage of social security to wages and a reversal in trends towards income equality. Within the union movement there has been an uneasy debate over the solidarity between the employed and unemployed. Some unions, led by the Industriebond–FNV, concede that certain aspects of the welfare state need to be modified and that priority has to be given to industrial recovery and pricing people back into jobs. Understandably, this position has never received much support from civil servants' unions.

Continuing high unemployment combined with barriers to entry triggers off processes which enlarge the area of the economy outside the scope of collective representation and bargaining. The responses of employees are among these processes. If labour markets, under the present standards and conditions of employment, fail to absorb a sufficiently large number of new entrants and people becoming unemployed, several consequences will follow. There will be pressure towards more flexible and generally lower standards of protection on hiring and firing, minimum and maximum hours, overtime, minimum wages and social benefits. This implies a loss of union power, even if in some corners of the economy unions may still be able to mobilize members.

The structure of interests and power, within and outside the union movement, militates against the centralized and solidaristic wage and working-time policies of the past. Although precipitated during the 1980s recession, current decentralization tendencies are also a response to long-term changes in product and labour markets. These changes are occurring worldwide and are likely to increase the importance of flexible specialization which may, under certain conditions, be combined with high levels of wage and employment security, and of union and worker involvement, but only in some parts of the economy.

It is true that employers have been the prime mover in decentralization and are likely to gain most from it. But skilled employees in competitive firms may at least share some of that gain, even if it impairs the capacity of the union movement at large to defend its general redistributive aims. Nor is it likely that governments will or can reinstate the centralized policies needed to regenerate the tightly linked income guarantees. Currently, not even the Labour Party demands restoration of the high and extensive standards of protection and welfare of the 1970s.

The enfeeblement of the Dutch trade movement is unlikely to be a temporary phenomenon. It can be shown that the shrinking of union representation was a long-term process which, obscured by the rise in public sector unionsim, started long before the 1980s and is related to de-industrialization, the decline of manual labour, the deconcentration of production processes, the changing skill-structure of the workforce, and the rise of new services and (white-collar) professions. These processes will continue, together with a public sector which has ceased to expand and needs restructuring. The growing assertiveness of employers, the reversal in government policies and the weakening of nationwide concertation did certainly not help the unions, but the retrenchment of labour did not result from exclusionary policies. It should be recalled that, in the Netherlands, there have been no legal changes making it more difficult for unions to organize, bargain, strike or picket. Nor have facilities been withdrawn from unions.

Perhaps membership figures will stabilize and the present downturn will come to an end. Membership losses were small in 1986, and in 1987 all confederations made membership gains. However, compared with the increase in employment union density has continued to decline. There are yet no signs of a turnaround, and I feel confident in predicting that in the next decade or so a density rate of 20 per cent is more likely than the 40 per cent of the past.

Should my prediction prove correct, sooner or later the representativeness of trade unions as an influential sociopolitical institution in Dutch society will be questioned. In many ways the traditional FNV and CNV unions must make a new start. However, the very foundations from which to start have become less solid. Their traditional membership among manual workers has aged and is nowadays less central in social life and economic production. Dutch trade unions share with union movements abroad an under-representation in private services, but their weakness in manufacturing is exceptional. Union membership is heavily biased towards the public sector, but civil servants are not likely to replace the traditional leadership of the metalworkers, and if they did the result would be an entirely different social movement.

Clearly, vital elements in Dutch industrial relations are being changed and, on balance, I would argue that the centrifugal forces are uppermost. The main reason is that one can detect no or only weak counter-forces: the union movement has been seriously weakened and its main political ally defeated. Within the broader labour movement, the idea of a centrally co-ordinated policy inspired by a class solidaristic understanding of interests has lost appeal, and the organizational structures supporting concerted action have weakened. In present circumstances, employers may be under a strong temptation to defy the unions. If they believe that unions no longer hold bargaining power, employers might wish to bypass them or strike deals with whoever agrees. The recent settlements in banking, at Philips and Heineken, or in the public sector, in which the FNV and CNV unions were simply asked to take or leave the contract signed with staff employee unions, are examples of this novelty in the post-war history of Dutch industrial relations. On the other hand, many employers are reluctant for good reasons to destabilize their time-honoured relationships with trade unions: adding insult to injury might unsettle forty years of peaceful labour relations.

Some larger industrial unions define the present situation as one in which their survival is at stake. Seeking out new clientele is perforce the first commandment of organizations which are cut off from resources to which they have been used. Servicing members and assisting in supervising technical and structural change in firms have been areas in which Dutch unions have a poor record. In my view there is no way around the strengthening of works councils as a first step on the road to rehabilitating unions. Unions would have to reinvest their still considerable resources in structures that facilitate contacts with and between councils, and enhance their bargaining and recruitment capacity. Only by rebuilding strength where it counts for employers can Dutch unions regain the crucial role they played in the first thirty-five years of post-war industrial relations.

References

Akkermans, T. and P. Grootings (1978) 'From Corporatism to Polarisation: Elements of the Development of Dutch Industrial Relations', in C. Crouch and A. P. Pizzorno (eds), *The Resurgence of Class Conflict in Western Europe*, vol. 1: *National Studies*, London: Macmillan.

Albeda, W. (1985) 'Recent Trends in Collective Bargaining in the Netherlands', *International Labour Review*, 124.

Albeda, W. (1986) 'Regeringsbeleid en CNV. De spanningsvolle relatie tussen CNV en de Nederlands overheid 1977–1986', in J.C. Looise, J. Paauwe and H.J. van Zuthem (eds), *Vakbeweging in verandering. Dilemma's en Uitdagingen*, Deventer: Kluwer.

Bergeijk, C. van and A. de Grip (1984) 'Bestaan en ontwikkeling van interne arbeidsmarkten', *Sociaal Maandblad Arbeid*, 6.

CBS (1977–87) *Sociaal-Economische Maandstatistiek*, The Hague: CBS.

CBS (1979–85) *Statistiek van de Vakbeweging*, The Hague: CBS, biennial.

CBS (1980–6) *Statistisch Zakboek*, The Hague: CBS.

CBS (1985) *Vijfentachtig jaren statistiek in tijdreeksen 1899–1984*, The Hague: CBS.

Corpelijn, A.W.F. (1986) 'Beweging en stabiliteit op de arbeidsmarkt', *Economisch-Statistische Berichten*, 71.

CPB (1980–6) *Centraal economisch Plan*, The Hague: CPB.

CPB (1986) *Macro-economische Verkenningen 1986*, The Hague: CPB.

DCA (1987) 'De betekenis van CAO's in kwantitatieve zin', *Sociaal Maandblad Arbeid*, 11.

Fase, W.J.P.M. (1980) *Vijfendertig jaar loonbeleid in Nederland. Terugblik en perspectief*. Alphen: Samson.

Flanagan, R.J., with D.W. Soskice, and L. Ulman, (1983) *Unionism, Economic Stabilization and Incomes Policies: European Experience*, Washington DC: Brookings Institute.

FNV (1985) *FNV Jaarverslag 1985*, Amsterdam: FNV

FNV (1986) 'De FNV over veertien jaar', unpublished report, Amsterdam: FNV.

FNV (1987) *De FNV in het jaar 2000*, Amsterdam: FNV.

Geelhoed, L. (1983) *De interveniërende staat*, The Hague: Staatsuitgeverij.

Huiskamp, R.J. (1983) 'De CAO-structuur in de Nederlandse industrie', *Economisch-Statistische Berichten*, 72.

Kalma, P. and M. Krop (1983) 'Herverdeling van de arbeid en klasse(n)compromis', in J. Bank, M. Ros and B. Tromp (eds), *Het vierde jaarboek voor het democratische socialisme*, Amsterdam.

Korpi, W. (1983) *The Democratic Class Struggle*, London: Routledge and Kegan Paul.

Lammers, C.J. (1984) 'Rebellion of a Loyal Elite', paper presented at EGOS AWG on Trade Unions, Amersfoort, 11–13 October.

Lehmbruch, G. (1982) 'Introduction: Neo-corporatism in Comparative Perspective', in G. Lehmbruch and Ph.C. Schmitter (eds), *Patterns of Corporatist Policy-Making*, Beverly Hills and London: Sage.

Lijphart, A. (1968) *The Politics of Accommodation*, Berkeley: University of California Press.

Looise, J.C. (1985) 'Medezeggenschap via de CAO', *Tijdschrift voor Arbeidsvraagstukken*, vol. 1.

Looise, J.C. and F.G.M. de Lange (1987) *Ondernemingsraden, bestuurders en besluitvorming*, Nijmegen: ITS.

Ministry of Economic Affairs (1982) *Budget 1983*, The Hague.

Ministry of Economic Affairs (1986) *Budget 1987*, The Hague.

OSA (1986) *Arbeidsmarktgedrag ten tijde van massala werkloosheid*, Tilburg, Organisatie voor Strategische Arbeidsmarktonderzoek.

Peper, A. (1975) 'The Netherlands: From an Ordered Harmony to a Bargained Relationship', in S. Barkin (ed.), *Worker Militancy and Its Consequences, 1965-1975*, New York: Praeger.

SAE (1983-7) *Rapportage Arbeidsmarkt*, The Hague: Department of Social Affairs and Employment, annual.

SAE (1986) *Financiële Nota Sociale Zekerheid*, published with *Annual Budget*, The Hague: Department of Social Affairs and Employment.

Schmitter, Ph.C. (1981) 'Interest Intermediation and Regime Governability in Contemporary Western Europe and North America', in S. Berger (ed.), *Organizing Interests in Western Europe*, Cambridge. Cambridge: University Press.

Streeck, W. (1985) 'Co-determination: The Fourth Decade', in B. Wilpert and A. Sorge (eds), *International Perspectives on Organizational Democracy*, Chichester: Wiley.

Streeck, W. (1987) *Industrial Relations in West Germany: Agenda for Change*, Wissenschaftszentrum Berlin, discussion paper 87/5.

Teulings, A. (1981) *Ondernemingsraadpolitiek in Nederland*, Amsterdam: van Gennep.

Teulings, A. (1985) 'Prominenten en Volgers. Recht, macht en invloed van ondernemingsraden op de besluitvorming', *Tijdschrift voor Arbeidsvraagstukken*, 1.

Teulings, A. (1987) 'A Political Bargaining Theory of Co-determination', *Organization Studies*, 8.

Vall, M. van de (1970) *Labor Organizations: A Macro- and Micro-Sociological Analysis on a Comparative Basis*, Cambridge: Cambridge University Press.

Visser, J. (1986) 'De crisis van een verouderend verzorgingsarrangement', *Namens*, 3.

Visser, J. (1987) *In Search of Inclusive Unionism. A Comparative Analysis*, unpublished doctoral thesis, University of Amsterdam.

Visser, J. (1989) 'Working-Time Arrangements in the Netherlands', in A. Gladstone, R. Lansbury, J. Stieber, T. Treu and M. Weiss (eds), *Current Issues in Labour Relations. An International Perspective*, Berlin: de Gruyter.

Visser, J.C. (1986) *Bedrijfsbezettingen. Het verleden van een actiemiddel*, Amsterdam: Internationaal Instituut voor Sociale Geschiedenis.

Vos, P.J. (1987) 'De vakbeweging: een stervende dinosaurus of schepper van nieuwe arbeidsverhoudingen', in A. Buitendam (ed.), *Arbeidsmarkt, arbeidsorganisatie, arbeidsverhoudingen*, Deventer: Kluwer.

Vroom, B. de and F. van Waarden (1984) 'Ondernemersorganisaties als machtsmiddel', *Economisch-Statistische Berichten*, 69.

Windmuller, J.P. (1969) *Labor Relations in the Netherlands*, Ithaca, NY: Cornell University Press.

Wolff, P. de (1983) 'Incomes Policy Developments in the Netherlands', *Industrial Relations*, 22.

Wolff, P. de and W. Driehuis (1980) 'A Description of Post-War Economic Developments and Economic Policy in the Netherlands', in R.T. Griffiths (ed.), *The Economy and Politics of the Netherlands*, The Hague: Martinus Nijhoff.

WRR (1980) *Plaats en Toekomst van de Nederlandse industrie*, The Hague, Wetenschappelijke Raad voor het Regeringsbeleid, Report No. 18.

Zimmermann, E. (1986) *Neokorporative Politikformen in den Niederlanden*, Frankfurt: Campus.

8

Trade Union Action and Industrial Relations in Portugal

Mario Pinto

1 Background: Portugal's recent accession to pluralist democracy

It was only after the coup of 25 April 1974 that a system of labour unions and industrial relations comparable to those of the other EC member countries emerged in Portugal. Under the previous regime there was virtually an official union system, controlled by the state, especially as regards union elections, collective bargaining and the resolution of industrial disputes. Strikes were totally banned.

In the wake of the coup in 1974 a revolutionary process was unleashed under the leadership of the far left (the Communist Party and other extremist military and civilian forces). In the process, socialism was proclaimed as the official ideology, the large enterprises were nationalized, and so on. During this revolutionary period the Council of the Revolution decided to proclaim, by law, a national confederation of labour unions called Intersindical National (IN), which was given the legal monopoly in the representation of working people in unions (Decree-law 215–A/75, 30 March 1975).[1]

This period came to an end on 25 November 1975 with the failure of an attempted military coup by the far left. The victory of the population and of the military moderates, among whom was General Eanes, gave rise to a period of more moderate politics that permitted the Assembly to proceed with its work and proclaim the new Constitution in April 1976. The Constitution enshrined trade union freedom as defined in Convention 87 of the ILO. And it is then, formally speaking, that Portugal's experience with free unionism and free industrial relations really begins. The effects of the revolutionary period were slow to disappear entirely, however, as far as a number of union and industrial relations matters were concerned. Since IN (which had changed its name to the General Confederation of Portuguese Workers–Intersindical National, or CGTP–IN) held fast to the earlier, revolutionary single-union concept, and since its policy orientation was determined by the Communist faction, at the end of 1978 a second confederation was founded by workers politically close to two major parties, namely the Socialist Party (PS) and the Social Democratic Party (PSD). This was the General Workers' Union (UGT). Practically speaking, then, the start of the 1980s coincided, in Portugal, with the start of the democratic, pluralist union experience. Any comparison of the current decade with the preceding period must take account of this enormous difference as well as of structural factors and the specific effects in Portugal of recession and the economic changes taking place on an international scale.

In analysing certain of Portugal's structural constitutional and legal arrangements, in both economic and social affairs, one must bear in mind the compromise produced by the parallel advance of the revolutionary process along with the Constituent Assembly. It should not be forgotten that the Assembly was held under siege by revolutionary militants, and that the latter succeeded in imposing two pacts on the political parties, that is, on the deputies of the Assembly: a compromise between Western-style, pluralist democracy and the principle of socialism, with Marxist-inspired collectivist features.

2   The context of the 1980s

The economically active make up about 47 per cent of the total population. Those engaged in agriculture still constitute a fairly large share, though the trend towards a reduction of the labour force in the primary sector has been clear-cut throughout the 1980s, amounting to about 1 per cent of total employment annually (Table 8.1).

The decline in farm employment has not necessarily meant a shift of labour into the other sectors, and it may result from retirement, especially on the part of older workers. One of its effects is the very high percentage of pensioners: 1.9 million as against just 3.6 million active workers contributing to the social security system (the most lopsided ratio in the EC). This extremely grave situation, however, also has historical, political causes. The growth of pensioners is displayed in Table 8.2.

During the 1980s the workforce employed in the mining, manufacturing and construction sector held comparatively stable. The services sector has expanded by almost the same amount as the agricultural sector has diminished, or at a pace of about 1 per cent of total employment annually.

The composition of the workforce shows a large proportion of

Table 8.1 *Structure of labour force, Portugal and EC, 1986*

Sector	Portugal (1st quarter 1986)	EC average
Primary	21.7	7.2
Secondary	33.7	38.4
Tertiary	44.6	54.4

Source: Ministry of Labour

Table 8.2 *Economically active population by sectors, Portugal, 1970–85*

	Contributors	Pensioners
1970–5	+ 39	+ 530
1975–80	+ 14	+ 189
1980–5	− 0.2	− 3.9

Source: Ministry of Labour

farm workers and unskilled workers. In a total population that still has a 20 per cent illiteracy rate, 72 per cent of the labour force has at least six years of schooling. In the employment structure, upper and middle executives (8.2 per cent of total employment) have a better education, but only 3 per cent have university degrees. In general there is a shortage of skilled manpower.

The overall economic and social context of the 1980s has been marked by economic problems (recession), the vicissitudes of Portugal's new-born democracy, and also, most notably, by the cultural–ideological and 'institutional' universe handed down by the previous period, which has nonetheless evolved significantly. Two major economic questions have dominated this period: one, truly structural, concerns the enlargement of the private sector; the other, recession and modernization.

The question of expanding the private sector arose not just because the Constitution of 1976 had greatly reduced it by ratifying the major nationalizations of the revolutionary years (banking, insurance, chemicals, petroleum, transportation, steel, ship-building, breweries, and so on) but also and mainly because the constitution had enshrined the principle of the permanence of the nationalizations and the principle of the reservation of the 'basic sectors' of the economy for the state (that is, the exclusion of private entrepreneurs from them).

Action on this crucial question of the structure of the economy has gone through two phases, demarcated by the revision of the Constitution in 1982. In practice, the first corresponded to the policy of the governments of the parliamentary right, the second to that of the 'centre bloc'. The revision of the Constitution itself turned on the issue of purging the document of the Marxist ideological slant of the 1976 text. The preamble to the portion of the charter dealing with 'economic organization', for instance, read: 'The economic and social organization of the Portuguese Republic is founded on the development of socialist relations of production by means of the collective appropriation of the principal means of production and funds as well as natural resources, and on the exercise of democratic power by the working classes'. This wording was replaced by a less ideologically charged and more flexible version in the 1982 revision.

During the first phase, the Democratic Alliance governments tried unsuccessfully to end the state monopoly, specifically by opening a private bank. They were blocked by the Military Council of the Revolution, which had the powers of a constitutional court. After the constitutional revision, which abolished the Council of the Revolution and created a proper Constitutional Court, the 'centre bloc' government attained this objective.

The structural issue is much broader, however. The problem of compensation for the nationalizations of 1974–5 is still open; the seizures of property were largely not paid for. The privatization of many small businesses that were nationalized indirectly (subsidiaries of large firms that were taken over) is still at issue, and so are other aspects of the general problem. The question became more relevant still in 1987, because since this year the Assembly has had powers of constitutional revision. Some position statements (the Secretary-General of the Socialist Party, for one, has come out in favour of abrogating the clause establishing the irreversibility of nationalizations) point to a fierce debate with the Communist Party, the only force that defends the 1974–5 approach.

The second great concern in Portuguese economic life in the 1980s has been the serious economic and social problems produced by recession and also by the repercussions of previous developments. Some of the key macroeconomic variables are shown in Table 8.3. Portugal's economic performance over recent years has diverged considerably from the average for European countries and for the OECD as concerns unemployment and inflation.

So far in the course of the decade, the unemployment rate has risen from 7.6 per cent (based on labour-force surveys, which do not correspond to the ILO standards) to 11.0 per cent in 1986.

Table 8.3 *Macroeconomic development, Portugal, 1980–6*

	1980	1981	1982	1983	1984	1985	1986
GDP (% growth)	4.1	0.5	3.2	− 0.3	− 1.6	3.3	4.3
Balance on current account (bn US dollars)	− 1.251	− 2.852	− 3.245	− 1.640	− 0.623	+ 0.369	+ 1.135
Balance on current account (% of GDP)	− 5.1	− 11.7	− 13.5	− 8	− 3.1	+ 1.8	+ 3.9
Price inflation	16.6	20	22.4	25.5	29.3	19.3	11.7
Real wages (% increase)	6.6	− 0.3	− 2.5	− 5.1	− 7.9	+ 2.0	+ 5.0
Unemployment (broad)	7.6	8.8	7.2	10.5	10.9	11.1	11.0
Unemployment (ILO definition)						8.5	8.4

Source: Banco de Portugal and Ministerio do Trabalho

These must be considered quite a good performance given the general state of the economy. The explanation for this, the only variable in which Portugal has out-performed the European average, lies partly in the rigidity represented by workers' legal protections, which makes dismissal difficult. Dismissal for economic reasons ('collective dismissals' under Portuguese law) is not easy, in practice, because it must always be justified in writing, and the ultimate decision rests with the Minister of Labour (who is obviously subject to substantial political and union pressures). This difficulty, it is widely held, explains the bizarre phenomenon of 'late paycheques'. Many firms in difficulty do not pay their employees' wages punctually, and even when firms have to cut back or altogether halt production, the workers stay on, but do not receive their salaries.

The fluctuations in the inflation rate are certainly attributable to the instability of the political system, which has swung back and forth between election-oriented, expansionary policies and restrictive policies, the latter introduced to halt rapid inflation and a worsening trade deficit. In the 1980s Portugal's stop–go fiscal and monetary policies have already produced three distinct phases: go (1980–2), stop (1983–5) and go again (1985–6).

Only a few industries have successfully modernized (above all such export-oriented ones as textiles). But even they have generally not made any major organizational innovations. In the services (above all banking, communications and insurance) the introduction of new technology has begun without serious union opposition.

3   The actors and their relations

3.1   The state

Since the revolution of 25 April, four major parties have come to dominate the Portuguese political scene: on the right, the Social Democratic Centre (CDS), a Christian-Democratic-oriented formation; on the left, the Portuguese Communist Party (PCP); on the centre-right the Social Democratic Party (PSD); and on the centre-left the Socialist Party (PS), a member of the Socialist International. These descriptions do not correspond either to the parties' respective programmes or to their self-definitions. The latter would make the CDS a centre party and all the others leftist. The two left-wing parties, PS and PCP, depending on the political situation of the day, label the other two parties the 'right' and leave the 'centre' out of the picture entirely. All the elections since 1975 have given the largest vote to the two more centrist parties of the spectrum, the PSD and the PS. The CDS and the PCP have always had a much less substantial representation (see Table 8.4).

Table 8.4   *General election outcomes, Portugal, 1976–85*

	1976		1979		1980		1983		1985	
	Share of votes (%)	No. of seats	Share of votes (%)	No. of seats	Share of votes (%)	No. of seats	Share of votes (%)	No. of seats	Share of votes (%)	No. of seats
CDS	16.00	42	42.49[1]	121	44.91[1]	126	12.55	30	9.96	22
PSD	24.38	73					27.23	75	29.87	88
PRD									17.92	45
PS	34.86	42	27.33	74	26.65	71	36.11	101	20.76	57
PCP	14.35	40	18.80	47	16.75	41	18.07	44	15.49	38

[1] In 1979 and 1980 CDS and PSD ran in an electoral alliance with the tiny Popular Monarchist Party (PPM).

In the 1985 elections, however, a fifth party was formed, the Democratic Renewal Party (PRD), sponsored by the President of the Republic, General Eanes. The PRD took a position in the centre of the spectrum, winning votes from the PS, which lost ground.

From 1974 to 1979 Portuguese political life was in constant turmoil. After a series of six provisional governments (until the proclamation of the new Constitution in April 1976), there was a succession of minority governments, except for a brief seven-month period. In the early part of this period, 1976–8, two governments were formed by the PS, which had won the most popular votes in the 1976 elections. Next in 1978–9, came three so-called 'Presidential confidence governments' headed by independent prime ministers chosen by the President of the Republic. This pattern of minority governments with brief tenures in office in a time of economic crisis and a turbulent social climate did not continue into the 1980s. In this decade Portugal has had governments based on a majority coalition, except the latest Cavaco Silva cabinet from 1985, a minority PSD government.

Between 1980 and 1986 political life went through three sub-periods. The first, 1980–2, saw three governments under the same majority coalition, the Democratic Alliance between PSD and CDS, the right-wing parties, with a few independents and a small monarchist and ecological party. The second, 1983–5, was dominated by a 'centre bloc' government of PSD and PS, the two largest parties. The third period began with a minority PSD government installed in late 1985.

Throughout the 1980s, Portuguese governments continued to restrict pay rises agreed in collective bargaining, but employing different legal means from those used in the previous decade. The law which set a ceiling on wage gains had been repealed in December 1979.

In view of the importance of the public sector for the Portuguese economy, both general government and the nationalized firms, government actually plays a key role in setting salaries. In public corporations, in effect, the government can monitor collective bargaining, because ministers have tutelary powers. And in general government it is the government itself that unilaterally sets wage rates, after consultation and bargaining with the civil service unions. In practice, ministers have always controlled collective bargaining in the public enterprises. And generally speaking the private sector has followed the pattern set by the nationalized firms. So government has strongly influenced practices in the private sector.

The question of social concertation was raised, as a practical matter, by the 'centre bloc' government in June 1983. Enjoying the sympathy of the UGT, the government formed the Permanent Council for Social Concertation (CPCS) by decree-law in March 1984 (No. 74/1984). It is a tripartite organ, including government representatives plus those of the employer and union confederations. The two successive governments under Soares and Cavaco Silva consistently sought the consensus they needed within the

Council. Such consensus was simply not obtainable, however, for the reform (that is, liberalization) of the labour laws; it was found only on incomes policy. In this sphere, agreement was first achieved in 1984 on the government's draft 'programme for financial and economic recovery'. But the true, decisive advance in Portugal's experience with tripartite concertation came in June 1986 with an agreement on incomes policy for 1987.

3.2 The unions

Since 1979, as noted, Portugal has had two major, national union confederations: the CGTP–IN and the UGT. The former was initially the sole recognized confederation (that is, it had a legal monopoly on union activities) for all Portuguese working people. It has always been dominated by Communists and Communist sympathizers (at present its top leadership includes just one Socialist and a few independents). With the adoption of the Constitution in 1976 this legal monopoly was done away with, and in October 1978 the UGT came into being. It was formed by workers (politically close to the PS and PSD) who refused to accept Communist domination of the CGTP–IN. As a consequence of the political agreement on which its creation was based, UGT has retained an internal organization founded on political affiliation, with the Socialist and Social Democratic tendencies being equally represented in confederation bodies for the first few years. Later, the results of internal elections were accepted, and now the Socialists are slightly in the majority. About 20 per cent of Portuguese unions do not belong to any federation. The former corporatist union structure was highly decentralized both organizationally and in terms of collective bargaining.

After the revolution all the unions had to revise their statutes. Yet the earlier model was largely maintained: the nationwide confederation (which was very influential in the political sphere). The UGT kept the largest unions of the old corporatist regime (banking, insurance, office and service employees). But it also had to create new unions, especially in industry. These are large national, industry unions, which means that in a sense they run counter to the established practices (for example, in textiles, metal and engineering, chemicals and construction).

The structure of the CGTP–IN is thus rather traditional, based on individual unions grouped in industry-wide federations and co-ordinated by regional organizations. The UGT, on the other hand, is based on large national or regional unions, with no federations (save three exceptions, each for specific reasons, which have developed a role as technical back-up to collective bargaining).

The UGT has no regional co-ordinating organizations.

Official statistics from the National Statistical Institute show that in 1984 there were 352 base unions (varying widely in territorial extension: 105 national, 39 covering the autonomous regions, 99 covering more than one department, 104 intra-departmental, 2 inter-city and 3 municipal). Of these, in 1986 141 were affiliated with the CGTP–IN, 3 to the UGT and 5 independent. There are forty regional labour councils, none belonging to the UGT.

Under the law union members in a company may form a company local there. The unions also have the right to name union delegates at the workplace. Delegates from the same union can form a union committee at the company level, and this is the basis of labour union organization at the workplace.

The two confederations have widely divergent positions and often conflicting relations. The CGTP–IN, which considers itself *the* 'united labour movement', has always been, both in theory and in practice, highly ideological – against capitalism, for nationalization and agrarian reform, hostile to social concertation, advocating 'mass, class-conscious unionism', opposing all the governments formed since the passage of the Constitution (even when the Socialist Party has been in power) as right-wing. It has special relations with the socialist-bloc countries, and strongly criticizes the United States. In addition, it opposes Portugal's membership in the European Community. The CGTP–IN has never recognized the UGT, which it brands as 'splitters'.

The UGT explicitly favours the reform of society 'in keeping with the principle of respect for the free will of all citizens'. It also favours trade union freedom and advocates the active participation of all working people and citizens in politics. The UGT has always accorded full freedom to internal factions. The idea of social concertation and Portugal's experience with the practice are primarily the product of the UGT's belief in them. The union has consistently been an outspoken advocate of this path. Unlike the CGTP–IN, the UGT favours relations between the two major confederations and has repeatedly called for joint action. The UGT is affiliated with the ICFTU and the ETUC.

Portuguese unions are not highly centralized. Decentralization is part of the legacy of the corporatist political regime, in which there were no union confederations but just craft or industrial unions, severely restricted territorially, grouped into regional or national federations or councils. Collective bargaining was carried on by the base unions or by the federations.

Functionally, collective bargaining is principally at the industry level and also the company level. Bargaining is conducted either by the federations or by the base unions. The confederations have a supporting role, in addition to their political one. They have never signed a collective bargaining agreement, but in July 1986 the UGT did sign, within the CPCS, an 'agreement on incomes policy for 1987'. This agreement with employer organizations and the government is not, legally speaking, a collective bargaining contract. It does nevertheless set a very important precedent, as a 'gentlemen's agreement' on collective bargaining signed by a confederation.

Portuguese wage- and salary-earners number about 3.25 million. The CGTP–IN, at its most recent congress in May 1986, claimed to represent about 1.35 million. The UGT claims membership of 1.1 million. Going by these claims, then, the unionization rate would be 75 per cent, which is manifestly too high. Public estimates offered in trade union circles never go above 60 per cent, and even this seems too high. The real unionization rate is less than 40 per cent, but it is hard to determine it any more accurately than that. It is universally acknowledged that in the last few years the overall unionization rate has declined. The UGT, however, is still growing.

The highest unionization rate is found in the nationalized enterprises. The situation is uneven in this sector, but probably ranges from 40 per cent to nearly 100 per cent according to industry; in the nationalized banks, for instance, union membership can be presumed to be virtually universal, thanks to the sick pay and medical coverage and the pensions regime. The lowest rates of unionization are to be found in the smaller private firms. Such industries as metal and engineering, textiles and glass have traditions of politicized unionism, with rates of unionization estimated at higher than 40 per cent.

3.3   The employers
Employer organizations are recognized and regulated by law – Decree Law No. 215–C/1975, 30 March 1975, known as the law on employer associations. The legislation formally distinguishes between business enterprises in general and firms under an employer (that is, enterprises that ordinarily have employees working for them): only the latter can belong to employer associations. The distinction derives from the old corporatist regime, which was very rigid in both industry and commerce.

After the abolition of the corporatist *gremios* (the employer associations of the old regime), three new employer associations arose: the Confederation of Portuguese Agriculture (CAP), the Confederation of Portuguese Industry (CIP) and the Confederation of Portuguese Commerce (CCP). The old industrial and commercial associations (which dated back to before the corporatist regime and kept apart from corporatist integrations insofar as they limited themselves to somewhat marginal representation of economic interests) continued to exist and did not merge with the employer movement. The result is that Portugal has a dual structure: trade associations (the old industrial and commercial associations) on the one hand, and employer associations (the successors of the former corporatist *gremios*) on the other, organized by industry and also often on a local or regional basis.

The most representative farmers' organization, the CAP, was founded in November 1975. It represents seventy-six regional farmers' associations, sixteen specialized associations and twelve co-operatives. The base associations are organized into four federations which largely correspond to the main agricultural regions of the country. All told, CAP groups more than 100,000 farmers. In areas where there are no associations, farmers can join the confederation as individuals. CAP has been a constant presence in Portuguese political life and debate, demanding a pro-farmer policy (which it has not obtained) and also strongly criticizing the collectivist approach to agrarian reform and the socialist guidelines laid down in the Constitution. CAP's closest political ties are with the PSD and CDS. However, the strength of the farmers' confederation does not correspond to the weight of farmers in the Portuguese economy, because Portuguese farmers – mostly small peasants – are individualistic and not inclined to step out of line. The membership of the confederation varies greatly from region to region.

Collective bargaining is not very common in agriculture. After 1974–5, collective bargaining was suspended and resumed only in 1980, and even then negotiations were limited to just a few areas. Since collective bargaining has little place in farming, CAP has a minor role in 'industrial relations'. It is very active in the Concertation Council, however.

The industrialists' organization, CIP, was founded in 1974. It represents seventy-nine industry and regional associations with more than 30,000 member firms. The number of persons employed by the member firms is estimated at 820,000. The base associations may form sections and may also create sector federations. In some cases 'technical associations' have been formed in parallel with the representative bodies. Given the non-participation of the large nationalized firms, CIP represents a rank and file conspicuously lacking in large employers. Further, the sectoral associations have considerable autonomy, and the participation of enterprises is generally not very strong. In short, the representative strength of the CIP is not great. Perhaps this is why it has steadily maintained a very hard-line political position with regard to the rigidity of labour legislation and to the socialist tendencies of the Constitution, always calling for greater consideration of the worth of private initiative. It has strongly criticized the nationalized firms as loss-makers, uneconomic enterprises living on state subsidies.

For years the CIP rejected the idea of concertation on the pretext that the problems of the day required a legislative solution, which was up to Parliament (and hence the political parties) and not to business and labour organizations. This position was viewed as an attempt to pressurize the government, which needed tripartite concertation to defuse the conflict likely to be provoked by certain restrictive measures (1983–4). At last the CIP agreed to take part in the CPCS, the Concertation Council, and it now appears to be willing to continue to do so.

The CIP faces quite difficult conflict with Portugal's two major industrial associations, one covering the north with headquarters in Porto, the other in Lisbon. Both are powerful, because they sponsor and run industrial fairs and carry on permanent training programmes. Fairs are a very large source of revenue, permitting them to maintain a technical apparatus that far overshadows that of the confederation.

The commercial confederation, CCP, was founded in 1974. It has 137 affiliated associations with 125,000 member firms (about half of Portugal's commercial businesses). A few federations play the role of liaison between the confederation and the base associations. The picture is highly diversified: some of the associations are very strong, others very small and ineffective. The image of the CCP is more conciliatory, more dialogue-oriented, than that of the CIP. It has not taken up the battle against nationalizations as militantly as the CIP, but it has pressed for the liberalization of labour legislation. It is not plagued by internal battles with trade associations, perhaps because these are not as powerful as their industrial counterparts.

In 1979 CAP, CIP and CCP formed the National Council for the Portuguese Economy (CNEP) with the objective of co-ordinating the positions of the three confederations. But it has certainly not eclipsed the three confederations as protagonists. All in all, the affiliation rate of the three employer confederations is low. Their organizational level is viewed as poor, because of the lack of effective participation by the member firms and the lack of financial means. On the political scene, however, the presence of the employer organizations has gradually gained in importance.

The main issues they have raised are compensation for nationalization and the need for greater flexibility in labour legislation (dismissal, strikes, working hours, and so on). The experience with concertations in the CPCS, where only the confederations sit (not the individual associations nor the federations), has helped strengthen their role and forge greater unity among them. There have also been movements in the other direction, however, such as the Northern Entrepreneurs' Council, a regional organization.

4 The processes

4.1 Collective bargaining: institutional aspects

Collective bargaining in Portugal (regulated by law) still has the same structural model as under the corporatist regime, in the sense that there is no diversification, no hierarchy of applicable agreements. Contracts may be either industry-wide or restricted to a single company; there are no inter-industry agreements. If the two contracts conflict, the law recognizes the company-level contract. This means that when a company signs an agreement with one or more unions, this contract can, if need be, supplant the industry contract in its entirety. Thus the substance of company agreements is formally equivalent to that of industry agreements.

Collective bargaining is decentralized, in that the negotiations are conducted by the base unions themselves. The federations, when they participate, do so as representatives of their member unions. The confederations do not engage in collective bargaining. But in practice they (and the federations as well, in the case of CGTP–IN) do play an increasingly important role owing to the unions' need for technical assistance and because negotiations need to be fitted into the framework of economic policy and the social and economic situation. They have the role of co-ordination and representation, especially in discussion of economic and social policy at the highest political levels.

The prevailing pattern, deriving from the old corporatist regime, is that only a few of the largest firms sign company agreements. The unions have sought to negotiate agreements with the largest private employers, but employers' policy is to avoid developing collective bargaining at this level. Nonetheless some private firms in economic difficulties have negotiated somewhat informal protocols for dealing with their problems.

Collective bargaining in the nationalized firms is controlled by the government, the responsible ministers having power of ratification. As part of the policy of controls on wage increases and reducing the public firms' losses, this power has been used to contain union pressure, which is stronger here than in the private sector. The result has been the development by the companies' management councils of expedients to reconcile these two opposed pressures. Some have included such measures as a sort of across-the-board promotion in their company contracts, while others have resorted to unofficial, parallel internal agreements (underground collective bargaining). Another consequence is a higher incidence of industrial conflict in the public enterprises. In the public services the law requires negotiations, or collective bargaining, but the negotiations are concluded with a unilateral act on the part of the government, not a collective bargaining contract. The civil service unions have relatively little clout or means of pressure, and real wages in the civil service have declined.

Collective bargaining contracts cover virtually all workers in industry and in the tertiary sector, because ministerial decrees have regularly extended collective agreements to non-union workers. Any contract may be so extended; there is no requirement of union representativeness. If, for instance, there are two different agreements, corresponding to the two major unions, as a rule the Minister chooses so to extend the first contract signed. The Minister of Labour has the power to issue labour regulation decrees (a sort of substitute for contracts) when negotiations are boycotted and in industries where union and employer organizations are lacking. Very few such decrees have actually been issued, however, and this power is resorted to less and less. It too was handed down by the old regime, by which it was used against the unions.

The law provides for optional mediation and arbitration of labour disputes. Mediation is very common, but arbitration is rare. An arbitration decision is as binding as is a collective contract. For public firms, arbitration may be made compulsory by the Ministers of Labour and of Social Protection. But they have not exercised this power except in a very few cases – and even these failed to yield satisfactory results, owing to a lack of union co-operation in designating the arbitrator.

Since 1974–5 the law has limited the validity of collective bargaining contracts in some respects. The limitations concern, among other things, reduction in hours (these must be authorized by the Minister of Labour, who will grant them on grounds of productivity gains), increases in annual vacations (maximum thirty days), holidays and excused absence, and private supplements to social security. On the other hand, the law prevents collective bargaining contracts worsening the terms of previous contracts, unless they explicitly state that as a whole the new terms are more

Table 8.5 *Variation in real wages (%), Portugal, 1980–6*

1980	1981	1982	1983	1984	1985	1986
+6.6	−0.3	+2.5	−5.1	−7.9	+2.0	+5.0

Source: Banco de Portugal

advantageous for the workers covered. This rigidity has scarcely encouraged the use of collective bargaining to help introduce the changes needed for industrial reorganization.

Collective bargaining contracts are legally permitted to adjust wages yearly and to modify the other provisions every two years. With few exceptions, the substance of the contracts has not been greatly affected by the changes in the labour market. Real wages, as fixed in contracts, have evolved in correspondence with government economic policy (see Table 8.5).

The most significant change in collective bargaining practices, in this regard, was that brought about by the tripartite agreement on incomes policy reached in the Concertation Council in 1986, which modified the basis for calculating wage adjustments. Previously the unions had lodged their wage claims based on the past year's inflation; now the government forecasts an inflation rate for the coming year, and business and labour (the UGT and the employer confederations) agree to bargain on the basis of that forecast. The pact had some practical effect in 1986, in that collective bargaining immediately changed its way of calculating wage adjustments.

Another highly significant consequence was the reversal of the two union confederations' positions. With this agreement, the UGT became the more important in collective bargaining, insofar as the CPCS agreement provided a basis for the prompt, peaceful conclusion of collective bargaining agreements. The CGTP–IN, which rejected the tripartite accord, attempted to establish even higher wage claims, but the settlement of contracts with the UGT removed the CGTP–IN's ability to mobilize, since the contracts signed were applied to all workers in any given firm. Thus the UGT, which only began collective bargaining after the turn of the decade, had become truly dominant in collective bargaining by 1986–7.

4.2 The emergence of concertation

Unquestionably the key event of the 1980s for the Portuguese industrial relations system has been the country's first social pact, the 'tripartite agreement on incomes policy for 1987', signed within the Permanent Council for Social Concertation by the government, the UGT and the three employer confederations. Such an inter-industry accord is simply unprecedented in Portuguese history. Before it, relations still adhered to the conflictual pluralism model, with little or no concession to the varying needs of companies to adapt to crisis or recession. Afterwards, the UGT came to be predominant in collective bargaining and succeeded in enforcing the concept of overall negotiations (economic and social questions being dealt with as a package). The UGT proposal for a modernization pact would institutionalize the three-tier bargaining system – on the inter-industry, industry and company levels. This would mark the first time the Portuguese industrial relations system has been reformed by the bargaining partners on their own initiative and not by law.

Concertation does not take place solely at the national, inter-industry level within the CPCS, however. The Lisnave company agreement is a key case in point. The largest Portuguese ship-builder, and a symbol of union radicalism, it was on the brink of bankruptcy. Wages had been reduced by 50 per cent, and even these were not paid on time (indeed, the company was a year in arrears). So the UGT, which represented only a small minority of the company's workers, proposed and signed a contract with management. The CGTP–IN opted to sign as well. The Lisnave pact contains a no-strike clause, the suspension of some rigid job classification rules, and provisions on internal mobility and adjustment of working time. The agreement was renewed, and in the election for the company council the UGT won an absolute majority.

4.3   Industrial conflict

The pattern of industrial conflict in the 1980s is most interesting (see Table 8.6). There was a sharp increase in the number of strikes in 1981, the second year of the Accion Democratica coalition, when CGTP–IN conducted a militant political opposition prompted by the reduction in real wages. Since then the number of strikes has declined steadily, except in 1984, which was a dramatic year with a cut in real wages of more than 10 per cent. But in 1985, when the 'centre bloc' governed until November, strike activity fell back to its 1980 level in terms of number of strikes and even lower in terms of number of workers involved and number of days lost.

This reflects the diminishing ability of the CGTP–IN, in the course of the 1980s, to carry on an effective political opposition, and a stronger participatory and representative role for the UGT, which is more moderate and strongly in favour of a participatory, reformist unionism, against a strategy of simple trade union militancy.

Table 8.6 *Industrial conflict, Portugal, 1980–6*

	No. of strikes	Workers involved (000s)	Days lost (000s)
1980	374	398.6	734.5
1981	756	403.9	749.7
1982	563	262.5	456.1
1983	532	273.6	650.7
1984	550	230.5	269.7
1985	504	199.0	275.4
1986[1]	211	112.9	117.8

[1] First six months.

Source: Ministry of Labour

The central issues in bargaining and conflict can be summarized under a variety of headings.

4.3.1 Wage arrears Portugal has witnessed this bizarre phenomenon in recent years. A growing number of troubled firms began to defer wage payments to their employees, who kept working (because they were aware of the companies' difficulties) unless the business came to a total halt. Eventually many tens of thousands of workers were affected, and special legislation had to be passed to provide welfare payments for them. One interpretation blames the phenomenon on the difficulty of dismissing excess personnel. Collective dismissal, which must be authorized by the Minister of Labour, was virtually impracticable for political reasons, while individual dismissals are not allowed except for grave disciplinary offences, which must be justified in writing and are subject to review by an administrative tribunal.

The latest available figures show 274 firms with significant wage arrears. The number of workers affected is 31,795, and the back wages due amount to the equivalent of 13,376,310 US dollars. The back-pay problem is decreasing somewhat, but it is also true that new cases are continually being discovered.

4.3.2 Employment and training policy It was in 1980 that the principal legislation to foster employment was passed. There was a law laying down the general principles of employment policy and specific laws for the promotion of employment and the creation of jobs (Decree-laws Nos 444/1980, 445/1980 and 416/1980). Some measures had been taken in 1979, mainly to facilitate geographical mobility. But 1980 marked the beginning of a new phase. Since then state incentives and subsidies have proliferated: funding of self-employment projects: protected jobs (for the handicapped); incentives to create jobs for young first-job seekers; local job initiatives; temporary jobs for youth and subsidies for the long-term unemployed; programmes for the employment of unemployed youth in socially useful projects a.id so on. All these measures have had an impact that is hard to quantify. Some have had to operate under severe budget constraints. These employment measures, together with the large number of retired persons and the rigidity of the workforce suggest why, despite its severe economic problems, Portugal still has a comparatively low unemployment rate. At the same time, a vocational training policy was introduced.

4.3.3 The issue of flexibility Reforming labour legislation to enhance flexibility is a crucial issue in Portugal, because of the great rigidity and worker protection enshrined in law, especially the provisions on dismissal and on the right to strike. The prevailing opinion now is that this reform is possible only through talks within the Concertation Council. In the meantime, employers are resorting to term employment contracts as a way of avoiding the application of the job-security protection enjoyed by workers on standard contracts. The latest statistics show that more than 70 per cent of new employees are on term or temporary contracts, which cannot be extended for a total exceeding three years without being automatically converted into standard contracts.

The positions of the unions on this issue have evolved. At first, the flexibility-enhancing reforms advocated by the Mota Pinto government in 1979 were rejected by both CGTP–IN and UGT. Since then, UGT has said repeatedly that flexibility measures could be introduced, but with limitations and concessions from the other side. The CGTP–IN has steadfastly opposed any such measures. But the union positions have progressively moderated over time, and eventually some agreement on the issue within the Concertation Council is probably to be expected.

4.3.4 Working hours Since 1974 the shortening of work hours either by collective contract or by individual agreement has been prohibited by law (Decree-law 505/1974) except by Labour Ministry authorization in cases in which the industry's economic growth justifies it. Working hours (which in principle are set by employers but are also often fixed by collective bargaining contracts) are limited by the principle of the eight-hour day. In 1986 the government submitted to the Concertation Council draft legislation whose main provision would permit a ten-hour day and a fifty-hour week with no increase in the number of working hours per year. But this flexibility measure failed to win the endorsement of the Council. The employer confederations favoured it, but the UGT set a condition that annual working time should be reduced. The CGTP is strongly opposed to the proposal in any form.

5 Levels

The tradition inherited by the revolution was political centralization and relative decentralization in industrial relations (that is, industry-level contracts). With the creation of the workers' committees (essentially factory councils, with participatory and consultative powers) and the development of company locals within the unions, the system has been somewhat decentralized. However, the law – which is decisive in institutionalization – delegated no collective bargaining powers to these structures. Thus the craft and industrial unions at industry level are still the protagonists of bargaining. On the other hand, the confederations have not taken part in negotiations, except as consultants. But the process of social concertation has augmented the importance of both union and employer confederations. One may even note the growing importance of the confederations and the declining role of the workers' committees, with few exceptions, and conclude that the trend is towards centralization. Table 8.7 summarizes overall developments.

At the company level, however, a large number of informal agreements have apparently been concluded. One is tempted to speak of parallel or underground bargaining, or company-level bargaining for crisis management in troubled firms. The extent of this practice is not clear, nor are the precise terms of the agreements reached. What is known is that private employers avoid formal bargaining at the company level.

The entire system of collective bargaining is thus in transition. And if the UGT's proposal, as set forth in the modernization pact, is approved, there will be a more formal institutionalization of multi-level bargaining: inter-industry, industry and company. We can only wait and see.

Finally, as to the actors themselves, the CGTP–IN alone has a centralized organization (democratic centralism). The UGT may be excessively decentralized (having even institutionalized internal factions). The employer confederations are highly decentralized. The progress of social concertation may accentuate an already existing tendency towards greater centralization that has been set in motion by the decisive role of the confederations as against the membership structures.

Table 8.7 *Changes in the industrial relations system, Portugal since 1980*

Type	Pre-1980 (1974–9)	Post-1980
A(a) National concertation	Non-existent; rejected by sole union Intersyndical; political climate conditioned by radical left; model of pluralism with maximal conflict	Despite opposition from Communists, Socialist and Social Democratic parties, government and unions reached agreement on institutionalization of social concertation in Permanent Council (1984), in which employers' bodies would also be represented
A(b) National bargaining structure	Union legitimacy based on law; tradition of corporatist regime until 1974 resumed by new forces dominant after revolution. Role of unions within public administration limited because of government unilateral action. But unions have right to strike	Little change, but UGT given more important role at national level
B Decentralized collective agreements	Sectoral bargaining; firm-level bargaining in big companies and state sector; no national inter-industry bargaining; dynamic of conflictual pluralism	Unions tried to increase firm-level agreements in big companies, but employers seek sectoral agreements. Tripartite pact of 1987 on incomes constitutes an example of national-level bargaining. But in firms in difficulty, many informal company-level agreements
C(a) Worker participation via unions	Very rare; only in a few firms in difficulties and then very informal (except during the revolutionary period when such participation had sense of workers' control)	No change. Employers prefer not to give union representatives such a role, except when they want to share economic difficulties with union delegates

Table 8.7 *contd.*

Type	Pre-1980 (1974–9)	Post-1980
C(b) Participation without unions	Workers' commissions created by law and Constitution with rights to consultation and information	No changes, but the commissions less important
D(a) Individual contracts with collective agreements undermined	Yes, in several sectors especially in black economy	Perhaps growing, in black economy
D(b) As D(a) but in secondary labour market	Yes, in several sectors especially services	Perhaps growing with the scale of the activities

Note

1 Other regulations were established in line with the concept of union monopoly and state socialism (the labour union law passed as Decree-law 215–B/75, 30 March 1975).

9

Transition and Crisis: The Complexity of Spanish Industrial Relations

Jordi Estivill and Josep M. de la Hoz

1 The overarching trends

1.1 Trade unionism in retreat: a subaltern role

Spanish trade unionism entered the 1980s in a defensive, subordinate posture. Effectively, notwithstanding the fact that the labour movement had been the spearhead of the struggle under the Franco regime, eventually succeeding in dismantling the vertically structured labour organizations, the unions had been compelled by the political transition to democracy to play a subordinate role. Politics dominated virtually the entire social scene. A good illustration is the 1977 Moncloa Agreement, from which both employer associations and trade unions were excluded.

Spanish labour unions could hardly follow the European-wide pattern of soaring expansion in the 1960s in connection with unprecedented economic expansion and industrial development. Forced into clandestinity, they could not spread and consolidate their membership, their influence with rank-and-file workers, or their internal structures (federations, union services, strike funds, and so on) by counting on their external relations (institutionalized role, relations with political parties, the media, public opinion, and so on). Nevertheless, in 1974–7 the unions sparked and lent momentum to the strongest mass movements of the democratic opposition to the regime. In 1976 and 1977 the number of strikes revealed a significant peak following Franco's death, and according to union sources 5.5 million joined the attempt to take united labour action through the CDS (Social Democratic Centre).

However, trade union divisions (resented by rank-and-file workers, but polarizing at each successive election – 1978, 1980, 1982, 1986), together with the inability to form a true services network for members and above all the consequences of economic recession, caused a loss of membership and influence. In 1983 union membership was estimated at 1,768,000, and in 1985 all unions together had 780,500 members, or less than 10 per cent of Spanish wage- and salary-earners. The unions have not passed the

Table 9.1 *Main economic variables (percentage change on previous year), Spain, 1980–6*

	1980	1981	1982	1983	1984	1985	1986
Private consumption	0.9	−0.5	0.9	1.2	−0.8	1.0	3.6
Public consumption	4.4	1.5	6.3	3.9	3.0	5.0	4.0
Gross capital formation	3.9	−5.1	−1.8	−2.7	−3.2	5.0	12.0
Domestic demand	1.8	−1.2	0.9	0.7	−0.8	2.0	5.7
Exports of goods and services	1.6	6.5	6.8	7.8	15.4	1.5	1.1
Imports of goods and services	3.1	−2.8	4.6	0.5	1.0	3.0	16.0
GDP	1.5	0.4	0.9	2.5	2.3	2.1	3.0
Prices	15.5	14.6	14.4	12.2	11.3	8.8	8.0
Wages		15.4	14.0	13.7	10.0	9.2	8.0

Source: Anuario Estadìstico of the INE (Instituto Nacional de Estadistica)

acid test, that is, the need to show working people that they have the power to improve wages and working conditions. Since the first concertation agreement in 1977, wages have failed to keep pace with inflation, which averaged over 15 per cent in 1980 (see Table 9.1). Recession struck the Spanish economy severely, and the main victims were wage-earners. The public sector deficit and the balance of payments deficit soared, exports lagged and above all unemployment swelled, from a position slightly under the European average in 1977 (5.2 as against 5.4 per cent) to well over it in 1980 at 11.5 per cent.

Given this poor labour market, despite their new legal and institutional status similar to that of organized labour in the rest of Western Europe – recognized by the Constitution (1978), by the decree-laws on union participation in government institutions (1978–9) and the 'Estatuto de los Trabajadores' (Workers' Charter 1980) – the unions' role shrank in collective bargaining, in industrial action at the company level, in worker protection and in wage claims. They sought to make gains with the inter-confederal union–employer agreement of 1980 (Acuerdo Marco Inter-confederal, AMI – see Table 9.2), but the labour movement was in retreat. Its role at the turn of the decade was an increasingly subordinate one.

1.2 Economic change and labour market deterioration
In the new decade, some economic variables improved. The Socialist government's economic policy proved successful, from 1982 on, in lowering inflation to under 10 per cent, righting the balance of payments (see Table 9.3), and increasing exports. GDP

Table 9.2 *Development of concertation, Spain, 1979–86*

	Agreement	Wage rise range set (%)	Change in consumer price index (%)	Signatories
1979	Acuerdo Básico Interconfederal (ABI)	–	–	CEOE UGT
1980	Acuerdo Marco Interconfederal (AMI)	13–16	15.5	CEOE UGT USO
1981	Acuerdo Marco Interconfederal (AMI)	11–15	14.6	CEOE UGT USO
1982	Acuerdo Nacional sobre el Empleo (ANE)	9–11	14.4	Government CEOE UGT CCOO
1983	Acuerdo Interconfederal (AI)	9.5–12.5	12.2	CEOE UGT CCOO
1984	–	6.5[1]	11.3	–
1985	Acuerdo Económico y Social (AES)	5.5–7.5	8.8	Government CEOE UGT
1986	Acuerdo Económico y Social (AES)	8	8.3	CEOE UGT

[1] Government decree for public sector.

Table 9.3 *Balance of payments on a transactions basis (million of US dollars), Spain, 1975–86*

	1975	1980	1981	1982	1983	1984	1985	1986[1]
1 Imports	15,193	32,306	31,086	30,513	27,543	27,063	28,524	32,357
2 Exports	7,807	20,581	20,971	21,332	19,871	22,727	22,643	26,758
3 Balance of trade	−7,386	−11,725	−10,115	−9,181	−7,672	−4,336	−5,880	−5,598
4 Services, net	2,755	4,489	3,443	3,476	3,814	5,226	6,323	9,577
of which:								
5 Tourism	3,096	5,720	5,709	6,122	5,942	6,882	7,141	10,545
6 Net transfers	1,143	2,048	1,692	1,581	1,180	1,118	1,143	984
7 Balance of payments on current account	−3,488	−5,188	−4,981	−4,125	−2,679	2,008	1,586	4,962
8 Long-term private capital movements	1,788	4,020	3,598	763	2,153	2,799	1,146	−659
9 Long-term public capital movements	15	174	639	1,009	953	532	394	2,074
10 Total long-term capital movements	1,803	4,194	4,236	1,773	3,106	3,331	1,540	1,415
11 Basic balance of payments	−1,685	−993	−744	−2,352	428	5,339	46	3,547
12 Short-term capital movements, errors and omissions[2]	930	445	−577	−791	−1,359	−2,246	120	178
13 Monetary movements (increase in holdings indicated by minus sign)	755	548	1,322	3,155	931	−3,093	–	–
of which:								
14 Changes in reserves	120	758	757	3,121	301	−4,560	−1,304	2,843

[1] Provisional, estimated.
[2] Including domestic banks' foreign currency accounts.

Sources: Ministry of the Economy, Ministry of Commerce

Table 9.4 *Government budget and borrowing requirement on a disbursements basis (billions of pesetas), Spain, 1982–6*

	1982	1983	1984	1985	1986[4]
Total revenues	2,636	3,277	3,868	4,422	5,484
Tax revenues	2,162	2,745	3,204	3,731	4,632
Direct taxes	1,159	1,431	1,670	1,917	2,231
households	937	1,142	1,341	1,519	1,779
firms	222	289	329	398	452
Indirect taxes	1,003	1,314	1,534	1,814	2,401
Other revenues	474	532	664	691	852
Total expenditures	3,695	4,567	5,320	6,062	6,910
Current expenditures	2,839	3,559	4,216	4,867	5,792
Staff costs	1,073	1,189	1,191	1,303	1,453
Purchases of goods and services	151	170	230	205	212
Current transfers	1,536	2,025	2,390	2,626	3,233
Other	79	175	405	733	894
Capital expenditures	856	1,008	1,104	1,195	1,118
Fixed capital formation	290	438	445	433	414
Capital transfers[1]	566	570	659	762	704
Accounting item[2]	122	120	253	180	
Budget out-turn	− 937	− 1,168	− 1,199	− 1,460	− 1,426
Non-budget transactions	− 130	− 63	− 141	− 28	
Overall balance	− 1,067	− 1,231	− 1,340	− 1,488	− 1,426
Net financial transactions[3]	− 53	− 264	− 744	67	− 40
Borrowing requirement (−)	− 1,120	− 1,495	− 2,084	− 1,421	− 1,466
Financing					
Bank of Spain	808	268	968	393	
Net foreign borrowing	106	146	186	− 286	
Net domestic borrowing	206	1,081	930	1,314	

[1] Including small amounts carried forward from previous budgets.

[2] Including the difference between appropriations and disbursements plus residual items carried forward but not yet assigned to specific accounts.

[3] Including a small increase in minting of coins.

[4] Budget.

Source: Ministry of Finance

grew at an annual average rate of more than 2 per cent (see Table 9.1), but this was still less than the EC average. Bank profits were very large. Direct investment from abroad, the public sector and tourism continued to fuel economic activity.

Nonetheless, despite some reprivatization, the incidence of state economic intervention increased and the public deficit soared (see

Table 9.5   *Labour market (000s), Spain, 1980–6*

	Labour force	Employment	Participation rate (%)	Unemploy-ment	Unemploy-ment rate
1980	12,858	11,376	48.7	1,482	11.5
1981	12,864	11,017	48.2	1,847	14.4
1982	12,999	10,882	48.2	2,117	16.3
1983	13,122	10,786	48.1	2,336	17.8
1984	13,188	10,472	47.8	2,716	20.6
1985	13,265	10,355	47.5	2,910	21.9
1986	13,905	10,961	47.9	2,944	21.2

Source: INE

Table 9.4). The worst deterioration was in the labour market. The labour force continued to expand despite a declining birth rate and the ageing of the population. Total employment, however, declined steadily (see Table 9.5 and Figure 9.1). Whether one judges by recorded or by estimated (Table 9.6) unemployment figures, the rate doubled between 1980 and 1986, from about 11 to over 20 per cent. At the end of 1986 the number of registered unemployed was more that 2.9 million. By industry (Table 9.7), the worst was construction (35.2 per cent), followed by manufacturing industry (16.2 per cent) and agriculture (11.5 per cent). The services sector, by contrast, in line with the European trend, was the only sector with a positive balance between the creation and destruction of jobs.

So despite definite government and employer measures to make the labour market more flexible, industrial conversion, stagnation in some sectors and the lack of private investment continued to exclude the weakest groups and prevent the integration of the younger generation into the workforces. In June 1986 about one in every four Spaniards between the age of sixteen and twenty-five was unemployed, making a total of 1.5 million jobless young people. Thus of the unemployed all told, about half were young people under twenty-five, while in all age groups women were the worst hit (see Table 9.8). In the rural regions (Andalusia, Estremadura) and in the working-class districts of the big cities (Barcelona, Madrid, Bilbao), a growing number of people under thirty have never held a steady job and have no real hopes of doing so. These groups have very poor education (failures, drop-outs, absenteeism), negligible vocational skills, poor individual and collective socialization, and usually a passive, when not active, resistance to involvement in any long-term cultural, political or trade union initiative or project. One may see the signs of an

Table 9.6 *Unemployment and unemployment benefits, Spain, 1973–86*

	Registered unemployment (INEM) (000s)	Registered unemployment rate (%)	Estimated unemployment (INE) (000s)	Estimated unemployment rate (%)	No. unemployed receiving benefits	Index of benefit coverage (%)
1973	129	0.96	323	2.40		
1974	196	1.45	398	2.94		
1975	302	2.26	623	4.66		
1976	448	3.39	697	5.27	278,611	62.19
1977	662	5.00	832	6.28	337,885	51.04
1978	908	6.90	1,083	8.23	423,854	46.68
1979	1,130	8.59	1,334	10.14	524,659	46.43
1980	1,416	11.01	1,620	12.60	689,026	48.66
1981	1,744	13.53	1,988	15.39	750,094	43.01
1982	2,151	16.53	2,235	17.06	721,660	33.55
1983	2,342	17.80	2,434	18.43	612,433	26.15
1984	2,604	19.70	2,869	21.69	686,675	26.37
1985	2,732	20.50	2,934	22.00	884,348	32.37
1986	2,902	21.00	2,944	21.20	921,095	31.74

Source: Ministry of Labour; INE

(000s)

Figure 9.1 *Employment, labour force and unemployment, Spain, 1981–6*

Source: INE

emerging urban culture of implicit rejection of the work ethic, the value of striving, effort, saving or common struggle. In addition, there is the reappearance of marginalization and spreading poverty in a country that is still far from the level of social assistance or protection provided by other Western European welfare states.

Such familiar European phenomena as the decentralization of production, labour-market segmentation, the underground

Table 9.7 *Labour market by sector (000s), Spain, 1980–6*

	Agriculture				Industry				Construction				Services				First-job seekers
	A	B	C	D	A	B	C	D	A	B	C	D	A	B	C	D	
1980	2,211	2,104	107	4.8	3,341	3,089	252	7.5	1,327	1,019	308	23.2	5,371	5,076	295	5.5	520
1981	2,106	1,982	124	5.9	3,279	2,953	326	9.9	1,301	941	360	27.7	5,430	5,063	367	6.8	670
1982	2,038	1,927	111	5.4	3,186	2,789	397	12.5	1,291	927	364	28.2	5,589	5,164	435	7.8	810
1983	2,039	1,921	118	5.8	3,143	2,722	421	13.4	1,275	900	375	29.4	5,664	5,163	501	8.8	921
1984	2,038	1,887	201	9.9	3,123	2,652	471	15.1	1,226	789	437	35.6	5,677	5,108	569	10.0	1,033
1985	2,018	1,786	232	11.5	3,065	2,560	495	16.2	1,152	745	406	35.2	5,708	5,175	533	9.3	1,244
1986	1,975	1,705	270	13.7	3,114	2,662	452	14.5	1,224	877	347	28.4	6,399	5,718	681	10.6	1,194

A: Labour force.
B: Employed.
C: Unemployed.
D: Unemployment rate (%).

Source: INE

Table 9.8 *Unemployment rates by age and sex (%), Spain, 1977–86*

	Age 16–19			Age 20–24			Age 25–54			Age 55 and over		
	Total	Men	Women	Total	Men	Women	Total	Men	Women	Total	Men	Women
1977	15.3	14.5	16.3	10.2	10.5	9.8	3.5	3.8	2.5	2.4	3.0	0.6
1978	21.6	19.9	23.9	14.4	15.0	13.7	4.4	4.7	3.7	2.9	3.7	0.6
1979	26.3	25.3	27.7	18.0	18.3	17.7	5.5	5.8	4.6	3.5	4.4	1.0
1980	34.9	32.9	37.6	24.1	24.4	23.7	7.3	7.8	6.0	4.5	5.5	1.5
1981	43.0	41.5	45.2	29.6	29.2	30.0	9.1	9.6	7.5	5.7	6.8	2.0
1982	47.6	46.5	49.2	33.5	33.3	33.8	10.4	10.6	10.2	6.4	7.7	2.4
1983	51.1	49.7	53.0	37.1	35.7	38.9	11.8	11.8	11.8	9.7	8.2	2.6
1984	55.6	54.4	57.1	42.1	40.5	44.1	14.2	14.3	13.9	9.2	10.9	3.8
1985	55.9	54.1	58.6	44.6	42.2	47.8	15.8	15.6	16.3	9.8	11.5	4.8
1986	52.4	48.5	57.5	43.7	40.9	47.6	14.9	13.9	17.3	10.5	12.0	5.8

Source: EPA (INE)

economy, and especially the increasing precariousness of jobs (more than a million irregular workers) are more severe in Spain. The problems of an economy halfway between north and south, acting as turntable between the two, persist. The new international division of labour, indeed, has exacerbated them, although the government's prudent economic policy since 1982 – public sector investment and extended unemployment benefits (Table 9.6) – has helped prevent a still sharper deterioration.

2 The actors

The electoral victory of the Spanish Socialists in 1982 came at a time when similar governments held power in the Mediterranean countries of Europe. The Socialist Party ruled most large cities and eleven of the seventeen regional governments. The same year the Uniòn General de Trabajadores (UGT) for the first time won a plurality in the union elections. This favourable international scene and domestic domination, together with the election campaign promises, raised hopes of substantial change, especially welcome a year after an attempted *coup d'état* that had revived the ghosts of the past and shown the reluctance of the traditional power centres to disappear. Except in Catalonia and the Basque country, where nationalist parties held their own against Socialist growth, the conservatives (Alianza Popular, AP) were in the minority, while the Communist Party, wracked by internal conflict, managed to get just four deputies elected and went into a political crisis whose only countervailing feature was the strength of the Comisiones Obreras union (CCOO).

The latest elections, in 1986, fundamentally confirmed those results. The Socialist Party again won an absolute majority, though losing a few seats in the Chamber. The conservatives also lost a few seats. In the course of the year their most important leader had to resign, the opposition coalition broke up and the Christian Democrats (PDP) pulled out of it. The Social Democratic Centre (CDS), the Party of the former President, gained, as did the nationalist parties, while the Communist Party split was deepened. The principal reasons for worry for the government were (in foreign affairs) the referendum over NATO membership and the question of Spain's African redoubts, and (domestically) the Basque country and student revolt. The government nonetheless has the reins of power firmly in hand.

In the most recent elections (local, regional and European) in June 1987 the Socialists were again the leading party, but their popular vote decreased by 1.5 million and the Party lost its absolute majority in a number of major cities (Madrid, Valencia, Seville, Zaragoza) and regions (the Canaries, Valencia). Regional autonomy and nationalist parties made further gains, and so did the CDS. The Communists recouped some of the ground they had lost, and the AP consolidated its position with a modest loss. Spanish politics is gradually diversifying from a bipolar situation.

2.1   The state

Taking the lesson of the failure of French Socialist economic policy to heart, the government adopted a programme of moderate growth, seeking to curb both inflation and wages, improve the flexibility of the labour market, shorten the working day (planning an annual working time of 1826 hours), foster exports and private enterprise, and rationalize corporations. All in all, except for the last, these objectives have been attained. The programme amounted to 'getting the economy ready to advance faster when the world economy recovers'.

The global recovery, however, failed to live up to expectations through the entire period 1980–6, which narrowed the scope for manoeuvre. Nevertheless, early on the Socialist government nationalized the Rumasa holding company and tackled industrial conversion in Asturias, Cadiz, Galicia, Valencia and the Basque country, at the cost of considerable social distress. Later it enacted liberalization measures affecting foreign investment and the labour market (in August 1984 and March 1986 respectively), acted to stimulate private initiative and increased taxes (VAT).

In the past decade more than eighty measures concerning the labour market have been promulgated. The Labour Relations Act of 1976 established a rigid contract system, but some margin of flexibility began to emerge with the Moncloa Agreements of 1977, the Workers' Charter in 1980 and the Basic Employment Act of 1980. The Socialist government, beginning in 1982, introduced a set of measures (Law 1984, Decrees 1989, 1991, 1992, 2104 and others) whose effect was a far-reaching liberalization of the labour market. This is manifest in the large number and variety of forms of atypical employment contracts used today in Spain: new business contracts, cyclical contracts, services, apprenticeship, trainee, job creation, group contracts, temporary contracts, homework contracts, socially useful jobs, and so on.

Spain's accession to the European Community in 1986 was certainly one of the crucial economic events of the decade, but it is much too soon to judge the overall impact. However, it is already clear that some industries (textiles, steel, dairy products) and some regions (Asturias, Galicia) will suffer and others (food-processing among industries, Valencia and Andalusia among regions) will benefit. In any case, integration in this larger economic and social sphere is a major challenge to Spanish society and the Spanish economy.

Partly out of conviction, partly because of the paucity of social movements at the time of their electoral victory, the Socialist government threw itself into a campaign to modernize the state. Measures were taken to rationalize the educational and judicial systems and the civil service, and in this framework the idea of a more all-embracing welfare state arose. The concept was to compensate, by a social wage, for the loss in purchasing power of the individual workers' wage. But this ran up against the difficulty of increasing government spending. The enormous deficit of the Spanish social security system raised doubts about the possibility of any substantial progress. Even so, despite the development of social services and some types of welfare (old age and unemployment benefits), social policy failed to close the gap between Spain and the rest of Europe (unemployment benefits were short in duration, no minimum wage, no family allowances, and so on).

Another important strong point in the government's social and labour policy has been employer–union agreements. These emerged at first with markedly political colouring, the explicit aim being to reinforce the democratic system. The need was to set some limits on the action of a labour movement that was highly politicized, with an anti-capitalist ideology and a great ability to mobilize workers. In return, unions were offered institutional recognition and some social and economic advantages. As the recession made itself felt, this concertation turned more strictly economic in content, although the government continued to take part. Since 1979 all Spanish governments have favoured such agreements, and in 1982 and 1985–6 they were actually cosignatories to them. This shift has taken the form of agreements on wages, jobs and productivity. Since the 1970s the number of strikes has diminished, the rigidity of contract forms has declined, dismissals have been made easier and salary ranges have been set for collective bargaining. On the whole most government, business and union leaders have strongly supported concertation, and public opinion surveys show that the majority of the people favours them as well.

2.2 *The employers*
The Spanish employer class has changed dramatically in the course of the last ten years. At Franco's death, Spanish employers had no organization to represent them; they were on the defensive at a

time of major industrial conflict, subject to ideological attacks that denied their legitimacy, and with an uncertain future. Their first task was to organize, and based on industrial and territorial associations they founded the Spanish Confederation of Employers' Organizations (CEOE). The CEOE is relatively supple in structure, and is able to carry on and conclude major labour agreements (thanks to its broad representation among employers) and to conduct relations with the unions.

In the first two years after its foundation in 1977, the CEOE's relations with the UCD government were strained, owing both to the makeup of the Party in power and to government policy (expansion of the public sector, tax reform, labour legislation, and so forth). Starting in 1979 relations improved and became more functional. Relations with the subsequent Socialist governments have also had their ups and downs. For the most part the CEOE has supported the government's monetary and financial measures, its industrial programme and policy of curbing wages, and the decision to join the EC, although it has been less satisfied with the recent tax increases. Meanwhile, the employers' organization has criticized the rise in public spending (especially that for nationalized enterprises), the funding and management of the social security system, and the hesitancy of labour-market reforms.

This ambivalence produced a series of actions by the employers' leadership ranging from support and endorsement of present government economic policies to opposition to other measures. Officially, the CEOE was non-aligned with respect to all political parties, and with rare exceptions the organization made no directly political pronouncements. That does not mean that some of its interventions did not tend to favour, in more or less covert fashion, right or centre options, or exert pressure against the left. However, the local employer associations showed their sympathies more openly. This was the case in the regional elections in Galicia in October 1981 and Andalusia in May 1982, as well as in Catalonia and the Basque country, where the strength of regionalist parties divided the sympathies of employers.

The Constitution included endorsement of the principle of the free-market economy, which reassured employers. Their social legitimacy was buoyed by the value placed on the concepts of innovation, risk, competition and profitability, which won a broad consensus in political circles and in public opinion.

Thus the business community overcame an initial uncertainty and retreat, owing to the new conditions brought about by the political transition, to consolidate its position and then go over to the offensive. Obviously, tripartite concertation and the weakening of the trade union movement helped pave the way for this. The basic task of the employer community with respect to the unions is to seek, and find, a valid bargaining partner with whom feasible, effective agreements can be reached. Employers recognize the demands and bargaining role of the unions but not their aspirations for social transformation. Predictably, this strategy, adopted in 1979 and continued through the 1980s, led the CEOE to develop a privileged relation with the UGT and to move away from the CCOO. The UGT was credited as a serious, responsible bargaining organization, while the CCOO are discredited as politically controlled, ideological and socially radical.

Spanish employers as a whole seek not to eliminate unions from industrial relations, but to shift them on to a terrain in which wages can be linked to productivity, in which unit labour costs are as low as possible, and in which the labour market is thoroughly liberalized. This does not mean, of course, that on some occasions and in some companies employers have not sought to bar union participation or sponsored company unions or urged individual employment contracts.

Though at times employers have been sceptical of the outcome of nationwide bilateral agreements, for the most part the results have proved positive, in that they have curbed wage rises, eased the earlier conflictual climate (reducing the number of strikes) and strengthened the employer position. Actually, the CEOE was the sponsor of the first agreement with the UGT in 1979, and it has been present in all the bilateral agreements since.

2.3 The unions

The trade union panorama has seen a significant clarification and simplification. Some unions – Confederación Sindical Unitaria de Trabajadores and Sindicato Unitario – have disappeared. Some independents have joined UGT and Unión Sindical Obrera (USO), while others have lost influence. Also, a government attempt to define union representation (the 1984 Organic Labour Relations Act, Ley Orgánica de Libertad Sindical – LOLS) excludes minority unions from most representative machinery. Thus strategies are clearer. UGT backs the government, though at times criticizing it, as in May 1985 and January 1987, and appears as the concertation union. ELA–STV (Solidaridad de Trabajadores Vascos, the Basque union) stresses bargaining and its role in the Basque country, refusing to sign pacts. Intersindical Gallega (INTG) adopts the same line for Galicia, though it engages more freely in confrontation. USO bargains where it is present. And finally, the CCOO oscillate between criticism of and opposition to the government and a reluctant participation in agreements (the Acuerdo Nacional sobre el Empleo (ANE), or national agreement on employment, and the AI, Acuerdo Interconfederal) (see Table 9.2).

Clarification, however, does not mean unity or consolidation. Divisions are still sharp, and with very few exceptions (joint demonstrations on social security in 1985 and NATO in 1986), disagreement and even clashes are the order of the day. Despite some efforts (the USO strike fund), and with the exception of ELA–STV, the membership services provided are scanty and ineffective (legal defence, help with tax returns). the unions' participation in social and economic bodies has brought them little benefit indeed.

Moreover, the largest unions remain the targets of action by the political parties. They are used by the latter for their own tactical purposes, and they are having great difficulty in overcoming this subaltern role. The room for labour action is increasingly narrow, and workers are channelling their demands into the political system. In these conditions, the possibilities for exchange between the unions and the political system are scarcely visible. In Spain, the unions are the objects rather than the subjects of political and social life.

Last but by no means least, trade union action is hemmed in by the fixed intervals set for wage increases by tripartite contract agreements and by the impoverishment of the content of collective bargaining. At the company level, it is vitiated by economic troubles, which have hit industry hardest. The unions have no ideological defences or strategic response to unemployment, the increasing insecurity and precariousness of the workforce of the underground economy. More and more, their action is limited to the defence of workers in large corporations and in companies that are still growing. All in all, workers are drawing away from the unions, which are seen as distant, mediatory institutions. Workers are increasingly spectators rather than actors on the social scene.

This has produced a significant loss of dynamism and of membership. Though statistics on dues-paying members, local affiliates and so on are none too reliable, some significant figures well illustrate the general picture. Between 1977 and 1985 practically all unions lost membership. In the euphoria of 1977, Spanish unionization was claimed to be at 'European' levels. In 1985 it was well below the French rate. A provisional estimate gives present union membership at about 10 per cent of Spanish wage- and salary-earners.

Another, indirect indication of workers' growing disaffection is participation in union elections. From 1978 to 1982 abstentionism grew steadily. In the first year, for all of Spain the number of union delegates elected was 193,112; in 1980, 164,617; in 1982, 140,770; and in 1986, 162,800. The government did not hold the elections in 1984. Official sources report slightly decreased abstentions in 1986. As to the election results, in the first year the CCOO led with 34.47 per cent of the total; UGT had 21.70 per cent, USO 3.87 per cent and independent delegates 32 per cent. The independents waned rapidly in importance. In 1982, they amounted to 21 per cent, and in 1986 just 6.67 per cent. In 1982, UGT superseded CCOO as leading union by a margin of 3.3 percentage points, and in 1986 it remained in the lead with 40.82 per cent, closely followed by CCOO at 34.48 per cent. USO held its 3.7 per cent. A CNT collective also took part in the elections. The nationalist unions, ELA and INTG, which began in 1978 with 11.65 per cent and 7.62 per cent respectively, in 1986 took 34.9 per cent in the Basque country and 20.86 per cent in Galicia.

Looking at the various unions' representation in collective bargaining, one finds that in 1983, a year after the national political and union election, UGT outstripped CCOO. In 1986, however, the latter regained its former strength, while ELA and INTG enlarged their influence. These shifts, plus the regional disparities, the varying unionization and relative influences depending on industry, on public or private sector, on company size and so on, show just how fluid the trade union situation still is. The great weakness of the unions, however, the one that has forced them into strategic retreat, is their lack of following among Spanish workers.

3   An uncompleted model of industrial relations

The still ongoing processes affecting Spanish industrial relations, both internal and external, make it impossible to speak of a fully fledged, consolidated model.

At the grassroots, one finds some plants (mainly small businesses) managed by old-style, 'Manchester school' production, technical and social standards: despotic employer control, no union, no contracts, subsistence wages, worker submissiveness, with occasional violent outbreaks, and so forth. At the other extreme are technically advanced firms (mainly multinationals) with new technology, skilled labour, collective contracts, a strong union presence, high salaries and good fringe benefits (insurance plans, housing, company store and so on). In between, a varied constellation of conditions in a labour market where the strongest trend appears to be towards greater precariousness.

Nevertheless, there are a good number of elements characteristic of the pluralist model. The actors are independent. Collective bargaining covers the large majority of industrial wage-earners. There are established rules, and a significant number of strikes indicating a pattern of industrial dispute that does not threaten the system as a whole.

On the other hand, a number of elements suggest the corporatist model. First is the long series of concertation agreements: 1979, Acuerdo Básico Interconfederal; 1980–1, Acuerdo Marco Interconfederal; 1982 Acuerdo Nacional sobre el Empleo; 1983, Acuerdo Interconfederal; 1985–6, Acuerdo Económico y Social (see Table 9.2). There have also been efforts to keep other unions out ('closed shop' legislation in 1983, LOLS in 1984) and to accord institutional recognition and acceptance to those unions deemed 'representative'. There has been increasing state intervention in social and economic life, while at the summit a group of elites has been formed which negotiate among themselves and derive political and social legitimacy from their rank and file through representative democracy.

The coexistence of these two conflicting sets of elements, these two possible interpretations, shows the limitations of the two models, as well as the incompleteness and complexity of Spanish industrial relations. Actually the independence of the actors, while proclaimed in law and vigorously asserted by the protagonists, is quite debatable, given the growing intervention of the state and the unions' financial dependence on the government (subsidies, allocations to union funds), the steady convergence of viewpoints among the actors and their rapprochement with the political system.

The number of contracts signed rose from 2584 in 1980 to 3805 in 1985, then declined to 3013 in 1986. The number of firms and of employees covered by collective bargaining contracts peaked in 1982 at 889,300 and 6,262,900 respectively. In 1986, the figures were 710,800 and under 5 million. But it is above all the content of the bargaining, together with extension contracts in time (every two years rather than annually) that shows its impoverishment. It is increasingly limited to discussion on wages, the range of which has already been set by national agreements, and on the working day (Table 9.9).

It can be seen that the average amount of wage rises granted has diminished over the years, and that wage gains have failed to keep pace with inflation, while respecting the ranges set by nationwide concertation. Increases have been unequally distributed. From 1981 to 1984, industry contract rises exceeded company contract rises by 4 percentage points. Also, the more labour-intensive industries

Table 9.9 *Collective bargain agreements, Spain, 1977–86*

	No. of agreements	No. of firms covered (000s)	No. of workers covered (000s)	Average contract wage rise (%)
1977	1,349	557.1	2,876.4	25.01
1978	1,838	637.1	4,629.2	20.59
1979	2,122	657.8	4,959.6	14.10
1980[1]	2,564	877.7	6,069.6	15.26
1981[2]	2,694	672.7	4,435.2	13.06
1982	3,385	889.3	6,262.9	12.02
1983	3,665	869.7	6,226.3	11.44
1984	3,791	836.9	6,180.8	7.67
1985	3,805	843.3	6,088.2	7.41
1986[3]	3,013	710.8	4,825.3	8.16

[1] Excluding Catalonia and the Basque country.
[2] Excluding Catalonia.
[3] January–November.

Source: Based on Ministry of Labour data

(textiles, construction, shoes, catering and hotels, education, health) have had higher than average rises. What hinders a linkage between wages and productivity, however, is the criteria for determining the composition of wages. Thus base pay plus seniority rises and other fixed components accounted for over 60 per cent of effective wages in 1981 and about the same (63.6 per cent) in 1986. On this point, then, the unions' aim (as much as possible, fixed wages) has held its own against the employers' aim of increasingly variable wages. Seniority within the firm continues to be rewarded more than productivity, and turnover has held steady at about 5 per cent. In 1983, the average seniority of the workforce in large firms was 14.5 years, much higher than in most advanced industrial countries (comparable figures were 6.7 years in the US, 8.6 in the UK). In 1983 the government set the number of hours of work at 1826 a year. The tendency in collective bargaining, albeit stronger in the public than in the private sector, is to lower this figure still further. In the last three years contract working hours have settled at about 1800 a year, just under forty hours a week. Overtime has also diminished. The unions have pressed for both of these improvements in the belief that they will help create jobs, though this is not at all evident, at least in the large firms.

Strike activity is greater in Spain than in most European countries. Until 1979 industrial conflict was linked with the political situation (1976) and the inception of collective bargaining. Thus from 743 strikes involving 303,000 workers and 1 million days lost in 1973, the figures rose to 3662 strikes, 2,556,000 workers, and 13,750,000 days in 1976. The next year the number of strikers rose to nearly 3 million and days lost to 16,641,000. In 1979 strikes numbered 2680, while the number of participants and days lost peaked at 5,713,000 and 18,917,000 respectively From then on, all three figures declined progressively. In 1985 there were 1275 strikes, involving 1,608,000 workers and causing the loss of 2,958,000 days.

Thus progressively strike activity has waned, especially in terms of days lost, and strikes have concentrated in large firms and in some regions particularly affected by industrial restructuring. At present, the main issue in most industrial disputes is job protection.

An interesting question is what effect the lack of a social concertation agreement in 1984 and 1987 had on strike activity. In the former year there was a rise in the number of strikes, strikers and days lost, but all in all a fairly insignificant one. Does not this suggest that concertation is more and more *pro forma*? To a large extent, it has become the ritual signature of a pay rise accord, the only clear point usually involved. For the rest (such issues as jobs, absenteeism, productivity) the accords have been vague and ambiguous enough to draw criticism from all their signatories.

As to territorial range, industrial relations are subject to conflicting tendencies. Some forces work in favour of centralization (concertation, the concentration of decision-making powers at the top level of union and employer organizations, economic and financial policy and so on). But the constitutional arrangements governing politics and administration accord some powers to regional governments. In the Basque country, the regional authorities and the largest union both seek to develop an autonomous labour-relations framework for their territory. Also, some labour struggles have broken out at the local or regional level. Collective bargaining is ambiguous as well. There are some nationwide industry contracts (banking, chemicals and others), but most agreements are for a given industry at the provincial level.

3.1   An irony: institutional recognition and union decline

It is hard to say whether the subordinate role and the defensive posture of the labour movement in the 1980s signals the onset of a structural crisis or simply a bad moment. What is undeniable, at any rate, is that Spanish unions have lost much of the power and influence they enjoyed in the later 1970s. But the period of strength was brief, and had not been, as in the rest of Europe, the result of sustained economic growth, prosperity and political freedom; rather, it came about at a time of political transition, once the economic recession had clearly emerged. The irony of the Spanish situation lies in the fact that this union decline has occurred at a time of institutional and legal recognition; or, to be precise, at a time when the effects of a favourable legal framework should have made themselves felt, when democracy was being established and a party with pro-labour origins and programme came to power.

Most of the legislation governing Spanish labour relations had been passed in the immediately preceding years, and it ensured a substantial union presence both at the company level and in social policy. When these Acts were passed, some employers' voices were actually raised in protest at what they called the unionization of economic life and the annihilation of private initiative. Some employer spokesmen even cited the constitutional clause endorsing the market economy, implying that this legislation bordered on the unconstitutional. Other observers noted the open, more progressive nature of this legislation compared to that in other European countries. In reality, the current legal framework of labour relations in Spain resembles that found in most of the rest of Europe in giving unions considerable scope for action, though some problems of institutional confirmation have been raised.

The introduction of democracy and the consolidation of progressive power after 1982 might have led one to think that the unions would find fertile terrain for growth and development. Yet democratic legitimacy and the strong points it implied did not make for large-scale union participation in social, political and institutional decision-making. The weakness of organized labour kept it from really wielding influence on the political scene, and unions seldom overcame a certain facelessness during political exchange. The few times they did, it was mainly owing to the interests of their friendly parties, not to their own strategy.

This was true of the CCOO, which although – or perhaps because – they were stronger than the Communist Party, were neutralized by the internal battles and schisms of the Party, which were replicated within the union. The CCOO only managed to exert some influence in the campaign of opposition to the government's economic policy, to the pension law and on the occasion of the NATO referendum. As for the UGT, its room for action was restricted by the Socialists' governing role. The policies of curbing wages and fostering labour-market flexibility drove the UGT towards opposition, but given its strategy of institutional participation and social concertation, and given the provenance of its functionaries, it was unable to go very far in that direction. Only very recently has the union managed to distance itself to some extent from government economic policy, seeking to distinguish among responsibilities and politicians within the Socialist structure.

At the local and regional level, perhaps, union power has been more successfully exercised. In some circumscribed disputes (Sagunto, Puerto Real, Reinosa, Asturias and others) the unions have largely determined the course of the conflict and often the outcome. In these cases the eventual agreements – often not much to the liking of the groups that initiated the action – involved negotiations with local and regional parties and governments. In the Basque country, one could perhaps speak of true social policy negotiation. This is suggested by the hegemony of ELA–STV, confirmed in the latest elections, by the common objectives of the union and the ruling Basque party, the Basque Labour Relations Council, and by their condemnation of violence. Yet ELA–STV is against social compacts and the Basque employers' association and the UGT oppose a separate Basque labour relations system, while the polarization of politics around nationalism prevents further progress along those lines.

All in all, despite the institutional recognition of its legitimacy, Spanish trade unionism is in a subordinate position, which is due more to a combination of economic factors and internal weakness than to the action of anti-labour political or social forces. Thus minor adjustments to recoup strength along the old lines will not suffice. A sweeping transformation of the old approach is needed.

What, then, are the external and internal challenges to Spanish unionism? Economically, Spain is midway between south and north, though more closely resembling the pattern of the latter in that it has considerable industrial potential while the services have grown rapidly in recent years. This role as turntable in the international division of labour has led Spain to export raw materials, especially farm products, and labour, when emigrants succeed in finding jobs in the more advanced countries, while offering the workers of urban Europe a rest and recreation vacation area. On the other side, Spain imports high technology and exports intermediate goods, acting as a testing ground for Japanese and American multinationals seeking to enter Europe and for Europeans getting ready for a move into Latin America.

All this is reflected in the structure of the economy and in the labour market. Industrial restructuring, imposed by external constraints (limits on steel output, Asian competition in textiles) and internal limits, has struck most heavily where union strength was greatest (steel and engineering, mining, shipbuilding, textiles). Large plants have shed labour or shut down, while entire districts

(Asturias, Galicia, Sagunto) have witnessed the disappearance of their principal industries. The decentralization of industry has sapped the 'workers' strongholds' where blue-collar workers had managed to impose their own style of work organization, of bargaining and of union representation.

The introduction of new technology has shifted large numbers of wage-earners into jobs further removed from direct production. Marketing, planning, financial services, advertising employ growing numbers of workers, who are neither attracted nor motivated by traditional unionism and its culture. Moreover, some of the most dynamic sectors of the Spanish economy (including tourism and food-processing) have very little union tradition and great organizational difficulties. The underground economy, which is very extensive, is another obstacle to unionization (in shoes, toys, textiles and so on), as well as the classic industrial 'minifundia' widespread in many industries and regions.

Above it all, there is unemployment, underemployment, multiple employment, difficulty in finding a job in line with one's qualifications, more than a million precarious workers. All this generates mistrust, lack of solidarity and actions in defence of narrow group interests, undermining working people's cohesiveness and ability to organize. The only safe, stable area appears to be public employment in these circumstances, the unions' ability to exert pressure in the labour market has diminished, as has their capacity to defend diverse, and sometimes conflicting, interests and aspirations. How can the jobless and the employed, ailing and dynamic industries, precarious and secure workers, the skilled and the unskilled be brought together in a single strategic design? The strikes and demonstrations of the spring of 1987 are significant in this regard, for they marked both the inception of a number of spontaneous worker groups and the raising of specific demands that did not issue forth in broader social movements.

Yet to note only the external factors in union decline is in a way to hide one's head in the sand, blaming circumstances largely outside union control for the internal strains and incompetence that explain their present state. Recently the unions have been engaged in a critical re-examination. Summing up their analyses, a first inference is that the unions that have best weathered the political transition are those that were best adapted to the democratic process (UGT and ELA–STV). In other words, the unions in which the anti-Franco resistance weighed most heavily (CCOO and USO) have been slow to revise strategy and organization. The debate within the CCOO on whether to opt for being a sociopolitical movement or a straight trade union, USO's faith in its independence from domination by political parties, and the persistence in both organizations of habits linked to clandestinity are presumably instances of the inability of some union leaders tempered in battles prior to 1976–7 to understand the new state of affairs. In the case of the UGT, by contrast, most of the leaders and officials only appeared in the course of the last few years.

Generally speaking, the unions had expectations of greater progress and social change than have actually been achieved. They organized and devised strategy and tactics according to these expectations, but they soon found themselves facing an unfavourable balance of strength that compelled them progressively to tone down their pronouncements. In the process, a good many militants were 'burnt out'. Tactics and slogans had to be modified. Long-term shifts in content presented a confused and disorienting image to working people.

Thus the CCOO, for instance, started out with the self-image of a broad-based social movement, intending to represent the interests of all working people. Initially, their position was a rejection of all pacts, but gradually they shifted to the scheme of the free trade union with close relations to the Communist Party. They accepted the Moncloa Agreement (1977) and were signatories to the ANE (1982) and AI (1983), swinging back and forth between acceptance of bargaining and opposition. The UGT detached itself from the Moncloa Agreement and eventually became Spain's major pro-concertation and pro-participation union shifting somewhat from strong fraternity with the Socialist Party (PSOE) when it was in opposition, and thus stressing its socialist character, towards its more recent detachment, while seeking to voice the dissatisfaction of some workers with government policy. The USO stressed the socialist path, worker self-management and independence, while opposing agreements, until 1980. In that year it signed the AMI accord, and since then has dropped a part of its ideological position and allowed for independent unions to join, with the slogan 'a union for everybody'. All these very considerable position changes affected workers, for whom the day-to-day, concrete matters of union presence consisted in wages, working conditions, the inter-union committee and the union local within their firms.

These practical concerns kept workers from identifying with the increasing disunity and even polarization of the unions, when they had always experienced the concept of trade union unity, the older image of the industrial union and the union at company level, as strongly positive. In the last few years on the few occasions that the unions acted together worker participation was stronger. By contrast, rivalry between unions, recurrent hostility during union election periods, accusations and so on have alienated a good many workers, who do not understand the strains and see them as the defence of the petty interests of the individual unions if not of the personal interests of union officials.

Turning to another sphere, the trade union movement's analysis of the recession and its consequences was tardy and partial. The unions were not alone in this, of course, but it seriously affected their scope for manoeuvre and action. Indeed, when their membership began to soar in 1979, they were quite unprepared to organize or retain the new mass of members. In some cases – CCOO and USO – they continued to insist on acceptance of the principles of the union, that is, on an ideological selection process. None of the unions built up services to meet the real needs of workers. Partly out of incompetence and partly out of underestimation of the need, none of the unions except ELA offered anything but legal advice and assistance in filling out tax forms. By the time they realized their mistake and reacted by intervening in other areas (holidays, insurance, stores and cafeterias) it was too late. Having counted on passion and militancy rather than concrete interest, and failing to win substantial advantages in collective bargaining, they could not retain the members they had attracted.

These are certainly not the only factors accounting for the present situation. Other key elements are the hegemony of the political parties and their use of the unions as battleground, tactical support and pool of officials at all levels of management. It must be said, however, that the unions have been signally lacking in ability to respond independently or to preserve their autonomy in the face of these pressures. This has diminished the vitality of trade union life. Again, the unions are not alone in this; indeed, most of the social movements of the 1970s have suffered a similar fate.

3.2 An unsteady concertation

Some observers hold that the dominant model of industrial relations in Spain is Type A in the project's general model (Table 9.10), that is, simultaneously with collective bargaining at the grassroots there is a vast process of negotiation between national employer and union organizations. It is even argued that all in all Spanish society has entered the corporatist era, and that social and industrial concertation is one of the most telling pieces of evidence for this thesis.

Unquestionably, while concertation practices have been weakened or even eliminated in some European countries in the 1980s, in Spain they only began in 1977 with the Moncloa Agreement, which was more political in nature. They were consolidated

Table 9.10 *Changes in the industrial relations system, Spain since 1980*

Type	Pre-1980	Post-1980
A(a) National concertation	Inception of concertation in framework of transition to democracy, mainly political in nature	Pacts more social than political, signed each year except two, with varying formulae and results
A(b) Industry-wide collective bargaining	Some national, industry-wide collective bargaining contracts (chemicals, banking)	More difficulties in reaching industry contracts nationwide
B Decentralized collective bargaining	Considerable increase in provincial and local contracts. Company-level contracts raised wage minimums	Continued increase, in dynamic industries and companies. Elsewhere, adherence to the limits set in concertation accords. Some troubled companies and industries are exempted from the norms
C(a) Worker participation via unions	Significant role played by union sections (locals) and inter-union committees at company level. Limited experience in participation in management	Weakening role of union committees, still sharper weakening of locals. Union participation in social and economic agencies, plans for participation in public sector
C(b) Worker participation without unions	Little importance. Occasional meetings	Some efforts by firms, in connection with 'human relations'. Spread of co-operatives
D(a) Simple contract (no unions)	Common in the services sector and for technicians and higher officers	Increasingly frequent, thanks to the development of these groups
D(b) Simple contract (no unions) in secondary labour markets	Traditional in the informal economy (textiles, construction, toys, shoes)	Expansion, because of growth of underground economy. More than a million precarious workers

with the BI in 1979 and generalized from 1980 onwards with the AMI, ANE, AI and AES. This variance from the broader European pattern poses a twofold question. First, how can overall agreements be reached if the economic resources to legitimate them and provide real substance are lacking? And second, are such agreements really the product of the true balance of strength at a given moment? Or are they not, rather, a way for the signatory organizations to gain a representativeness and strength that they have not attained by other means? In any event, the unsteadiness of concertation in Spain is underscored by the discontinuity of the national agreements, the variety of signatories and forms, the diversity of content and the dubious chances of their being made effective.

First, since 1979 there have been two years, 1984 and 1987, in which no concertation agreement has been signed. In 1984 this was due to the employer confederation's non-negotiable 6.5 per cent wage-rise proposal, the government's decision to opt for a more focused incomes policy (a medium-term economic plan and a decree applying the 6.5 per cent figure to the public sector), and the weakness of the unions. Actually, wage agreements reached in free collective bargaining provided for rises of 7.5 and 8 per cent, while prices went up 11.3 per cent. The number of strikes was higher than in the years preceding or following – owing mainly to restructuring – although the increase was not as marked as had been expected when the concertation talks broke off. In 1987 there was no tripartite agreement, and again the number of strikes rose, in connection with restructuring (in Reinosa, Puerto Real, Hunosa), demands by particular categories (doctors), and to a lesser extent contract bargaining (RENFE, IBERIA).

Second is the vast array of variants in concertation accords. The Moncloa Agreement of 1977 was a straight political pact, with neither employer nor union organizations signing; it was complemented by an imposed incomes policy (the April Decree) and labour-relations compromises (wage rises, temporary contracts, social security). The ABI agreement in 1979 was a bilateral accord between CEOE and UGT. The AMI in 1980 was a two-year, three-way agreement between CEOE, UGT and USO. The ANE in 1981 was a one-year, four-party, tripartite accord: government, CEOE, UGT and CCOO. A year later, the same parties, less the government, signed the AI. And finally came another two-year pact, in which the government participated but the CCOO did not (the AES for 1985–6). This seemingly never-ending flux is an unmistakable sign that the concertation process is not yet firmly established.

The substance of the pacts also changes over time, though the idea of setting wage scales within which collective bargaining must operate has always prevailed. The pacts variously contain: tax compromises (AES), clauses on mediation, arbitration and conciliation (AMI, AI, AES), accords to be developed in legislation (ANE, AES), vague or specific references to job creation (AES), more or less explicit provisions on productivity, absenteeism, retirement, working time (AI).

The positions taken by the various actors have also been subject to modification. The ANE, for instance, was signed by government and employer and union organizations under the impact of the attempted coup in 1981. The main arguments on behalf of the agreement were the need to ensure the stability of democracy and of social consensus. The CCOO accepted these arguments and overcame their hostility to concertation agreements. The next year, however, resistance resurfaced with respect to the AI, although the pro-Communist union eventually signed. Two years later, the CCOO were practically excluded from the AES.

The union most in favour of concertation is the UGT. Indeed, a good part of its strategy depends on concertation, although its attitudes vary with the political and economic situation. The USO was present at the AMI talks and later signed the agreement. Since then it has been left out of other negotiations, while both ELA–STV and INTG oppose broad government-inspired agreements and the very idea of concertation itself, preferring direct collective bargaining.

The employer organization, the main architect of the pacts, supports concertation agreements in certain circumstances. Spanish employer organizations take a pragmatic stance. That is, they take part when they can obtain substantial concessions either from the unions or from the government. The government itself has been a direct participant in agreements twice in the course of the 1980s. The first time, in 1982, was for political reasons; the second, in 1985, as part of economic planning. The present government much more clearly favours concertation, but it also advocates the independence of the two sides in industrial relations. The government's worry is that employers and unions may send it the 'bill' for the agreements, restrict its decision-making discretion, and criticize it afterwards for the signatories' failure to comply with the accords.

This indeed, is a fourth characteristic of concertation in Spain. What happens is that within a few months of the signature of an agreement, and sometimes even prior to it, the various participants begin to distance themselves from it, going on to reciprocal accusations of non-compliance (job creation, institutional representation and so on). The follow-up committees have not worked, not to mention special working-groups. They have turned into forums for criticism when they have not been neutralized and superseded by events. One could conclude that both sides are more interested in the talks leading up to the agreement and in the almost ritual act of signature itself than in the actual contents and potential consequences of the accord. More than once it has been insinuated that behind the formal agreements there are much meatier, secret pacts between the signatories.

However that may be, social concertation in Spain has affected some of the variables comprising the model of industrial relations. The negotiating process both before and after signature of the pact has obliged the various partners to get to know one another better, to understand the other side's point of view and accept some of its arguments. This continuous contact, at least at the top leadership level, has brought about a rapprochement in positions at the same time as it centralized decision-making. Some accords sought to correct the fragmentation of collective bargaining with a clause calling for nationwide bargaining for each productive sector. Also, the Workers' Charter of 1980 set a minimum threshold of union representation for the signature of conventions. Those ratified by unions totalling 50 per cent of total membership are universally applicable. The 1984 Labour Relations Act (LOLS) further reinforced the legal recognition of the UGT–CCOO duopoly on union representation in Spain to the exclusion of other unions.

The Moncloa Agreement in 1977 provided for union participation in the management of the social security system, in public corporations and in the general committee on prices, in proportion to the results of union elections. The Constitution, Article 129, explicitly recognizes the unions' right to take part in the social security system and in other public bodies. Later, a set of decree-laws laid down the specifics of this participation. With the ANE agreements in 1982, para. IV, the mode of union participation in most of the state's social and economic agencies and a schedule for implementation was specific. And, notwithstanding the slowness, administrative difficulties, internal resistance and failure to abide by the schedule, this agreement constitutes a highly significant institutional recognition of the unions' role and a strengthening of their ties with the state.

Another major step in this direction taken by the ANE agreements is the introduction of a direct government subsidy to the unions, 800 million pesetas being disbursed in 1982, 1983 and 1984. At the end of 1984 the government paid out another 1 billion pesetas to UGT, under the notion of devolution of the unions' patrimony. This has had a tonic effect on the budgets of the unions, whose self-financing through voluntary dues is very limited, while the effort to institutionalize the automatic dues check-off by negotiated agreements (1981–2) largely failed. Although all the unions have sought to computerize the payments system and collect dues through bank receipts (some are paid directly by the firm), they have never ceased to have financial and liquidity problems. The CCOO, for instance, are currently having trouble meeting the social security payments. The level of external financing for the unions is high, most of it coming from the state.

All in all, social concertation has traced out a path of increasing institutionalization of the major unions in a tripartite system that fully recognizes their legitimacy. There has been no particular desire in Spain to exclude them, as there has been in some other parts of Europe. Even the UCD government up to 1982 gave no signs of any such plan, despite its dubious labour and union policies; still less so the Socialist government.

The employers have not only gained in political space and public legitimacy but have also strengthened their internal unity. For this reason the employer confederation has favoured concertation, even though this meant making some concession to its bargaining partners. These partners were necessary to stabilize the labour scene and bring down the level of conflict. This does not mean that the CEOE has not given preferential treatment to the UGT, sometimes keeping the CCOO out of agreements, or that it has refrained from exerting pressure through provincial or industry-level collective bargaining.

The halting progress of concertation has had its effects. One has certainly been the lowering of the expectations harboured by Spanish working people at the time of the transition to democracy. Another factor in this lowering of sights has been wage moderation and wage restructuring.

Before the Moncloa Agreement, wage pressure was strong, and rises were equal across the board for all categories. The Moncloa accord laid down that at least half the salary be raised in accordance with the same, linear standard. Later, with subsequent agreements and the type of collective bargaining that arose, wage differentials between categories widened. The salary range broadened, as did intersectoral differentials. The faster-growing industries, such as electric power and banking, offered better wages. This stemmed partly from the fact that the standard agreed to and recommended in all the agreements for determining salary increases was productivity. The concertation agreements set overall margins within which collective bargaining contracts could vary. The argument on behalf of these margins is that they allow each industry, region or even company to adapt to its own conditions. This flexibility is only relative, however, since the margins are narrow (as a rule, no more than 2 percentage points) and the pattern of wage rises in the broader contracts produces union pressure for local negotiations to set minima. On the other hand, the AMI agreements allow great flexibility to firms that are being converted or restructured or that already had collective bargaining agreements in previous years. In both cases, the absence of the obligation to follow the limits fixed in their downward movement means that there is a downside flexibility corresponding to the upside flexibility accorded in the agreements in which government intervention ensured legislative enactment. The Moncloa Agreement itself introduced temporary employment. ANE included atypical contracts (part-time, trainee, temporary and practice) and sought to encourage the hiring of some social groups using these types of contract. AES, finally, ratified and extended these compromises to create employment. The legislative and industrial flexibility in labour relations is still controversial. The employers contend that it is still insufficient and must be enlarged. The unions, by contrast, are beginning to argue that it is already excessive. The former adduce the high cost of dismissals or attrition of jobs and the burden of social security contributions. The latter point to the more than one million precarious workers, wage moderation and the rarity of private investment creating jobs.

The government is a strong partisan of concertation, citing the success of some contract forms, the development of some social welfare benefits (pensions, unemployment and so on) and the slower growth of unemployment. The discussion will certainly continue, for it is hard to tell to what extent increasing flexibility is behind redundancies and the expulsion of workers from the labour market and to what extent, by contrast, it leads to job creation. And concertation will predictably continue to provoke debate and renewed efforts for its development. Regardless of cyclical phenomena, for the time being both business and labour organizations find more benefits than costs, especially in terms of internal unity and strategy, control of industrial relations as a whole, and outside recognition. What is more, the political continuity that has prevailed since 1982 (though wear and tear is beginning to show) in the government and opposition parties, the subordination of collective bargaining to concertation, centralization and impoverishment, and the lack of impetus in other means of social and labour integration (co-management, worker participation and so on) all foster social concertation.

The factor hindering the development of concertation in Spain is the difficulty of renewing economic growth, which implies a relative contraction in what there is to distribute by means of central accords. This in turn threatens a loss of legitimacy (among the membership and the broader constituency they seek to represent) on the part of the signatory organizations. This means the unions have tougher problems in satisfying the rank and file and in exercising effective control over industrial action (as seen in the strikes of the spring of 1987). Nor are they all in agreement with the practice of concertation, some preferring direct collective bargaining with employers. Some employers too complain that the agreements benefit the large companies and fail to take account of the problems of the small ones or the problems specific to given situations. Finally, workers, partly out of narrow self-interest, partly because they see no offsetting benefits against wage moderation, are drawing further and further away from the unions, which always have to consider general and long-term interests as well as immediate gains.

3.3 Flexibility the magic formula

To some extent, the machinery of worker protection in Spanish industrial relations under Franco was based on powerful state intervention and obstacles to discretionary dismissal by employers. The corporative union protected the individual interests of workers. Starting in the early 1960s, through collective bargaining, which developed over the next quarter-century, some forums for the representation and discussion of worker and employer interests were brought into being. In the late 1960s there was a limited, timid experiment in worker participation in the boards of directors of companies with more than 500 employees.

As noted, under democracy the rigidity of the old system was done away with, both as regards wages and as regards labour market regulations. Lately, in the face of growing unemployment, 'flexibility' has become the new vogue, a kind of magic incantation underpinning extravagant hopes. Everyone is talking about it. The government expects a positive impact on jobs from the new regulations on atypical employment (temporary, part-time, apprenticeship and so on), from the liberalization of store opening hours, from early retirement and from tax relief for new hiring. It has also facilitated geographical mobility and functional mobility, as demanded by the employers, hoping for the rehiring of those moving in districts designated as urgent targets for reindustrialization. These are financed by 'funds for the creation of employment'. Beyond these measures, early in 1988 the government began floating the idea of a three-year agreement to increase available jobs and foster greater solidarity and better competitiveness.

For their part the employers, the main beneficiaries of this set of measures, maintain that dismissal is still difficult, that severance pay is too high and social security contributions excessive. Generally, companies have taken advantage of this greater flexibility just to replace permanent employees by those holding temporary jobs.

Some multinationals and service enterprises have introduced individual contracts. Management in the multinationals seeks to introduce the Japanese model of labour relations. The large corporations are subcontracting to small or underground companies the less profitable stages of production. New technology, especially computer technology, is being rapidly introduced in banking, the services, department stores and so on, while productivity is rising without stabilizing employment. The employers' organization for the Spanish textile industry, which employs some 400,000 workers, has recently put forth a plan for 1992 calling for some financial and tax measures but also for negotiated modifications in the working day and for other innovations such as the possible suspension of permanent employment contracts for up to ninety days, the early termination of temporary contracts and more early retirement. The only countervailing commitment on the employers' part would be to maintain the present level of employment. Proposals of this sort are not legion. Banking employers have sought to introduce geographical and job mobility, but so far the concessions offered in exchange have not persuaded the unions.

Finally, while some employer spokesmen have opposed social agreements that block external flexibility by setting general conditions, the CEOE has gone on record as being in favour of the government's latest proposal for a three-year agreement.

For their part, the unions do not favour measures aimed at enhancing flexibility. They are convinced that the recent legislation is one-sided, all to the advantage of employers, and that the agreements they have signed have had little perceptible effect on employment. Both UGT and CCOO stress the direct relationship between flexibility and the state of the labour market. As the deterioration of the latter weakens the unions, they can no longer admit any dismantling of the protections (against dismissal) offered under the Franco regime. These regulations are still a guarantee of job security for workers and of stability for the unions where they are solidly represented. And this leads the unions to concentrate their efforts still more heavily on workers who still have jobs, steadily losing contact with the unemployed even while their programmatic statements are concerned with the most vulnerable groups. In a word, they are caught in a vicious circle.

Young first-job seekers, women, the long-term unemployed (over a year) are little by little being left out of the culture of the labour movement, which is concentrated in the traditional union industries (chemicals, textiles, steel), among civil servants and the new, dynamic industries. For those left out, the unions have tried, but with little success, to create auxiliary organizations (unemployed federations and associations, women's rights committees). They have also put pressure on the government to expand welfare benefits, improve pensions and create jobs. For those still employed, the unions have sought to develop bargaining demands attractive to technicians, white-collar workers in the services and lower-level management. Apart from the fact that these groups have organizations of their own, the programmes and slogans of the main worker unions have had very little success in appealing to these groups.

If the unions have had some success in defending the interests of certain groups of workers, the fostering of social solidarity has run up against the government wage-curb policy and its financial difficulties. On the other hand, though they have become clearer, bargaining and participation are not as strong as formerly. The company-level union locals, and still more so the committees, were the leading elements in the labour movement. Often their functions were not apparent, and following the signing of collective bargaining contracts their substance was defined. Even such restricted practices as employee participation in boards of directors (a law of 1962, a 1965 decree) provided some opportunities for mobilization over the question of information and representation.

Today, despite the efforts of the unions, the company-level union sections are making very little headway. The inter-union company committees are often the scene of confrontation between different unions and have thus largely lost their unifying role. Their dynamism has also been greatly limited by the restrictions hedging round collective bargaining – both the general rules laid down in tripartite negotiation and the poor economic state of most of industry.

Union participation in the social and economic agencies of the state offered some possibilities, but so far hopes have been disappointed by a paucity of results. The unions, and especially the UGT, have also asked to be involved in the management of the public corporations, which have considerable importance in the Spanish economy. The AES agreements in 1986 mentioned the possibility of enlarging union rights in this sphere. On 16 January 1986 the government and UGT signed a renewable agreement initially valid until December 1987. It recognizes the union right to participate in the management organs of public enterprises with more than 1000 employees. It is too early to give an assessment, but this agreement may point to a way forward that is not negligible.

It is premature to predict which path Spanish industrial relations will take in the future. Concertation (Aa), despite difficulties (economic problems and problems of legitimacy), still enjoys broad consensus among the industrial relations actors, first and foremost the government. All parties have benefited from the signature of the tripartite agreements. Collective bargaining, both general (Ab) and decentralized (B), is perhaps losing impetus but certainly has not disappeared. It continues to help determine working conditions and wages for the majority of working people. Union participation (Ca) in company decision-making depends on economic, social and political factors that are in decline today, while more institutional participation is still a recent experience limited to a few cases, both from the firms' viewpoint of interest and human relations, and from the workers' viewpoint of saving their jobs. Direct worker responsibility (Cb) remains an exception, despite some gains.

10

Changes in the Swedish Model

Gösta Rehn and Birger Viklund

The worldwide, post-OPEC inflation appeared in Sweden as increases not only in prices but also in profits, which in turn provoked very high wage increases. Thanks to these, the real wage level peaked in 1976. Reductions followed, when national and international cost increases hit, with some lag, consumer prices. By 1980, therefore, the real hourly income for industrial workers had declined from the 1976 level by nearly 10 per cent.

Even if we remember that Swedish workers are probably well aware of the risks connected with reductions of competitiveness in the world market (unemployment) and therefore may be prepared to accept caution in wage policy, it may seem surprising that the reduction in real wages, which finally reached nearly 10 per cent below the 1976 levels did not lead to any strong reactions among union members. Of course the fact that the bourgeois parties lost government power to the Social Democrats in 1982, and that the latter suffered a setback in 1985, can be interpreted as expressions of misgivings about economic development. But the increase in unemployment (albeit rather limited) and the slow return to full employment also contributed to these electoral events.

One explanation for the limited reaction against the reduction in real wages may be that the peak in 1976 came about rather suddenly and that people had not accustomed themselves to a higher consumption pattern before inflation eliminated this temporary boom. Another is the fact that the possibilities for compensating oneself through wage drift were often considerable; money earnings, despite all self-restraint, actually grew by around 10 per cent in most years.

But there were, of course, tensions and Sweden's long-standing labour peace came to an end in 1980 with a gigantic labour conflict. For several months after the 1979 agreements had expired, SAF, the Swedish Employers' Federation, practically refused to discuss any increase in wages whatsoever. Towards the end of April, the Trade Union Confederation, LO, gave warning of strikes targeted on a few strategic areas of employment. SAF answered by a lock-out of almost all employees in manufacturing.

After a week, however, the dispute was settled through an agreement that gave a general wage increase of about 5 per cent, despite the employers' long-held position of 'zero growth'.

Some observers wanted to explain this conflict as an accident caused by the clumsy interference of an inexperienced Prime Minister in the bourgeois government. Others have declared it to be 'the end of the Swedish model', formerly characterized by a peaceful, rational and pragmatic willingness to foresee the outcome of costly production stoppages. Still others have declared that the rapid settlement demonstrated the unbroken strength and vitality of that very same model of industrial relations. Be that as it may, the conflict was settled after one week, since everyone – not least the employers – realized that it was a mistake. The President of SAF, widely regarded as a hawk, who had come in a few years earlier to take over after a reign of inflation-soft doves, had to excuse himself before his members by declaring the costly lock-out to be an 'investment in the future', that is, a warning to the unions that they should not expect to get wage increases too cheaply.

1 General economic developments and their effects on industrial relations

Throughout the 1970s, there had been a constant increase of employment in public service, particularly for women working part-time. Together with an active labour-market policy, this growth contributed both to holding the unemployment figures down to about 2 per cent and to increasing the activity rate (total labour force as a percentage of total population between 16–64 years), despite an approximate 15 per cent decline in employment in manufacturing during the same period. In 1980 the activity rate approached 80 per cent, the highest level in OECD countries; and it is still growing. In 1986 it has reached 83 per cent.

Developments since 1980 have been marked by two broad features. On the one hand, there has been the fight against inflation and unemployment, wherein the government has tried to get the labour market organizations to slow down the growth of money wages so that Sweden would not become uncompetitive in international markets – on which she has become increasingly dependent, imports having grown to one-third of GDP. On the other hand, major changes have occurred in labour-market structure, in particular in the relative growth of the service sectors, both the private and, particularly, the public, in relation to the goods-producing sectors (manufacturing, and building and construction). There is a relationship between these two aspects: the importance of the internationally competitive sectors, with respect to their part in the total production of goods and services, has grown; but because of greater productivity increases in these sectors, their part in the active population has declined relative to the home-market sectors. Among the 'home-market unions', concern for pricing oneself out of the (international) market is not so well ingrained as among the unions of 'competition industries'.

It is symptomatic that the conflicts leading to work stoppages after 1980 have all, except for the SIF strike in 1988, concerned public sector groups. As already indicated, the bourgeois government of 1976–82 succeeded for some years in keeping the unemployment rate down to about 2 per cent or lower, despite the international slow-down and restraint policy which led to a considerable growth of unemployment in most of the industrialized world. Their success in this respect was due to a combination of subsidies to preserve jobs, the nationalization of declining industries and the continuation and reinforcement of an active labour-market policy. There were times when nearly 5 per cent of the labour force was engaged in temporary works, adult training courses, sheltered workshops or subsidized employment, and thus protected from unemployment. A number of devaluations also contributed to this.

Faced with budget deficits, of the order of magnitude of 10 per cent of GDP for the consolidated public sector, and an international current balance deficit of about 5 per cent, the government finally applied a policy of restraint in 1980–2. This policy, despite a 10 per cent currency devaluation in 1981, brought unemployment up to nearly 3 per cent, primarily due to restraint in the growth of public sector employment.

The Social Democratic Party won the elections in 1982 and formed a new government. Practically its first action was to undertake a new devaluation, this time by 16 per cent. It also started to reduce the budget deficit by reducing the subsidies to declining industries and further slowing the growth of the public sector. Initially, unemployment showed a further increase in 1983, but has since again gone down, to below 2 per cent in 1987.

It could be foreseen that the devaluation would lead to further price increases. It was an amazing feat of persuasion that the government convinced the representatives of pensioners and wage- and salary-earners not to demand immediate full compensation for these increases in the cost of living.

All the time, now as during earlier periods, the government has tried to engage the trade unions in a sort of informal concertation policy aimed at reducing the growth rate of both prices and money wages to levels similar to those in competing countries, where lower wage and price inflation is achieved via a high rate of unemployment, something not 'permitted' in Sweden. In discussion with union leaders, the Minister of Finance has been trying to get unions to accept 'caution' and 'responsibility'. In 1985 he even offered a premium – a direct tax reduction of 600 SEK per person – if the unions would keep contractual wage increases at a maximum of 5 per cent as indicated in central discussions. Although the unions only partially met the Minister's conditions, the 600 SEK were paid. Anything else would have been political suicide. This Swedish experiment with 'Tip' (tax-based incomes policy) has not been repeated.

In November 1985, a group of labour economists, representatives from the Nordic trade union centres and social democratic parties, with the Swedish Minister of Finance as one of the leading participants, published a programme for a 'negotiated incomes policy'. The basic notion was that the government, in give-and-take reasoning with the trade union federations or their bargaining cartels, would be able to come to a consensus about non-inflationary wage developments, year by year. What the unions would achieve by accepting this invitation to negotiations was not made very explicit. But the inference was that specified actions could be taken against unemployment and price increases; and that improvements in social policy or reforms in taxation would be considered.

In the so-called revised budget bill, of April 1987, the Minister of Finance went one step further. He declared that he would apply a cash limit of 3 per cent on wage increases for state employees. If they wanted more, the consequence would be a reduction in employment (either directly or through productivity increases. He encouraged the other public service employers (municipalities and provinces) to follow the same principles. Apparently, this is expected to set an example for the private sector as well.

The reactions of labour and employer organizations and their leaders, both to the proposal of the Nordic group of labour economists for a negotiated incomes policy and to the new declaration that 'cash limits' would be applied in next year's negotiations for public service employees, were largely negative. The freedom of the negotiating parties to make decisions based on their own responsibility, without state interference, was widely stressed. On the other hand, everyone is open to government participation in discussions, without submission to government directives.

The government apparently still hopes to be able to exercise influence through persuasion. The leaders of the central labour confederations certainly share the government's view that inflation has negative consequences for the workers. The government hopes that the union leaders, on this basis, will be able to keep order in the union ranks and discipline even those unions whose leaders frankly declare that they have no responsibility towards the economy at large, only towards their own members.

The crucial question is, of course, whether this is a realistic proposition, and whether it will remain so even if Sweden maintains the low level of unemployment which is regarded as a policy goal, below 2 per cent. Already, the gradual reduction from 3 per cent in 1983 to 2 per cent in 1987 seems to have led to imbalances, with a high rate of wage drift and pressures for extra wage and salary increases in order to attract qualified persons to occupations in short supply. There is some tolerance among unions for special income increases in particular categories, but this is rather limited.

2 Processes and developments within industrial relations

2.1 The solidaristic wage policy

All through the war and post-war years, particularly between 1959 and 1976, there had been a successful attempt to reduce wage differentials of all sorts (the solidaristic wage policy). This ideology had its origin in working-class solidarity within LO; but with the growth of low-income groups within salaried employees' unions, it spread even to TCO (Central Organization of Salaried Employers' Unions) and, less explicitly, to the professionals in SACO/SR (Central Organization of Unions of the Professions). The difference between the average wage in the industrial branch with wages below the general average and that in those above the general average declined from 30 per cent in 1959 to 13 per cent in 1979, where it has since stabilized.

The principle of wage solidarity has always been contested by neo-classical critics of this and other egalitarian policies – without much success, at least not until 1980. Internally, here and there within the trade union movement, there has been a certain reluctance to push equalization too far. This reluctance has come not only from the highly qualified professionals, but also from LO unions (particularly Metal), who argue that if differentials for skill and work stress were reduced too far, it might hamper recruitment to important jobs, or cause skilled workers to move to white-collar unions in order to get higher status and salaries as technicians. This concern, together with wage drift in specific occupations where labour is in short supply, explains why the trend to equalization has not continued since 1976, despite the fact that central agreements have consistently contained a low-wage emphasis (that is, provisions for special increases for low-wage groups inside each organization).

In addition to the moral and ideological arguments about solidarity and equality, trade unionists also present economic arguments for wage solidarity. 'Is it not quite possible', they ask, 'that a wage system based on profitability would slow down overall economic growth (and thus hurt real wages) by braking the expansion of efficient firms, through high wages, and the decline of inefficient firms, through low wages? And might not this slowing-down effect be greater than any benefits possibly gained by workers being lured by increasing wage differentials?' We can expect unions to continue to apply the solidaristic principle of equal wages for jobs with comparable work content, regardless of profit differences. Connected with this policy is a request that the government apply a labour-market policy to help workers leave industries and regions with low productivity and declining employment opportunities and switch to jobs with higher productivity and a better future.

Like stabilization policy the solidaristic wage policy has had to struggle with wage drift. When the agreements have provided for extra high wage rises for low-wage categories, part of the effect of this on the wage dispersion has been counterbalanced by wage drift being stronger for skilled workers in short supply. In spite of this the differentials-reducing policy has been the strongest element. As indicated above, all sorts of differences have been very strongly reduced, particularly during the period from the late 1950s to the mid-1970s.

In principle the solidaristic wage policy, as it has been defined in various LO publications, should take into consideration the differences in requirements of skills, stress and other demands on the worker in each type of work. One should try to establish a 'rational wage structure', that is, such wage relativities that a supply–demand balance could be achieved in all sorts of jobs, in other words application of a job evaluation. But various trials with a view to defining such a wage differentiation have hitherto failed not least because of disagreements between those who in such a system would find arguments for an improvement of their relative wage position and those who find themselves in the opposite situation. In practice, therefore, the endeavour of the trade unions has been to improve the wage position of the low-paid groups, irrespective of the reasons for their low wages.

2.2   Labour law reform

Another aspect of the concertation of the industrial relations system was co-operation between the central confederations on issues other than wages. There were agreements on the promotion of female participation in income-earning work, industrial training, work environment and safety, technical progress and so on. On the white-collar side, there were also agreements about old-age insurance. The blue-collar workers of LO tried to arrive at a general old-age insurance system, but the result was so meagre that they preferred to go to the government and ask for legislation. A system for supplementary pensions (on top of the old 'people's pension' system) was passed in Parliament in 1959 after an unusually intense political fight.

During the 1970s co-operation between the unions and the government (until 1976 LO was led by Social Democrats) resulted in a number of new laws, aimed at improving the situation of workers and limiting the prerogatives of employers. There was an attempt to move society more in the direction of economic and industrial democracy and to improve the quality of working life. The following laws were important:

Co-determination: A framework legislation inviting the organizations on both sides to establish agreements about more detailed implementation. The law gives employers a duty to inform their personnel about important events or plans to give the unions a fair chance to negotiate such plans with them. However, final decision-making powers still rest largely with the owners.

Employment security: This act gives employers a duty to give advance notice about dismissals. Dismissals are also permitted only for 'reasonable cause', and not, for example, because of personal animosity, or the organizational or political activity of the worker, and so forth.

The right of workers to exercise trade union activities: A certain amount of paid time can be used for trade union meetings and shop-steward work.

Trade union representatives on corporate boards: Two seats on the board of any company with twenty-five or more employees.

Safety and health activities in the enterprise: Elected safety delegates received increased powers, including the right to stop work they consider dangerous to workers' health and safety, prior to an investigation by safety inspectors.

Job security and employment promotion: Employers must notify the employment service about vacancies, even if hirings are undertaken through other channels. The employment service agencies have the right to discuss with employers the placement of persons with handicaps. Employment promotion had, of course, always been a central government activity; for example, through public works, training and mobility allowances and wage subsidies for disadvantaged groups and underdeveloped areas. In the early 1970s the government declared as a principle that the first line of defence against unemployment should be drawn inside the 'factory gates'. Later, even under the bourgeois government of 1976–82, this principle was further developed through a varied set of subsidies for both protecting existing jobs (in connection with the worldwide setback experienced by Sweden's most important industries) and creating additional jobs.

Educational leave: With due notice, a worker can take time off for training courses or other educational activities. The above laws, all considered part of the co-determination system, gave rise to a wave of educational activities by both trade union and employers' organizations.

In addition, there were also several laws aimed at more general social reform introduced in the 1970s.

Annual holiday entitlements: These were increased from four to five weeks with right to accumulate the fifth week for up to five years, making it possible to take a longer vacation intermittently. Various rights to leaves of absence were introduced or increased, for example parental leave to be used by either parent in connection with childbirth, leave for care of sick children. The conditions of sickness and unemployment insurance were also improved.

Elastic retirement rules: Possibilities were increased for an individual to determine his retirement, between the ages of sixty and seventy, with actuarial adjustment of the pension level. It was also made possible to get early pensions (without adjustment) for combined reasons of health and labour-market difficulties, or to take part-time retirement.

The various bourgeois governments which were in power from 1976 to 1982 modified some of these laws and social insurance arrangements, but to a limited degree. There was a softening of the employment protection law to allow temporary hirings, as this law was alleged to hinder the hiring of additional workers because employers were afraid of getting stuck with a worker once hired.

During the years before 1980 the employer organizations also attempted to counterbalance the influence of workers, through unions and political power, by greatly expanding their educational activities directed to their members and their propaganda activities directed to the general public. This activity was partly inspired by the fact that the labour movement had established the above legislation to strengthen the workers' position in the economy, pro-labour legislation being used when experience or foresight found negotiations to be insufficient. However, an extra impetus was provided by the plans, proclaimed by the LO at its 1976 convention, for the introduction of employee capital funds. The employers saw such funds as a semi-revolutionary attack on the market economy, a plan to confiscate their profits and to use the money to buy away their ownership and give it over to the trade unions. In effect, by 1980 the SAF and the SI (the Confederation of Swedish Manufacturers) had taken over from the bourgeois political parties a large part of the task of directing propaganda against the Social Democratic Party, in order to prevent its return to government.

2.3   Tug-of-war over employers' prerogatives

The labour law reforms of the 1970s have in many ways limited the employers' old prerogatives. By international standards, the gains may not appear very remarkable, since for many years of labour government Swedish unions concentrated on social goals, full employment and social security and left the running of the enterprise to the employer. (Note, for example, the famous para. 32 of the SAF constitution, which stated that only those enterprises could be members of SAF where management had unlimited right to hire and fire and direct and distribute the work.) This was part of the 1905 compromise, in which the unions had accepted these employer prerogatives on the understanding that the employers would accept unions and not promote union-free environments.

Over the years these prerogatives have of course become modified by every new collective contract governing work rules and other conditions in the plant. In theory, however, the employer still upheld those rights stated in para. 32. During the first post-war period, with its high economic activity, full employment and considerable wage gains, there was, perhaps understandably, no union pressure to change this situation. Instead, union judges in the Labour Court (established in 1928 to interpret law and contracts) upheld the traditions established with the first decisions of the court in the early 1930s. Hence, the employer prerogatives were not changed to accommodate new political and social thinking.

The legislation of the 1970s, in particular the Security of Employment Act and the Co-determination Act, drastically changed the picture and represents a major move forward for trade union positions. The labour law reforms were preceded by the supplementary pension system financed by employer contributions to central funds and followed by the wage-earner investment funds, which further attacked the employers' power over capital markets.

Recent employer strategies, such as individual profit-sharing, the decentralization of wage bargaining, quality circles and the like, must therefore be seen as an employer defence policy – even if the ingredients of the policy are the same as can be found in countries like the USA where they represent more an offensive against unions.

The union answer to this defence policy seems to be to maintain centralized collective bargaining with respect to wages while at the same time encouraging worker involvement in the running of the local enterprise. This need not mean that the workers identify with the company, but it does mean that they identify with the economic success of the community. Of course, employers are likely to try to exploit the worker's interest in keeping his job and to attempt to identify this interest with the company interest. The union answer to this tactic is to negotiate rights to various forms of educational leave and to press for community training and retraining facilities in order to secure employment even in periods of rapid technical progress and structural change.

2.4 Renewal funds: limited co-determination

A union effort to tag on to the idea of profit-sharing without giving up ideas of collective savings and solidaristic wages is the so-called renewal fund. According to a new law passed in 1985, companies have to pay 10 per cent of their profits above 500,000 SEK to a blocked account in the central bank. This money can be used in the company for training, research and development. Both sides can veto the use of the money, that is, the union in the company and management must agree on how to use it. If there is no agreement the funds stay in the bank without interest.

The law is not very detailed about the use of the funds, but at least the LO has recommended to its members that the main part of the funds should be used for training of workers with little educational background, those who are most vulnerable during structural change, that is, women and immigrants. It is very clear from the short experience so far, that employers are most interested in training technical staff in the use of new technology.

The law should be seen as a new and more powerful form of industrial democracy than the Co-determination Act, which after information and negotiations have been completed gives the full right of decision-making to management. During the first year of the renewal fund (payments in 1986 on the basis of the 1985 profits – no decision has yet been taken to continue the system) 5.1 billion SEK were delivered to the central bank. Out of these so far (March

1989) 4 billion have been earmarked for projects approved by local unions and management.

Evidently most companies have had enough liquidity to make the investments they wanted without mobilizing these funds. It seems that the local unions have not been very clear about how to use the money for training. There also seems to be a need for more leadership and initiative from central trade unions in this matter. However, the renewal-fund idea offers a new solution to the problems that the unions sought to solve by introducing the system of wage-earner funds. There is a direct benefit to the individual in access to training and upgrading necessary to cope with new technology.

3   Levels of collective bargaining

Table 10.1 shows that during the post-war period Sweden developed a rather centralized collective bargaining system led by the two dominant confederations, LO and SAF. Contractual wage increases were largely determined by 'recommendations' based on agreements between them. The affiliated branch-of-industry unions followed these recommendations nearly 100 per cent, the recommendations giving them some leeway for specific applications through national or local bargaining, for example for sharing out the wage increases among different member groups in each union.

Gradually, there had also developed a system of 'cartels' of unions from TCO and SACO/SR for bargaining purposes. Often these co-operated with each other and with the big unions for public sector workers in LO concerning the standpoints to take before and during bargaining sessions with the respective employers' associations. However, this sector has grown to the point where negotiations in general are no longer completely centralized but cover different large sectors of the economy. The three main sectors are the private sector, the state sector and the local government sector. Even in these, negotiations are not fully co-ordinated. In addition, negotiations also take place at a national level in the banking and insurance sectors where the individual national trade unions negotiate. SALF – the Foremen's Union – has tried with varying success to be independent after once having been among the founders of the private sector white-collar union cartel, PTK. SACO/SR unions have their own cartels for negotiations with the state and local government respectively.

In the private sector the LO as the national centre negotiates for some 1.4 million members. Also in the private sector the PTK, with some 500,000 members, is an important bargaining organization.

Table 10.1 *Changes in the industrial relations system, Sweden since 1980*

Type	Pre-1980	Post-1980
A(a) National concertation	Tried by successive governments. Sometimes temporarily established	Tendencies in both directions
A(b) Industry-wide collective bargaining	Firmly established tradition but under strong leadership by central confederations and cartels; modifications by local bargaining	Endeavours from employers (some organizations and big companies) to promote decentralization and differentiation, partly and temporarily successful
B Decentralized collective bargaining	Local modifications of national sector agreements (institutionalized wage drift)	Employers are (unilaterally) introducing additional modifications, profit-sharing, convertibles, options
C(a) Worker participation (in production planning, technological change and so on) via unions	Promoted by laws and law-stimulated agreements	Slow progress but some indications that it contributes more to the increase of efficiency than to delays by bureaucratization
C(b) Worker participation without unions	Unions were present practically everywhere	Some cases of small new enterprises with advanced technology where employers and salaried technicians co-operate directly
D(a) Simple contracts without union	Rare	See above
D(b) Simple contracts (no union) in secondary (black or grey) labour markets	Occasionally but of relative importance in some sectors like painting, building repairs and so on	Some growth tendencies, but limited

While the agreements reached by the PTK are binding for its affiliated unions, those concluded by the LO are presented as recommendations to be accepted or not by the individual unions, though the recommendations have been followed practically 100 per cent.

On the employers' side, alongside the SAF in the private sector there is also SFO, which negotiates for state-owned companies, and KFO, which negotiates for companies owned by consumer co-operatives. The state-owned companies are considered to be private sector companies for the purposes of the collective bargaining structure.

The respect given to the LO/SAF negotiations was not only due to their strength in numbers. It was broadly accepted as logical that those enterprises and workers who were most closely linked to the world market had to lead since they had the strongest feel for what was possible with respect to the need to remain competitive in the world market. During the 1970s and 1980s, however, when the membership coverage of the other organizations had caught up with that of LO, this leadership came to be contested. In one bargaining round, the public sector negotiating parties even took the lead, formally in order to speed up a particularly slow negotiation process. We can present the wage-making process as it actually has been shaped in recent decades in no less than five stages as follows.

First, discussion between the government, unions and employers about the economic situation and the economic policy as foreseen by the government.

Secondly, negotiations between LO and SAF as well as between the cartels of white-collar and public sector workers and their respective counterparts (the SAF for salaried employees in the private sector, the Federation of Municipalities, the Federation of Counties and the central government agency for negotiations with their respective groups). Outside these categories are only relatively limited groups.

Thirdly, branch-level negotiations about more detailed applications and modifications of the central agreements. In LO it is formally the national unions which sign the agreements.

Fourthly, company-level negotiations. Partly these are invited by the central agreement, which may also deliberately leave scope, not only to national, but also to local union branches to distribute extra increases among their members; partly it may be called 'institutionalized wage drift', that is, additions to what the national industry contracts have stipulated. Despite the threat of SAF to expel member firms which give too much, such additions are often given either as an attempt to over-bid for manpower in a high-employment situation or for fear of wildcat strikes. The latter increased during boom periods from the 1960s onwards despite the fact that workers can be fired by the Labour Court if they strike to amend a valid contract (according to a law of 1928).

Fifthly, wage drift through individual wage increases with or without involvement of local shop stewards. This is the original form and concept of wage drift, which first became important when the war had created full employment. With time it has become a normal element of earnings determination. Since the 1960s about half the total increase in hourly money earnings in manufacturing industries has been wage drift. The anticipation of wage drift for workers with 'elastic' wage systems and for those in short supply has led to 'compensation for wage drift' being given to those with more rigid wages both in individual enterprises and in branches of industry. Differences in wage drift create conflicts which threaten good relations between trade unions and provoke catching-up demands which cannot be satisfied without a rather rapid movement of the whole wage structure.

4 Actors

4.1 The state

Both employers' and workers' organizations have always been anxious to be free from government intervention in their affairs. The permanent mediation agency and the special mediation commissions, appointed by the government in situations where large organizations appear to be having difficulties in reaching agreements through negotiations, have been accepted as service organs with the task of helping the bargaining parties to solve a difficult problem through some compromise, but not as government envoys trying to induce the parties to carry out a government policy. The famous 'Saltsjöbaden agreement' (1938, still in force with limited amendments) established rules for solutions and negotiations so as to show that the organizations could keep order in their own ranks and avoid careless conflict damaging 'third parties' and society as a whole in an irresponsible way.

In spite of this, once, in 1973, when a broad conflict occurred in the public sector, mainly involving SACO/SR and affecting essential public services (doctors, nurses, customs officers and so on), government and Parliament passed a law forbidding further strikes. This was also a way for the government to avoid carrying out its own threat to declare a far-reaching lock-out (which would even have affected army officers).

It is symptomatic that this happened in the public sector. Public employees, who had earlier lived without any right to bargain and to strike (this as a *quid pro quo* for their high employment security and pension rights) had received these rights as recently as 1966. The groups in question had for a long time had a rather advantageous position on the relative salary scale, but because of a changing market had begun to lag behind the LO and TCO groups. Not being too experienced in industrial relations, they moved into a blind alley in the form of a very unpopular conflict. Their lack of support in public opinion made it possible for the government to go to the unprecedented action we have noted.

Largely respecting the rule of non-intervention in substantive negotiations over wages, the government has always tried more indirect ways of influencing overall wage developments. Often the Minister of Finance has been invited to speak about the economic situation at sessions of the representative body of LO (about 150 union leaders) when these have gathered to plan wages policy for the coming year. On several occasions the government has offered tax concessions, price subsidies or other advantages in order to gain acceptance of some sort of incomes policy (wage restraint or even a virtual wage freeze) in order to break inflation. In 1973 and 1974, to create a real-income increase without high wage increases, the government applied a direct tax reduction financed by an increase of the general payroll tax to reduce profits and incite employers to resist labour-cost increases. The results of these experiments were, however, not very encouraging because of the overwhelming force of the international inflation and its effects on profits and costs of living.

In those cases when the unions have actually accepted and fulfilled a government proposal about an efficient incomes policy action, this has after some time been followed by a wage–price explosion. This makes it difficult to agree without reservation with the statement, often met in foreign observers' comments, that Sweden's centralized wage-bargaining system has implied a sort of incomes policy of particular efficiency in the fight against inflation. On the whole prices in Sweden have followed international inflation. Opportunities for utilizing situations of lower Swedish costs developments for revaluations of the currency have not been realized. Instead the post-OPEC exaggerations of wage increases compelled the government to undertake devaluations while accepting a somewhat higher inflation in Sweden than abroad.

This inability to sustain anti-inflationary incomes-policy actions is partly due to the fact that actual earnings developments were not determined only by the contracts but also by wage drift, that is, additions given locally or individually outside the control of the national organizations (although it has sometimes happened that the SAF has fined members who have too ostentatiously deviated upwards from the contracted wage increases).

4.2 The unions

In 1980 the three central trade union confederations: LO with 2.3 million members, TCO with 1.2 million members and SACO/SR with 250,000 members, all reached about 80 per cent coverage in their respective fields – blue-collar, white-collar and academic professions. By 1986 they were at about 85 per cent coverage. Particularly remarkable is the capacity of the unions to attract women as members. The number of women in trade unions has increased dramatically, not only due to the increased participation of women in the workforce but also because of the greater coverage of women in unions, despite the fact that many women work only part-time.

The greatest growth has been recorded in the local government sector, due to the rapid increase of employment in this sector and to the long-term levelling off or decline in employment in manufacturing. The largest LO union is now the Municipal Workers' Union, SKAF. The unions of white-collar workers, mainly in TCO, have also shown rapid growth, thanks to increasing employment and by building on the high degree of unionization earlier reached by the blue-collar workers in LO. There is also a tendency for blue-collar workers to become white-collar workers because of upgrading in connection with the introduction of new technology.

As indicated earlier the attitudes of unions and their willingness to follow the leadership of LO in both wage policy and in other respects have been modified by changes in the structure of the labour market, particularly the growth of the public and private sectors and of the white-collar and academic categories. This means that the possibilities of obtaining and maintaining a consensus about wages policy have been reduced or at least that such endeavours have met new problems.

The wage-bargaining round for 1986 and 1987, like previous rounds, was very much dominated by the debate about *följsamhet* (parallelness): that all groups have a right to wage increases similar to those of other groups. This demand from public service unions implying a request for compensation for the wage drift among workers with more elastic wage systems released violently antagonistic debates at the 1986 LO congress between the leaders of the two largest unions (local government and metalworkers).

A group of trade union leaders and experts (all in LO) then, in

June 1987, presented a report on wages policy which recommended an intensified utilization of job evaluation for the whole labour market (and not only inside individual companies or for the members of LO). It also requested improvements in wage statistics for the same purpose. It indicates that there is need for a broader co-ordination of wage negotiations than the solidaristic wages policy which is applied inside each confederation or each bargaining cartel. It notes that unions with many low-wage members have greater difficulties than others in improving wages. Thus it is noted that the wage levels for workers with similar jobs can still be very different despite the long-term application of the solidaristic principle. Experience suggests, however, that it is very difficult to get those who would be required by a strict job evaluation to take a relative cut in wages to participate in the necessary investigations.

During earlier parts of the post-war period there was constant economic growth, which made it possible to allow considerable wage increases every year. Within this framework it was possible to rectify inequities by extra wage increases for disadvantaged groups and for groups of employees with straight hourly or monthly wages, that is, for groups which did not benefit from much wage drift. Thus women's wages in local government service jobs have been lifted to a level not far below those of production workers in industry, actually well above 90 per cent of those male industrial earnings obtained mostly through different forms of incentive systems. The industrial conflicts in the early 1980s were the result of a fundamental change in the economic situation with very low or no economic growth, high government costs to cushion structural change in industry and a continued need for the wage policy to take care of groups and individuals who were falling behind.

4.2.1 Demarcation disputes Demarcation disputes, which in some countries have frequently been a source of trouble for the unions, have traditionally been peacefully solved by arbitration provided by the central confederations. Suddenly, however, such a problem has led to an open conflict. In the background is the introduction of new technology and the private and public employer strategy of buying services from private service companies. As such this phenomenon is not new. There is, for example, an almost thirty-year history of industrial companies buying cleaning from cleaning firms, thus avoiding paying industry wages to cleaning staff. The multinational, private or government firms that sell the services are organized by the Building Maintenance Workers' Union, the contracts of which are far cheaper than, for example, those for the engineering or steel industries. On occasion the change in classification of these jobs from 'industry' to 'service' has led to strikes among the cleaning staff. These strikes have had only lukewarm support from the typically male industrial unions.

The most recent case involves the Transport Workers' Union and the Municipal Workers' Union (Kommunal). Land-based cranes in the harbours are owned and run by the municipalities. Crane drivers are thus organized by the Local Government Workers' Union, the largest in LO with over 600,000 members. Now new technology involving container traffic and container ships and many more cranes on board the ships calls for new forms of work organization, leading to an integration of the municipal and transport jobs in the harbours. This development has been met by the municipalities by a more independent management of the harbours in the form of 'harbour companies'. The Transport Workers' Union and the Municipal Workers' Union have agreed that crane operators in large harbours should be organized by the latter union while small harbours would be the domain of the Transport Workers' Union. There was, however, a dispute over whether the harbour at Köping was large or small. The question of the size of 'large' harbour was referred to the LO executive, which according to the LO constitution has the final say in demarcation disputes. LO decided that the harbour in question, with eleven crane operators, was to be considered a small harbour and thus to be organized by the Transport Workers' Union, which then signed a contract for the entire harbour with the Stevedoring Employers' Federation. However, the Municipal Workers' Union did not accept the LO decision and took their members out in a strike supported by sympathy strikes of workers in two other harbours, including the main Swedish port, Göteborg. This is the first case in modern times in Sweden of a demarcation dispute leading to a strike against a third party. An added problem is the fact that most stevedoring workers in Sweden have broken away from the Transport Workers' Union and formed an independent Port Workers' Union outside LO.

Irrespective of how this case is solved it points to continued problems in the future with public sector unions trying to keep members, who – for reasons of new technology and work organization – have ended up in private or publicly owned companies, who sign or want to sign wage agreements with unions in the private sector. If these problems cannot be solved inside the blue-collar workers' confederation, LO, but are allowed to lead to strikes hurting the general public, the credibility of LO and the whole trade union movement will be negatively affected.

In the longer perspective there will certainly be similar or worse conflicts involving white-collar unions, which with the advent of computer technology attract more and more skilled blue-collar workers, for example the lathe operator turned numerically-controlled-machine programmer. Already there is a steady stream of metalworkers joining the union of salaried and technical employees in industry, SIF – a shift from an LO to a TCO union.

4.3   *Employers*

It is against this background that we have to judge the employers' industrial relations strategies. Here the period 1980–7 has seen clear efforts at a development away from centralized bargaining over wages and towards a new decentralized form of bargaining over the management of work practices. The outcome can be seen in the changes noted in Table 10.1.

The major organization on the employers' side is the highly centralized Swedish Employers' Confederation, SAF, with about 40,000 member firms, mainly from manufacturing. Separate associations for other sectors look very much to SAF for leadership. Central and local governments of course have their own separate agencies for the negotiation of wages and other working conditions. This is also the case with the consumers' co-operative movement.

However, it is not clear who are the decisive actors on the employers' side. In the 1950s SAF took the initiative over centralized wage bargaining and today by the very nature of its centralized organization and constitution, it must strive for central control over the bargaining system. Thus SAF can, and does, fine employers who pay more than they have to according to the contract. But inside the SAF there are both strong branch organizations, first of all the engineering industry federation, and big individual employers, for instance Volvo and its charismatic president Pehr Gyllenhammar, who maintain a very independent line and also voice personal opinions on political questions, which do not always square with those of the SAF. Both the Engineering Employers' Federation and Gyllenhammar have advocated a decentralization of the wage-bargaining process. In 1984 the Engineering Employers' Federation also managed to win over the Metalworkers' Union to its strategy – this was when the metalworkers got their extra wage class for skilled workers. But the experience of this breakaway from the traditional LO policy of wage solidarity was not very positive for the metalworkers. They are now back in the LO fold and in the 1985–6 wage-negotiation round supported the idea of centralization, this time showing their independence through verbal attacks on public sector employees, for example at the LO congress 1986.

The metalworkers' dilemma is compounded by the growing tendency of large employers, like Volvo, to pay extra through profit-sharing schemes, which so far are not considered disloyal by the SAF – probably because they come under another employer strategy: to woo employees away from the unions through different forms of scientific management. Individual profit-sharing is also a tool of flexibility – another employer strategy – since it is a one-sided employer decision which can be nullified in a year in which there is a lower profit. There are different forms of profit-sharing; direct cash payments, presenting employees with shares in the company, crediting them with sums of money on accounts blocked for a few years, offering to buy options or 'convertibles', making them shareholders later on. There is also a publicity drive to engage small savers to place their money in company shares without direct connection with their own workplaces. The intention is clearly to make ordinary wage- and salary-earners interested in the promotion of profits in private enterprise. The power of the big shareholders to continue having the decisive influence in the respective companies is hardly reduced, rather increased, by an increase in the number of small shareholders.

Beside this, there are other features in the employers' counter-offensive to reconquer the power they lost through the pro-labour legislation of the early 1970s and the 1980s. The most important are probably the management-consulting activities of the technical department of SAF. A series of projects on the development of a more democratic work organization had been conducted in the 1960s under the then existing Joint Consultation Agreement. The agreement was terminated when work began on the new Co-determination Act, but the employers continue this development work without union participation. The initiative in the socio-technical field was thus taken by the employers, who understandably introduced their ideas of bonus payments instead of straight monthly salaries and who saw the experiments more as a means of reducing absenteeism and turnover and increasing quality and productivity than as a way of democratizing worklife. True, the unions are also interested in a positive development of production, but the overriding trade union goal is, of course, a more human and democratic worklife.

After the Co-determination Act had been introduced and the Agreement on Development and Productivity concluded, the development of worker participation in production returned to the joint consultation system in a new programme of management–organization–co-determination (LOM). In the meantime the employers have developed their theories and practices (the Volvo experiments), while the unions have concentrated on co-determination negotiations, perhaps disregarding the fact that progressive worker participation calls for both negotiations and participation in project groups. For this latter strategy to work unions must base their participation on increased competence in production questions. While it is obvious that they are catching up with the employers in the sociotechnical field, including quality circles, autonomous work groups and so on, they are not in command of the profit-sharing developments. Leading trade unionists are annoyed by the obvious effect that the solidaristic wages policy will be undermined, which in turn will create splits in the labour movement.

The employer strategy in the field of co-determination over production questions is also one of decentralization. The Co-determination Act called for agreements on practical forms of worker participation. The employers effectively blocked such agreements until 1982, when the Development Agreement was signed. In the meantime, 1976 to 1982, the employers' organizations developed management programmes without participation from LO or PTK. The best-known example of this is the Volvo Kalmar factory, where work organization has been decentralized at the same time that production quotas and major management decisions have been centralized to Volvo headquarters. This has led to higher quality and increased productivity without really sharing any of the major decisions with the workers and their unions.

The Development Agreement came at a time when there was a general decentralization trend in society, and as a consequence now the joint consultation machinery under the Development Agreement is in practical use only at the plant level. The national unions and LO take almost no part in regulating through law or agreements the way joint consultation is handled in the workplaces. The only way the unions can influence co-determination practices is by providing wage-earner consultants and through union education activities.

5 Concertation through negotiations

Structural change, changes in trade union membership (a shift from unions in private manufacturing to public service) and changes in employer strategy do not in the Swedish case lead to a decreased role for the trade union movement or any weakening in its bargaining position. On the contrary increased overall trade union membership and a new role for the unions in production questions rather indicate an increased union role. The only development which could limit this would be internal division and a decentralization, which could go further than is really in the union interest.

The most difficult adjustment is the one that calls for changes in trade union structure. If it is agreed that the system of three unions in a workplace does not help them deal with technical changes, it can be seen that there would need to be new forms of co-operation between blue- and white-collar workers' unions. There is also a need for support from the central unions in negotiations about production problems. Here the national union structure with very large regional branch organizations does not lend itself to union participation in decisions over production questions. Instead there is room for local labour councils with resources in the form of technical consultants, researchers and direct links with local governments and universities. They could help union representatives in small workplaces deal with non-wage issues.

In a period of rapid structural change – plant closures, introduction of new technology, opening up of new markets for more or less sophisticated products, which may not have a long life-span – the unions will have to be active at several levels at the same time. They have to find political allies and exert political pressure at both a national and a regional/local level in order to secure full employment. They also have to participate at the national level in some form of centralized wage negotiations without which a low-inflation, full-employment policy cannot function. This political role must be made credible through an active trade union presence at the plant level. The labour law reform and the co-determination agreements following the labour laws have provided tools for such local participation. The more unions take responsibility for production questions and get involved in traditional employer concerns, the more they will be listened to when they give political advice or formulate tough demands.

There is no real crisis facing Swedish concertation practices. The strains experienced now are not new. There is rather a long tradition in Sweden of employers' organizations in export industries (the engineering industry federation in particular) pushing for independence: being allowed to pay lower wages to beginners and higher wages to skilled workers and opposing concertation policies involving public sector workers. But in the past inter-union solidarity has been strong enough to ward off this threat to concertation. A new feature, however, is the increasing independence of some very large export firms – Volvo, Ericson, Electrolux, SKF – which because of their size can almost blackmail government, central and local, and also stay more and more independent of the employers' federation.

This tendency is further promoted by government action: in the absence of an industrial policy in Sweden the government's major strategy when facing regional employment problems seems to be to give very large tax concessions to the giant companies to induce them to place some form of production facility in the depressed areas. Local governments usually provide all sorts of *gratis* infrastructure.

Profit-sharing schemes, which at least equal the annual wage increases in size, are allowed by the employers' federation and difficult to oppose for the national unions or LO/TCO. This is, of course, not in conformity with a wage policy of solidarity. Still, by international comparison, the wage levels in these 'profit machines' are rather low. The individual profit-sharing schemes can also be seen as an employer's line of defence against ideas about collective profit-sharing into wage-earner investment funds.

Centralized wage bargaining and other concertation practices in the Swedish environment are seen as necessary elements in the pursuit of the long-term targets of full employment, steady economic growth with a low inflation rate and a wage policy of solidarity. Central wage negotiations are also seen as the only way of keeping the government out of the wage formation process. So far this strategy has succeeded in the private sector. It has not succeeded in the public sector, where the government does not quite distinguish between its role as an employer and its political role. This seems to be a major reason for the public sector conflicts in 1984 and 1986. The Swedish concertation practices, therefore, are both offensive and defensive: they are defensive in the sense that without concertation practices the government would certainly become more directly involved in the wage-negotiation process, and long experience shows that with government involvement – even with mediation – the finer points in free collective bargaining tend to be lost. Only when the two sides have time to find the solutions in bargaining can necessary adjustments of wage abnormalities be found, groups that are lagging behind be brought forward and individuals who deserve it be lifted up to the wage level where they belong.

The offensive long-term goals of centralized bargaining are part of the solidaristic approach of the labour movement: to pay decent wages to all workers irrespective of the economic success of the enterprise and to help workers affected by plant closures and regional economic problems – on occasion caused by wage levels that individual firms could not pay – with active manpower programmes.

This policy, which also intends to make Swedish industry

competitive on the world market, could not be pursued if it were not part of a solidaristic concerted wage and economic policy. By 1982 the Co-Determination Act of 1977 finally led to an agreement promoting participation and productivity in the enterprise. While the top union organizations had meanwhile advised local unions not to agree to any new local agreements on worker participation before the central agreement was concluded, this same agreement gives very general recommendations about local activities to develop the co-determination practices in accordance with local conditions. As discussed above, this new line of approach was even more underlined when the participative research programme, LOM (management–organization–co-determination), was formulated to promote the development agreement.

Unions have responded to all this in different ways, trying to make 'flexibility' mean also a more flexible working life for the workers. Agreements have been reached about more shiftwork and shorter hours for workers agreeing to participate in continuous and other forms of shift work. In retail trade the unions have had little support from the general public in trying to limit the hours that shops are open to the public. The unions have not been able to convince the legislators to forbid Saturday–Sunday work and they are now concentrating their efforts on trying to prohibit Sunday work. Employers have no problems in finding unorganized part-time workers to keep the stores open over weekends even where they have agreements with the union members that they need not work over the weekend.

Unions agree that there is a need for flexibility in the work organization to promote efficiency, a better job content and democracy in the workplace, but maintain that employment and social security should not suffer. However, the two sides seem to agree that detailed regulation is not possible. Increased flexibility will have to be found through decentralized bargaining. Above all the plant union needs more time, financed by employers, to prepare itself and its members for participation in project groups planning for new investments and changes in the production technology.

By and large during the period under review Swedish unions have held their own in spite of structural changes both in the economy and in the trade union movement and in spite of the decrease in real earnings for which members could have blamed the unions and the whole labour movement and tried to seek solutions outside traditional concerted efforts.

True, statistics seem to indicate that wage differentials have not continued to shrink since 1976, and for a couple of years unemployment grew to 3 or 4 per cent, although declining toward the traditional 2 per cent in 1986–7 and less than 1.5 per cent in 1989. But considering the international trend and internal pressures from market forces such a virtual *status quo* on these points could be considered a victory for the unions.

However, the changed union structure – growth of public sector unions and a roughly unaltered membership of blue-collar unions in industry – has led to a change in union attitudes and policies. The unions in private industry – mainly the Metalworkers' Union – from having been the leaders of social reform inside the labour movement now appear as more self-centred and 'red-necked'. They play no role in the uphill fight for equal opportunity between the sexes, which many consider the most important issue on the labour market; they have come to accept employer proposals for higher wage differentials; and they have joined the liberal criticism of the public sector, using a rather tough language against their fellow workers. The unions in the manufacturing industries certainly face great problems in their efforts to adapt to new technology. Given the Swedish union structure with one blue-collar and two separate white-collar unions in industry (foremen and other salaried employees), one has reason to fear a situation where considerable efforts will be directed to an organizational competition between the blue- and white-collar unions.

The initiative in social reform in the Swedish labour movement has shifted to the public sector and other service unions. This change has taken place at the same time as a decision has been taken by the Social Democratic Labour Party to phase out collective union affiliation to the Party. Through this system the unions in manufacturing have played a leading role also in local politics. Even if some form of union financing of local political activities continues, the automatic financing of the Party disappears. There are those who fear that in the long run this can make unions like the metalworkers, the chemical workers, food workers, wood workers and building workers more concerned with their own immediate craft and employment interest, less with general social questions, and less prepared to act in the interest of the total labour movement. But such developments cannot be taken for granted and they may anyway be offset by increased 'socialization' of white-collar unions.

If no solution is found to the problem of blue-collar workers advancing in their job out of an industrial union into a union of salaried employees simply to get better pay, we may however see a continued concentration on the interests of the skilled workers by the industrial unions, leading to larger wage differentials.

A continued growth of the public sector, as we have seen in the past and particularly in the 1970s, is in the interest of the trade union movement, at least seen in a purely organizational perspective, since trade union membership in the public sector is almost automatic, and wages in the public sector are relatively high. If instead the growth takes place in the private sector services (an inevitable development if one is to judge from the US example), an increase in union membership will not so automatically follow and wages and other conditions of employment will in consequence not be as favourable. Already various forms of franchising are creating insecurity for the workers and much extra work for tax authorities and for unions.

11

United Kingdom: The Rejection of Compromise

Colin Crouch

Three developments in industrial relations have been particularly important in the United Kingdom during the 1980s. First, the almost complete rejection by the Conservative government of the search for national compromise in industrial relations that had characterized the policy of all parties since at least 1940 and, arguably, since the early twentieth century. Secondly, the installation of a tough legal framework for trade union action, marking the final end of the so-called 'voluntarist' tradition that dates back to 1871. Thirdly, in several sectors of the economy, the emergence of the company as the most important level for industrial relations activity, replacing the branch, shop-floor and state levels that had previously competed for importance within the British system.

These processes can all be seen as the consequence of the rather dramatic events of British industrial relations of the past two decades: the gradual and insistent spread of shop-floor power within the labour movement, leading eventually to widespread militancy; the frantic and only occasionally successful search by governments for some kind of neo-corporatist framework for achieving order in wage bargaining; since the end of the 1970s, the double defeat for organized labour in the simultaneous growth of mass unemployment and near collapse of the Labour Party as a serious political force.

In some respects the three developments are linked: one aspect of the rejection of compromise has been the installation of the legal framework, and both provide much of the scope for employers' company-level initiatives. On the other hand, the individual elements are not inevitably joined. Extensive legislation governing the conduct of industrial relations can be found in several countries where governments have long followed concili-atory policies, and the pursuit of company-level industrial relations is compatible with a wide range of political and legal contexts. It is important to bear this in mind when, below (section 5), we consider how lasting the changes of the 1980s are likely to be. While the following account of events will draw attention to the interrelated character of the main changes, their futures could well be very diverse.

1 Structural problems

While the British economy has shared the general conjunctural crisis and the more long-term restructuring problems of all Western industrial societies, three special factors have distinguished its experience. First, it was still undergoing its own particular secular decline when the current general crisis broke, exacerbating its problems of adjustment. Secondly, the unusually predominant role of the financial sector has intensified the shift of employment and output away from manufacturing. Thirdly, in common with Norway, Britain has benefited from the exploitation of North Sea oil. This gave the government unprecedented freedom from constraint on the balance of payments and on tax revenues. However, since it also raised the value of the pound sterling on the foreign exchanges for much of the period, the gain has been largely at the expense of the competitiveness of the manufacturing sector.

These factors, together with some real productivity gains resulting from restructuring, have combined to produce a particularly acute relative contraction of both output and employment in manufacturing (see Table 11.1).

Table 11.1 *Output and employment, by sector (%), United Kingdom, 1975–85*

	1975		1980		1985	
	E	P	E	P	E	P
Agriculture	2.7	2.4	2.6	1.9	2.6	1.6
Mining, etc.[1]	1.5	1.6	1.4	5.3	1.2	6.6
Manufacturing	31.0	26.3	28.3	23.5	23.8	22.6
Public utilities	1.4	2.6	1.4	2.7	1.3	2.6
Construction	6.6	6.1	6.5	5.4	6.0	5.3
Trade, etc.	18.2	11.4	19.3	11.0	21.2	11.5
Transport and communications	6.4	7.2	6.3	6.2	5.8	6.0
Financial services	6.5	14.5	7.3	15.4	9.1	17.2
Community and social services	25.5	4.8	26.7	4.6	28.9	4.5

E: Employment (including self-employed) as percentage of total civilian employment.

P: Sector's percentage share of gross domestic product.

[1] During the 1980s this sector has included the output of the North Sea oil fields.

Source: OECD and ILO

For many years the UK has been a net importer of food and primary products, but during the 1980s it has also become a net importer of manufactures. This has been made temporarily tolerable by earnings from North Sea oil, but there is anxiety whether, as oil resources are depleted, the economy can depend on the tertiary sector (primarily tourism and financial services) to compensate for the deficit in the other two sectors.

Little has been done to offset this tendency for several reasons. The high value of the pound sterling, while encouraging imports and hurting the export sector, has been of considerable help to the government's counter-inflation target. (Indeed, in mid-decade industry began to make some competitive gains when the decline in oil prices eased the upward pressure on sterling.) Further, it has been widely accepted that much of British industry required major change of a kind that did not seem to be happening under previous policy regimes. There was therefore some attraction in a kind of 'cleansing' process through major bankruptcies and unemployment, after which some 'fresh starts' might be made. This form of restructuring policy was also well suited to the Conservative government's aversion to state intervention in the economy.

Finally, manufacturing is, along with the public service, the main centre of trade union strength. Union power having been identified by the Conservatives (and indeed by many others) as a major political problem, widespread insecurity in that sector during a time when the government wanted to make changes in the role of unions offered several advantages. It should also be remembered that the old manufacturing industries are concentrated in geographical areas where the Labour Party is dominant, so political damage to the Conservatives was limited.

The other key unionized sector, the public service, has received special attention. As elsewhere in Europe, there has been widespread agreement that it could not be fully protected from the retrenchment taking place elsewhere, implying reductions in employment. While this issue has had to be grasped by governments of various kinds, British Conservatives had by the late 1970s developed an ideology of opposition to public spending and publicly provided services that made them tackle the task of cuts with enthusiasm. However, as Table 11.1 indicates, change has been far slower here than in manufacturing. The community and social services sector, which is overwhelmingly public, has continued to grow in both relative and absolute terms.

In addition to the sectoral changes in employment, there has been, as in other industrial countries, a decline in manual against non-manual employment; a rise in part-time and temporary

Table 11.2 *Gender ratios in employment, by sector, United Kingdom, 1975–86*

	Ratios of male to female employment		
	1975	1980	1986
Agriculture	4.1	4.1	4.4
Mining, etc.	23.1	18.0	17.1
Manufacturing	2.4	2.4	2.5
Public utilities	4.2	4.0	4.0
Construction	15.8	12.8	9.9
Trade, etc.	0.9	0.9	0.9
Transport and communications	4.9	4.4	4.1
Financial services	1.3	1.2	1.2
Community and social services	0.7	0.7	0.6
Aggregate	1.6	1.5	1.4

Source: ILO

contracts (Millward and Stevens, 1986:10–14, 205); and a rise in employment within smaller workplaces, though not necessarily in smaller companies. Some of these processes are associated with the emergence of a segmented labour market (ibid.: 210ff), with different kinds of workers enjoying very different employment conditions and levels of security.

Overlapping with this category, some changes are associated with the increasing participation of women, especially married women, in the labour force (see Table 11.2). Male participation has meanwhile been declining. At first sight this rise in the apparently more 'disposable' part of the labour force during a recession is surprising, until one reflects that it is precisely this disposability that is often attractive to employers. Married women are far more likely than men to accept part-time work and temporary contracts, and at a time of business uncertainty compare favourably in employers' eyes with male workers, especially after the great gains in security of employment that workers secured in the 1970s.

While in the long term the most crucial issue for the UK will be the competitiveness of its 'post-oil' economy, the most politically salient indicators have been the inflation and unemployment rates. In common with other countries, the UK has seen major improvements in the former offset by deterioration in the latter (see Table 11.3). In this context the re-emergence of powerful wages pressure in the late 1980s has been strange.

Table 11.3   *Inflation, unemployment and changes in earnings (%), United Kingdom, 1980–6*

	Inflation[1]	Unemployment[2]	Increase in earnings[3]
1980	18.0	6.6	18.6
1981	11.9	9.9	7.9
1982	8.6	11.4	6.9
1983	4.6	12.5	7.4
1984	5.0	11.7	6.1
1985	6.1	11.2	8.4
1986	3.4	11.1	–

[1] Annual increase in consumer price index.

[2] Unemployment according to standardized ILO definitions.

[3] Increase in average annual earnings, all persons in employment.

Source: OECD

2   Issues and processes in industrial relations

2.1   Political and institutional developments

The Conservative government has been highly and radically active within industrial relations. Its measures and policies may be summarized under four straightforward headings (a more detailed account will be found in Crouch, 1985).

2.1.1   Actions designed simply to weaken the power of the unions and/or of workers in relations with employers   These include: (i) the general macroeconomic policy of not taking action to reduce unemployment or prevent redundancies; (ii) the imposition of fairly strict 'cash limits' on public sector pay, reducing the scope for political bargaining; (iii) the introduction of changes in the law to make more difficult the use of union strength; and (iv) minor reductions in the legal rights of individual workers.

One effect of (i) was to make workers afraid of striking or taking other actions that might put their jobs at risk. In the early 1980s workers rejected union strike calls in some important disputes, mainly in the motor industry. Union leaders, accustomed to being criticized by their members for their lack of radicalism, were now accused of the opposite.

The importance of (ii) has been that the government announces each year how much money is available for public sector pay increases. If workers in any part of the sector achieve a higher level of pay, their employing agency has to make up the difference through manpower cuts or improved productivity. The policy has been used to push public sector pay (apart from special favoured categories, such as the police and the armed forces) below that of previously comparable occupations in the private sector. It has been a form of incomes policy, but since it has simply been imposed by government authority within the public sector, the government has not had to seek union (or even employer) co-operation in its implementation.

Among the legal changes under (iii) and (iv) the most important have been those affecting picketing and secondary action. These have become legally hazardous activities (Wedderburn, 1986:536–48; 597–606). The automatic effect of a ban on secondary action, and the particular limitations imposed in the picketing legislation (which enables workers to picket only their own *place of work* – that is, not their own *company*) is to reduce the chances of workers at one firm (or even of one plant within a firm) doing anything to help colleagues at another. This is of considerable importance within an economy where most employment takes place in companies that themselves have the resources of multi-plant and often multinational operations. In addition, of course, employers can further supplement these resources with those of the police.

2.1.2   Actions to reduce the institutional regulation of conflict in order to expose industrial relations more directly to market forces   A number of institutions designed to develop conventions for fixing pay and conditions without recourse to conflict, especially in the public services, have been abolished. Among the main examples were the Pay Research Units established in 1953 to fix civil servants' pay; mechanisms for ensuring certain minimal standards for low-paid workers, some of which date back to the late nineteenth century; and systems for ensuring the extension throughout a sector of employment of pay and conditions negotiated within it by employers' associations and unions, dating back to the Second World War. In 1987 school-teachers lost the right to negotiate their salaries, having to accept instead ministerial control. Further, having dispensed with incomes policy in the private sector and not seeking union co-operation in the administration of the public sector policy, the government has been under no pressure to pursue a consistent line in the implementation of 'cash limits', and has therefore avoided the creation of institutions and shared understandings.

One can also include under this heading the policy of preferring to withstand long strikes rather than reach compromises, a policy more reminiscent of US than British industrial relations, of which the year-long miners' strike in 1984–5 has been the most dramatic example. An additional political motive for this has been the

Conservatives' perception that the public blames unions (and, by extension, the Labour Party) for the disruption caused by prolonged strikes. This constitutes a change of major significance. For many years British governments saw it as important to restrain the scope of industrial disputes, lest an amalgamation of issues conflate into uncontrollable conflict that might damage at least the government's own standing and possibly civil peace as well.

2.1.3 Actions designed to reduce the legitimacy of trade unions as participants in national political life The range and number of contacts between ministers and union leaders, which had grown steadily since 1940, declined immediately the Conservative government took office. The government has also announced that unions would henceforth no longer be regarded as a major interest meriting representation on public bodies considering matters of general importance; their advice would be sought solely on questions directly affecting the work interests of parts of the labour force. There has also been a gradual abandonment of the doctrine that union recognition by employers constitutes 'good industrial relations'. Ministers regularly treat union recognition as just one of the means by which employers might choose to tackle relations with their employees. So far, however, there has been only one case of the government itself refusing to permit union membership among its employees (at the intelligence-gathering centre, Government Communications Headquarters (GCHQ)).

2.1.4 Legal measures to increase the power of union members and/or workers in general against union organizations The rights of workers not to join a union where 'closed shops' exist was introduced in the Employment Act 1980. The same act encouraged unions to use secret postal ballots in elections for officials and votes on strike calls. This was strengthened by the Trade Union Act 1984, which enables employers to take legal action against a union calling a strike without a prior ballot. Two curiosities of this provision are (i) that, having held a ballot, unions are free to continue with the strike even if a majority has voted against it; and (ii) that the law does not apply to unofficial strikes. However, subsequent case law has shown that this latter provision cannot be used by unions to encourage unofficial strikes instead of calling official ones, as they will be expected to demonstrate that they have done all in their power to discourage the unofficial strike. The same act also requires unions wishing to maintain political funds to resubmit the decision to do so to a secret ballot of the members every ten years.

A further measure, the Employment Act 1988, establishes, *inter alia*, rights for individual workers: to try to secure ballots to prevent their unions from calling strikes; and, in the event of a strike, to escape union discipline for disobeying the strike call. It will be noted that these rights only assist workers seeking to prevent or weaken union action; there are no reciprocal rights working the other way.

These policies work at the widely acknowledged gulf that had emerged between union leaders and their members during the 1970s. But the law on ballots to approve union political funds (designed to destroy the financial base of the Labour Party, which could not survive without union contributions) back-fired. By early 1986 all unions with political funds had held ballots among their members. Without exception these produced very large majorities in favour of keeping the funds.

The government may well have lost this issue by trying to go too far. In designing this law it had been acting on the basis of fairly strong evidence that most workers were rather opposed to their unions being 'political' (Moran, 1974; Roberts et al., 1972). But the form taken by the law was to require unions to have the support of a ballot of their members in order to be allowed to spend money on any political activity at all, not just affiliation to a party. For a union member to vote against political funds meant voting to deny his or her union any right to take political action. Clearly, the majority of union members did not want to weaken their unions' freedom to act in this way. By seeking a complete political emasculation of trade unionism, the government secured the reverse of its aims, as union political action now has a renewed legitimacy. Indeed, five unions that previously had no political funds acquired them under this legislation, though no additional unions have actually affiliated to the Labour Party.

2.2 Developments within industrial relations

2.2.1 A summary of wage developments Although the overall context has clearly been one of union weakness, the detail is more complex. The proportion of the workforce covered by collective wage agreements has *risen* during the 1980s, though solely because of the growing relative size of the public sector (Millward and Stevens, 1986:225ff). Within manufacturing industry there has been a decline in collective bargaining, partly because some employers took the opportunity of the economic and political climate to stop dealing with unions, but more importantly because the recession mainly hit large firms rather than small ones. Collective bargaining is concentrated among the former.

Table 11.4   *Changes in earnings, whole economy and*
manufacturing, United Kingdom, 1980–6 (1980 = 100)

	1981	1982	1983	1984	1985	1986
Whole economy	125.8	137.6	149.2	158.3	171.7	185.3
Manufacturing	123.6	137.4	149.7	162.8	177.6	191.2

Source: Department of Employment Gazette

In the early years of the decade, the height of the recession, unions' bargaining strength was particularly low. There were many cases of workers being unable to achieve any wage rises at all, even though inflation was running at high levels. At British Leyland, the state-owned automotive firm usually at the heart of militancy, workers went four years (1978–81) without a rise in real wages, and this despite strike action in 1981.

However, from late 1983 onwards, when the incomes of those in work again began to rise faster than either inflation or productivity, unions began to secure some bargaining gains. From 1984 the rise was most noticeable in manufacturing, the sector that had been most hit by the recession (see Table 11.4).

These developments may partly reflect the fact that, even during a period of unemployment, Britain's poor training system has produced considerable shortages of skilled workers. But there may also be support for the argument that in much of manufacturing industry (Batstone, 1984) and indeed generally (Batstone and Gourlay, 1986) little has really changed in collective bargaining. In manufacturing shop-steward organizations and local bargaining arrangements just waited quietly during the worst of the recession, and by mid-decade had begun to be active again. In other areas of employment, where the recession was less severe, the overall experience may well have been of continuing growth in the union role (ibid.:ch. 3).

Also supporting this thesis is the fact that the main grounds for wage increases have continued to be increases in the cost of living, a typical trade union demand (Millward and Stevens, 1986:296–7). While it is true, as we shall see below (section 3.2) that some employers have been taking important new initiatives in industrial relations, these reminders of stability caution us against exaggerating the significance of the new.

Public service employees, being highly unionized but rapidly falling behind in incomes, became increasingly militant. They also faced the most aggressive changes in management strategy, as public employers responded to government policies more readily than private employers, who often took a less political and more long-term view of their relations with their employees (Batstone and Gourlay, 1986). As will be discussed below, most of the major disputes of the 1980s have been in that sector.

2.2.2 Bargaining over job losses and reductions in work time While unable to resist job losses, unions have had a little more success in negotiating their terms, but within narrow constraints. In the old heavy industries, such as mining, shipbuilding and steel, and also in the motor industry, redundancies have been widespread and virtually non-negotiable. The annual number of redundancies, which had been running at around 190,000 at the end of the 1970s, leapt to over half a million by 1981. They then declined, but were still around a quarter of a million in 1986 (*Department of Employment Gazette*, monthly data). There is evidence that, in many cases, unions preferred to trade job losses for improved working conditions, pay and skill levels for the workforce that remained (Batstone and Gourlay, 1986).

The TUC tried to co-ordinate a general campaign for a reduction in working hours, though the targets were unspecific and the campaign made nothing like the national impact of similar events in Germany, Denmark and elsewhere. Average working hours for manual workers in manufacturing declined in 1981 to 98.7 per cent of the previous year, but then began to rise and by 1987 were running at 103.4 per cent of the 1980 figure (*Department of Employment Gazette*, monthly data).

But these data reflect changes in overtime working as well as in the length of the standard working week. The distinctive British characteristic of large amounts of overtime working has remained, further widening the gap between those in work and the unemployed. Average overtime among manual workers in manufacturing declined from 11.8 hours per week per worker working overtime in 1980 to 8.2 hours in 1981, but by 1987 had risen slightly to 9.3 hours (ibid.). The main change in standard hours was a reduction from the previous norm of forty to thirty-nine hours per week. By 1986 15 per cent of manual workers still had standard hours of forty or more, and about 10 per cent had negotiated reductions below thirty-nine, in some cases as low as thirty-five (for example, print workers in provincial newspapers). (Non-manual workers with standard contracts normally have a 35- or 37.5-hour week.)

Unions in the engineering industry negotiated reductions in the working week in 1981 and again in 1986. However, some employers resisted this. By 1987 the management of British Leyland 'clawed back' fourteen minutes each day by reducing workers' rest periods, defeating strikes by workers against the move. Towards the end of 1989 there was further conflict in engineering as the unions demanded a 35-hour week in line with the general European union campaign.

2.2.3   Bargaining over 'flexibility'   The demand for 'flexibility' has become a major feature of British industrial relations. It has been essentially an employers' offensive, strongly encouraged by the government, though many unions have now found means of taking up the challenge and sometimes taking the initiative.

The employers' demands usually include a willingness among workers to switch between different jobs within the company. This breaks the old insistence on job demarcation that had once been the hallmark of British craft unionism, but in fact much of this had during the 1970s been negotiated away or had disappeared with the old craft to which it had been linked. However, during the 1980s further inroads have been made, with unions being forced to give up some important job controls. The Ford Motor Co., the Post Office and the shipbuilding industry saw important disputes and negotiations over such issues, but most dramatic were conflicts in the newspaper industry. This sector has the most entrenched union power and has been extensively affected by new technology, so it is not surprising that the question has been confronted most fully here. In the case of Rupert Murdoch's firm, News International, which publishes *The Times* as well as more popular titles, the employer went to the lengths of dismissing his entire workforce and moving to a new factory surrounded by barbed wire in order to make a fresh start with new flexibility.

Flexibility has also meant unions conceding long-established rights over working time and work organization. Those affected have included railway workers, miners, dockers, car workers and teachers. However, some researchers (e.g. Batstone and Gourlay, 1986) have reported some continuing success among unions in negotiating changes in work practices and in the introduction of new technology. They also suggest that in many firms employers and unions have been able relatively amicably to negotiate the implementation of change.

Employers have often also wanted flexibility in the form of different types of worker. In 1985 the Engineering Employers' Federation said that they wanted work divided in the following ways: (i) ancillary services, such as cleaning and catering, could be contracted to specialist firms: (ii) many semi-skilled workers should be on temporary contracts so that their employment could vary with the state of the product market; (iii) other semi-skilled workers would be on standard contracts; (iv) workers with scarce skills would be offered superior terms with guarantees of security, in exchange for complete job flexibility and, preferably, representation by only one union. Some progress on this and other aspects of flexibility was being made in 1986, with the Confederation of Shipbuilding and Engineering Unions accepting much flexibility over job description, overtime and shift-working in exchange for reductions in working hours. The main sticking point seemed to be single-union representation, an issue made important only by Britain's unusual union structure. Eventually this deal was rejected by the workforce.

2.2.4 Participation and industrial democracy The issue of industrial democracy as such disappeared from the British political agenda on the election of the Conservatives. But the general area of worker involvement and consultation has continued to be a very lively one. There is considerable variety of responses within individual sectors and firms. There has recently been debate among observers whether firms have used the recession to dispense with various forms of joint consultation and participation (Cressey and McInnes, 1984); or to *intensify* consultation but as a means of avoiding and diminishing the importance of unions (Chadwick, 1983; Terry, 1983; Edwards, 1985); or merely to improve their relative position within an essentially stable industrial relations framework that assumes that unions, shop stewards and the rest will be virtually permanent features of employee relations (Batstone, 1984; Marchington and Armstrong, 1985).

Different researchers have found evidence of all three variations, and this is not inconsistent. Different firms face different labour markets, different kinds of trade unionism, maintain different personnel policies and entertain different expectations about the long-term future. Increased 'worker involvement' has often been a feature of the 'Japanese' approach to management adopted by some managements (see section 3.2 below). Unions have often been involved in the negotiation of such arrangements, though they have usually had to agree that the participatory devices themselves should not involve unions directly. It is likely, however, that the number of firms making highly elaborate and thoroughgoing changes is relatively limited (Batstone and Gourlay, 1986:125–7). More common is the relatively uncoordinated, piecemeal introduction of elements of new approaches.

To summarize these developments in collective bargaining, there has been a far more mixed pattern than the stereotype of a

Table 11.5 *Industrial conflict, United Kingdom, 1980–8*

	A	B	C	D	E	F	G
1980[1]	1,348	833.7	0.04	11,964	0.52	618	14.4
1981	1,344	1,512.5	0.07	4,266	0.20	1,125	2.8
1982	1,538	2,102.9	0.10	5,313	0.25	1,376	2.5
1983	1,364	573.8	0.03	3,754	0.18	421	6.5
1984[2]	1,221	1,464.3	0.07	27,135	1.28	1,199	18.5
1985	903	791.3	0.04	6,402	0.30	876	8.1
1986	1,074	720.0	0.05	1,920	0.09	672	2.7
1987	1,016	887.0	0.04	3,546	0.16	873	4.0
1988	781	790.0	0.04	3,702	0.17	1,011	4.7

A: Number of disputes.
B: Number of workers involved (thousands).
C: Workers involved per 1000 workers employed.
D: Number of days lost (thousands).
E: Days lost per 1000 workers employed.
F: Average size of disputes (that is, workers involved per dispute).
G: Average length of disputes in days.
[1] There was a prolonged dispute affecting the whole steel industry during 1980.
[2] There was a prolonged dispute affecting the coal-mining industry for nearly the whole of 1984.

Source: ILO (for 1986–88, *Department of Employment Gazette*)

weakened trade unionism might suggest. As discussion below (section 3.3.) will show, the evidence from statistics of union membership is mixed, and so is that from conflict data (Table 11.5). Overall the number and volume of strikes have clearly declined, though within this overall total there have been some major disputes, such as those in the health and civil services and the state mining and steel industries. What is only partially clear from the statistics is the changing shape of conflict. In place of the short, shop-floor strikes for improvements in pay and conditions, or to settle a grievance, that dominated in the 1960s and 1970s, there is now likely to be a defensive struggle waged by a union, often to try to prevent job losses. There have been some unusually long strikes, though average strike length has recently declined – not because the workers have been gaining their objectives quickly, but because they have accepted defeat.

Also, as the four examples cited above indicate, the big conflicts have been in the public sector, where the unions and the government confront each other directly over a combination of economic and political issues, and where the oligopolistic nature of production gives unions some power even during a recession. But all this may change as the government privatizes much of the public sector.

Between 1961 and 1981 government statistics distinguished between official and unofficial strikes. The original decision to make the distinction was essentially a political one, as in the early 1960s both government and many employers wanted to draw attention to the large amount of conflict not under union control. In 1981 the Department of Employment suddenly ceased producing these statistics. It is probably significant that the Conservative government elected in 1979 was no longer interested in unofficial strikes, but saw the most important militancy as that which came from union leaderships themselves. As a result of this change it is no longer possible to say whether there has been any major shift from unofficial to official action. However, since about 95 per cent of strikes was usually unofficial, the sharp decline in the number of strikes must largely represent a reduction in shop-floor action.

3 Actors

3.1 The state

As the account in section 2.1 makes clear, the present government has engaged in some radical departures from past political practice in British industrial relations. It has finally imposed a legal framework restricting union freedoms, an issue which had been actively discussed in the country for two decades. More surprisingly, it has reversed the whole long-term trend in which governments tried to moderate workers' militancy by incorporating unions. However, in making this assessment, it is important to put these policies into perspective and to appreciate the limits of this 'exclusion' strategy.

By themselves many of the legal changes could have been pursued within a variety of general contexts. The relative absence of legal constraint on union workers' industrial action that previously existed was unequalled in any other industrial country, except perhaps Italy. And in theory even a government intending to co-operate closely with unions might well have wanted to weaken and constrain them first.

Paradoxically, perhaps, although the government has had very strong ideas in its determination to weaken trade unions, it has had fewer fixed ideas than most of its predecessors on what constitutes a desirable system of industrial relations. It has certainly jettisoned the previous all-party orthodoxy which maintained that 'good' industrial relations must involve recognition of trade unions by employers and the elaboration of bargaining procedures, but it has not replaced this with a clear alternative. It is the government's policy that employers – and not governments or trade unions – should have power in industrial relations. Employers should not be presented with any one dominant model of personnel relations, but should enjoy a legal framework that enables them to choose from a variety of potential approaches. If employers want to maintain familiar policies of institutionalized collective bargaining, the government has no objection. But it equally has no objection if they refuse to recognize unions altogether – by dismissing workers who demand a union or, if they prefer, by installing personnel policies that seem to replace some of the functions of union representation. To discern more of the government's own preferences we need to consider further aspects of overall policy.

The policies designed to reduce the legitimacy of trade unions as participants in national political life (section 2.1.3 above) mark the clear breach of the Conservative government with any strategy of neo-corporatism, of trying to co-opt the unions into sharing overall economic responsibility. Unions are simply not wanted for anything of the kind. In this respect, the most significant feature of the policy of extending balloting and other means of strengthening union members' rights over their union officers is the assumptions it embodies about the respective militancy of union leaders and their members. The former are seen by contemporary Conservatives as militants leading reluctant members against their will. A few years previously the opposite analysis was made: union officials would be criticized for not showing qualities of 'leadership' when faced with shop-floor demands for militancy.

There are, however, some important exceptions to this trend, which demonstrate that the government's rejection of relations with unions has its limits. Some tripartite regulatory agencies, such as the Health and Safety Commission and the Advisory, Conciliation and Arbitration Service, still exist and function; the government has not tried to abolish them, nor have the unions boycotted them. But it is primarily the Manpower Services Commission's (MSC) chequered career which reflects the ambiguities of government policy. The MSC had the task of administering the system of employment exchanges through which unemployed people try to find jobs and, more important, of developing training and retraining opportunities.

Established in 1973 by a previous Conservative administration, encouraged and developed by the subsequent Labour government, the MSC was for several years given a significant role by the Thatcher government. And it continued to attract widespread co-operation. Although it was used by the government as a device for imposing low wages on young workers, it retained the support of most trade unions. A creature of the Department of Employment, its interference in the territory of the Department of Education and of local education authorities (LEAs) initially occasioned only mild protest. While the 1986 teaching dispute saw school teachers and their unions refusing collaboration with the government and most of its agencies, co-operation with the MSC's plans for linking school education with vocational training progressed unimpeded.

Soon after the 1987 general election the re-elected Conservative government announced that it would be doubling employer representation on the MSC, but not that of the unions. It was also clear that the MSC would be playing a major role in the government's new young people's training scheme, under which school-leavers who refused a place in a temporary training or work-experience course would be denied unemployment benefit. The unions were bitterly opposed to this, as they considered it to be a move towards compulsory labour and an artificial means of securing reductions in the unemployment statistics. There were therefore moves within the Trades Union Congress (TUC) for union representatives to resign from the Commission. However, these moves were defeated, which indicates the strength of the TUC's commitment to the MSC.

Then, in early 1988, the government announced its intention of replacing the Commission by a much more narrowly defined Training Commission. By the end of the year this too had been abolished. The government took the opportunity of a vote by the TUC annual conference to withdraw from co-operation with the new youth training scheme to abolish all union participation in the management of official employment and training policy. Measures were then taken to place all responsibility for these policies in the hands of local employers, working primarily through private firms specializing in the organization of training schemes. Unions and local education authorities (the usual providers in the past of much vocational training) are permitted to participate only if local employers permit them to do so. From its early days the MSC had embarked on an initiative-taking, interventionist role, with Scandinavian active manpower policy as its obvious model. The scope was limited, as employer and government representatives on the Commission ensured that it responded only to firms' expressed demands for skilled labour; it could not plan. However, its abolition has seen the final end of any attempt in Britain either to use manpower policy as a means of involving unions in economic policy or to organize training on any basis other than employers' calculations of their immediate needs.

3.2 Employers

Discussion in previous sections has already made clear the considerable variety of responses being made by British employers to the changed political situation. At the level of formal organizations the contrast could for several years be seen in the different positions of the main peak organization, the Confederation of British Industry (CBI), and the smaller, more propagandist, Institute of Directors. The CBI welcomed most of the government's industrial relations policies. It had come to believe by the late 1970s that unions had too much power and were exercising excessive constraints over firms; it set up a committee on the balance of power in industry to propose measures to restore power to employers. The CBI has therefore been broadly in favour of the new legal controls being imposed on trade unions. But it remained cautious.

For this caution it was criticized very heavily by the Institute of Directors. The Institute does not carry the large burden of business representation that is borne by the CBI. In previous years it was mainly a social club for company directors, but during the 1970s it became an important focus for businessmen critical of the CBI's willingness to co-operate with the Labour government. In particular it attracted supporters of Margaret Thatcher and her new-right faction within the Conservative Party. The Institute now acts as a very vocal propaganda group. It provides optimistic statements about the state of the economy and gives vigorous support to the government's policy of legal controls on trade unions – often advocating new tougher measures. As the Thatcher government has grown in success, so the CBI has increasingly adopted a more similar tone. Representing mainly firms in the manufacturing sector, it remains worried that government policy on the currency and interest rates continue to hurt this sector, but its criticisms are very muted, and it refuses most attempts by the TUC to orchestrate joint initiatives on the issue.

The CBI is by far the bigger and more important of the two employer bodies, but it is not entirely clear which of them speaks for the larger proportion of British business interests. Neither organization has much power. The Institute, which lacks any public-policy role, can wield no authority over firms, but even the CBI can use only persuasion and the provision of information to influence firms' industrial relations policy.

Overall, British employers are responding to the government's invitation to pursue whatever industrial relations policies they like. Many, awaiting a revival of union power, continue as they have acted for years. Since large-scale surveys have failed to pick up much evidence of change (Batstone, 1984; Millward and Stevens,

1986), this group probably constitutes the majority. However, others have responded to the possibilities of change. Some have learned from the experiments in Japanese and some American firms of various means by which employers can take the initiative in personnel relations, building up loyalty and commitment among the workforce and offering them limited forms of participation. Sometimes this includes a policy of incorporating union representatives; at other times it is a means of excluding unions.

Other firms again have taken more crude advantage of the political and labour-market situation either to get rid of unions altogether or, more often, to push them to the margins and deprive of them of many of the powers they had won in previous decades. There has been some evidence of US 'union-busting' consultants operating in Britain. Again, not much of this yet shows up in aggregate statistics.

Particularly interesting is the position of public sector employers, including the important group of recently privatized firms. It has not, with very few exceptions, been government policy to try to prevent union membership or recognition here, so public employees are becoming a larger proportion of the union movement. But it has been government policy to encourage tough, uncompromising industrial relations policies, often to an extent not being followed in most of private industry (Batstone and Gourlay, 1986). For example, the previously state-owned automotive firm, British Leyland, and, in particular, the National Coal Board (NCB) have marginalized union influence through a series of hard confrontations. At GCHQ the government abolished union representation altogether.

3.3   The unions

By the end of the 1970s one could discern three broad currents of thinking within the union movement. There were those who saw no better alternative to, and several positive gains in, co-operating with neo-corporatist policies, especially if there was a Labour government. There were those who just wanted to get on with normal collective bargaining and not become entangled in politics. And there were those who wanted to mobilize the growing militancy of British workers to make concerted political challenges.

The election of the Conservatives, who were not interested in neo-corporatism, cut the ground from under the first group. The second experienced something of a revival with the end of incomes policy, except that they were now negotiating during extremely unfavourable labour-market conditions – or, in the public sector, a continuation of *de facto* incomes policy. The only strategy being argued with any conviction was that of the militants, represented most prominently by the President of the National Union of Mineworkers (NUM), Arthur Scargill. In 1973–4 the NUM had defeated a Conservative government in a memorable strike, and it remained the view of the union left that this was the kind of strategy likely to defeat the Thatcher government.

The defeat of the NUM in the year-long strike of 1984–5 has discredited the extreme militant line within British trade unionism, leaving all shades of opinion now in disarray. The strike was a particularly bitter one, with considerable violence being exercised by both pickets and police, a small number of deaths of both striking and working miners, large divisions between sections of the industry that continued working and those that struck, and in the end considerable hardship among miners' families, forcing the miners to return to work. In the aftermath the National Coal Board (NCB) took very harsh action against prominent strikers, and a rebel union, the Union of Democratic Mineworkers, was established in the regions that had opposed the strike. The NCB is now able to play this union off against the NUM in any dispute.

Militancy and shop-floor unionism, the forces that destroyed TUC power in the 1970s, have now joined it in weakness. If the vacuum within the union movement is being filled, it is by a quite different force, and one congruent with the developments in employer strategy discussed above. As was discussed above in connection with bargaining over flexibility, some unions have started signing special company agreements with individual firms that embody a new conception of trade unionism. In addition to single-union recognition, acceptance of various forms of flexible working methods and understandings about not calling strikes, these agreements typically also provide for the installation of various company-controlled forms of employee participation and the abolition of distinctions between manual and non-manual staff. They also feature pendulum arbitration, a Japanese device under which arbitrators are not permitted to compromise but must support either the employers' or the unions' position; it is intended to moderate initial bargaining positions. (For a useful, if journalistic, account, see Bassett, 1986.)

Most of these agreements are in the new high-technology sector. The main union to take advantage of them has been the EETPU, followed by the AEU. Other unions have been watching developments closely, suspicious of the threat posed to their own capacity to recruit members and critical of the no-strike agreements, but envious of the progress being made in securing recognition in a growing area of employment. For example, in 1986 the General,

Municipal and Boilermakers' Trade Union (GMBATU, later GMB) set itself up to 'help' companies with personnel matters, offering also acceptance of flexibility, binding arbitration and single-union recognition. The EETPU, however, took its advocacy of such deals to the point where it was reaching agreements with employers over the heads of other unions present in a company, who then lost recognition. The union was punished for this by expulsion from the TUC in 1988.

The rise of sub-contracted and temporary labour obviously creates problems for unions, as the employers' main aim in developing such categories is to avoid observing negotiated terms and conditions. However, by 1987 the Transport and General Workers' Union (TGWU), followed quickly by the GMB, began to develop means of recruiting and representing temporary workers. One method that they are using, yet to be tested extensively, has been to maintain a union register of people available for temporary work – a service for companies, but one which tries to secure a role for unions in this largely non-unionized sector. This has been done in the past by specialized groups, such as printing industry unions, but not in the low-skilled areas in which the GMB and the TGWU are active. An even more original initiative by GMB, in spring 1987, was to try to provide services for the self-employed. The experiment was launched first in north-eastern England, where many former GMB members have been trying to establish themselves in various forms of self-employment following the collapse of so many large firms in the region. This is often a spurious self-employment: people work in reality for an employer, but are given self-employed status so that the 'employer' can avoid tax and insurance liabilities.

Union membership has declined steadily (see Table 11.6). Unfortunately it is not possible from the statistics to distinguish between a decline consequent on employers refusing to grant unions recognition, workers simply finding unions of no help in the tough bargaining context, or the mere effects of high unemployment. The details of membership in individual sectors suggests that a good deal can be explained by the last. In fields where employment levels have remained high, there is little or no evidence of a decline in union membership (Millward and Stevens, 1986:60).

As has been mentioned above, union membership has remained high in the public service. There has also been a small but continuing rise in unionism in the financial sector. This is of course a sector of very rapid growth in Britain at present, but it is also one where in the past unions found it difficult to recruit. The workers are mainly non-manual, well-paid employees, and the employers

Table 11.6 *Trade union membership, United Kingdom, 1975–87*

	Members (000s)	Density[1]	Density[2]	No. of unions
1975	12,026	50.86	53.0	470
1980	12,947	52.77	56.4	438
1981	12,106	49.84	55.4	414
1982	11,593	47.92	54.2	408
1983	11,236	46.76	53.4	394
1984	10,994	45.26	51.8	375
1985	10,821	44.04	50.03	370
1986	10,539	42.54	48.54	335
1987	10,475	42.20	47.86	330

[1] Union members as percentage of total employee labour force.
[2] Union members as percentage of persons in employment.

Source: Department of Employment Gazette

(banks, insurance companies, finance houses) have traditionally been strongly opposed to union membership among their staffs. Most of them conceded union recognition during the 1970s, and it has been notable that, following a major reorganization of the structure of the financial sector (the 'City of London') in early 1987, some firms have been rejecting unions again.

In some sectors membership losses have been even more severe than might have been expected from unemployment. For example, the country's largest union, the TGWU, saw its membership rise from 1,500,000 during the 1970s to a high point of 2,000,000 in 1979, only to fall back to 1,500,000 by 1984, even though during that period the union absorbed the membership of several other unions, with original memberships totalling 200,000. The second biggest union, the AEU, which had for many years reported a membership of over a million, announced in 1987 that it had dropped to 800,000.

The number of unions in Britain, still high in comparative terms, has continued the decline on which it embarked over twenty years ago. The main cause of this is the disappearance of small craft unions, either as their distinctive crafts disappear or, more frequently, as they amalgamate with larger unions in order to achieve economies of scale. The decline has brought no real rationalization of union structure on industry–union lines. British unions, like those in Denmark and Ireland, remain unusual in this respect.

If anything, the structure becomes more complex as large unions become like conglomerate companies, with interests in several sectors. Thus during the 1980s the National Union of Agricultural Workers amalgamated with the TGWU, and the Boilermakers' Union, an old, declining craft union, joined the unskilled workers' General and Municipal Workers' Union to form GMBATU. Several unions, including the two general unions (TGWU and GMB) also have separate sections for non-manual staff. There has been one notable case of a union separation. The technicians' union TASS, which had several years ago amalgamated with the AEU, though always remaining a separate section, completely separated itself again.

4 Levels

The characteristic levels of British industrial relations have been: branch-level collective bargaining; shop-floor bargaining, often of an unofficial kind; and national-level tripartite discussion. Of these, the first, which had previously predominated, was gradually reduced in importance, first by the rise of the shop floor and second by the conflict between shop-floor action and state intervention. The state was trying to impose a new national-level framework of order to combat unofficial bargaining and conflict. The tension between these two opposed forces finally broke in January 1979, when a series of strikes, often official but led from the shop floor, broke the Labour government's incomes policy.

However, the result of this process was not the final triumph of shop-floor action. As we have seen above, from 1979 several major features of British industrial relations changed. Encouraged by government policies for placing the initiative with individual firms, and concerned at the inability of branch-level institutions to contain shop-floor action, many employers took the logical step of making the *company* the important level in industrial relations. Steps had in fact already been taken in that direction during the 1970s under *union* influence, as unions and shop-floor representatives constructed bargaining policies to deal with individual multinational enterprises.

The difference in the 1980s is that employers are taking the initiative. It is perhaps significant that the shift to the company as a level has been associated with a decline in more decentralized bargaining at the workplace (Millward and Stevens, 1986:231). To date it is too early to assess the overall direction being taken, or even to determine just how important the change is. In some sectors branch-level bargaining by employers' associations and national unions continues as it has for many years – though this has declined very sharply during the 1980s to the point where around 90 per cent of firms in the private sector were establishing basic pay at single employer level and 65 per cent doing so even for fixing hours of work (ibid.:240–2; CB1, 1989).

5   An interpretation of changes

The loss by trade unions of political 'citizenship' rights during the 1980s has been very striking; losses in bargaining rights have been considerably more modest. Table 11.7 presents the situation in terms of the project's model of types of industrial relations system. It summarizes the account that has been given above, but it is worth stressing that the clearest change has been the almost total eclipse of any elements of concertation (Aa). Always weak in practice, concertation had however been the goal of repeated policy attempts since the early 1960s. It has now disappeared from the political agenda, and virtually from the political vocabulary.

The organizational and political achievements of trade unionism during the 1970s moved in opposite directions from underlying political and economic trends; the UK experience is here probably the most extreme case of a more widespread phenomenon. Early in the decade the appearance of high inflation so soon after a growth in union militancy and power rendered governments who were committed to full employment dependent on union co-operation for maintaining economic stability. In Britain, at around the same time the Labour Party entered government, though on the basis of very low popular support. Unions were then able to make major gains in legislation and general influence as part of the price to be paid for their co-operation.

But the underlying conditions were far less favourable. While organized labour was building new rigidities into the labour market, employers were seeking a new degree of flexibility to cope with unstable product markets. While unions were trying to protect declining industries, new patterns of international trade and the growth of the newly industrialized countries in the Pacific were rendering those industries hopelessly uncompetitive. While labour was offering national co-operation, the growth of shop-floor militancy was reducing its capacity to deliver that co-operation. While the Labour Party governed, the Conservatives were growing in both public popularity and hostility towards the unions.

Matters came to a head in 1979, when the strikes of the 'winter of discontent' prepared the way for Conservative victory in a general election. Since then virtually all major events have strengthened the 1979 change of direction: the split in the Labour

Table 11.7 *Changes in the industrial relations system, United Kingdom since 1980*

Type	Pre-1980	Post-1980
A(a) National concertation	Encouraged by successive governments, but never stably established	Almost complete disappearance
A(b) Industry-wide collective bargaining	Widely established throughout public sector and in private manufacturing (especially manual workers), but under pressure from decentralized shop-floor movements	Declining as a result of shift from manufacturing to services, from manual to non-manual work and to some extent as result of managerial strategy; rising as result of growth of public services
B Decentralized collective bargaining	Widespread in several manufacturing industries (especially engineering) at plant level; growing in public services	Continuing to grow, but now as a result of managerial preference for *company*-level industrial relations
C(a) Worker participation via unions	Rare, but growing interest; some major experiments (especially in public sector)	Decline of 1970s experiments, but some new examples based on 'Japanese' models
C(b) Worker participation without unions	Unimportant; mainly among non-manual workers	Some growth; attracting much interest but, as yet, not widespread imitation
D(a) Simple contract (no unions)	Always important in private services, non-manual work (private sector) and small firms	Increasing as result of rise of sectors always associated with it
D(b) Simple contract (no unions) in secondary labour markets	Limited to some employments (for example construction, catering, cleaning, clothing, clerical) mainly among women	Spreading to an increasing number of industries and firms – especially as female employment grows

Party, the enhancement of the government's prestige through the war in the South Atlantic; the collapse of employment levels and of much of manufacturing industry; the defeat of the mining strike; the introduction of rapid changes in technology and work organization, giving management a chance to take advantage of the changed bargaining situation.

The political shift has been central in producing change; the shift in state policy has been very abrupt, and there is considerable evidence that the government would like employers to move faster and further than they are doing to deregulate and de-institutionalize the labour market. However, much would clearly have happened without political change: the demand for flexibility, the collapse of basic industries, the high unemployment, are only partly political phenomena. The economic processes at work have also been fundamental.

Most unions would probably now prefer a return to the concertative policies of the 1970s, as they experience the loss of both membership and influence that their political marginalization has imposed. Given that a Labour government would always return to a search for concertation, and given that the great majority of unions seek a return of a Labour government, the unions can be said to be committed to a return to concertative policies. However, only a small group of union leaders is willing to accept openly what that really means in terms of wage restraint and co-operation with government. Joint Labour and TUC policy still talks about the need for a 'national understanding' between unions, government and employers, while failing to be explicit about the constraints that this would involve for union behaviour.

5.1   Future prospects

The 1987 election confirmed the Conservative government in office and gave them the rare prize of three successive electoral victories since 1979. The Conservatives' share of the vote (42 per cent) was not particularly good for a British governing party, and the real development was not any gain in the popularity of Conservatism but the collapse of the Labour Party as a serious contender for government office. The government and employers had little to fear from the labour movement. One could therefore expect that existing policies would be strengthened rather than relaxed. Further legislation to constrain unions is indeed in progress, and some further dismantling of industrial relations institutions can be expected, though towards the end of 1989 there were marked signs of a political recovery by the Labour Party, which could inhibit employers from adopting positions hostile to unions.

Within days of the 1987 election the government further weakened the remnants of tripartite co-operation by downgrading the National Economic Development Council (it will meet rarely and not be attended by senior ministers) and by ending parity in representation to the Manpower Services Commission. But the final rupture came the following year when the MSC and all significant tripartism in training were stopped.

5.1.1 Employer strategy   As has been discussed earlier, until now the majority of employers with a unionized workforce have continued with arrangements of type A(b) or B though with a major shift towards themselves in the balance of power within the relationship. There has also been some clear preference for a shift from A(b) to B.

Examples of more dramatic shifts of policy, mainly to the two forms of type D but also to those of type C, can certainly be found and have attracted considerable interest, but so far they remain minor in their overall impact. It may well be, however, that the renewed stability of the new-right political regime will lead an increasing number of employers to imitate these developments and seek an American-style 'union-free environment'. Much depends on their analysis of whether unions are in a state of terminal decline or in one of *reculer pour mieux sauter*. The latter possibility argues for maintaining good relations; the former for more aggression.

5.1.2 The union response   As indicated in section 3.3, several of the major British unions are managing to move beyond mere defence and find answers to the challenges of changed employer strategy with respect to the three main ones: the shift to labour markets of type D(b) – where unions are seeking means of representing the new kinds of worker; the occasional introduction of worker-involvement schemes of type C – within which unions like the EETPU are trying to find a role; and the pressure for flexibility – where many unions have negotiated the introduction of new technology and flexible working methods, exchanging concessions for improvements in conditions, working time and union representation. Similarly, several are trying to become involved in equipping their members with new skills – whether through participating in the reform of training schemes or, in some cases, through the provision of training by the unions themselves.

To date it is difficult to assess the success of these measures; they have become prominent only during the past two years. We do not yet know whether they have had any effect on the continuing decline in union membership or on the willingness of employers in new sectors to recognize unions.

The great decline in manufacturing employment in the early 1980s has now probably slowed down, so (unless there is a rise in employer aggression) the membership decline should also slacken pace. Similarly, however, the rise in public employment from which unions gained has also slowed; it has also been considerably affected by privatization. Unions are making some progress in representing workers in the new private services area, but only very gradually. The rise in the female proportion of the workforce presents a challenge to which they have been responding well. The picture therefore remains mixed.

To the extent that new union recruitment strategies succeed, they will ironically have serious implications for the capacity of the unions to constitute anything of a 'movement' for the general defence of working people as opposed to a series of sectional groupings. Indeed, British unions have never been very good at generalized defence; that is a task they have delegated to the Labour Party. Unions themselves have usually been at their best in highly specific occupational representation. It is this that has constituted their characteristic strength: deep shop-floor roots and a high degree of responsiveness to problems at the workplace.

Even when the Labour Party was very weak the unions showed no sign of being able to fill the vacuum of general representation, though many of the challenges facing workers are of a general, and sometimes political, kind. The TUC, the main focus for co-ordination, has only ever acquired an important role when relations with government either require it or make it possible; at present neither is the case. Meanwhile, all the new initiatives by unions mentioned above are exceptionally particularistic, involving deals with, usually, individual companies. The TUC tries to issue guidelines and give advice, but its role is marginal. Most important, one feature of the emerging new system – deals whereby unions exchange recognition for single-union representation – is divisive and imposes a considerable strain on inter-union relations.

On the other hand, in some respects British unions remain strangely unified: only in Austria is there a similar absence of divisions based on *either* politico-religious *or* occupational differences. The great majority of unions, manual and non-manual, are members of the TUC and show no sign of wishing to separate from it. Of course, the price of this unity, and the great contrast with Austria, is that it means very little: there is so little overall co-ordination that unity poses few constraints. The fact that unions of senior civil servants, managers and university teachers are all part of the TUC does not mean that British unions have succeeded in establishing cross-class solidarity, but rather that they make no demands for it. However, it is a strength of a kind: it pools resources, it prevents wasteful inter-confederal conflict and occasionally it does make joint action possible.

Changes in employment patterns are important here. Neither white-collar workers nor skilled manual ones in the new industries identify themselves as part of a labour movement; nor do they have any particular allegiance to the Labour Party. They view their union in the same way they might view a motoring organization or some other service agency. British unions are reasonably successful in recruiting this kind of worker, but in doing so they dilute their own political identity and sense of being a 'movement'. It is significant that membership growth has been concentrated in those unions that have not affiliated to the Labour Party – not because workers deliberately choose non-party unions, but because the party's affiliated unions are concentrated in declining sectors.

Meanwhile there have been signs that the Party considers the unions' unpopularity to hinder its own search for electoral success. Union leaders were noticeably absent from Labour's 1987 election campaign, and in 1989 the Party committed itself – with much union support – to ending the block vote.

However, the unions remain deeply interested in macroeconomic policy and industrial relations law. Rank-and-file members might not feel part of a movement in any emotional sense; but leaders and officers are aware in a practical way that the idea of 'business unionism' ignores the realities of the political economy. It is notable that the EETPU, so often a rebel among the unions and now expelled from the TUC, remains strongly committed to the Labour Party and to a union political influence. Similarly, the main officers of such non-partisan unions as the National Union of Teachers (NUT) or the National and Local Government Officers' Association (NALGO) are usually Labour supporters.

It is likely that in the end a looser but still clear association between Party and unions will emerge. Each will try to avoid sharing the other's unpopularity; there will now be an attempt at amending the cumbersome way in which union block votes control the Party conference and elections to its National Executive Committee; unions will learn not to presume on their members' political commitment. But, provided they do nothing that the bulk of their members actively oppose, they will be given ample leeway by those members to continue playing a political role and a party one.

If nothing else, the fact that the Conservatives have now chosen to define themselves unambiguously as hostile to trade unions while the smaller opposition parties remain indifferent to them will guarantee a continuing Labour involvement for British unions. Similarly, the shift to the right of the US Republican Party has led American unions to a closer identity with the Democrats than before.

Oddly, therefore, the great shifts in employment patterns now taking place in the advanced capitalist economics will have fewer implications for British unions than for their more powerful counterparts in Scandinavia. One issue that could strengthen trade union unity might be training and manpower policy. To the extent that successful manpower policy requires an overall national approach rather than piecemeal action, unions share an interest in lobbying for it together as well as separately within their individual industries.

As an inchoate group of organizations, British unions will retain a power and a presence in the British economy: uneven, illogically structured and excessively decentralized as always, rather weaker than before but of continuing importance. It is at the national political level, where their own scope for initiative is weak and where they face the government in Europe most hostile to trade unions, that their fall from the influential years of the 1970s has been most dramatic and where continuing decline seems most likely.

References

Bassett, P. (1986) *Strike Free*, London: Macmillan.

Batstone, E. (1984) *Working Order*, Oxford: Basil Blackwell.

Batstone, E. and S. Gourlay (1986) *Unions, Unemployment and Innovation*, Oxford: Basil Blackwell.

CBI (1989) *The Structure and Process of Pay Determination in the Private Sector, 1979–86*, London: CBI.

Chadwick, M. (1983) 'The Recession and Industrial Relations: A Factory Approach', *Employee Relations*, 5(5):5–12.

Cressey, P. and J. McInnes (1984) paper presented to ESRC conference on 'The Recession and Industrial Relations'.

Crouch, C.J. (1985) 'Conservative Industrial Relations Policy: Towards Labour Exclusion?', in O. Jacobi, B. Jessop, H. Kastendieck and M. Regini (eds), *Economic Crisis, Trade Unions and the State*, London: Croom Helm.

Department of Employment Gazette (monthly), London: HMSO.

Edwards, P. (1985) 'Managing Labour Relations Through the Recession', *Employee Relations*, 7(2).

Fatchett, D. (1986) *Trade Unions and Politics in the 1980s*, London: Croom Helm.

Fosh, P. and C.R. Littler (eds) (1985) *Industrial Relations and the Law*, London: Gower.

Marchington, M. and R. Armstrong (1985) *Joint Consultation Revisited*, Discussion paper 13, Glasgow: Centre for Research in Industrial Democracy and Participation, University of Glasgow.

Millward, N. and M. Stevens (1986) *British Workplace Industrial Relations 1980–1984*, London: Gower.

Moran, M. (1974) *The Union of Post-Office Workers: A Study in Political Sociology*, London: Macmillan.

Roberts, B., R. Loveridge and J. Gemard (1972) *Reluctant Militants*, London: William Heinemann.

Terry, M. (1983) 'Shop Stewards Through Expansion and Recession', *Industrial Relations Journal*, 14(3).

Wedderburn, Lord (1986) *The Worker and the Law*, 3rd edn, Harmondsworth: Penguin.

William, P. (1986) *Technological Changes, Collective Bargaining and Trade Unions*, Oxford: Oxford University Press.

Afterword

Colin Crouch

When, some time between 1968 and 1972, there was an extra-ordinary resurgence of industrial conflict in nearly every European country, there was a reversal of what many observers had believed to be a major historical trend. In the 1950s and early 1960s scholars had written books with titles like *As Unions Mature* (Lester, 1958); had spoken of a withering away of industrial conflict, with strike action gradually becoming reduced to intra-union disputes (Ross and Hartmann, 1960); or had seen strikes as a form of action indulged in only by rather unusual kinds of workers, living in 'isolated masses' (Kornhauser et al., 1954). As union membership in many countries stagnated at the same time, it seemed to some that the whole business of autonomous organiza-tions representing a workforce had become outmoded. What price such theories from the vantage point of the early 1970s, in the wake of 'les événements de mai', 'l'autunno caldo', the extra-ordinary rise in shop-floor conflict in the United Kingdom, or the clear ending of the years of virtual absence from strikes in West Germany or Scandinavia, in the context of rising union member-ship throughout western Europe?

Therefore, when in 1972 Alessandro Pizzorno and the late Serge Mallet convened an international research team to consider what was happening to industrial relations in the then member countries of the European Community plus Britain, the group was under a strong temptation to dance on the graves of those North American scholars of an earlier generation. Marxist observers were parti-cularly concerned to be able to refute claims that the maturation of capitalism was associated with a *reduction* in social tension. But Pizzorno dissuaded us from replacing simple linear theories of declining conflict with equally simple and linear ones proclaiming its inevitable intensification. We lacked any mechanism for arguing such an inevitability, he argued, and therefore would run the risk of being proved mistaken by subsequent events in precisely the same manner as those we were now rejecting.

Fortunately we saw the wisdom of his argument. While the two volumes that resulted from the project (Crouch and Pizzorno, 1978a and 1978b) are replete with criticisms of Ross and Hartmann and the rest, they contain no assertions of a necessarily upward-spiralling trend, and include articles by Pierre Dubois (1978) considering the 'wavelike' character of industrial conflict, by David Soskice (1978) on the unusual features of the late 1960s economy, and by Pizzorno himself (1978) on the way in which conflict intensifies at periods when new, or excluded, collective identities are demanding some form of recognition – all arguments that avoid the trap of extrapolating future developments from recent trends.

Now of course we are living in the new period that should have been anticipated if there were indeed specific or, more interestingly, wavelike characteristics to the earlier resurgence. Conflict did not continue its constantly exacerbating course. Outside Scandinavia, industrial conflict in European and other industrial societies is at lower levels than in the later 1960s and the 1970s. And again the extrapolators of linear trends are at work. There is now no shortage of observers pronouncing the final end, not only of industrial conflict, but of trade unionism (that is, autonomous representation of employee interests) and of labour politics in general.

Are these predictions any better founded than the earlier ones? Is there, on the other hand, any evidence that industrial conflict is indeed wavelike and should be expected to return?

The papers in this collection allow consideration of three different explanations of the current decline: a conjunctural explanation concerning the recession of the early 1980s; a structural one concerning changes in the labour force and system of production; and a political one concerning the balance of forces in late-twentieth-century political economies.

The first of these is that which most easily supports 'wave' theories. The relationship between economic conjuncture and workers' militancy is not simple: during recessions strikes tend to become larger, longer and more bitter, but there may be fewer of them as the small-scale, opportunistic strikes typical of periods of expansion decline. In that case a decline in the archetypically opportunistic strikes of the 1968–80 period was only to be expected. On the basis of wave or cyclical theories such as those of Cronin (1979), Dubois (1978) or Shorter and Tilly (1974), a new rise in conflict should be anticipated as the economic cycle turns, especially as workers seek to remedy grievances that have built up during the years of recession. If European unemployment levels sustain their recent and hesitant fall over the next year or so, some rise in conflict levels should therefore be expected. There is perhaps already a little evidence of this in some countries.

However, the structural theory would suggest that any such recovery of militancy will be limited. This thesis points to the rapid decline, in all European societies except those that might be considered still to be industrializing, of employment in the mining and manufacturing sectors of the economy, and of manual work in general. These are the sectors that have in the past provided the backbone of union membership and union militancy.

This is powerful and goes beyond a mere extrapolation. However, the theory leans rather heavily on certain static assumptions about the kinds of employee most likely to be militant. In fact, both historically and comparatively there has been more variety in this than such an argument implies. British coal miners have traditionally been particularly militant; the French have not. There was a time when skilled workers were seen as the heart of trade unionism; by the 1960s this position was occupied by assembly-line workers.

It is undoubtedly true that major *changes* are introduced into trade unionism when manual workers in manufacturing industry become a minority of the workforce, but it cannot be assumed that change embodies an end to unionism or organized dissatisfaction with the terms and conditions of employment as such. Already it has become evident in many countries that public service employees, often including non-manual ones, can replace manual groups in the forefront of militancy. This trend may be reduced by the privatization of public services, but not necessarily. Sometimes it is the character of the work (large scale of operations; natural monopoly) that determines workers' behaviour here rather than the identity of the employer. And to the extent that the presence of the state is relevant, this may remain true even after a service is nominally privatized.

The growth of private non-manual employment in the tertiary sector does seem to be more generally associated with a decline in unionism, or at least a decline in militancy, but even this is not a universal tendency. Scandinavian private service employees have a high rate of union membership, albeit in unions unconnected with the bulk of the labour movement; in the Republic of Ireland bank employees have often been among the most strike-prone groups. There is much here that is non-determined, that is vulnerable to change and variation.

The same applies to some of the manual groups whose numbers are surviving economic restructuring but who lack the strong traditions of the declining heavy industry sector: office and factory cleaners, the staff of fast-food outlets, for example. It should not be assumed, however, that these groups remain indefinitely incapable of being organized, just as organization spread from the skilled to the unskilled at the end of the last century. The employees in these categories often belong to groups with social identities that are particularly underrepresented or in some other ways occupationally problematic – such as women, ethnic minorities and young people in general. Their role in the formation of new collective identities formed a part of the analysis in the Crouch and Pizzorno studies, but in some respects their role is more prominent now than in the period we studied. It is doubtful that their industrial relations story is yet complete.

When one considers that, at different times and places, groups as diverse as air-traffic controllers, motor-industry paint-shop workers, primary school teachers, refuse collectors and junior magistrates have all been in the vanguard of action, one becomes wary of predicting that any particular occupational change marks an irreversible decline in trade unionism. True, major changes in the structure of a population will lead to changes in the kinds of action pursued within it; peasant revolts no longer occur once the peasantry has passed into history. But the process we are witnessing today is less radical than that. There is no elimination of the role of the *employee* in prospect. This role is at any time likely to generate a demand for representation; and such a demand is likely to encounter a varied pattern of opposition and institutionalization from employers and governments.

With European unionization rates ranging from a Scandinavian 90 per cent to a French 15 per cent, and with degrees of centralization running from the Österreichischer Gewerkschaftsbund to the British shop-steward system, the range of present variety is enormous. It is likely to increase.

More problematic is whether this diverse group of modern employees is capable of being welded into any kind of basic unity. Unions may have a long-term future, but do union *movements*? There will be variation, as there is already, in the extent to which different unions and national confederations succeed in solving problems of both initial recruitment and subsequent moulding.

This raises the final theme: of political action, of the scope for strategy by a variety of participants. One of the things that both the writers of the 1950s and those of us commenting in the 1970s overlooked was the scope for reaction by adversely affected interests. Human groups rarely take punishment lying down, but try to respond. Unions in many countries responded capably to their membership decline of the 1950s; employers are now responding effectively to the loss of initiative they suffered during the waves of militancy after 1968. Unions – or, rather, some of them, because we must never lose sight of the scope for variety of response here – are trying to respond to their problems today, in ways described in some of our chapters.

More immediately we should consider those changes induced earlier, and still in progress, by government and employers. The papers in this volume have shown the relevance of national politics for industrial relations. This is not entirely straightforward. Where a system of organized labour is producing outcomes that employer and other established interests find relatively satisfactory (as in Germany today or Sweden at the end of the 1970s) they may do little to disturb overall patterns. Where the power of labour is proving a problem, even pro-labour governments may adopt tough policies (as in Spain today). However, in general it remains possible to argue that where government is either friendly or (as in Italy) at least non-hostile towards organized labour, there will be limits to the kinds of political attack that will be launched against it. A contrast between, on the one hand, the hostile governments of Britain, Denmark and, to a certain extent, the Netherlands and on the other the remaining countries in our group demonstrates this.

Governments enjoy considerable discretion at a time of recession, when labour is economically weak: do they offer unions help to maintain their organizations (perhaps in exchange for various kinds of co-operation)? Do they remain broadly neutral and let market forces take their rather hostile course? Or do they set out to exacerbate the impact of those forces, taking advantage of the conjuncture to weaken labour's position even further? The outcome is not determined; there is scope for variation; there is unlikely to be any overall convergence.

Employers also have options. Do they broadly accept the structure of institutions established at an earlier period, when perhaps union strength was greater? Do they take advantage of a more abrasive economic climate to reduce workers' rights and institute a much tougher, harsher managerial regime? Do they adopt more skilful, if more difficult, policies of winning workers' loyalty and identity through the application of management techniques that seek co-operation and involvement without the intervention of unionism? The first we are likely to see where employers are both reasonably satisfied with existing outcomes and fearful of what would happen if and when labour recovers strength, were the institutional barriers that had previously been so painfully erected to be broken down. Such employers do not take full advantage of the current situation and therefore reduce the prospects of the changed employment context having any major long-term effects on industrial relations.

The second group, the so-called macho-management, play for far higher stakes. If they win, they might rid their firms of unions and non-compliant workers for a long period. If they lose, as the first group of employers fear, they may unleash a backlash unprotected by institutions of mediation when labour recovers strength. It is employers of this type who maintain the momentum of the cyclical or wavelike character of strikes. It is significant that many wave theories originated with studies of France. A country where employers are least likely to accept institutionalized relations with union representatives, France has seen a long-term series of major manifestations of dissent, followed by long periods of relative quiet while workers suffer defeat, accumulate grievances which they can do nothing about, recuperate and seek to rectify grievances in a new mobilization. This is the most dramatic case, but similar patterns can be seen in Britain and elsewhere.

The third group of employers seek to avoid both the long-term disruption of this and the failure to take advantage of the changed balance of power that the former permit. They are a prominent group of employers because of the novelty of their ideas, but so far they account for a rather small minority. IBM and similar US multinationals are the most notable; Japanese firms are strongly identified with the phenomenon, and so are several French ones. The strategy is not necessarily hostile to unions: the pure Japanese model incorporates unions of a certain kind; US versions are less likely to. To adopt such a strategy means to devote great care to industrial relations, at a time when there is ostensibly not much need to do so.

An interesting irony of this approach is that it fragments and depoliticizes representation, encouraging what the Germans call *Betriebsegoismus*. As a result, should conflict enter the situation, it is likely to be of the atomized kind of which employers complained so much in the 1970s. The same is true for many other characteristics of the late-twentieth-century workforce, including the growing prominence of non-manual workers.

In summary, then, industrial relations at the present time are capable of a variety of fates. Some of these do include the possibility of a continuing, irreversible decline in unionism and conflict: where employers in the private sector with largely white-collar employees work very hard to construct involvement policies that exclude unions; where unions can find no strategy for offsetting this; and where governments make a union-exclusion policy legal and feasible. Such an outcome will certainly persist and succeed in many individual firms, perhaps whole branches of the economy, just possibly in some entire countries. These cases make it possible that occasionally an extrapolation of the trends of the 1980s will be valid.

But there will be many other contexts where that particular combination will not appear. Some combination of the structure of employment, unions' skill, government policy and employer preference will continue to make possible the autonomous representation of employee interests. In those cases trade unionism of various kinds will be likely to persist. To the extent that the employee body being represented will be more heterogeneous than in the heyday of manufacturing-sector unionism, it may well often be a less 'manageable' unionism. Occasionally – and open conflict is rarely more than an occasional experience – such situations will enable strikes and lock-outs to continue their long-established wavelike pattern of recurrence.

References

Cronin, J. (1979) *Industrial Conflict in Modern Britain*, London: Croon Helm.

Crouch, C.J. and A. Pizzorno (eds) (1978a) *The Resurgence of Class Conflict in Western Europe since 1968*, vol. 1: *National Studies*, London: Macmillan.

Crouch, C.J. and A. Pizzorno (eds) (1978b) *The Resurgence of Class Conflict in Western Europe since 1968*, vol. 2: *Comparative Analyses*, London: Macmillan.

Dubois, P. (1978) 'New forms of Industrial Conflict 1960–1974', in C.J. Crouch and A. Pizzorno (eds), *The Resurgence of Class Conflict in Western Europe since 1968*, vol. 2: *Comparative Analyses*, London: Macmillan.

Kornhauser, A., R. Dubin, A. Ross (eds) (1954) *Industrial Conflict*, New York: McGraw Hill.

Lester, R.A. (1958) *As Unions Mature*, Princeton: Princeton University Press.

Pizzorno, A. (1978) 'Political Exchange and Collective Identity in Industrial Conflict', in C.J. Crouch and A. Pizzorno (eds), *The Resurgence of Class Conflict in Western Europe since 1968*, vol. 2: *Comparative Analyses*, London: Macmillan.

Ross, A.M. and Hartmann, P. (1960) *Changing Patterns of Industrial Conflict*, New York: Wiley.

Shorter, E. and Tilly, C. (1974) *Strikes in France: 1830–1968*, Cambridge: Cambridge University Press.

Soskice, D. (1978) 'Strike Waves and Wage Explosions, 1968–1970: An Economic Interpretation', in C.J. Crouch and A. Pizzorno (eds), *The Resurgence of Class Conflict in Western Europe since 1968*, vol. 2: *Comparative Analyses*, London: Macmillan.

Index

Note: The names of organizations are given in their English forms, followed by the abbreviation used in the country of origin. For the full name as used in the country of origin, see the list of abbreviations on pp. ix–xvi.

Index compiled by Peva Keane